COLLINS GUIDE
TO ALPINES AND ROCK GARDEN PLANTS

COLLINS GUIDE TO

ALPINES

and Rock Garden Plants

ANNA N. GRIFFITH
M.A., F.L.S.

PHOTOGRAPHS BY
VALERIE FINNIS

CHANCELLOR
PRESS

First published in Great Britain in 1964 by
William Collins Sons & Co Ltd

This edition published in 1985 by
Chancellor Press
59 Grosvenor Street
London W1

© Anna N. Griffiths 1964

ISBN 0 907486 81 9

Printed in Czechoslovakia
50586

CONTENTS

Preface, *page* 11

5

Contents

6

Contents

7

Contents

8

Contents

9

Contents

PREFACE

The love of alpine plants is apt to become more and more absorbing: the charm of the miniature, the romantic association with the mountains which are their traditional home, the satisfaction of the many easy and floriferous species and (to the expert) the challenge of those which are difficult, all help to explain their attraction.

Strictly speaking, alpine plants are those found in mountainous districts, that is, in the high alpine pastures above tree line and in the actual rocky cliffs rising from them. For the purpose of this book, however, they are taken to include any species suitable for growing in the rock garden or unheated alpine house. In general, this means plants which are reasonably hardy, perennial, and compact in habit (usually six inches or less, occasionally up to a foot). It must be confessed that a few are described because they are so widely seen in the European Alps by the increasing number of plant lovers on holiday there, even though they are rarely (sometimes surprisingly so) seen in gardens. Annuals are almost non-existent at great heights and the few suitable for the rock garden can be counted on one hand. "Improved" garden hybrids are not, in most cases, appropriate in association with true alpines, although notable exceptions occur in the large group of Kabschia saxifrages. In addition, certain small wild plants from the woodlands are included for the shadier or damper corners, as are some other species which look in character although they do not in their local habitats grow at great heights.

To describe all the species listed in the catalogues of alpine specialists alone would fill several volumes this size—indeed a library would be needed if one added those many other exciting plants which, for one reason or another, are not in the current lists. It seemed most useful, therefore, to include as many genera as possible so that, if the actual species sought cannot be found, at any rate a good idea can often be formed of the sort of plant it is likely to be. In looking up an unknown plant, therefore, the generic description (see note on nomenclature, page 37) should always be read before that on an individual species. As for the selection of species I have tried to choose those characteristic

Preface

of the various sub-groups into which they naturally fall. On the other hand, some genera are monotypic, i.e. have only a single species, such as *Loiseleuria procumbens*.

From amongst such a wealth of material it has been difficult to make a selection for this book, but I have tried to make the interest as wide as possible by including representatives of four classes of plant. Firstly, there is the cream of those many alpines which are free-flowering and also easy to grow, with no fads and fancies. The majority fall into this group, give certain simple conditions of cultivation. Then there are those which are undoubtedly difficult and provide a challenge to the cultivator. In some cases these are inconstant and capricious in their demands, so that occasionally a beginner may succeed with one which has pined under the experts. This adds, of course, to the thrill for the beginner and disconcerts the expert. I have also included reminders of some beautiful species which were in fairly general cultivation before the war and are overdue for reintroduction; and a very few recent introductions which seem likely to be amenable to cultivation.

I am very grateful to all my friends who have helped me by checking and proof-reading and must particularly thank Valerie Finnis for providing the photographs from her extensive collection; Dr. P. F. Yeo for his most kind advice on taxonomy; and my two sons for their encouragement and suggestions.

Preface to Second Edition

Unlike most other forms of horticulture the rock garden is concerned almost exclusively with wild species and therefore the owner is not faced yearly with "improved" cultivars vying with each other to oust established favourites. Botanists, however, have a disconcerting habit of discovering an earlier recorded plant name which takes precedence over the familiar one by which it is now well known. Alterations have therefore been made in a few places to bring the nomenclature up-to-date.

It is likely that within the next decade more species may merit inclusion. Plants from the Southern Alps of New Zealand are proving more amenable to cultivation here lately, helped by improved methods of obtaining freshly harvested seed, and plant-hunting expeditions to various areas of the world still little explored botanically offer hope of fresh exciting species, but time is needed to show which will prove permanent in cultivation and become available commercially.

INTRODUCTION

ROCK GARDENING IN THE PAST

We tend to think that the serious study and cultivation of alpine plants began with Reginald Farrer, and I would be the last to underestimate the impetus given by his enthusiasm and vivid descriptions, of a liveliness which will probably never be equalled, but it is amusing and sometimes instructive to hunt out references to the plants and their cultivation in much earlier gardening literature.

The first mentions of the rock garden were often synonymous with the rootery, this being the decaying stump of a felled tree, planted up with small ferns and the like. However, even in 1838, in *The Flower Garden* by Charles McIntosh, there is a chapter on Rock-work and Root-work, which begins with a warning against the use of "irregularly formed flints, the scoriae of forges and large bits of coke", which might have been written by Farrer himself. The chapter ends with a long list of suitable rock plants, and, although there are a few we would not admit today, it is surprising to find how many familiar names are already there, including several which we still find a challenge in cultivation. Much of his advice on soil, construction, etc., is still practical, but although some plants spring to mind which might appreciate the cave he recommends as an adjunct to the Rock-work, I do not think many of us would go to his length of surrounding it with ivy and installing a "couple of horned owls" as an added attraction!

Culture of alpines in pots and pans, at least, one would consider a present-day development, but a hand-coloured plate in *Botanical Lectures*, part III, by William Curtis (1804) represents "a very ornamental wall for exhibiting Alpines and other hardy plants", this being a modern-looking three-tiered, brick-walled bed, "with the pots plunged in gravel or sand". And indeed "if expense were no object" he recommends raising it to five or more rows.

13

Plant Collectors

The Little Library, written for children, in its volume *The Garden* (1831) although very reprehensible in the clinker, dull-corner conditions advised, hints at plants once plentiful now out of cultivation when it portrays as a suitable plant for a child's rock garden the lovely blue-green form of *Iris persica*, in cultivation until the 1930s, though rare, but apparently not yet rediscovered on any of the recent expeditions to Persia and Turkey.

The Floral World for 1869 includes an article on 'Collecting and Cultivating Alpine Plants', in which the author gives an impressive list of plants flourishing in her garden after eight years including such temperamental beauties as *Ranunculus glacialis*, *Campanula excisa* and *Gentiana* 'IMBRICATA'. Its advice on collecting, establishing and growing is careful and exact, and would be considered sound today.

Many of the flower books of the late eighteenth and early nineteenth century include a surprising number of alpine plants among their (usually) beautifully hand-coloured plates. For example, Curtis's Botanical Magazine, vol. XI, 1797, contains amongst others a most delightful plate of *Ranunculus parnassifolius*, and the early volumes of Maund's Botanic Garden (1825 onwards) whose full-page illustrations consist each of four exquisite small hand-coloured engravings, show a large proportion of alpine plants, which sometimes fill complete pages.

These old books become scarcer and scarcer, especially since so many have been ravaged for calendars and Christmas cards, but it is still possible occasionally to find examples at a reasonable price on bookstalls, especially when they are the odd volumes of a set.

PLANT COLLECTORS

More than any other gardener, the grower of alpine plants is directly indebted to the plant collector. Our border plants and our vegetables are mostly so far removed from their wild prototypes as to be almost unrecognizable. Not so with the alpine plant: the specimen in our garden is usually the exact counterpart of that which caught the collector's eye when growing in its wild fastnesses thousands of miles away. In some cases it *is* the actual plant, which has been sent by a collector or distributed by a nursery, or at any rate it may be that first remove, a plant from wild collected seed. The work of the hybridizer is not entirely lacking, but in all but a very few genera it is negligible. The notable exception is the genus Saxifraga, especially

Plant Collectors

in the Kabschia group, where we should all miss the many colourful and floriferous hybrids produced since the turn of the century. Another genus which abounds in hybrids, by reason as much of their own propensity as man's intention, is that of the lewisias, which have so readily fraternized that it is nowadays difficult to obtain several of the original species true, even from wild collected seed. There are a few isolated cases of hybrids in other genera, which will be mentioned later, but in general one finds in the wild species a grace and elegance— a magic in fact—that is often blurred in the hybrid.

Some of the early introductions were made by men not primarily botanists, in the course of their ordinary avocations abroad, among them the French Jesuit missionaries in the Far East. Later came the professional collector, often financed by botanical institutions or by some of the enterprising firms of those days, especially the famous nursery of Messrs. James Veitch. Their task was not always easy or even safe. Robert Fortune, introducer of many new plants, was sent to China by the Horticultural Society of London in 1843, and writes: "On our voyage up the coast we were attacked by fleets of pirates on two different days, and had I not been well armed we must have fallen into their hands, where in all probability my career would have been soon terminated. I had a severe attack of fever at the same time, and altogether was in a most deplorable condition when I reached Chusan. Having the greater part of my collections in the country near Shanghai, I was most anxious to know in what state they were, and finding an English vessel about to sail for the Yang-tse-Kiang I immediately crawled on board in the best way I could and, with a fair wind, we soon reached our destination." (*Journal of the Hort. Society of London*, 1846.) There is no space here to enumerate even the most famous names, but some are commemorated in the plants they introduced, as for example Georg Wahlenberg in the genus *Wahlenbergia*, Reginald Farrer in the species *Gentiana farreri*, and the two French priests, Pierre d'Incarville (1706–57) and l'Abbé Jean Delavay (1834–95) in *Incarvillea delavayi*.

Since the beginning of the century expeditions to Central Asia have brought us hundreds of new plants, including many primula species and dwarf rhododendrons. Recently exploration in Asia Minor has brought delightful dwarf tulips, irises and other bulbs, but it is as yet too early to know how kindly they will take to cultivation. Exciting new plants are appearing from Patagonia; and the Andes offer some of

15

our familiar genera in most unfamiliar guise, such as the rosulate violas, which have the appearance of a sempervivum sprouting with little violets.

LEARNING ABOUT PLANTS

Lucky are those who live near some Botanic Garden, specialist nursery, or keen alpine gardener, for nothing can compare with seeing the actual plant, in all its stages and correctly named. For those able to attend them, the fortnightly Shows of the Royal Horticultural Society at Vincent Square, London, are a source of delight and information, as there is hardly a show without at least one stand devoted to alpine plants, and during the spring and early summer (and especially at the Chelsea Show in May) there are always many such exhibits by specialist nurseries, which are tightly packed with treasures. The shows of the Alpine Garden Society in London and the provinces, always display a magnificent collection of well-grown specimens, ranging from everyday rock plants to the greatest rarities.

A list of specialist nurseries is given on page 319, from any of whom catalogues can be obtained. Better still, visit them.

A further help is to join one of the alpine garden plant societies. These issue illustrated journals, of interest to the beginner as well as the expert, hold shows in London and elsewhere and offer seed lists of over 2,000 species, many unobtainable commercially. There are local groups in many districts, with lectures illustrated by colour slides, and discussions and other activities. Advice, mountain holidays, and a good alpine library are among the other advantages offered to members. For addresses see page 320.

GROWING ALPINE PLANTS

Even in the earliest days of the Alpine Garden Society it was recognized that there were two extreme types of alpine plantsmen. There are those for whom a rockery is primarily a pleasant and colourful addition to the garden, and those whose delight is in the fascinating detail of each particular small plant—an enjoyment enhanced by segregating them in pots and pans and in bringing them nearer eye-level in alpine house, raised frame or bed. The latter are often those who enjoy the challenge of the rare or difficult plant. Naturally, there is no sharp division between the two approaches.

16

Growing Alpine Plants

Soil. The foremost essential for almost all alpine plants whether in the garden or in pots, is a very well-drained soil, rich in humus. As long as it possesses these qualities, the exact proportions can vary, but a suitable compost would be one-third good loam, one-third peat and/or leaf-mould, and one-third coarse sharp sand, mixed with $\frac{1}{4}$ to $\frac{1}{2}$ its bulk of stone chippings. Eventually the whole is top-dressed with a $\frac{1}{2}''$ layer of the same chippings. This conserves moisture in the soil, tends to prevent the accumulation of moisture round the neck of the plant, and helps to discourage weeds. Small pea-gravel can take the place of chippings in the bulk of the soil, but should not be used for top dressing if avoidable as its yellow colour makes a less attractive background for the plant.

For those living on an alkaline soil who wish to grow some of the very attractive ericaceous and other plants which are calcifuge (and these, one should note, do not merely dislike lime; most will not survive at all in a soil containing it) the preparation "Sequestrene" can help to overcome their difficulty. Diluted according to instructions, and well watered into the ground or pot, it can have a wonderful effect in making available the iron in the soil, which was inhibited before by the presence of the lime. The usual sign of iron deficiency is shown by first the paling and then the yellowing of the leaves. In most cases within two or three weeks of administering the "Sequestrene" the plant will have recovered its natural deep green.

Where individual species have special soil requirements these are mentioned in the text.

The Rock Garden. The simplest form of rock garden is seen where an existing slope is maintained by rocks, or even bricked terraces, and planted, in its natural soil, with aubrietas, alyssums, dianthus, and campanulas. Such a site can give cascades of mauve, purple, and gold in the spring, followed by the pinks and whites of dwarf dianthus in early summer and the blue of campanulas from July onwards, with the minimum of trouble and little expense. Sooner or later, however, one wants to construct a garden which will cater for the needs of plants which require rather more care than do the easy-growing ones mentioned above.

Having chosen the site, which must depend on each individual garden, but which must not be under the drip of trees, the first and most important condition to consider is the provision of the very

Growing Alpine Plants

sharp drainage which is so essential. This can be obtained by excavating for some inches below ground level (unless you are building upwards on a fairly steep slope, when bottom drainage will look after itself) and filling the depression with large pieces of stone, broken brick, etc., and by having above this drainage layer a compost which is heavily laced with stone chippings or gravel (see above).

With regard to siting the rock garden, a natural slope, where available, is the easy solution, unless it is north-facing, which would restrict the choice of plants. If a flat site has to be used a plan may first be made, according to the size and shape of the garden, and contours may be provided by digging to make a depression and building up the sides. A winding path may be sunk between raised banks, thus providing varied aspects for plants, and in some neighbourhoods the sunken space may provide a damp area which will suit moisture-loving plants. In such a case a path can be made by stepping-stones.

The method of building up is by a series of small tiers, starting from the base, with retaining walls of the available stone, and rising in a series of irregular bays and terraces, filling in with the compost as one goes. If the stone is stratified the strata should be arranged horizontally, or in slightly inclined parallel lines, and where possible upright crevices should be formed between adjacent rocks. The lowest course of each terrace should be firmly embedded in the soil and the rocks set to slope slightly backward.

Wall Gardens. The wall garden is simpler in design than the conventional rock garden, merely consisting of a raised bed, entirely contained by walls built up of stone. It is usually rectangular, but of course need not be, and I have seen two very attractive curved beds of this kind forming the boundary of a terrace and a sloping lawn. There is a splendid example of the long straight wall garden in the Savill Gardens, Windsor.

The compost is the same as for the more normal rock garden, and a few isolated rocks may be used on the surface for effect (and also provide a cool root run) but they are not essential. If stone is not easily available the walls may be built up with disused railway sleepers (as in the stock beds at the University Botanic Garden, Cambridge), which look well and are quite satisfactory. Ideally the crevices between the blocks should be planted up as one is in process of building, and

18

this should be done as far as possible, but as one usually acquires plants gradually this is rather a counsel of perfection.

Crazy Pavement. A platform of crazy paving adjoining a house can provide a congenial home for quite a number of rock plants, which appreciate getting their roots under the stone and rarely if ever dry out. It is essential to choose rather compact – growing plants and the best results are from seeds sown in the crevices.

Sinks and Troughs. This form of rock gardening has an appeal of its own, as there is scope for building individual units, whether for pictorial effect, with built-up rock and plants which can be trusted to flower well and over a longish period each year, or as a frame for plants, for example, of one particular genus, or, if one has brought· any small treasures from abroad, for the mountain gems from one particular locality. The old stone sink or trough is becoming more and more difficult to find, and more expensive when found, though of course it is much to be preferred if available. It is sometimes rather shallow, but can be built up to some extent by irregular pieces of rock unobtrusively cemented to the back of the sink and to each other, which not only gives a little more depth, but a slope towards the front which can be broken into a terrace by one or more embedded pieces of rock. The drainage hole must be covered with crocking—and for perfect drainage it is wise to tilt the sink very slightly in the direction of the hole. It can be supported on brick tiers, or sturdy sawn tree trunks can be used if available and last long, being protected under the sink. The compost is as before, and small stones throughout it are an added advantage. Glazed sinks are not attractive (though so much more easily obtainable), and I have not yet found a satisfactory method of disguising their glossy white sides. Containers of rough-cast reinforced concrete are occasionally procurable, or can be made by the handy gardener, and these are almost as suitable and attractive as the natural stone troughs. Watering is sometimes a problem, as surface water, during a dry spell, is apt to run off without penetrating. A good method is to sink an upright short pipe, or tube made by removing both ends of a narrow tin canister, near the opposite corner to the drainage hole, and filling it with water as necessary. It can be hidden by a piece of rock laid over the opening and has the added advantage of taking the water where it is most required—to the roots. One of the flat, slatted wooden trays, easily obtained from most fruiterers, is useful to protect against scorching sun, and also in season, if necessary, against the depredations of birds.

Alpine House. The alpine house is basically an unheated greenhouse with very ample ventilation. Its main asset is that it gives protection from overhead moisture in late autumn and during the winter to those plants which need it. These include many of the woolly-leaved plants, such as several of the helichrysums, certain of the small cushion plants which may be also hairy or woolly, like the aretian androsaces, and other plants, often tap-rooted, which resent dampness round their crowns during the season when growth is more or less dormant. The lewisias are examples of this last class.

For the well-being of the plants the ideal staging is formed by beds of sand or ash, in which the pots and pans are embedded, if possible to the rims. This has the advantages of preserving a more equable moisture and temperature for the roots (and some protection from frost) and of minimizing watering. It does however add a great weight to the staging, especially as the sand must be contained by upright edging and a metal base which allows for draining (corrugated iron may be used), and it does create a difficulty in exchanging pots or pans of differing sizes. A compromise may be made by standing them on a shallow layer of fine gravel, settling them slightly into the gravel. To prevent small pots from drying out too rapidly they may be set in a seed-box (or similar receptacle) of sand or ash, on the staging. Watering is a problem in the winter, and the best advice is "when in doubt, don't". In any case it should be done very sparingly, avoiding the crowns of the plants. If the pans are plunged, water is only needed rarely, and even then it is often sufficient to water the sand around them. Certain plants which are not very dependent on light may be kept under the staging in winter. Such are the ramondas and haberleas, ferns, etc.

When it becomes really warm, spraying is very much appreciated and also tends to discourage pests, especially red spider. But almost all plants are the better for being moved outdoors for the summer months. My own routine is to bring in first of all, in autumn, those plants which need protection from excessive winter damp and then later, in early spring and for my own pleasure, the early flowering species as soon as their buds are forming so that the whole delightful development may be watched and enjoyed. In this connection the Kabschia saxifrages in their great variety give a very long flowering period and a wide range of colour. Then, as summer approaches, by degrees almost all the pans are moved outdoors to open frames or to tables on the north side of an open hedge, where they are in light shade for part of the day.

The question of supplying heat to an alpine house is controversial. There is no doubt that the more hardily alpine plants are grown the more they are likely to maintain their native character of dwarf, compact, and sturdy growth, and that some plants brought to the show bench, while beautiful specimens, have a lush growth and a looser form and greater height than they would ever display in the wild, the result of glasshouse treatment in far from spartan conditions. On the other hand, it must be remembered that one of the chief threats to the true alpine plants in our lowland winters is the alternation between comparatively warm, muggy, often damp spells, encouraging new growth, and severe frosts which may be sudden and at times prolonged. In their native haunts they are liable to be covered with a snow blanket continuously from September onwards (according to altitude) until the following spring or even early summer. This not only ensures stable conditions, but also protects them from very severe frosts, as the normal temperature at ground level under deep snow is about freezing point or even a degree or so above it. Therefore, any attempt we can make to encourage this long period of dormancy is not providing "unnatural" conditions, and an alpine house with temperature thermostatically controlled not to fall below freezing point can hardly be criticized on that score.

Frames. One of the most useful adjuncts to rock gardening, the alpine frame, is almost indispensable when raising cuttings or when establishing collected or imported plants, and the majority of plants in pots or pans over-winter more satisfactorily in a frame than in an alpine house, and with less need of attention. Watering is rarely necessary throughout the winter, and a greater degree of protection (by polythene, sacking, bracken, etc.) is possible than in the case of a completely unheated alpine house. In fact, the greatest advantage of the latter is that it gives a certain amount of protection to oneself. A north-facing position is the most generally useful, but an extra, south-facing frame is invaluable for those bulbs, and a few other plants, such as the rhizomatous irises from Asia Minor, which require a summer baking, as they can there enjoy all the sun there is and can be kept completely dry for months. If the frames can be raised to a height of 2½ to 3 ft. this adds very much to one's comfort in dealing with their plants. The most usual way is to set them on bricks or split sleepers, filling the lower space with rubble and soil and the top foot depth with fine gravel and sand, spent ash, or peat and sand. The pots or pans are then plunged to their rims in the bed so made. During dry open weather, except in severe frost, the frames should be opened by day, and watch should be kept for any sign of mildew. This is, indeed, necessary in the alpine house too. Any affected leaves, etc., should be removed at once and the plant sprayed with fine sulphur dust.

LENGTH OF LIFE

A well-known Swiss authority on plants from his own native mountains has suggested that the *average* life of a high alpine plant is seven years. Length of life varies considerably between the individual species, which may be divided into three groups, annual, biennial or monocarpic, and perennial. Extremely few annuals grow at great heights and of those from lower altitudes only a very small number are suitable for the rock garden and are included here. A biennial is a plant which, when grown from seed, forms leaves the first year but does not flower until the second year, after which it dies. Several plants found described in lists as biennial are really only monocarpic; that is, once having flowered they die. They may flower in their second year, like a true biennial, or they may grow for some years before flowering, but after so doing they surely die, usually leaving as a legacy prolific seed. Some will always need many years of development before they produce blooms (for example, *Saxifraga florulenta*); others, such as *Sedum pilosum*, are variable. This last germinates readily, forming comfortable woolly rosettes, a proportion of which will flower the second year and die. Others will wait until the third spring or even longer so that, starting with seed from the first instalment, it is easy to keep a succession of flowering plants of this most delightful sedum through the years.

Among the perennials some are naturally short-lived, such as *Linaria alpina* and *Erinus alpinus*. Fortunately these and others have the engaging habit of seeding around themselves, and so perpetuating

Growing Alpine Plants

the species. Others, such as some crucifers, reach the zenith of their beauty in the second year, after which, although they survive, they become progressively woody and dishevelled. These are best treated as biennials and replaced with young plants from seed, which is usually plentifully set. There are also those plants which are so nearly completely hardy that they will withstand most winters but may succumb to an exceptional one or an abnormal pattern of weather (such as a sudden very severe frost following a long mild spell). We can provide against their loss by collecting seed or establishing cuttings in a frame.

Of the main body of perennials most will continue in good health for a great number of years and need little individual attention, except the cutting out of dead growth (especially in the shrubby species) or the occasional division of a plant which is obviously suffering from overcrowding. This is often necessary with some primula species. A few plants resent disturbance when once established, and these are so noted in the text. Many perennials are herbaceous, that is, the current year's growth dies down after flowering, leaving small resting buds through the winter, to unfold in spring forming the new flowering plant. In most plants these "noses" are readily visible, in which case the only precaution (although a very necessary one) is to protect them from the ravages of slugs and snails, especially during a mild damp autumn and in early spring; in other instances the dormant buds are formed just beneath the soil and are often very small. A word of warning is due here, as it is not unknown for a new and unfamiliar plant from a nursery to be thrown away after flowering, under the impression that it was dead, whereas a little very cautious investigation of the top of the root system just below the soil would probably have disclosed the small hard resting buds awaiting the return of spring. Never, therefore, abandon hope or throw away an apparently dead plant from pan or garden until at least the summer of the following year, as some of these plants with such determined dormancy (for example, some of the rarer silenes) do not show signs of renewed life until late spring. A very few species, including some hardy orchids, actually remain completely dormant for a whole season, reappearing again and flowering with renewed vigour the second year.

SUCCESSION OF FLOWERING

Given propitious weather, the year may open with *Erica carnea* vars.,

23

Succession of Flowering

Crocus laevigatus, Helleborus niger, Cyclamen orbiculatum vars., and a precocious *Daphne mezereum* already in flower. These may be followed rapidly by Snowdrop (*Galanthus*) spp., *Eranthis hyemalis* and *E. cilicica, Crocus tomasinianus* and *C. sieberi, I. danfordiae, Iris histrioides* var. *major,* and *I. bakeriana*, some of the earliest Kabschia saxifrages, heralded by *S. kellereri*, and, by the end of the month, the pale, china-blue buds of *Scilla tubergeniana.*

FEBRUARY

Many of the foregoing will still be in flower, unless a frozen January has held them in dormancy, and they will be joined by:

Anemone blanda
Colchicum luteum
Crocus chrysanthus in var.
Cyclamen orbiculatum and vars.
Erysimum helveticum
Hepatica spp.
Iris reticulata and vars.
N. asturiensis (*minimus*)
Narcissus cyclamineus
Polygala chamaebuxus
Primula altaica
P. auricula forms
P. clarkei
P. marginata forms
Saxifraga apiculata
Saxifraga, Kabschia and
    Engleria spp. and vars.
Scilla siberica
Tulipa humilis group, including
    pulchella and *violacea*
Tulipa turkestanica

MARCH
Adonis amurensis
Alyssum saxatile in var.
Androsace carnea
Anemone apennina
Muscari spp.

Narcissus bulbocodium
Omphalodes verna
Primula allionii
P. clarkei
P. denticulata
P. pubescens group
P. rosea
P. rubra
Aubrieta in var.
Chionodoxa luciliae
Draba spp.
Erythronium dens-canis, etc.
Pulmonaria spp.
Saxifraga oppositifolia
Kabschia saxifrages in var.
Tulipa aucheriana
T. griegii
T. kaufmanniana

APRIL
Adonis vernalis
Androsace chamaejasme
A. helvetica, imbricata, etc.
Alyssum spp.
Arnebia echioides
Aubrieta in var.
Fritillaria spp. and vars.
Haberlea spp.

24

Narcissus rupicola, etc.
Primula auricula
P. bhutanica and other
Petiolares primulas
P. farinosa
P. halleri
P. marginata
P. x *marven*
Pulsatilla vernalis
P. vulgaris
Ramonda spp.
Shortia galacifolia
S. uniflora

MAY
Aethionema spp.
Aquilegia spp.
Armeria spp.
Dianthus spp.
Dryas octopetala
Erigeron spp.
Erinus alpinus
Gentiana acaulis
G. verna
Geum montanum
Iberis gibraltarica
Iris cristata and *I. c.* var.
  lacustris
I. gracilipes
Linaria alpina
Lithospermum oleifolium
Lynchnis viscaria
Omphalodes luciliae
Phyteuma comosum
Polemonium spp.
Potentilla aurea and *P. verna*
P. nitida
Pulsatilla alpina
P. sulphurea

Saponaria ocymoides
Trillium spp.
Tunica saxifraga
Late tulips (*T. australis,*
  T. hageri, etc.)
Viola spp.

JUNE
Achillea spp.
Androsace sarmentosa and vars.
A. sempervivoides
Aster alpinus
Coronilla cappadocica
Edraianthus spp.
Erodium spp.
Geranium spp.
Gypsophila repens
Helianthemum vars.
Incarvillea spp.
Leontopodium alpinum
Linum spp.
Onosma tauricum
Phlox spp.
Saxifraga, spp. of the Aizoon
  group
Sedum spp.
Thymus serpyllum
Veronica spp.

JULY
Acantholimon glumaceum
A. venustum
Atragene alpina
Campanula spp.
Cyclamen europaeum
Dianthus seguieri
Gentiana septemfida
Gypsophila cerastioides
Hypericum spp.

25

Succession of Flowering

Penstemon spp.
Sempervivum spp.

AUGUST
Ceratostigma plumbaginoides
Crassula sarcocaulis
Dianthus knappii
Gentiana farreri
Oenothera spp.
Polygonum spp.
Sedum spp.
Silene schafta
Tunica saxifraga

SEPTEMBER
Colchicum spp.
Crocus sativus
C. speciosus
Cyclamen neapolitanum

Gentiana sino-ornata
'PRAECOX', and other
Asiatic spp.
Lapeirousia cruenta
Sternbergia lutea
Zauschneria californica
Z. microphylla
Zephyranthes candida

OCTOBER
Crocus kotschyanus
Cyclamen cilicium
Gentiana sino-ornata
Nerine filifolia

NOVEMBER
Crocus laevigatus
Erica carnea, early vars.

DECEMBER
Ranunculus calandrinioides
Helleborus niger

N.B.—The times given are the normal months in which flowering commences. From year to year, and in individual gardens, these times may vary earlier or later up to three or four weeks, especially in the case of the early spring flowers. In many cases the flowering period is long and may well last through the ensuing month. A few plants notable either for long-lasting individual flowers or for a long succession of flowers are:

Acantholimon spp.
The cushion androsaces (A. helvetica, etc.)
Alyssum species, especially A. saxatile 'FLORE PLENO'
Aubrieta in var.
Cyclamen europaeum, C. neapolitanum, and C. orbicutalum
The cluster-headed dianthus
The varieties of Erica carnea, especially 'EILEEN PORTER'
   which remains in good flowering condition for up to three months
Erodium spp.
Geranium spp.
Helichrysum spp.

26

Propagation

Helianthemum spp.
Omphalodes luciliae
Polygala chamaebuxus
The potentillas, especially the shrubby spp.
Primula altaica, P. rosea, and *P. denticulata*
Ranunculus calandrinioides
Saponaria ocymoides
Scilla tubergeniana
The Aizoon and Kabschia groups of saxifrages, which not only have long lasting flowers, but are attractive throughout the bud stage.

PROPAGATION

In propagating, one can only be positive that one is getting exactly the same variety if one propagates vegetatively, i.e. by actual division, layering, cuttings (stem, root, or leaf) bulbils, etc. In fact, one must use a part of the original plant, in which case one is said to have a clone. With seedlings, on the other hand, although many plants do come reasonably, or almost exactly true from seed, this correspondence varies right down to instances where one is likely to obtain only a small proportion, or none, exactly like the parent plant. This is strikingly so with special forms of *Pulsatilla vulgaris* of which seedlings can be had in colours quite distinct from the purple of the type. Seeds from named varieties themselves perhaps deep red, pale pink, or even white, will yield plants of a wide range of colour shades, not necessarily producing even one matching the parent. In some cases the original shade is more likely to occur in the second generation.

Seed. This is the most general method of propagation and the means by which many new species are introduced. The seed lists of the various Alpine Plant Societies (see page 320) offer many rarities not available commercially.

Many alpine seeds benefit by being frozen. It was interesting to note the number of outdoor plants of high alpines which produced self-sown seedlings after the exceptionally long icy spell in the spring of 1963, which lasted from December to the end of February. Also certain species, for example most members of the Order Ranunculaceae germinate freely if sown when first ripe, but tardily and spasmodically if kept until the spring or later. Others, such as many of

27

Propagation

the Asiatic primulas, will not germinate at all unless sown immediately on ripening, which in some species is even before the capsule turns brown or splits. Because of this the spectacular *Primula sonchifolia*, although long known, was not brought into cultivation until air transport was available. It is a good plan, therefore, if there is enough material available of any rare or difficult plant, to sow a pinch as soon as it is gathered or received, and the rest in February.

The simplest soil mixture to use is John Innes Seed Sowing Compost, to which a little sand may be added. Otherwise, a mixture may be made up from one-third each of sandy loam, leaf-mould or peat, and sharp sand. For ericaceous and woodland plants the proportion of leaf-mould or peat should be increased. A 3″ pot is usually large enough for the purpose and should be scrupulously clean and also well crocked. It should be filled to within ½″ of the rim and the surface levelled and slightly pressed. Then it should be stood in a vessel of water until the darkened surface shows that it is completely moistened. Small seeds should be sown directly on the surface; with exceptionally minute ones it is a good plan to mix them well with a little silver sand before sowing. This helps uniform distribution by showing clearly which parts of the surface are already sown. Large seeds such as dwarf lupins should be lightly covered to their own depth and "feathered" seeds, if few enough to make it practicable, placed upright with the tail erect. Over the surface is sprinkled a thin layer (barely to cover the compost in the case of very small seeds) of fine chippings. These may be of limestone (except for lime-haters), granite, ⅛″ gravel or even fine "grains" of coal. The last discourage the growth of moss or liverwort on the surface. I myself use the very finest flint grit, about ⅛″ in diameter. This is obtainable from any store keeping products for poultry-keepers. All these surfaces conserve moisture, help to maintain stable conditions, and discourage weeds. After sowing, the pots may be stood in a closed frame or under small individual sheets of glass, "tongue" glasses (the small glass bowls used for various potted foods), or even cork mats, although in this case they must be examined frequently and brought into the light when germination has started. Watering should be by immersion or by very fine spray.

Transplanting should take place when the first true leaves of the plant have developed, but with rare seeds sown sparsely, or with very small seeds sown closely, it may be left until later. In the latter

28

Propagation

case it is sometimes advisable to pot on tiny congregations of seedlings. Bulb seedlings should not be transplanted until at least their second year.

Quite an appreciable number of alpines delay germination until the second year or even longer, particularly if the seed is not sown immediately upon ripening, or soon after. No seed pan, therefore, should be discarded until at least two years after sowing. If space is available it is wise to keep them even longer in cases of rare and particularly desired species, if a shady, slug-free corner can be spared where they can be left plunged to the rim in sand or spent ash, but quite exposed to the weather. Seeds of *Androsace helvetica*, for example, germinated very freely in the spring succeeding the long, cold spell of 1963 from a cushion which had died and been left in its pan, and forgotten, in a shady corner of my garden three years before.

Division. Many plants are readily divided and these are generally recognizable, usually having an extensive system of fibrous roots. A tap-rooted plant can never be divided. In a few cases, division should not be attempted even if appearances suggest it; certain plants resent disturbance when once established, and this is noted in their individual descriptions in the alphabetical list. The most simple of all are those plants which, like many of the Asiatic gentians, form clumps of separate individual shoots and thongy root systems which need only a little teasing apart to divide into a number of separate plants. Others, like several of the primulas, form a mat of creeping rootstocks with many fibrous roots attached, and in this case the rootstock must be cut or broken, care being taken that each portion has an adequate supply of roots. A large fibrous-rooted plant may be divided by driving two upright handforks, back to back, across the centre of the clump and levering them apart. Division is best made after flowering.

Cuttings. Most alpine plants can be increased by this means and, unless a large number are required it has the advantage over seed that one often gains by a year's growth. The cuttings may be taken by detaching a small branch with a "heel". This should be trimmed, and the bottom leaf or two removed at least to a point which will be above soil level when the cutting is planted. If there is no branch small enough for this method to be used, a cutting may be made by slicing at an angle with a sharp knife, just below the axil of a leaf.

Propagation

Within reason the smaller the cutting the better; it is more manageable, more likely to strike, and will probably make a better shaped plant. For example, with androsaces and Kabschia saxifrages single rosettes should be detached, and with *Erica carnea* small side twigs of less than an inch. The cuttings should be firmly inserted in damp sharp sand, or sand mixed with one-third fine peat. They should be kept close in a frame, in which, if it is kept for cuttings alone, they may be planted direct, or they may be inserted in a pot of sand or sand and peat, which is then placed in a polythene bag and closed at the top. They should be kept in the shade and never be allowed to dry out. If a frame is used, an occasional fine spraying is beneficial. Careful watch should be kept for any appearance of mould, and if it is seen the affected part should be removed at once. The time taken by different plants to strike is extremely variable, but when a cutting is found to be making good growth (below as well as above soil) it should be potted on into a richer mixture, especially if it was previously growing in sand only. Cuttings should not normally be taken of shoots in bud or flower. However, if no other material is available from some much desired plant the actual buds or flowers should be carefully removed; in some cases unnoticed and hitherto dormant small growth-buds may develop, and it is worth taking the chance.

Leaf Cuttings. Some plants, for example ramondas and certain crassulas and sedums, may be propagated by leaf cuttings. In the case of those with petioles, such as the ramondas, the leaf is held near the base and sharply pulled off, detaching the whole of the leaf including its stalk. The base is then shallowly inserted in the rooting medium (sand and peat), and it is useful to anchor it by placing a pebble on it. This must be lifted from time to time to see if new growth is starting, after which it must be removed to give light and air. Until this happens, the soil must be kept damp and the atmosphere moist, either by being kept close in a frame, or in a pot enclosed in a polythene bag, or by constant spraying. Certain crassulas and sedums with sessile leaves are so eager to produce leaf cuttings that any small succulent leaves, accidentally knocked off, root almost immediately in the soil on which they fall.

Root Cuttings. Portions of the roots of some plants may be used as cuttings, and this is fortunate as several of them are species which are not easy to propagate by normal methods. *Phlox nana* var. *ensifolia* is one of these. Other suitable subjects are *Morisia hypogaea* and *Weldenia candida*. They must be plants with rather fleshy, thongy roots, and the procedure is to cut a thong into 1″ lengths, inserting them in the usual sand and peat compost, either erect, with the top just level with the surface, or almost flat, with the bottom end slightly embedded and covered with a stone. It is imperative to plant them the right way up, i.e. with the end nearest the body of the plant uppermost, and if this is not obvious by their tapering it is helpful to cut the further end (nearer the tip of the root) at an angle, to remind one when planting.

Layering. This is suitable for certain shrubby species with whippy branches that can be bent down to ground level. A nick is made in the under surface of the branch, which is bent backwards at that point, and the angle so formed is pressed below the surface and pegged there with a bent wire or angled twig or, if more convenient, it may be covered in soil and a stone placed on it. *Daphne blagayana* lends itself to this treatment. Layering is a very slow process, and the junction must not be disturbed until one is sure roots have formed. *Daphne cneorum*, for example, will probably take at least two years to root from layers.

Another natural method of propagation in special cases is by rooted suckers, cleanly cut from the parent plant. *Euryops evansii* is a plant which kindly provides these occasionally in its pot or surrounding ground.

Most bulbous species divide to a lesser or greater degree into bulblets which are easily separated and grown on. *Iris danfordiae* is an extreme case where the wheat-like bulbs are so many and so small that it is years before they again reach flowering stage—if they have not already succumbed to the many-hazards on the way.

THE PLANT'S ENEMIES

Birds are the largest common enemy. They are most destructive at certain seasons, mainly in the spring when they are nesting, but also for a short period in the autumn—and are most active in the early morning. No plant of cushion formation is safe from them, even in the alpine house unless all openings are netted, not forgetting the doorway. I have watched a bird tear apart a prostrate plant in the open garden with the utmost ferocity, hurling the shoots rapidly in every direction, and there is evidence of the same savagery when the tufts of some precious androsace or tufted saxifrage in the alpine house are discovered spread in all directions quite a distance away from the mutilated parent plant. The only safeguard is the individual protection of each plant which one knows from experience is particularly likely to be the object of attack, and this includes all those of a tight cushion or mat-forming habit. Although tedious to manipulate, black cotton criss-crossed from upright twigs can be effective and this is the only way possible with such plants as the early small crocus species and some of the early primulas, both of which are particularly vulnerable. Over a whole sink of small treasures, close mesh chicken-wire may be bent into an arched cover. For individual plants, whether in the open or a pan, there is sometimes obtainable a light, latticed plastic fruit-punnet which, when weighted against wind (or cats), is effective; for larger pans the separate hemispherical halves of a plastic lettuce-shaker, to be had at any kitchenware store, serves the same purpose. All these are more or less unsightly, but I know no other effective way. Bird scarers are also unsightly and may be a nuisance to neighbours, and in any case soon become familiar features and lose their power to alarm.

Mice can be a menace to the small bulbs and corms, especially the crocus and cyclamen species. As the damage is done underground it is often widespread before it is discovered. They have even been known to nibble the top-growth of sedums and cyclamen under staging in an alpine house, but it is usually the actual bulbs or corms of plants which are attacked. In a closed space, such as an alpine house or frame, ordinary mouse-traps are effective but elsewhere, unless adequately protected, there is the fear of a bird being the victim and the same reason forbids the use of poisoned bait.

Slugs and Snails are perhaps our most devastating enemies. Others, large or small, only exceptionally do more than mutilate and the plant may be nursed into recovery, but the slug is only too apt to devour completely. It is utterly infuriating to know that nothing on earth can recapture some rare and irreplaceable treasure from inside

The Plant's Enemies

the sleek and slimy marauder still crouched complacently near by. Whole pots of small seedlings may be eaten to ground level in a night, or all the tender growing points gouged from the resting shoots of herbaceous alpines waiting prepared for the spring. Some species, usually the most choice, are more attractive than others to these pests. Most campanulas, and especially the rarest, are irresistible to them. Generally the alpine house is safe, but not always; even there, from time to time, one finds the worst has happened. It seems that the enemy has come in, perhaps among the crocks of a pot brought from outside or perhaps hatched from an egg already in the soil. In these cases, the slug or snail can usually be found and destroyed by examining the sides and vent-holes of the invaded pot and those around it, but in the garden all one can do is to sprinkle the ground wholesale, but particularly where damage has already appeared, with any of the proprietary slug-poisons. These may be had in the form of small granules or flakes which are commercial alternatives to the home-made remedy of one crushed "Meta" (solid fuel) tablet mixed well with half a pint of bran, or as pellets, which are easy to distribute and keep their potency longer. After an attack in alpine house or frame, pellets should be sprinkled around and under the pots in the neighbourhood.

Aphids. Although we usually speak of them as greenfly, these little pests may also be black, yellow, or brown. They are more apt to attack plants in alpine house or frame than out of doors, but whether in or out they should be dealt with as soon as noticed as they increase at a tremendous rate. Spraying with one of the ordinary proprietary insecticides (diluted strictly according to the maker's directions), repeated after three or four days, should control the attack. Alternatively, a systemic insecticide can be used which, as well as being sprayed, may be well watered into the pot, whence it is drawn up into the tissues of the plant, rendering it poisonous to aphids and some other pests.[1]

A few groups of plants, of which primulas are an outstanding example, develop a form of aphis on the roots. This results in the formation of white chalky powder which is very conspicuous if the plant is gently turned out of its pot. The general unhealthiness of

[1] Users of this type of insecticide should bear in mind, however, that the effects on animal life can be devastating.

33

the plant is a warning sign to investigate, but sometimes the infestation is so great that a crust of chalky powder is seen above the soil around the woody rootstock. To deal with this root-aphis, wash the roots in soft soapy water or a dilute solution of insecticide, and then repot after placing a few small crystals of paradichlorbenzene above the crocking at the bottom of the pot. The aphids are fairly easily dealt with in the garden by spraying as indicated, but sometimes they are very intractable in the alpine house, especially among the hairy or closely tufted cushion plants where drenching with spray is not only bad for the plant but also does not reach among the tiny crowded shoots. In this case a fumigation of the house is necessary, closing tightly all windows and doors and burning one of the fumigating cones which can be had at any gardening sundries shop. The dimensions of the house must be measured and the size of cone chosen according to the volume. One must keep a constant lookout in the alpine house, with a magnifying lens if necessary, on the very small plants and seedlings. If aphids are discovered in ones and twos, it is then often possible to remove them with a small camel-hair brush which has been dipped in suitably diluted insecticide. This at the same time applies a protective covering against immediate fresh invasion.

Caterpillars. These are not so frequent and are usually removed by hand as soon as seen. Watch should be kept, however, for curled leaves, or even curled young shoots. Examination will generally show that each contains a small grub enveloped in a little cocoon of leaf and fine web. These also must be removed by hand.

Earwigs. These are sometimes troublesome in the alpine house but are seldom numerous enough to be beyond the control given by a visit with a hand torch in the early dusk, as that is when they seem to emerge to feed.

Red Spider Mite. These insidious little pests are very minute and congregate on the backs of the leaves. The attack is usually only spotted when the plant begins to look unhealthy, the foliage at first turning pale and yellowish, and eventually shrivelling up altogether. Directly it is suspected the plant should be well sprayed with an insecticide having a paraffin base. They are encouraged by hot, dry conditions, and copious spraying of the alpine house during the summer

Collecting Plants

helps to prevent an attack. Outdoor syringing is also helpful in every way during scorching weather, but it is in the alpine house that conditions are more likely to encourage this pest.

Ants. From time to time we all of us suffer an infestation of ants, sometimes actually in a pot or pan but generally in the garden. They are usually controlled by putting little dabs of Nippon on small pieces of slate, dotted about the area.

Yellowing of leaves (chlorosis). When the foliage of a plant becomes yellow, this means that chlorophyll is being produced in reduced amounts or not at all. The production of chlorophyll by the plant is a delicate process which can be upset in several ways, in particular by lack of magnesium or iron.

With lime-hating plants in chalky soil, the lime interferes with this process. The baleful influence of the lime can be reversed to some extent by watering it with a dilute solution of Epsom salts, which contain magnesium. But, better still, water the plant with a solution of the commercially available chemical "Sequestrene" (see page 17). This contains iron (and also some magnesium and manganese) in a form particularly favourable for counteracting the effect of the lime.

COLLECTING PLANTS

Now that so many take their holidays abroad among the mountains of Europe, the menace of indiscriminate collecting may become a real threat to the natural prodigality of the mountain flora, which contributes so much to the enchantment. Most countries, or separate cantons within a country, have lists of prohibited plants publicly displayed, often by posters with delightful coloured reproductions of the protected plants. It should also be remembered that no plants may be brought back into England except under a special permit from the Ministry of Agriculture, and that without this any plant found in one's possession will be confiscated by the Customs. Further, the majority of the very high alpines are both resentful of transplanting and difficult in cultivation, and in inexperienced hands will often not even survive the journey home. No plant should ever be touched near well-trodden paths, or where it is locally a rarity, whether it be on the forbidden list or not.

35

Collecting Plants

Even where a plant is locally abundant, if a specimen is taken it should, if possible, be a small plant or seedling. Even apart from other considerations, a young plant has a much greater chance of survival. Loose earth should be gently disentangled from the root system, which should be as complete as possible, and damp, not soaking, moss wrapped round up to the crown of the plant. An appropriately-sized rectangle of waxed paper—and none is so good as the inner wrapping of cereal packets—is now rolled round the moss, folding up the base after about two turns, making a test-tube shape which is then secured by a rubber band. This will also hold a small label with the name and any other required information, such as colour, locality, etc. Do not despise the label. It is astounding what distinguishing details, vivid in the field, can be blotted from one's mind by the return home. The separate packets should be placed upright in a polythene bag, secured at the top with a rubber band (or by knotting the top of the bag), in such a way as to include a certain amount of air so that the plants are not crushed together. They should be kept in a cool, light place (not in sunlight), and in these conditions will remain fresh for two or three weeks. They should be examined every few days for any sign of mould (in which case the affected part or plant should be removed), or undue moisture condensed on the inner surface of the bag (when the bag may be left open for a little while). If one can bring oneself to do so, it is better to remove most of the flowers from the plants, unless one wishes to keep a few in the hope of seed.

Once home, cut off the bottom ends of the "test-tubes" and stand them upright in a shallow dish of water for a short while. Then remove paper and moss, tidy the roots a little if they are very tangled or straggling, and plant in a shaded frame in sharp sand, or better still a sand and peat mixture, which holds moisture better. This should be kept closed for a week or ten days, and then opened for increasing intervals each day, the times depending on the weather conditions and the appearance of the plants. In most cases it is advisable to leave them undisturbed in the frame until the following spring, especially when they are in a mixture including peat or fine leaf-mould. A deep wooden lidless box, two-thirds filled with the sand-peat mixture and covered with a sheet of glass can quite adequately take the place of a frame. In frame or box care must be again taken to remove any sign of mould if seen, or rotting leaves.

36

A Note on Nomenclature

If one arrives home in warm, gentle and persistent rain, any species known not to be fastidious may be planted direct into a raised bed or trough in which the soil has a good proportion of sand and humus. This reduces trouble for oneself and avoids an extra move for the plant. However, one needs to be alert to the danger of the weather changing suddenly to heat and searing sun, when the necessary precautions of shading and watering must be taken. An upturned flowerpot, watered upon as well as around, both protects from the sun, and, through evaporation, helps to cool the atmosphere surrounding the plant.

A NOTE ON NOMENCLATURE

The plant kingdom is divided for reference into wide classes, which are further divided and subdivided. The last two of these main categories are the genus and the species, and a plant is identified by its generic and specific names in latin. The generic name comes first and has a capital letter; the specific name comes second, without a capital letter, e.g. *Gentiana verna*. Below the level of species, three categories commonly used are sub-species, variety and forma, though the first of these has been avoided in this book. Below these, modifications which do not qualify for botanical names are treated as garden varieties or "cultivars", although some of them may have been found wild. Cultivar names may be in latin or be fancy names: in either case they are distinguished by being enclosed in single quotation marks, and they have capital letters, e.g. *Anemone nemorosa* 'ROBINSONIANA'.

A multiplication sign indicates a hybrid between two species; such hybrids have names of their own, but the parentage (or 'hybrid formula') is often given in brackets after the name, e.g. *Gentiana* 'CAROLI' (*farreri* × *laurencei*).

The names of plants are governed by two codes, The International Code of Botanical Nomenclature and the International Code of Nomenclature for Cultivated Plants. Dr. P. F. Yeo has kindly brought the names in the book into agreement with these two codes, as far as possible. In many cases where synonyms exist the choice between them is optional; our choice of accepted names and synonyms has been influenced by the names currently used by nurserymen rather than by any desire to be strictly up-to-date with nomenclature.

37

Alphabetical List of Plants

ALPHABETICAL LIST OF PLANTS

The country of origin of each plant is given, also the approximate height and time of flowering. These last two may vary considerably according to the local physical conditions, including the weather, and in the case of size according to the spartan nature or otherwise of the soil. A plant in its home in the mountains is usually dwarfer and more compact than in the garden, where conditions are generally easier. Almost without exception the more congested the growth produced, the more the plant is truly in character.

Methods of propagating alpines are described in general on pages 27–31: any special requirements or difficulties in the case of individual plants are noted with their descriptions in this alphabetical list.

For the sake of those with little botanical knowledge, botanical terms have been used as sparsely as possible, and where a genus or species has a familiar English name in common use it is also given as a guide. To help the reader further, there is a short glossary on page 307 and a list of familiar names on page 310.

ABBREVIATIONS

* Especially desirable species and varieties.

D Plants liable to be difficult in cultivation.

P Plants needing a certain amount of protection, if only from overhead damp in winter.

ACAENA *Rosaceae*

This is a genus mainly indigenous to New Zealand, although a few species are found in South America and Polynesia. It includes mat-forming evergreen sub-shrubs, with small, dense foliage, irregularly pinnate and usually more or less silvery. Their prostrate habit and neat little briar-like leaves make the species very suitable for growing between paving-stones or as a general ground cover, especially for dwarf bulbs. The small globose heads of flowers are insignificant but they are followed in late summer by conspicuous spiny burr-like fruits. There is little to choose between them when not in fruit, and three usually grown are:

A. buchananii. South Island, New Zealand. Grey-green foliage and yellowish burrs. 1″–2″. Summer.

A. novae-zelandiae. New Zealand. Silky hairy foliage, and large purplish burrs. 1″–2″. Summer.

***A. microphylla.** New Zealand. The gem of the family, with little briar-like leaves of grey, shading to bronze, and freely produced fruits which in sunshine glisten like many spiny burrs of ruby spun glass. 1″–2″. Summer.

ACANTHOLIMON *Plumbaginaceae*

A genus of dwarf perennial plants with hard, usually grey, spiny leaves and tufted cushion-like growth. Natives of hot, dry countries from Asia Minor eastwards, they need a sunny, raised position, and very sharp drainage. They are attractive at all seasons by reason of their tufts of needle-like leaves, and have the pleasant habit of remaining neat after flowering, owing to the persistent calyces.

***A. glumaceum.** Armenia. Makes cushions of ¾″ dark green needles. 4″ close spikes of pink flowers. Summer. (Pl. 1)

***A. venustum.** Cilician Taurus. A beautiful plant, with 6″ rather loose tufts of silver-grey spiny leaves, and spikes of clear pink flowers held well above them. More difficult and less permanent than *glumaceum* and difficult to propagate. Seed if obtainable, otherwise cuttings, which do not strike easily. Summer.

ACHILLEA *Compositae*

Yarrow or Milfoil. Those species suitable for the rock garden owe much of their value to their finely cut foliage. Most are aromatic and all are easy to grow in sun or shade. Foremost among the many suitable are

A. ageratifolia (*Anthemis aizoon*). N. Greece. Close rosettes of lanceolate toothed leaves, and neat daisy-like flowers. One of the best. 4″. Summer.

A. clavennae. E. Alps. Tufted growth. Leaves oval, twice-pinnate, hoary white. Large white flowers in a loose corymb. A parent of several good garden varieties, valued for their grey or white foliage. 6″. Summer.

*A. 'Lewisii' ('King Edward'). A good garden hybrid of *clavennae*, free- and long-flowering. Sulphur yellow. 6″. May to September.

A. 'Kellereri'. Another hybrid. Finely cut grey foliage and white flowers. 6″. Summer.

A. nana. The charming tiny yarrow of the High Alps, with small tufts of hoary fern-like leaves, and a distinctive few flowered head forming a neat ball. The white ray petals are short and wide around a small dusky yellow disc. 2″–3″. Summer.

A. rupestris. S. Italy. An attractive free-flowering plant; white daisies with greenish disc above narrowly spoon-shaped leaves. 4″–6″. Summer. (Pl. 1)

ACONITUM *Ranunculaceae*

Most of the species are really too tall for any except the very large rock garden, but the following are so continually met with in the mountains that they must be mentioned. All have the characteristic hooded Monkshood flower, and all have leaves palmately cut.

A. lycoctonum (*vulparia*). Wolf's Bane. Europe, N. Asia. Leaf segments wider and not so deeply cut as in the following species. Each flower tall and narrow, variable but usually pale yellow. A woodland plant, but has been found up to 7,750 ft., varying in height with locality. Up to 3 ft. June–August.

A. napellus. Monkshood. Asia and Europe (including Gt. Britain). A very variable species, found up to 8,200 ft. Flowers usually purplish-blue, occasionally white. Up to 3 ft. Summer.

A. paniculatum. S. Europe. A taller plant, from lower altitudes (5,000 ft.), with larger, handsome, violet-blue flowers in a less close spike. Up to 4 ft. July–August.

Although these are so tall as only to be admissible in the background

Actinella, Adiantum, Adonis

of a large rock garden, there are in the Himalaya a few desirable really dwarf species, such as *A. hookeri* (2″–8″) with few, large, hairy, blue or purple flowers, and in N. America one or two more, such as *A. uncinatum* (4″–8″) with lilac flowers. These are from time to time available in cultivation, and are well worth growing, although not very long-lived.

ACTINELLA *Compositae*

A. grandiflora. The most striking member of this genus (usually listed as *Rydbergia grandiflora*) is a native of N. America, and over a tuft of meagre, narrowly-cut leaves, produces a single gaillardia-like head, enormous for the size of the plant, on a 4″–6″ stem. It can be grown from collected seed (Rocky Mts.) but is not long-lived, which is perhaps why so spectacular a plant is so rarely seen in gardens. Summer.

ADIANTUM *Polypodiaceae*

The Maidenhair ferns are in general too tender for the open garden, although the type plant *A. capillus-veneris* is a rare British native on a few sheltered coasts. The handsome *A. pedatum*, an American and Asiatic species, is hardy and will flourish and spread in leafy soil in half shade, but is tall—up to 2 ft.

A. venustum. Himalaya. Although reputed tender, this charming species, which is like a fine Maidenhair of spreading, almost prostrate growth, has not only survived in East Anglia, but spread mildly in leafy soil in half shade for several years, including the punishing winter of 1962–63.

ADONIS *Ranunculaceae*

Three of the species of this genus which are suitable for the rock garden are superficially very similar. They all have leaves divided in three, with each segment much subdivided into linear divisions to the base. They are entirely herbaceous and the first sign of life in the New Year is the fat flower bud guarded by the undeveloped leaves. The flower opens before the leaves are fully developed, and is a conspicuous feature in early spring with its ample yellow petals and boss of golden stamens. The following are all under 6″ when the

43

flowers first open, but later the leafy stems develop to their full height of 10″–12″, forming a densely feathery clump.

*A. amurensis. Japan. The earliest. This also has a double form, which is more easily obtainable but perhaps not quite so attractive as the type, as there is a lot of green in the yellow petals. February. (Pl. 1)

*A. brevistyla. Himalaya. Silky blue buds, rising from whorls of much cut, deep green leaves, open into solid white chalices. In Scotland the blue is very pronounced, and makes this a very beautiful and striking plant. In the south the blue tends to be paler or may even be an indeterminate grey. This may be due as much to the nature of the soil as to latitude. Cool, leafy soil. 6″–8″. May.

A. pyrenaica. Pyrenees. Golden chalices with central boss of stamens. first opening at 3″–4″. 8″–9″ eventually. June–July.

*A. vernalis. Europe. The best of all, being earlier and more dwarf than *A. pyrenaica*, and having larger flowers. 7″–8″. March–April.

AETHIONEMA *Cruciferae*

These charming little sub-shrubs from the Mediterranean region bear a strong family likeness to each other. Most have a neat, bushy habit, the much-branched stems bearing many narrow, rather succulent little leaves, usually of a lovely blue-grey which is very pronounced in some species. The individual flowers, in shades of pink, are small, but they are borne in many headed clusters at the ends of the branches. They are easy to grow in any light, well-drained soil, with a little lime, in full sun. Easy from seed, and likely to self-seed in a pleasant way. Early summer flowering.

A. armenum. Armenia. One of the smallest, making a neat mat of blue-grey foliage, with 4″ clusters of pink flowers.

A. coridifolium. Asia Minor. Often confused with the very similar *A. pulchellum*. Grey-green leaves and heads of medium pink flowers. 6″–8″.

*A. pulchellum. Asia Minor to Persia. Even more attractive than the foregoing, with almost blue foliage and longer heads of brighter pink flowers. 6″–8″. (Pl. 1)

*A. 'WARLEY ROSE'. A lovely hybrid, probably of *A. coridifolium*, with deep pink flowers. 6″. (Pl. 1)

Ajuga, Albuca, Alchemilla
AJUGA *Labiatae*

The Bugle tribe is not a distinguished one, but it provides one or two hearty rampers that will grow anywhere, and are useful as a ground cover. They make a carpet of strong prostrate rooting stems, with ample ovate deep green leaves and neat 3″–4″ spires of hooded flowers. The three most useful species (all from Europe) are

A. genevensis. Less stoloniferous than *A. reptans*, and very attractive in flower, with spikes of deep, almost pure gentian blue. 3″. Summer.

A. pyramidalis. This is often confused in lists with the foregoing, but is quite distinct. Its oval, slightly hairy leaves form a regular four-sided pyramid up the stem, continuing as leafy bracts between the smaller, paler flowers, regularly to the apex. Its attraction is the colour of the bracts, which gradually shade from green at the base of the stalk to a conspicuous reddish purple at the apex. Found freely throughout the Alps, but always in ones or twos. 3″–4″. Summer.

A. reptans. Bugle. Very stoloniferous, offered by nurseries in varieties with blue, rose, or white flowers and in *A. r.* 'MULTICOLOUR' ('RAINBOW') with glossy, variegated leaves. An attractive and carefree ground cover, but too invasive to introduce among more choice plants. 2″–3″. Summer.

ALBUCA *Liliaceae*

Most of the albucas are too tender for outdoor growing and too tall for the rock garden, but a very dwarf species has come into cultivation during the last few years, and is offered as *Albuca* sp., from Basutoland. This is a delightful little plant, with linear leaves and solid little faintly flushed white goblets on 3″–4″ stems, in June, rather like little upturned snowdrops.

ALCHEMILLA *Rosaceae*

Lady's Mantle. A genus of dwarf perennial herbs, with heads of very small flowers, either yellow or greenish. Some people find a quiet charm in their palmately-lobed leaves, which are covered with adpressed silvery hairs, especially on the backs, and fold their segments to show this silvery sheen. But if admitted at all it should be to some unobtrusive corner, as they readily seed around and are likely to become a nuisance. For garden purposes, *A. alpina, pentaphylla, sericea,* and *vulgaris,* are so similar that it would be unwise to admit the invasion of more than one. All of these are natives of Europe. 6″–10″. Summer.

ALLARDIA *Compositae*

Attractive small bushy plants with much-cut ferny foliage and daisy-like flowers.

A. glabra. Himalaya. Strongly aromatic green foliage, pale pink flowers. 6″. July.

A. tomentosa. W. Himalaya. Similar, but with white, woolly foliage. 6″. July.

ALLIUM *Liliaceae*

A genus of over 300 species widely distributed over the northern hemisphere, but not so often seen in gardens as their good temper and availability warrant. This is probably mainly due to the family taint, the smell of garlic, which is present to a greater or lesser degree in most of its members. (*A. cepa* is the onion; *A. sativum,* garlic; *A. schoenoprasum,* chives. The last is a charming little plant with delicate heads of pinkish mauve.) This odour, however, is hardly ever noticeable unless the plant is bruised. A few species tend to reproduce themselves to the extent of becoming weeds, not only by seed but also by means of bulbils produced underground or, in some instances, among the inflorescences. The following are among the least in stature and are delightfully graceful little plants with a good range of colour. Flowering as they do from early to late summer, they can bridge the gap between the spring and autumn bulbs. Most have narrow, linear leaves, and have flowers in umbels held well above the leaves. Almost every shade but scarlet is represented, and several other suitable species may be found described in *Collins Guide to Bulbs.*

A. amabile (*yunnanense*). N.W. Yunnan. A slender, tufted plant with rich, deep-rose to purple flowers. 4″–8″. Late summer.

*A. cyaneum. Kansu, China. Close heads of slightly pendent, bright blue flowers. Summer. 9″–12″. June–July.

A. flavum 'MINOR'. S. Europe, Caucasus. Yellow, glistening, campanulate flowers. 4″. Mid-summer.

46

*A. karataviense. Turkestan. Large for our list, but must be mentioned as it is such a striking plant, especially in its foliage. In spring it produces a pair (usually) of very broad, flat leaves, which develop most beautiful metallic shades of· blue-grey and reddish-purple. The large globular flower-head, borne on a sturdy stalk, is a variable light mauve. 6″–8″. May–June.

A. mairei. Yunnan. A delightful little plant, very similar to *A. amabile*, but with paler pink flowers. 4″–5″. Summer.

*A. moly. S. and S.W. Europe. From a spreading pair of wide, blue-green leaves rises the stem bearing a many-flowered umbel of golden-yellow flowers. 6″-10″. June–July.

*A. narcissiflorum. N. Italy, Caucasus. From a flat rosette of linear leaves rises the stem, bearing an umbel of bell-shaped flowers of bright rose. A beautiful plant. 8″–12″. June–July.

A. oreophilum var. **ostrowskianum** (*ostrowskianum*). Turkestan. A handsome plant with large globular heads of carmine-pink. 8″–12″. June–July. (Pl. 32)

A. sphaerocephalum. Europe and Asia Minor. Although rather tall in most of its forms, this must be mentioned as its dense heads of dark purple bell-shaped flowers are such a frequent feature of the Central European Alps. A foot or more. July–August.

A. tibeticum. A charming dwarf from Tibet, with large, deep blue tubular flowers, few to the umbel. 6″. Summer.

ALSINE. See MINUARTIA

ALYSSUM *Cruciferae*

A genus of small annual or perennial herbs, leaves small and often silvery hairy. The four-petalled flowers are almost invariably yellow. Desirable small shrubby species are

A. alpestre. S. Europe. A small spreading plant with little oval, hoary leaves, and heads of small flowers with rounded yellow petals. A variable species. 3″. Early summer.

A. montanum. Europe. The most common alyssum in the Alps, rather larger than *A. alpestre*, with bright yellow flowers having notched petals. 4″. Early summer.

*A. saxatile. Gold Dust. Europe. Very floriferous and the treasure of the rock gardener who is not concerned with rarities but only aims at bringing gaiety to a steep slope which happens to lie in his domain. For such a purpose either the type, or *A. s.* 'FLORE PLENO' with double flowers, which is both

47

more compact and longer flowering, combined with a couple of varieties of aubrieta (for example, the old but unrivalled dark purple 'Dr. Mules', and a good medium mauve) will create a beautiful effect, and the flowering season may be prolonged by interplanting with tufted dianthus and one of the easy and prolific campanulas. Nothing could be simpler or more lovely, and almost all the care needed is to cut back the alyssum and aubrieta, especially the latter, after flowering.

*A. s. 'Citrinum' is a clear pale yellow. (Pl. 1)

A. s. 'Dudley Neville' has flowers of quite an attractive shade of light buff.

A. serpyllifolium. Spain, Mont Cenis, etc. An attractive tiny prostrate plant, sometimes considered a variety of *A. alpestre*, with hoary leaves and compact heads of bright yellow flowers. It is a long-lived plant, and the little stems become quite woody with age. 1″. June onwards.

*A. spinosum (*Ptilotrichum spinosum*). A tiny intricate shrublet with the persistent petioles forming fine spines. Clusters of small whitish flowers. 4″–8″. Summer.

A. s. 'Roseum' has pale to deep rose flowers. 4″–8″. Summer. (Pl. 2)

AMARACUS. See ORIGANUM

ANACYCLUS *Compositae*

The few species in cultivation come from the Atlas Mts. in N. Africa. The two most readily obtainable are:

*A. depressus and ***A. maroccanus.** These are quite hardy, and will grow well in any well-drained soil, preferably in the sun, and both make attractive prostrate rosettes of much-cut carrot-like leaves. In spring they bear many white, daisy-like flowers, at the ends of stems which are prostrate for most of their length, the tips bearing the flowers becoming erect. The backs of the ray florets are a bright crimson, and this makes the plant very striking when buds and flowers are displayed at the same time. A rather larger plant than either, with even more striking scarlet-backed ray florets is **A. atlanticus* var. *vestitus*. (Pl. 2)

ANAGALLIS *Primulaceae*

Our own native *Anagallis arvensis*, Scarlet Pimpernel, or Poor Man's Weather Glass, can sometimes be found in deep blue, although much

Anarthrophyllum, Anchusa

more rarely than its usual pillar-box red, and although one does not find it offered as a rock plant, I think we are most of us loath to weed it out when it appears uninvited.

A. linifolia (*grandiflora*). Mediterranean regions. Perennial at home, usually of annual duration here, but easily kept going by seed, often self-sown. The type plant, prostrate, is very like our own native Pimpernel, except that it is a little larger in all its parts and sturdier, and has flowers of a deep gentian-blue with red reverse. Long flowering from early summer.

A. l. var. collina has rather stouter growth and rose-red or brick-coloured flowers. July. (Pl. 2)

*****A. l. var. monellii.** Spain. Has even larger flowers, of deep blue. July.

A. tenella. Bog Pimpernel. This is another native plant and of fairy-like proportions. Its frail stems never rise above about 1″, and are mainly prostrate, bearing most delicate little upturned bells of pale pink, often with deeper veins. It needs a boggy soil, and on such, in the heart of Dartmoor, runs happily about among the equally etherial *Wahlenbergia hederacea* with comparable pale blue bell-shaped flowers. A collected variety, even more lovely in its small way than the type, is *A. tenella* 'Studland variety'. Summer.

ANARTHROPHYLLUM *Leguminosae*

D**A. desideratum** is a plant newly introduced from Patagonia, and described as the Scarlet Gorse. It has short, spiny, grey-green leaves, rather suggestive of *Erinacea pungens*, and upstanding scarlet or orange flowers above a cushiony growth which in its natural habitat may be from 4″–12″. It will be an exciting plant if it proves amenable to English gardens. It is early days yet to know, but seeds have germinated and plants have been distributed. It withstood the 1961–62 winter (and flowered in the spring following).

ANCHUSA *Boraginaceae*

Most of this well-known genus are too tall for the rock garden, but quite the most beautiful of them is

DP*****A. caespitosa** (true). Very saxatile, in its native habitat (Crete), making starfish-like rosettes of deep green, bristly, strap-shaped leaves, and bearing many large almost sessile flowers of a deep, clear blue, intensified by a white eye. Introduced into cultivation in the 1930s, it is still a rare plant, as it is by no means easy. Propagation, when possible, is by cuttings. 1″–2″. Summer, long flowering. (Pl. 2)

Curiously, soon after its introduction another taller and much easier plant was shown under the same name. This has now been identified as *A. angustissima*, and makes a bushy clump of about 10″–12″, bearing many spikes of small, deep blue flowers. Summer.

49

ANDROMEDA   *Ericaceae Monotypic*

Arctic and temperate regions of the northern hemisphere.

*A. polifolia. Bog Rosemary. A charming little shrublet, with many fine but woody stems bearing tough little oval pointed leaves, dark green, either glossy or, in one form, matt-surfaced, with white tomentose reverse. The small flowers are urn-shaped, and may be either white or pale pink. It needs a shady position and leafy, lime-free soil. Two varieties even more compact than the type are *A. p.* var. *compacta* from N.E. Asia, with white flowers, and *A. p.* var. *nana* from Japan, with rose-pink flowers. 3″–5″. May–July.

ANDROSACE   *Primulaceae*

A genus of over 100 species, extending through Europe, Asia, and Pacific N. America. The floral structure is that of a primrose in miniature and all, except a few of the very small minority of annuals, are attractive. The very high alpine species, mostly European, are strongly saxatile, and make dense cushions of tightly packed leafy stems, bearing in the centre of each terminal rosette a single white or pink flower, sessile or on a stem up to $\frac{1}{2}$″. In the mountains the cushions are firm and often so crowded with flowers that these cannot open fully. In cultivation, however, it is by no means easy to keep them healthy and in character. Winter damp is fatal and overhead protection is then essential, although they are impervious to cold. A meagre, very gritty soil and a position in a chink between rocks help to keep the plants compact. A little lower the congested cushions give place to rosettes of usually hairy leaves either forming a small clump (*A. carnea*) or a loose mat of stolons (*A. chamaejasme*). These species are more good-tempered in cultivation. Some of the Asian androsaces are larger and also less needful of special protection. These and the two last groups bear their flowers in umbels. All need a well-drained soil with some humus. Seed germinates well, although sometimes tardily, but seed of the rarer species is not easy to obtain. Single rosettes of the cushion androsaces will strike as cuttings if one can bear to detach them. Those marked P need unheated alpine house protection in winter, or at least overhead protection, and are all of them delightful in pans. There are several more cushion forms of comparable difficulty to those mentioned, which attract and challenge the specialist.

50

Androsace

DP*A. alpina (*glacialis*). One of the most delightful of the Europeans, and widely found on granitic formations at 7,000 ft. and above. It tends to form a flat mat rather than a cushion, and the single flowers, pale pink to an occasional deep rose, are packed so tightly as to hide the foliage. Towards the Dolomites, it is found in a white form. A lime-hater, and difficult in cultivation, where, if it survives, it very rarely has the compact growth which is typical. 1″. Early summer and spasmodically later.

A. arachnoidea. See under A. villosa.

A. argentea. See A. imbricata.

A. carnea. Europe, from the Pyrenees to the Stelvio Pass. Very variable according to locality. Loose clumps of small narrow, pointed leaves with 1″–2″ scapes bearing umbels of pink flowers. This is the usual form, but it varies from a diminutive 1″ plant with tiny, palest-pink flowers (Maritime Alps) to the beautiful *A. c.* var. *laggeri* (Pyrenees), with wider, shorter leaves, and large, deep rose flowers with a golden eye (2″–3″). Other varieties are *A. c.* var. *brigantiaca* (Cottian Alps) with pallid flowers and *A. c.* var. *halleri* (France) with pink flowers and 1″ long leaves. All flower in early summer.

P*A. carnea ×pyrenaica. A charming hybrid forming a close 1″ cushion with pink, almost sessile flowers. Flowers over a long period, and is easier than most of the cushions. Early summer.

A. chamaejasme. Mts. of northern hemisphere. Rosettes of ½″ rather hairy, pointed leaves making a loose mat by connecting stolons. 1″–2″ umbels of small white flowers. Early summer.

DP*A. ciliata. Pyrenees. A delightful plant of close 1″, bright green rosettes of pointed leaves and single ¼″ flowers of deep rose. Early summer.

A. glacialis. See A. alpina.

DP*A. helvetica. Switzerland, Austria. Makes a solid dome (1″–2″) of tiny hairy rosettes, in the centres of which the solitary white flowers are almost sessile. Early summer. (Pl. 2)

DP*A. imbricata (*argentea*). European Alps. Habit of the foregoing, but the leaf rosettes are slightly larger and quite white with tiny adpressed hairs; solitary white, almost sessile flowers. Lime hater. Early summer.

*A. jaquemontii. Himalaya. A lovely recent introduction with small hairy rosettes (about 1″ across), and the habit of *A. chamaejasme.* Umbels of good pink flowers on 2″–3″ stems. Variable in colour. Early summer.

*A. lanuginosa. Himalaya. A late flowering trailing species, good for hanging over a rock face, with silver leaves and pale pink flowers in umbels. *A. l.* var. *leichtlinii* has white flowers with a red eye. July–October. (Pl. 2)

P*A. muscoidea. Kashmir. A neat little plant from over 13,000 ft., mat-forming, with small hairy rosettes and almost sessile, comparatively large white flowers. 1″. Summer.

A. obtusifolia. European Alps. Widespread, with small green rosettes and 1″–2″ umbels of white flowers, sometimes rather meagre. Early summer.

51

p**A. pyrenaica.** Pyrenees. Dense 1″–2″ domes composed of perhaps the smallest rosettes of all. Softly downy and bearing almost sessile, small white flowers. Early summer.

***A. sarmentosa.** Himalaya. A very variable species, but easy-growing in any situation and attractive in all forms. Considerably larger than any of the foregoing in all its parts. Mats of symmetrical rosettes, 1″–2″ across, of slightly hairy leaves, and umbels of good pink flowers on 2″–4″ stems. (Pl. 3)

Some named varieties are *A. s.* var. *chumbyi*, one of the best, densely tufted and very hairy: *A. s.* var. *watkinsii*, about half the size of the type; and *A. s.* var. *yunnanensis*, rather larger than *A. s.* var. *chumbyi*.

A. spinulifera. Central China, Yunnan. One of the largest in cultivation, forming a clump of rosettes of upright, rather coarse, 2″–3″ lanceolate leaves, broader towards the tips and often tinged with red. The flowers, nearly ½″ across, are borne in 5″–6″ umbels, and are pale pink with red reverse. When the leaves die back in winter they disclose the centres of the rosettes as hard flat cones of spiny leaves, rather suggestive of a small very dense sempervivum. Summer.

***A. sempervivoides.** Kashmir, Tibet. A charming and good-tempered little plant, making a mat of 1″, flat rosettes of bright green leaves connected by stolons, and bearing neat little umbels of bright pink flowers. 1″–2″. Early summer.

p**A. villosa.** Alps of Europe and Asia. Forms a dense mat or low cushion of small hairy rosettes connected by wiry stolons. Many umbels of delightful white flowers on 1″ scapes in early summer.

p***A. v.** var. **arachnoidea** is even more hairy than the type, and consequently whiter.

p***A. v.** var. **grandiflora** is similar but with larger and more solid flowers.

ANDRYALA *Compositae*

***Andryala aghardii.** Granatian Alps, Spain. Forms mats of mainly radical leaves, narrowly spoon-shaped to a pointed apex, and heavily felted with white hairs. Makes an attractive foliage plant for the alpine house. Its flowers are slender lemon "dandelions" on 5″–6″ stems. June.

ANEMONE *Ranunculaceae*

In this genus the petals are absent, the sepals, 5 or more in number, being coloured and petal-like. The flowers are usually solitary, but sometimes form an umbel. A characteristic is the involucre below the flower, which is formed by a conspicuous whorl of "leaves", usually tri-partite and again much slashed, corresponding with the true basal leaves which arise straight from the rootstock on long petioles. The carpels are separate and one-seeded, often ending in a long feathery awn. They are, in general, woodland plants rather than truly alpine, especially now that *A. alpina*, *A. pulsatilla* in all its forms, *A. vernalis*, and some others have been removed to the genus Pulsatilla. Most flourish best in a leafy soil and a cool position. Propagation by seed, sown if possible as soon as ripe.

A. alpina. See PULSATILLA.

*A. apennina S. Europe. A tuberous rooted species, in foliage rather like a more robust Wood Anemone, with upstanding many-sepalled flowers of a clear blue, making a wonderful sight where it has been allowed to naturalize. There are colour forms of mauve, pink, and white, which seem to occur spontaneously, and some semi-double, but none are as beautiful as the type. 6″–8″. March.

A. baldensis. Europe. A species of open high ground near the tree limit. Leaves bi-ternate, much divided, slightly hairy. The solid, white-sepalled flowers have about eight sepals, often bluish at the back, with a boss of golden stamens. It is not very tractable in gardens, and even where it grows freely it is a very spasmodic flowerer. 4″–6″. Summer.

*A. blanda. E. Europe, the Taurus. Rather like a very dwarf *A. apennina*, with even larger flowers of a rich purple-blue. It flowers before *A. apennina*, and dies away almost immediately afterwards, so that it is no nuisance to later flowering plants. It, also, shows colour variations. 3″. February. (Pl. 3)

A. caucasica. A. halleri. See PULSATILLA.

A. hepatica. See HEPATICA.

A. lesseri. N. America. Forms a bushy clump of many stiff stems bearing small deep pink flowers. The foliage is also stiff, and hairy, and the plant's chief merit is the bright and rather unusual colour of its flowers. 8″–10″. Summer.

A. magellanica. S. Chile. A creamy-white anemone with much-divided hairy basal leaves and involucre, sometimes considered a dwarf form of the following species. 6″. Spring.

A. multifida. N. America. A larger edition of the foregoing, with flowers which may vary locally to pinkish or yellow shades. 6″–12″. June.

*A. narcissiflora. Europe, Asia, N. America. The lovely Apple-blossom anemone of the Alps. It usually grows in damp meadows or light woodland, the bright green, softly hairy, much-divided leaves being beautiful in themselves. From the conspicuous involucre rises an umbel of bowl-shaped white flowers of solid texture, many of which are backed with soft pink. Hence its common name. It is not difficult to establish in leafy, fairly moist soil, but is not free-flowering in cultivation. 8″–12″. Summer.

Anemonella, Anomatheca, Antennaria

A. nemorosa. Europe (including Gt. Britain). The Wood Anemone of our English woods, with its myriads of white flowers opening to the sun. It varies in the wild, and almost any extensive patch would show some pink-backed sepals and probably flowers suffused with the colour. It also develops opalescent shades of luminous pale mauve, some of which forms have proved permanent and include *A. n. 'ALLENII', very early, with very large flowers of an exquisite lavender blue, and with less divided leaves than the type, and *A. n. 'ROBINSONIANA', with large, rounded, pale blue sepals, backed by soft cream. Other named varieties are offered and all are beautiful. There is also a double variety of the type plant, in which all the stamens have become petalloid, making a dense white boss in the centre of the flower. March.

*A. obtusiloba forma patula.** Blue Buttercup. Himalaya. Has the usual characteristic basal leaves, forming a flat rosette, from which the flowering stems radiate almost horizontally, bearing many buttercup-like flowers, which in the best forms are a beautiful deep blue. June. (Pl. 3)

A. pulsatilla. See PULSATILLA.

A. ranunculoides. Wood Ginger. Mid-Europe, Caucasus. Like a small and delicate Wood Anemone, except for the flower, which has fewer sepals, and is a bright yellow. This has also a double form. 4″. April.

A. sulphurea. See PULSATILLA.

*A. sylvestris.** Snowdrop Windflower. Europe to Turkestan. In appearance like a miniature edition of the so-called Japanese Anemone (*A. hupehensis*), with many satiny white, cup-shaped flowers in early spring, up to 1½″ across. A delightful and free-flowering early plant. 6″–10″. April.

A. vernalis. See PULSATILLA.

ANEMONELLA *Ranunculaceae Monotypic*

A. thalictroides. Rue Anemone. N. America. A most delicate and lovely little woodland plant, with the habit of a fragile wood anemone. The flowers are white, or much more rarely pale pink. The Thalictrum-like leaves rise from very small tuberous roots. It is happy in a woodland position where it is not smothered by coarser plants. There is a double-flowered form. 4″–5″. March–April.

ANOMATHECA now LAPEIROUSIA

ANTENNARIA *Compositae*

*Antennaria dioica** 'ROSEA'. The common antennaria of the Alps of Europe, Asia, and North America. It makes a dense mat of creeping stems,

54

Anthemis, Anthericum, Anthyllis

which root as they go, with many small silvery oval-pointed leaves, and upright stems of 2″–4″, bearing inflorescences of small rayless flower heads which vary from white to deep rose. They are all pleasant little ground coverers for an open situation, and forms selected for colour and fullness of flower-heads are very beautiful indeed. (Pl. 3)

A small variety is *A. d.* 'MINIMA' and particularly woolly forms have been distinguished as *A. d.* var. *tomentosa.* 2″–4″. May.

There are several other species, but these are very similar to the above, and not more desirable.

ANTHEMIS *Compositae*

A genus of many species, aromatic and having leaves which are usually attractive through being much cut, pinnately or twice pinnately. A few of the dwarf species are useful, mainly for their foliage, and good tempered in the rock garden.

A. aizoon. See **Achillea ageratifolia.**

*A. cupaniana. Italy. Makes a tumbled heap of beautiful silver-grey, ferny foliage, and bears for months on end large clear-cut white daisies singly on slender stems. Its only fault is its size, as it tends to cover more ground than the small rock garden can allow. 8″–10″. Summer.

A. montana. Europe, Syria. A very variable species, and basically a cushion plant of the mountains, with bi-partite, or more divided, leaves which vary from slightly hairy to woolly. Some of the forms have been given varietal names and one, *A. m.* var. *aetnensis,* has pinkish flowers. Others bear their white daisies in late summer.

ANTHERICUM *Liliaceae*

*A. liliago. Europe. This graceful lily carries its shallow white trumpets on foot-high stems rising from a clump of narrow radical leaves. Its size is intermediate between the handsome St. Bruno's Lily (formerly *A. liliastrum,* now *Paradisea liliastrum*) and the smaller, finer *A. ramosum (graminifolium)*, with still finer grass-like leaves and much branched sprays of much smaller white stars. They are both met frequently in the European Alps and are good-tempered plants in the garden, preferring a light, rich soil and part sun. 12″. Summer.

ANTHYLLIS *Leguminosae*

Two members of this genus for the rock garden form clumps or spreading mats of attractive pinnate leaves and clustered clover-like heads

55

and a third, a shrubby species, is very effective, though eventually rather tall.

A. hermanniae. Corsica. Forms a round shrub, with crowded grey-green, spine-tipped branches, almost hidden by the clusters of golden-yellow flowers. Up to 2 ft., in time. April. (Pl. 3)

*A. montana. Europe, S. Alps. A delightful plant, fluffy with silvery hairs, with large oval heads of shaded pink to deep rose. Hardy in a sunny spot in very well-drained gritty soil. 4″–5″. Summer.

A. vulneraria. Europe (including Gt. Britain). The Ladies' Fingers is similar to the foregoing, but without the conspicuous hairs. Flowers usually clear yellow, but varying to cream or even white in the Alps. There is also a beautiful rose-pink form. 4″–5″. Summer.

ANTIRRHINUM *Scrophulariacae*

p**Antirrhinum asarina** is a creeping, hoary snapdragon from S. Europe, with opposite, rounded, slightly lobed, velvety leaves, and quite large (1½″) yellow and white flowers. Coming from the Mediterranean regions it is on the verge of hardiness, but may survive or self-seed in the open rock garden. Once introduced into the unheated alpine house it will continue to reproduce itself by seed in odd corners on and under the staging, even when the parent plant succumbs to a severe winter. Early summer onwards.

APHYLLANTHES *Liliaceae Monotypic*

A. monspeliensis, a charming plant from the Mediterranean region, forms a colony of rush-like stems, from the tips of which unfold solitary six-rayed stars of deep blue, nearly an inch across. Once established it is hardy, but it resents disturbance. A lovely little plant for the alpine house. 4″–5″. June.

AQUILEGIA *Ranunculaceae*

The Columbine family is a wide one, being found in the temperate and mountainous districts of the whole of the northern hemisphere. The radical leaves are on long petioles, twice- or thrice-ternate, the segments lobed to a greater or lesser degree, in some species suggesting a Maidenhair fern. The flowers are usually nodding, occasionally solitary but more often on branched stems. Almost all are attractive plants, although some are too tall for all but the largest rock garden.

Aquilegia

They like a leafy, well-drained soil, and most resent disturbance when established. They flower in early summer. Like all Ranunculaceae the seed germinates most quickly and most freely if sown as soon as ripe. Otherwise it may take a year or more. The species are very prone to natural hybridization, and where more than one are grown one cannot depend on their coming true from seed.

A. atrata (*vulgaris* var. *atrata*). From the European Alps. This is dwarfer than *A. alpina*, with smaller, less conspicuous flowers, of a sombre reddish-purple or chocolate colour. 12″. Summer.

*****A. bertolonii** (*reuteri*). Italy. A delightful and easy little plant with dark green leaves and large rich blue flowers with incurved spurs, on stems of about 3″. May–June. (Pl. 3)

*****A. canadense.** N. America. An elegant plant, 1 to 2 ft. The flowers, several to a stem, are not very large, and appear slender as the sepals do not reflex as in most species, but they are conspicuous by reason of their bright scarlet sepals and yellow petals ending in scarlet spurs. There is also a pale yellow form, *A. c.* var. *flavescens*. Seed can sometimes be obtained from the specialist societies of *A. c.* 'NANA', which produces attractive midget forms down to 2″ or 3″. Summer.

*****A. discolor.** Spain. A very dwarf plant, with lobed leaves, spreading to make a cushion from which rise the 4″ stems, each bearing one or two short-spurred pale blue flowers with creamy-yellow cups. It is a delightful little plant for sink or alpine house. 2″–3″. Early summer.

A. ecalcarata. See SEMIAQUILEGIA.

A. einseleana. A European species related to *A. alpina* and *A. pyrenaica*, but distinct in appearance, being much more dwarf than *A. alpina*, and having neat flowers of blue-purple. 6″–8″. Summer.

A. flabellata. A Japanese species, usually met in gardens in the dwarf form *A. f.* 'NANA'. It is a beautiful little plant with solid, glaucous leaves which are almost blue-grey. The flowers have also a solid, sturdy look, and are a cool mauve-blue in the type. The white form, *A. f.* 'NANA-ALBA', is the one usually seen. 5″–6″. Early summer.

*****A. formosa.** N. America. Very like *A. canadense*, but with larger flowers. The colour varies from red and yellow to all yellow. 8″–10″. Summer.

*****A. glandulosa.** Altai Mts. The true plant is often offered, but much more rarely seen. It is a compact aquilegia of medium height, having many well-proportioned flowers with blue spreading sepals and white to deep cream petals with medium blue spurs. It is a very attractive plant, but, I think, not very permanent, which may account for its scarcity in cultivation. 8″–10″. Early summer.

DP*****A. jonesii.** This fabulous little plant from the Rocky Mountains is difficult

57

to obtain, to grow, and to flower. It created a sensation when first shown in London in 1932. That plant formed a rosette of little tufted leaves on inch petioles, of a lovely glaucous blue-grey. It bears solitary flowers, just above the foliage, very large for the size of the plant, with blue sepals and white or pale blue sepals with blue spurs. The flowers, unlike most aquilegias, face upwards. Seed is sometimes obtainable, but is usually long in germinating, and the plants are seldom kept to flowering stage. It appears to be a variable species. 2″–3″. Early summer.

A. laramiensis. Rocky Mts. Perhaps the smallest of all Columbines, forming prostrate 1″–2″ tufts of small, dark green, lobed leaves from which the creamy-white flowers, only about ½″ in length, barely emerge. Summer.

A. nivalis is only just coming into cultivation, although it has been pictured in Himalayan Floras for at least thirty years. It is to be hoped that it will establish well as it is a very distinctive little plant of 4″–8″, with small, sparse foliage, and comparatively large purple flowers, borne singly, with wide spreading sepals and short incurved spurs. The extruding stamens are almost black, which, with the spreading sepals, makes the flower look superficially rather like a delphinium floret. 3″–4″. Early summer.

A. pyrenaica. Pyrenees. A smaller, slenderer version of *A. alpina*. 9″–12″. A good rock garden plant. Early summer.

A. reuteri. See *A. bertolonii*.

A. saximontana. N. America. Another charming tiny Columbine, very little larger than *A. laramiensis*, with flowers which have been described as miniatures of the handsome tall blue *A. coerulea*, although plants I have seen have had white petals with blue spurs. It has the reputation in America of being a good perennial, which makes it curious that it is so seldom grown. 1″–2″. Early summer.

*****A. scopulorum.** Rocky Mts. Another very beautiful dwarf Columbine. All have lovely glaucous blue-grey, sometimes red-tinged, much cut and frilled foliage, but beyond this the species is very variable, both as to height, 3″–10″, and colour, which is usually a soft blue, with cream to primrose petals, but may vary to pastel shades of pink or mauve. Early summer.

A. viridiflora. Siberia, China. This, while otherwise following the family pattern, makes a complete colour break by producing flowers of a curious dark greenish-chocolate, almost black, with straight spurs. In spite of its sombre colouring, it is not unattractive. 8″–10″. Summer.

ARABIS *Cruciferae*

The well-known Snow-in-Summer (*A. albida*) is too invasive for the normal rock garden, although its double form is more restrained. But it is admirable for covering a rough stony slope, unsuitable for more choice plants, and well deserves its familiar name when in spring it forms a sheet of snowy blossom. There are, however, a few species which are very suitable for rock garden or alpine house and even, contrary to their relation, need care in cultivation.

A. androsacea. Cilician Taurus. A tiny rosette plant of the high mountains which superficially resembles *Androsace chamaejasme* when not in flower. Of no importance in the rock garden, but possible in a trough with other small fry. 1″. Summer.

*A. blepharophylla. California. In its best form a very attractive plant, bearing above its typical Arabis leaves 3″ spikes of flowers, large for the size of the plant. It is variable in shade from seed, but in its deep, rich rose form is a most desirable plant. Not very long lived. (One should be warned that there is a different plant under the same name, smaller in every way, and with tiny flowers of a dull pale pink.) Late spring. (Pl. 4)

A. bryoides. Greece. Forms a slightly heaped mat of small rosettes of less than an inch diameter, whose hairy leaves give it a silvery, hoary appearance. The flowers are small and white, on 2″ stems. Can make an attractive pan plant. Summer.

A. coerulea. European Alps. A tiny plant found in the High Alps, whose chief claim for notice is that its small flowers are in varying shades of purplish-blue. It is difficult to grow and keep, which is no deep cause for regret, though the deeper colour forms are attractive among the other small fry of the mountains. 2″–3″. Spring.

A. rosea (*muralis*). S.E. Europe. In effect a pink counterpart of *A. albida*, but not so invasive.

ARCTERICA *Ericaceae Monotypic*

A. nana. N. Asia (especially Japan). A small neat shrublet having dense wiry stems set with tiny box-like leaves in sets of three, and bearing freely its racemes of small, urn-shaped fragrant white flowers. It has been called "the ideal rock garden shrub", and is perfectly hardy. Requires a leafy, acid soil and partial shade, but is in no way difficult, and is often seen as a specimen pan in the alpine house. Eventually it forms a close mound 3″–4″ high. Early spring.

ARCTOSTAPHYLOS *Ericaceae*

A. uva-ursi, the Bear Berry, is found carpeting many woods in the Alps and in all the cooler regions of the northern hemisphere. It increases by rooting at the nodes of the prostrate shoots, and is a good ground cover for the shady, lime-free situations it demands. The small leaves are oval, shiny and leathery, and the small, urn-shaped flowers are pink or white. The fruits are comparatively large and of a brilliant red. May onwards.

A. nevadensis. N. America. A very similar species which is sometimes considered as a form of *A. uva-ursi*, but has downier leaves, especially on the young shoots. 4″–5″. Summer.

ARENARIA *Caryophyllaceae*

This genus includes many species of hardy, low-growing perennials, easy to grow in any well-drained gritty soil in an open position and all suitable, though not spectacular, for the rock or trough garden. They are small, almost moss-like plants and have five petalled star-like flowers on wiry stems, of glistening white—with one exception, *A. purpurascens.*

A. balearica. Balearic Is., Corsica, etc. A tiny creeping plant, happy when covering damp rocks in shade and admirable for the crevices of stone steps. It forms a film of very fresh green, which it bespangles with myriads of white stars from spring to early autumn.

*A. grandiflora. Alps of S. Europe. Forms a spreading mat, with bright green pointed leaves and large (1″) white flowers. 2″–3″. Early summer. (Pl. 4)

A. ledebouriana. Armenia. A good wall plant, with 6″ sprays of white flowers over ash-grey foliage. Early summer.

A. montana. France, Spain. This excellent plant is not so universally offered and grown as in times past. It is the most showy of the Arenarias, with large white flowers on 3″ pedicels. Early summer.

A. norvegica. Norway, Lapland, etc. A mat-forming species with white flowers on 2″ pedicels above bronzy-green foliage. Early summer.

A. purpurascens. Pyrenees, Spain. This has the exception to the usual white flowers of the species, and is a prostrate tufted little plant bearing purplish flowers, variable in shade, in twos or threes on 2″ pedicels.

    A. p. 'ELLIOTT'S VAR.' is a free-flowering pink form.

A. tetraquetra. Spain and the Pyrenees. A very distinct species with small leaves in four overlapping ranks, which gives almost a heath-like appearance to the short four-angled stems. The white flowers, from one to three, are at the tips of the stems. 1″–2″. Summer.

A. verna. See **Minuartia verna.**
Other very similar species will be found under the genus Minuartia.

ARISARUM *Araceae*

The amusing little tuberous plant **A. proboscideum** from the Apennines forms one or two arrow-shaped radical leaves, from which emerges the small green, arum-like spathe, which is shortly inflated and terminates in a long curved tail of 3″–4″. The appearance is of a colony of small mice disappearing into the leaves. A shady woodland position suits this curious little plant. Height 3″–4″. March–April.

ARMERIA *Plumbaginaceae*

The members of this genus form compact dense tufts of linear radical leaves, rather stiff in texture, and bear solitary, close, almost globular heads of pink (occasionally white) flowers enclosed in papery bracts, on leafless scapes. Their neat habit is attractive at all times, and they do especially well in sunny places.

A. alpina. See **A. montana.**

*A. caespitosa. Spain. Particularly valuable for the rock garden or alpine house. Its dense cushions, 2″ high, are covered with large flower heads, almost sessile amongst the short, rigid leaves. Prefers a light, well-drained soil. The type plant has pale pinkish-lilac flowers, but deeper forms have been collected, of which the best known is *A. c.* 'BEVAN'S VAR.' with beautiful flowers of a deep rose. There is also a white form. 2″–3″. May, June.

A. maritima. Europe (including Gt. Britain). The Thrift or Sea Pink, which is such a lovely feature of many of our own coasts. Very variable in colour, from white to rose, but the usual form is a pale lilac pink. Several forms have been given varietal names which are usually self-explanatory. 6″–8″. Summer. (Pl. 4)

    A. m. var. **corsica.** Corsica. An interesting and distinct colour break, the flowers being almost brick-red or terracotta. Summer.

A. montana (*alpina*). Mountain Thrift. Throughout the European Alps. Flowers of pinkish lilac; variable in height according to location, but intermediate between *A. caespitosa* and *A. maritima.* Summer.

ARNEBIA *Boraginaceae*

A. echioides (*Macromeria echioides*). The Prophet Flower. This is the only member of this genus one is likely to grow in the rock garden. In well-drained soil and in the sun it forms 9″ clumps of rough surfaced, hairy foliage from which rise the characteristic croziers of its Order, displaying widely funnel-shaped, five-petalled flowers of clear yellow, each with a conspicuous black spot. This, which is supposed to represent the Prophet's fingerprint, fades to a dull brown and eventually disappears leaving the flowers, in their last stages, a uniform lemon-yellow. 9″–10″. Summer. (Pl. 4)

ARNICA *Compositae*

D**A. alpina.** The Mountain Arnica. A prominent feature of the wild display of colour by the meadow flowers in the Alps in early summer. Over lance-olate, bright green leaves its almost leafless stems each bear two or three wide 2" daisies of the most vivid orange-gold. It is difficult to transplant and does not take kindly to cultivation. Acid soil. 8"–10". Early summer.

ARTEMISIA *Compositae*

This large genus contains a number of dwarf, often prostrate, species which are very suitable for sunny spots on the rock garden, or as pans in the alpine house. They are mostly aromatic or bitter, and some form the basis of liqueurs. Hence the reason perhaps for their appearance in some of the lists of protected plants. The flowers form spires of small rayless "buttons" and are of little account. They flower in late summer, but it is their silvery-white foliage which is their chief beauty.

P**A. brachyloba.** Mongolia. One of the smallest species, forming dense bunches of very silvery leaves much cut into very narrow linear sections. It eventually forms a mat of less than an inch in height from which rise 3"–4" stems bearing the small sessile yellow flower-heads. August.

P***A. glacialis.** Mts. of Central Europe. A low shrublet of 3"–6" with lower leaves twice-pinnate and upper ones pinnate. The foliage is silvery with silky hairs, and the small flower heads yellow, in terminal clusters. Summer.

A. lanata (*pedemontana*). Very like the above, and found in similar localities, but rather taller. Summer.

P***A. mutellina.** Mountain regions of S. and Central Europe. This small sub-shrub of 2"–3" is one of the most beautiful of the European species, with much-cut stalked leaves of a silvery whiteness on both surfaces. The flower-heads of pale yellow, few in number, are borne on erect stalks above the lacy foliage. 5"–6" in flower. Summer.

ARTHROPODIUM *Liliaceae*

A small genus of elegant lily-like plants from New Zealand and Australia. Only one is generally grown here.

A. candidum. New Zealand. Forms a clump of narrowly linear leaves, from which rise slender stems to about 10", bearing many rather small white stars. It needs a sheltered position and leafy, sandy soil. Early summer.

Asperula

ASPERULA *Rubiaceae*

A large genus of which several are well suited to the rock garden or alpine house. The linear leaves are opposite on the (usually) four-angled stems, but as they each have two or more leaf-like stipules the appearance is of a whorl. The corollas are narrowly tubular, with four pointed lobes, which gives a delicately starry appearance to the flowers. Individually, they are small, but the clusters are borne in great profusion. The foliage is fine and delicate and, in the woolly species, susceptible to damp in winter. Gritty, well-drained soil in sun.

A. arcadiensis. Greece. A rather difficult species. The dense woolly stems bear small bunches of waxy, rosy trumpets, 4"–6". Summer onwards. Good for a pan in the alpine house.

A. cynanchica. Squinancy Wort. Europe (including Gt. Britain). Weak, trailing stems with glabrous leaves bear heads of tiny pale-pink or white stars. As found in rather barren British soil, especially in cornfields, it is an inconspicuous plant of little attraction, but on the high ground in Central Europe, for example on the Mt. Cenis Pass, there are more compact and less prostrate forms with flowers which, although still small, form attractive sprays of deep pink. 3"–4". Summer.

A. hirta. Pyrenees. A pleasant little mat-forming species, the many 3" stems bearing whorled leaves, hairy, but deep green, with heads of small white flowers, fading to pink. July onwards.

p*A. lilaciflora** var. **caespitosa.** A recent introduction from the E. Mediterranean and a most valuable one, as it forms mats of deep green glossy, heath-like foliage from which rise the inch-high heads of the characteristic pink stars throughout the summer. Being so dwarf and compact, it is an admirable plant for a trough or pan in the alpine house.

A. odorata. Our own Sweet Woodruff, known in the country as New Mown Hay from its characteristic odour. This is more suitable for a shady corner where it can run about mildly. Its 6" stems have finely-toothed deep green leaves in whorls of eight, and, in early summer, flat, terminal heads of white stars, rather larger than the preceding. Summer.

p*A. suberosa** (*athoa*). Greece. Much resembles *A. arcadiensis*, but is more amenable to cultivation. When in good condition, it is one of the most attractive of mat-forming plants, forming a carpet of frail and lovely white-woolly foliage, covered with small, long-tubed stars of delightful pink. It makes a charming pan for the alpine house. Summer. (Pl. 4)

ASPHODELUS *Liliaceae*

DP**A. acaulis.** Algeria. The only member of this genus which is suitable for the rock garden (or alpine house). It forms a tuft of radical leaves, from 6″–10″ long, narrowly linear and grass-like, and almost prostrate. In spring, if one is lucky, one sees the beautiful, quite large, pale pink lily-like flowers, in such short-stemmed corymbs that they appear sessile in the clump of spreading leaves. It is by no means always free-flowering. It would seem that a summer baking is an advantage. The large fleshy roots require a good depth of sandy well-drained soil, and pots must be chosen accordingly, if they are to be grown that way. March, April. (Pl. 4)

ASPLENIUM *Polypodiaceae*

A very large genus of ferns, of over 600 species, widespread around the world, and containing several dwarf species which are hardy and most delightful in odd corners, in walls, and among rocks.

A. adiantum-nigrum. Black Spleenwort. World-wide (Gt. Britain, especially in the West). A little tufted fern with irregularly cut, rather stiff leaflets. Native form 3″–6″.

A. fontanum. (*halleri*) Rock Spleenwort. Europe, including Gt. Britain, Central Asia. Leafy tufts of wiry leaves with pinnate leaflets again cut and scalloped. 4″–6″. One of the prettiest of the dwarf ferns, but may suffer in a particularly hard winter.

A. ruta-muraria. Wall Rue. North Temperate Zone, including Gt. Britain. Found in crevices and walls where it must endure periods of absolute drought. A little tufted plant of 2″–4″, with stiff petioles bearing an indefinite number of irregularly fan-shaped thick-textured leaflets. Very variable in form.

A. septentrionale. Forked Spleenwort. North Temperate regions including Gt. Britain. In this curious little plant the leaflets are drawn out into practically linear segments, giving it a very un-fern-like look.

A. trichomanes. Maidenhair Spleenwort. "English Maidenhair", North Temperate regions, including Gt. Britain, and mountains of Tropics. Forms a spreading clump of erect, glossy, very dark brown, wiry stems with many opposite pairs of small, almost circular leaflets. Very plentiful in old walls, especially throughout the W. and N. of England. A delightful little fern of 3″–5″.

A. viride. Green Spleenwort. Northern hemisphere (including Gt. Britain). Like the foregoing, but with bright green petioles. A comparatively rare native, but more abundant on the Continent.

64

1

Acantholimon glumaceum
Adonis amurensis
Aethionema coridifolium 'Warley Rose'
(Below, *Iberis saxatilis* 'Little Gem')

Achillea rupestris
Aethionema pulchellum
Alyssum saxatile var. citrinum
(Below, *Thymus serpyllum* 'Silver Queen')

2

Alyssum spinosum roseum
Anagallis linifolia var. collina
Androsace helvetica

Anacyclus atlanticus var. vestitus
Anchusa caespitosa
Androsace lanuginosa

Aster, Asteriscus, Astilbe

ASTER *Compositae*

This huge genus provides many suitable members for the rock garden, and it is only possible to enumerate a few here. The characteristic daisy-like inflorescence of the aster differs from that of the Erigeron in having a single row of infertile ray flowers surrounding the disc of fertile flowers, instead of a fuller, overlapping set as in the latter genus.

*A. alpinus. The ubiquitous Alpine aster of the European Alps is as good tempered as it is beautiful. Forms vary, both in height, size of flower and colour of flower. All have stout lanceolate-spatulate radical leaves, and single flower heads on stiff upstanding stems bearing few small lanceolate leaves. The most desirable are compact and low growing with large solid flowers of bright purple rays surrounding a golden disc. Colour forms ranging down to white, and occasionally to pink, may be found. It has a mildly spreading habit. 4"–6". Early summer. (Pl. 5)

*A. farreri. W. China, Tibet. A handsome species with large violet-purple flowers with orange discs on 9" stems. Summer.

A. forrestii. See **A. souliei.**

A. likiangensis. Yunnan. A miniature edition of *A. alpinus* with blue flowers. 3". Summer.

*A. natalensis. A doubtful name, but the plant which carries it has deep green, shortly spatulate leaves with 3" stems carrying good blue flowers. Mat-forming. 6". Early summer onwards.

A. pappei. See **Felicia pappei.**

*A. souliei var. **limitaneus** (*forrestii*). Tibet. A very handsome aster with large purple-violet rays and orange disc. 6"–8". Summer.

A. thomsonii 'NANA'. W. Himalaya. A late flowering plant with showy lilac blue flowers. 9"–10". August–October.

A. tibeticus. Himalaya. A slender plant, with few lanceolate leaves. Flower-head usually solitary, bright blue, 1"–2" across. Height 6". Summer.

A. yunnanensis. Yunnan. Like an enlarged *A. alpinus* with mauve, orange-centred flowers. Handsome but tall except for the large rock garden. 9"–10". Summer.

ASTERISCUS. See ODONTOSPERMUM

ASTILBE *Saxifragaceae*

A genus of branched perennials, with two to three ternate, much divided fern-like leaves on slender petioles. The graceful plumes of many small flowers are found in shades of white, cream, and light to deep pink. They are all valuable for their late flowering habit.

*A. chinensis. China. Fluffy narrow spikes in a curious shade of deep pink flushed with purple. An easy plant, but prefers part shade in fairly moist soil. 8″–10″. July–October. (Pl. 5)

A. crispa. This name covers a group of dwarf hybrids with short stocky spikes of 6″–8″ in late summer. They have been given varietal names; 'PERKEO', pink flowers, very crinkled leaves, 'PETER PAN', deep pink flowers, etc.

*A. glaberrima 'SAXATILIS'. Japan. A most elegant little plant with much cut, dark green, sometimes bronzed, foliage and neat spires of pale pink and cream. Only 3″–4″. July–August.

A. simplicifolia. Japan. A plant of variable height (6″–12″) with sprays of white or pale pink flowers. August.

ASTRAGALUS *Leguminosae*

This genus is not widely represented in cultivation, probably because its members resent transplantation. Even a small plant on the mountains will be found to have a tough central tap root with wide-spread fine branched rootlets. Seed, which is slow to germinate, is the best means of propagation, sown where the plant is to grow. Once established, and left undisturbed, they are long-lived perennials. All have close heads of pea-shaped flowers and leafy stems radiating from a common root stock. The leaves are pinnate, usually with many pairs of lanceolate or long oval leaflets. The genus is nearly akin to Oxytropis, the critical small difference being in the shape of the seedpod. Summer flowering.

A. alpinus. This almost prostrate plant is often seen in the Alps and in N. Scotland, and has heads of rather pinched pea flowers of white, tipped with milky blue. 4″–6″. June.

A. aristatus. See *A. sempervirens*.

A. monspessulanus. Mediterranean region. Of spreading habit with tufted rosette-like growth on short branches. The flowers are usually a deep reddish-purple, but there is a white form. The foliage is attractive, being even more like *Asplenium trichomanes* than the rest of the genus. In rich damp soil it may grow a little tall for the average rock garden. 6″–12″. June

A. sempervirens (*aristatus*). (S. and Central Alps). A dense grey-green shrub, 10″–12″, quite distinct but the spiny appearance caused by the long persistent petioles of past leaves. Flowers, a pale ghost-like grey. 7″–10″. Early summer.

Astrantia, Athyrium, Atragene

A. utahensis (*halleri*). N. America. A prostrate bushlet of dense growth with many pairs (up to 20) of leaflets to the characteristic pinnate leaves. Heads of a few purple flowers. 4″–6″. Summer.

Several other Astragalus (and Oxytropis) are indigenous to the Rocky Mountains, and among seed received may be several garden-worthy plants, if they succeed in cultivation.

ASTRANTIA *Umbelliferae*

A genus containing some charming, although not showy, members. The radical leaves are palmately divided, on long petioles, and the compound umbels are borne well above them. Each umbel is composed of a bunch of tiny, short-stalked flowers, enclosed in an involucre of many overlapping pointed leaflets, which give it the appearance of a neat Victorian bouquet. Their colour is a more or less pink-flushed green. *A. major*, green, slightly flushed with mauve or pink, and *A. carniolicus*, which has an attractive form which is almost red, are both rather tall (a foot or more) for the average rock garden, but

*A. minor. European Alps, is a most fairy-like little plant. The stems are very slender and graceful, the leaflets narrow, and acutely dentate, and the umbels very delicate small bouquets of white and green. 6″–8″. Summer.

ATHYRIUM *Polypodiaceae*

The athyriums are mainly known by the species *A. filix-femina*, the Lady Fern, which is, in the typical form, much too large and rampant for the rock garden. There are, however, several dwarf and crested forms which may be found at specialist nurseries. The most delightful and good-tempered is:

A. filix-femina 'MINUTISSIMA'. This forms a dense clump, a miniature of the Lady Fern, of 3″–6″, according to position.

ATRAGENE. See CLEMATIS
67

AUBRIETA (often spelt AUBRIETIA) *Cruciferae*

So many and colourful are the modern hybrids in this genus that the original species cannot compete with them in splendour, and are little known in the rock garden. Most of the named varieties are spontaneous colour changes, or (more often) hybrids of *A. deltoidea*. They are too well known to need description, and range through all shades of pink, mauve, and purple. They are very easily raised from seed which, for a wide selection, should be obtained from a good firm, otherwise a large proportion will turn out to be an indefinite mauve. Desirable forms are very easy to increase by cuttings in late spring or by layering. After flowering they should be cut well back to encourage dense new growth for compact plants.

*A. deltoidea. Sicily to Asia Minor. Chiefly met in gardens in the forms *A. d.* 'VARIEGATA' ('ARGENTEA') (Pl. 5) and *A. d.* 'AUREA', both neat small-leaved prostrate plants with mauve to purple flowers, and leaves edged respectively with white and gold. Spring.

Of the very many garden forms any Alpine list will give a wide selection, and new varieties (often very little different from their predecessors) are constantly offered. A few good and distinct forms are:

'DOCTOR MULES', an old plant and still the best deep violet-blue.
'MRS. RODEWALD', large flowers of rich near-red.
'GURGEDYKE', deep purple.
'BRIDESMAID', pale pink with a deeper eye.
'CHURCH KNOWLE', large lavender flowers.
'BARKER'S DOUBLE', clear pink with a good proportion of double or semi-double flowers.

AZORELLA *Umbelliferae*

This genus includes a section of small-leaved, densely cushioned plants, which are sometimes obtainable and make interesting pans for the alpine house, where their symmetrical, fresh green mats are attractive in themselves.

A. gemmifera. Azores. Forms a hard green cushion, with insignificant flowers.

A. pedunculata. Ecuador. Tiny, crowded, dissected leaves, and small white flowers.

Bellidiastrum, Bellis, Bellium, Berberis

BELLIDIASTRUM *Compositae*

B. michelii is common among the European Alps, where it may be mistaken at first sight for *Chrysanthemum alpinum*. The Bellidiastrum has, however, a rosette of lanceolate leaves, rounded at the apices and slightly scalloped at the edges. The flowers are borne singly on slender stems, and often fade to a reddish hue. Pale pink forms are occasionally found. It will grow in a sunny well-drained soil, but is not a very long-lived perennial. 4″–6″. Summer.

BELLIS *Compositae*

The miniature daisies of garden origin, 'DRESDEN CHINA' (pink), and 'ROB ROY' (red) and others are charming little plants, but seem out of place in the rock garden. There is, however,

B. rotundifolia var. **caerulescens.** Atlas Mountains, which has ovate radical leaves and pale lavender flowers on 2″–3″ stems. It needs a protected semi-shaded position, and a hostage is best kept in a frame through the winter. Summer.

BELLIUM *Compositae*

B. minutum. Levant. A delightful miniature of our common daisy (*B. perennis*), whose tiny white flowers, backed with purplish-red, rise only an inch or so above the rosette of narrow spatulate leaves. Needs a warm, well-drained position. Summer.

BERBERIS *Berberidaceae*

Among this very large genus there are a few species which are eminently suitable for the rock garden or as specimen pans for the alpine house. They have many virtues. They have a pleasant bushy habit of growth, attractive clusters of bright yellow or orange flowers often followed by bright fruits, and some have purple foliage or take autumn tints. Also they are among the few rock garden shrubs which are not ericaceous, and therefore are very amenable to most soils.

*B. 'CORALLINA COMPACTA'. A dwarf form rarely attaining a foot in height and covered with red-budded orange flowers in spring; small spiny leaves. Evergreen. (Pl. 5.) Probably a form of *B. darwinii*. Summer.

*B. darwinii 'NANA'. Chile. A dwarf form of the well-known *B. darwinii* and with its characteristic orange flowers and tiny holly-like leaves. Evergreen. Summer.

B. empetrifolia. A new introduction from Patagonia. Red shoots and yellow flowers, followed by globose blue fruits. About 6". Evergreen. Summer.

*B. thunbergii 'ATROPURPUREA NANA'. Japan. A dense little bush of up to a foot, with elliptic leaves of reddish purple. Small yellow flowers, tinged red. Deciduous. Summer.

BERGENIA (*Megasea*) *Saxifragaceae*

The Bergenias are really more suited to the woodland than the rock garden, unless it is a very large one. Their crowded clusters of sturdy saxifrage-like flowers of pink or mauve are welcome in very early spring, but they all have large succulent leaves on stout stalks which look coarse unless seen in isolation from more delicate plants. The only species really admissible, and that only by reason of its early flowering, is:

B. schmidtii. (*crassifolia* × *ligulata*). Oval or wedge-shaped leaves and large pink flowers. Up to 18". The earliest, February–March. (Pl. 5)

BESSEYA *Scrophulariaceae*

B. alpina (*Synthyris alpina*). From a tuft of stalked oblong leaves with finely scalloped edges rise crowded one-inch spikes of small violet-purple lipped flowers. 6". Spring.

BETULA *Betulaceae*

*B. nana. Europe, N. Asia. The one really dwarf Birch and, in its most compact form, a most delightful little deciduous twiggy shrub, with many wiry branches set with tiny glossy orbicular leaves, round-toothed. These develop autumn colourings of gold before falling. Up to 1 ft. Suitable for a damp spot in the rock garden, or makes a charming pan in the alpine house.

BILLARDIERA *Pittosporaceae*

A genus of Australian evergreen climbers of which **B. longiflora** is the most dwarf member. It can be trained among foot-high twigs and has interesting

Biscutella, Blechnum, Bletilla, Boykinia

solitary pendent bell-shaped greenish flowers, often flushed with purple, but its chief attraction is its bright blue berries in October. It makes an unusual pot for the alpine house, trained around low twigs.

BISCUTELLA *Cruciferae*

B. laevigata. Europe. A biennial which is often seen in the Alps, and in that setting, and at their best moment, the heads of small yellow cruciform flowers (which are followed by very distinctive seed capsules forming pairs of adjacent flat circular pods) have a certain attraction. The moment is soon past, however, and it is not a plant worth introducing into the rock garden.

BLECHNUM *Polypodiaceae*

The Hard Ferns are so called because of their tough, leathery foliage.

B. penna-marina. S. Temperate and Antarctic. A hardy fern with almost prostrate barren fronds, long and narrow, with many rounded lobes cut almost to the petiole. The fertile (spore-bearing) fronds are upright (4″–6″) and dark in colour with much smaller, cramped lobes, which give them a shrivelled appearance. It spreads by rusty-scaled rhizomes.

B. spicant. Hard Fern. Northern hemisphere (including Gt. Britain). Similar in appearance to the above, but larger in all its parts (although the rhizome is not so spreading). It can, in congenial conditions, rise to foot-high clumps, but there are in commerce many dwarf, crested, and feathered forms available from firms which specialize in ferns.

BLETILLA *Orchidaceae*

B. striata. China. A charming orchid which is hardy in a sheltered position in peat and loam with leaf-mould and sharp sand, but it is safest in the alpine house, where it can be kept fairly dry in winter. It bears spikes of large, attractive orchid flowers of a rich reddish-purple. 10″–12″. Summer.

BOYKINIA *Saxifragaceae*

*B. jamesii. Pike's Peak, Colorado. A comparatively recent introduction, it makes a carpet of stalked, kidney-shaped, deep green, toothed leaves. It is not always free-flowering but when it produces its stocky 6″ spikes of deep cherry-red flowers in abundance it is a most delightful plant. Woodland soil, well drained. Early summer. (Pl. 5)

BRACHYCOME *Compositae*

A genus confined, with one exception, to Australia and New Zealand. The only species in general cultivation and suitable for British rock gardens is:

B. iberidifolia. Swan River Daisy. W. Australia. An annual, but a delightful little plant with many clear sky-blue daisies on much branched very slender stems. 6″. Late summer and early autumn.

BRIGGSIA *Gesneriaceae*

These near relations of the ramondas form more or less flat rosettes of rather thick crinkled hairy leaves and spreading, often prostrate, sprays of tubular, two-lipped flowers of shades of yellow, often green tinged. All are plants for the alpine house, in leafy soil and in a cool position. Not easy plants. The species most usually grown is:

DP***B. penlopii.** Bhutan. Quite attractive clear yellow flowers with orange markings in the throat. 4″. Summer. (Pl. 6)

BRUCKENTHALIA *Ericaceae Monotypic*

B. spiculifolia. S.E. Europe, Asia Minor. In effect a miniature of the Ling of our heaths and commons. It forms close mats of fine evergreen heather-like foliage and short spikes (about 6″) of small purplish-pink open bell-shaped flowers. It is a pleasant ground coverer in lime-free soil, and should be divided every few years if it tends to become straggling. Summer.

BRYANTHUS *Ericaceae*

This is now regarded as a monotypic genus, and the other previous co-members have been removed to Phyllodoce.

B. empetrifolia. See *Phyllodoce empetrifolia.*

B. gmelinii (*musciformis*). Kamtschatka and neighbouring islands, N. Japan. A tiny evergreen mat-forming heather-like shrublet, with ¼″ pink four-lobed flowers. Lime-free soil, cool position. 1″–3″. Summer.

72

Bulbocodium, Bupleurum, Calamintha

BULBOCODIUM   *Liliaceae Monotypic*

B. vernum. Alps to S. Russia. Nearly related to Colchicum. Its pinkish-mauve flowers are welcome when they push up from the soil in early spring, but the petals, unlike Colchicum, are divided to the base and tend to fall apart giving the plant rather an untidy look. The strap-shaped leaves follow later. It is an attractive plant when it first appears and is not so often grown as it might be. Not very permanent unless divided every few years. 2″. March.

BUPLEURUM   *Umbelliferae*

A widespread genus, represented in the high lands of Europe by two or three small members which have a charm of their own in a quiet way. These have narrowly lanceolate basal leaves, forming a neat clump, and heads of tiny greenish-yellow, very short stemmed flowers, enclosed in a circle of green bracts like a miniature Victorian posy. Among other rather similar species the two most universal in the Alps are:

B. ranunculoides. Linear leaves and small "nosegays" of greenish yellow flowers. Variable in height from 2″–12″. Summer.

B. stellatum. The most attractive of the genus as the yellow flower heads are more conspicuous owing to the encircling bracts being larger and wider. 2″–6″. Summer.

CALAMINTHA   *Labiatae*

A genus which includes several prostrate or nearly prostrate twiggy shrublets of easy growth, and useful for their late flowering habit (July–August). Although the thyme-like flowers in the axils of the leaves are small, they are very freely produced. All are easy plants, and suitable for a sunny, dry position.

C. alpina. The universal Calamint of the sub-alpine regions, especially in the southern ranges of Europe, covers itself with small, violet, lipped flowers over a long period in the summer. 4″–6″.

*C. grandiflora is often considered a variety of the foregoing, with larger, fatter, quite showy flowers, of a brighter and lighter shade. 4″.

CALANDRINIA *Portulacaceae*

A large genus, nearly akin to Lewisia, of which only one species is generally grown.

C. umbellata. Peru. Makes a rosette of narrow, succulent, pointed leaves, and carries sprays of many-petalled flowers of a shrill crimson-magenta. Suitable for the alpine house, where it may be kept fairly dry in winter. 4″–6″. Early summer. (Pl. 6)

CALCEOLARIA *Scrophulariaceae*

Of the dwarf members of this genus, a few are of borderline hardiness and need at least overhead protection in the winter. This applies particularly to the woolly-leaved species. The flowers are very distinctive, having a two-lipped corolla, the lower lip inflated and slipper-like. They are mainly natives of the mountainous regions of S. America.

PC. **arachnoidea.** Chile. Densely covered with white woolly hairs and having flowers of a peculiar dull reddish-puiple, in sparce racemes. It needs overhead protection or alpine house, and even so may succumb in a severe winter, but is worth care as the unusual colour of the flowers contrasting with the cotton wool of the foliage makes it an uncommon and, to many, an attractive plant. 8″–10″. June–September.

C. biflora. Chile. Basal rosettes of narrow ovate leaves and yellow flowers nearly an inch across on stems which may vary up to 10″ or 12″. Summer.

DP*C. **darwinii.** Straits of Magellan. One of the most striking and unusual of all rock plants. It forms a spreading mat and the large flowers are borne in pairs on 4″ stems. They are of a bright deep yellow, with maroon spots and across the prominent lip there is a wide band of glistening white, giving the flower a fantastic gnome-like appearance. It is hardy and can be grown from seed. It is, however, by no means an easy plant and a fairly rich leafy soil (no lime) in part shade seems to suit it best. It makes a most striking pan for the alpine house. 2″–4″. Summer. (Pl. 6)

DP C. **fothergillii.** Patagonia and the Falkland Islands. This barely remains in cultivation, but is a mat-forming species with many hairy, spatulate leaves and solitary pale yellow flowers with red or purple spots. Sandy leaf-mould, well-drained and in a cool shady spot would be advisable, if one were lucky enough to possess a plant of this 4″ species. Summer.

*C. **tenella.** Chile. A delightful little plant which runs about freely in a light sandy soil, with many small, almost circular leaves, and upright 4″ stems,

74

each bearing two or three ½" clear yellow, pouched flowers, with the usual crimson specklings. Fairly hardy, especially if planted in a sheltered position. Throughout the summer.

CALLIANTHEMUM *Ranunculaceae*

Very near Ranunculus and sometimes placed in that genus. The only member sometimes available is that found in the European Alps. This is:

D*C. rutifolium, which has attractive glaucous, almost succulent leaves roughly triangular in overall shape, but densely lobed, twice pinnate and again cut into deep rounded lobes, and often a lovely bluish-green. The single flowers of over an inch in diameter are borne on 3"–4" stems, and have a dozen or more solid pure white petals with central boss of golden stamens. Deep, well drained soil. Not very free flowering in cultivation. Summer.

CALLUNA *Ericaceae Monotypic*

C. vulgaris. (E.N. America, N. Europe, including Great Britain). The common Ling of our moorlands is very variable in height and habit. All flower from August–September, and any firm specializing in ericaceous plants may list up to 50 varieties, varying from white to deep purple, and from pygmies to bushlets of a foot or more. An acid soil is essential. A few of the most distinct varieties are:

C. vulgaris 'ALBA'. White Scottish heather.

*C. v. 'ALBA PLENA'. Nearly 1 ft. Fine double.

C. v. 'AUREA.' Purple flowers, golden foliage turning red in winter.

*C. v. 'FOXII NANA'. The best of the miniatures, forming a close 2"–3" cushion of dense, dark green shoots; by no means always profuse with its almost sessile purple flowers.

*C. v. 'H. E. BEALE'. A very good taller variety (1'–2') with many foot-long solid spires of crowded double pink flowers.

C. v. 'MINIMA' (Smith's variety). An even smaller plant than C. v. 'FOXII NANA', with cushions of only 2".

C. v. 'MRS. PAT'. Distinct dwarf habit (6") with pink tips to shoots.

*C. v. 'SILVER QUEEN'. Silvery foliage, mauve flowers. Up to 1 ft.

75

CALOCHORTUS *Liliaceae*

This large genus from California and Mexico contains many beautiful species with showy flowers, held erect on slender wiry stems of a foot or so. The three inner leaves of the perianth are enlarged and brightly coloured, often marked and bearded inside. These lovely and graceful plants are, however, only suitable for frame culture, except in a few especially mild and dry districts. About a dozen species out of 80 were in cultivation just before the war. Those who are prepared to take the precautions undoubtedly required to perpetuate these gay and ethereal beauties are referred to *Collins Guide to Bulbs* for detailed descriptions.

CALTHA *Ranunculaceae*

C. palustris, the King Cup or Marsh Marigold, is only suitable for a boggy spot adjoining the large rock garden, but there its foot-high sprays of glossy deep yellow cups so freely produced very early in the year, against its clump of dark green, shiny leaves make one of the gayest sights of spring. There are also white, pale yellow, and double forms, and a smaller form, *C. p.* var. *minor (radicans)*.

CALYPSO *Orchidaceae Monotypic*

DP***C. bulbosa** *(borealis)*. N. American woods. This entrancing little plant is one of the loveliest of the hardy orchids, with its single leaf and large solitary flower, having a deep-lipped rose pouch with crest of golden hairs, and upstanding sepals striped in brown and purple. Peat, sand, and leaf-mould, between rotting wood and in shade is recommended, but one is fortunate in seeing imported plants flower once, before they silently fade away, never to reappear. 3″–4″. Spring.

CAMPANULA *Campanulaceae*

The Harebell family is confined to the northern hemisphere and consists of about 250 species, at least half of which are suitable for the rock garden. The corollas are bell-shaped, from narrowly tubular

Campanula

to nearly saucer-shaped, with five joined petals varying from slightly recurved to being so deeply cut as to form a star. The colour is almost universally blue, the exceptions being white (sometimes specifically but more often as the variation in a blue species), occasionally tinted with pink, especially in the bud, and there is one yellow species, *C. thyrsoidea*. Many species are so nearly related and so variable within their own ranks that nomenclature has been debatable and subject to change. They need good drainage, and plenty of water in the growing season. They will stand a certain amount of shade and are in fact, with the exception of one or two high alpine species, easy plants and very floriferous. They also have the virtue of flowering from summer onwards, when the first tide of spring alpines is over.

ᴅ***C. allionii** (*alpestris*). French Alps, Piedmont, etc. Forms close clumps of upright leaves up to 2″, variable from short spoon-shaped to linear and also from green to silver grey. The flowers, like Canterbury Bells, are very large for the size of the plant and borne singly on 2″–3″ stems, upright or at an angle of 45° to the stem, variable in width of tube and in colour from light blue (a white form has been found) to deep purple. Scree and underground water. Rather difficult. It does well and then seems to exhaust its neighbourhood. Probably benefits from occasional breaking up and transplanting. 2″–3″. May.

***C. arvatica.** N. Spain. One of the charming small mat-forming species with trailing leafy stems and five-pointed blue stars. 2″. July. (Pl. 6)

***C. barbata.** Mts. of Norway and European Alps. The Bearded Bellflower sends many erect stems bearing 1–20 large inch-long bells, from a rather flat rosette of light green, slightly hairy leaves. The colour varies from mid- to pale-blue, with an occasional white, and the throat and lobes of the bell are covered with long, upstanding silvery hairs. Reputed biennial, but has survived several years in the garden and comes readily from seed. 3″–10″. Summer.

C. betulifolia. Armenia. A recently introduced species with pointed wedge-shaped toothed leaves and flopping, branching sprays with rather small, open bell-shaped flowers, white with pink reverse. Hardy, but the alpine house gives protection to its rather fragile stems. 3″–4″. Summer.

C. carpatica. Carpathian Mts. One of the best known of the trailing campanulas and obtainable in many distinct forms under varietal names. Flowers large, saucer-shaped or like a low, wide bowl. Corolla divided into broad pointed, very shallow lobes. Shades of blue and also white. Has given rise to several garden hybrids and varieties. 4″–6″. July–August.

C. cashmeriana. Afghanistan and Kashmir. A delicate trailing plant with small grey-green leaves on fragile stems. Tubular bell-shaped blue flowers. More hardy than its appearance would suggest, but not a long-lived plant. Scree. 5″–6″. Summer.

77

Campanula

D*C. cenisia. Non-calcareous. High Alps of Central Europe. A very high alpine from 8,000 ft. or more, where, among shaly scree and boulders, it fills every crevice with its hearty little rosettes of rounded, bright green leaves. The flowers are of a grey-blue which is difficult to distinguish from the grey rocks in a photograph, and are shallow five-pointed saucers. A most beautiful plant in nature, but difficult in cultivation, and short lived. The best chance is given by planting it in open, very stony, lime-free, scree, with added humus. One day's baking sun will kill an 8″ patch. 2″. Summer.

*C. cochlearifolia (*pusilla*). European Alps. The charming little Fairies' Thimbles are the most widely distributed and the best tempered of all the campanulas. With fresh green foliage of small circular or cordate stalked leaves they will take possession of a trough or scree by slender underground runners, but are easy to eradicate where not wanted. The little tubby bells on slender branched stems of 2″–3″ are produced in hundreds in summer and early autumn. there are colour forms, deeper and paler blue, a delightful pale slaty blue, and a white. (Pl. 6)

C. elatines. Piedmont. In effect a smaller *C. garganica*, with toothed, roundly cordate leaves and many small starry flowers. Makes a good pan for the alpine house. 2″–3″. July–August.

DC. excisa. S. Switzerland. A dainty small plant with narrow linear leaves and blue bells not unlike a narrow form of *C. cochlearifolia*, except that they have a curious punched hole at the junction of each pair of petal lobes. It will survive for some years in the scree bed, but it is likely to travel from its original position as though it had exhausted some necessary ingredient in the soil. In nature it fills the crevices between stones (usually granitic) very much as does *C. cenisia*. 2″. Summer.

*C. fenestrellata. Croatia. Like a congested finer *C. garganica* with small, toothed, glossy leaves of deep green and variable small starry flowers which can be a clear bright blue. 2″. July.

*C. formanekiana. Yugoslavia, Greece. Many of the E. European campanulas are monocarpic, i.e. die after flowering (although generally setting copious seed). Such is this species, forming a handsome rosette of lyre-shaped hoary leaves the first year, from which arise, the second summer, a stout central stalk of 12″ or more bearing single large white solid bells on long pedicels in the axils of the leaves, and also radiating prostrate stems each bearing one, or occasionally two flowers. A very handsome plant. June–July.

*C. garganica. Italy, Cephalonia. An easy and attractive plant, the type of a group of very similar species. From a rosette of long petioled, often downy, small ivy-shaped leaves the many flowering sprays of 5″–6″ arch upwards and outwards very gracefully, bearing a few small, sessile, ivy-shaped leaves and a long succession of starry blue flowers in late summer. (Pl. 6)

C. glomerata. Widespread in Europe (including Great Britain), temperate Asia. Very variable in size, but in habit a tufted plant of rough, oblong,

78

Campanula

irregularly dentate leaves and stiff erect leafy flower stalks bearing a crowded spike of deep blue-purple, funnel-shaped flowers. Size probably most dependent on environment as seed from our native 2″–3″ downland form will produce anything from 6″ to 2′ in the garden. A showy, handsome plant, though, curiously, not often grown. July–August.

*C. ×haylodgensis 'FLORE PLENO' (*cochlearifolia ×carpatica*). A neat little plant for crevices in walls or paving stones, in effect a very double-flowered *C. cochlearifolia*. One of the very few double-flowered campanulas. 2″–3″. Late summer.

P***C. isophylla.** N. Italy. The showy trailing campanula which used to be so popular in hanging baskets or tall pots in cottage windows, though it is almost hardy and has proved winter-proof in some sheltered gardens when planted high in wall or rock-work and allowed to trail. From a central root-stock it produces a tangle of spraying or prostrate much branched stems of up to 10″, with many roughly cordate, regularly dentate leaves on long petioles and in late summer practically covers itself with inch-wide shallow blue saucers. There is a white form *C. i.* var. *alba* and an attractive, rather woolly, variegated form, *C. i.* ' MAYI '.

C. mollis. Algeria, Central Spain. There is some doubt about the authenticity of the name of this plant, or whether the true species is actually in cultivation, but the plant usually offered under this name is like a much more compact edition of *C. isophylla*, with much shorter, stiffer curving branches and a long succession of rather tubby bell-shaped flowers, held erectly, and slightly woolly cordate, dentate leaves. Long flowering. 4″–6″. July–October.

D***C. morettiana.** S. Tyrol, Dalmatia. This delightful little plant forms tufts of tiny heart-shaped leaves on slender ½″ petioles in the narrowest cracks of the sheer Dolomite rocks and has quite disproportionately large bells of deep blue on wiry 1″ stems. There is also a white form. Difficult, but possible in the alpine house, between two stones or in a hole bored in tufa, in leafy, gritty soil. 1″–2″. Summer.

C. muralis. See **C. portenschlagiana.**

C. piperi. Rocky Mountains. One of the few American campanulas and a charming little plant to run between rocks, with glossy, almost holly-shaped leaves, and comparatively large blue, bell-shaped flowers on 1″–2″ pedicels. 3″. Summer.

C. pilosa. Japan. A very variable species, often in its country of origin given different varietal names in consequence. The form usually obtainable here is *C. p.* 'SUPERBA', a singularly hearty-looking little plant which makes a close mat of crowded lanceolate or spatulate bright green leaves and bears solid, upright, blue, funnel-shaped flowers on 1″–2″ stems. 3″. June–July.

*C. portenschlagiana (*muralis*). S. Europe. The well-known spreading campanula, completely hardy and very long-lived, with masses of deep green, broadly kidney-shaped, toothed leaves on 1″ petioles and, in late summer, un-

79

failing showers of light blue-purple, rather starry, bell-shaped flowers. 2″–3″, spreading.

*C. poscharskyana. Dalmatia. Like a larger and more rampant edition of the foregoing, with an even greater profusion of clear lavender-blue flowers in panicles. 3″–4″. Late summer.

*C. pulla. E. Europe. A charming little creeping plant forming masses of rosettes of glossy oval leaves, and upright thread-like stems of about 3″, each bearing a swinging bell of deep rich purple. Best divided fairly frequently, as in a congenial spot, well drained but never arid, it is apt to flower itself to death. Summer.

C. punctata (*nobilis*). E. Siberia, N. Japan. Not an easy plant, but very distinct, with a lax rosette of longish heart-shaped leaves and a central erect wiry stem bearing a few large, very long (up to 2″) tubular creamy bells. Very light gravelly soil. 12″. July.

C. pusilla. See **C. cochleariifolia.**

*C. raineri. Switzerland, Italy (very local). Forms a loose tuft of ash-grey, almost sessile leaves, and has wide, deep bowl-shaped flowers of a rich mid-blue, held erect on 3″ stems. Not easy to obtain true, but a very desirable plant. Summer. (Pl. 7)

C. rapunculoides. Europe. Only mentioned as a warning, as this lovely bell-flower, with its slender irregular spires of deep blue-purple, once introduced, is ineradicable, spreading by brittle cotton-like stolons and by fat underground tubers.

*C. rupestris. Greece. A rather tender species which in cultivation usually proves to be monocarpic. Makes an attractive pan for the alpine house, with clusters of rosettes of hoary, irregularly toothed leaves and erect campanulate pale lilac-blue flowers arising singly from the axils of the arching 4″–6″ stems. Summer.

*C. saxifraga. This and **C. tridentata,** both from the Causasus and Asia Minor, are very similar plants, forming dense clumps with many, rather long-petioled, oblong, slightly toothed leaves and comparatively large purplish-blue flowers, widely campanulate, with petals divided to about half the depth of the bell. Makes a handsome and effective pan for the alpine house. 5″–6″. Summer.

C. thyrsoides. European Alps. A curious and very distinct plant with few lanceolate basal leaves and a very leafy stout stem, which may be from 6″–12″ or more according to position, with a terminal very dense thick spike of pointed bell-shaped flowers of sulphur-yellow, the only campanula of this colour in cultivation. Often seen locally throughout the Alps, especially in meadow banks adjoining streams, where it reaches its greatest height. Summer.

C. waldsteiniana. Dalmatia, Croatia. A small neat tufted plant with many starry blue-violet flowers on 3″–4″ stems. One of the latest to flower. Rich gritty soil in the sun. (Pl. 7)

D***C. zoysii.** Italian Alps, Karawanken. A quaint and delightful little

3

Androsace sarmentosa
Anemone obtusiloba forma patula
Anthyllis hermanniae

Anemone blanda
Antennaria dioica rosea
Aquilegia bertolonii

4

Arabis blepharophylla
Armeria maritima alba
Asperula suberosa

Arenaria grandiflora
Arnebia echioides
Asphodelus acaulis

species, very saxatile, with creeping cotton-like stolons and many rosettes of tiny glossy leaves like miniature salt spoons. The relatively large flowers are usually borne nearly horizontally an inch or so above the leaves, and are of a curious shape, being rather narrowly bell-shaped, constricted before the mouth and then enlarging and again being puckered in at the lip, which gives them, when in flower, the appearance of a flight of tiny blue torpedoes. It is reputed to be very difficult but appears to be quite amenable to cultivation if grown in very gritty, chippy soil, with plenty of water in the growing season, and divided energetically at the first sign of ill-health (or even without). It dies down completely in the winter, but with the above treatment will almost certainly send up its tiny salt spoons again in mid to late spring. 1"–2". Late summer.

These are only a few of the many campanula species which are desirable for the rock garden or alpine house, but they include most of the more distinct. Many others will be found, often spasmodically, in the lists of specialist nurserymen, but several species are so much alike in general effect, especially when in flower, that no one, unless making a collection of the genus, would want specimens of all the very nearly related species.

CARDAMINE *Cruciferae*

The only member of this genus we need consider here is our own native Cuckoo Flower, or Lady's Smock, **C. pratensis.** This, in a fairly damp soil and part shade, is attractive in a quiet way when its rosette of pinnate leaves sends up spires of cool lilac cruciform flowers in April–May. The double form, *C. p.* 'FLORE PLENO', is a delightful plant, but scarce in cultivation as it sets no seed.

CARDUNCELLUS *Compositae*

C. rhaponticoides made a sensation when shown at the Alpine Society's International Conference Show in 1961. Recently collected in Morocco, it forms a thick flat rosette of lanceolate or narrowly spatulate leaves with a dark red midrib. In the centre sits a stemless, rayless thistle-head of purplish-blue. 1"–2". Early summer. (Pl. 7)

C. pinnatus is similar, except that the leaves are so slashed, especially at the base, as to appear shaggily pinnate.

CARLINA *Compositae*

C. acaulis, the Stemless Thistle of the Alps (and of our own downlands) is extremely attractive, with its sessile thistle-head set in the centre of a rosette of spiny, acanthus-like leaves. I have yet to see it repeating this habit in

Carmichaelia, Cassiope

cultivation, but know no reason why it should not do so, in sufficiently dry, sunny, well-drained, poor soil. 1"–2". Summer.

CARMICHAELIA *Leguminosae*

This curious genus from New Zealand has one species small and hardy enough for the rock garden or alpine house.

C. enysii. A twiggy shrub, with flattened leafless stems (the small leaves present in its young stages soon drop off) and erect racemes of tiny, violet, pea-shaped flowers in early summer. A light soil in full sun. No lime. 6"–8". Summer.

CASSIOPE *Ericaceae*

A very valuable genus for all who have a lime-free soil. All species enjoy a cool, shady position, not too dry, in peat and leaf-mould. All have thin, wiry branches closely set with tiny, pointed, adpressed leaves, giving the appearance of a very neat heather. Most are free flowering, in early summer, and nothing is more delightful than a well-grown specimen with its myriads of small white or pink-flushed pendent bells on wiry hair-like stems above the dense mats of close, dark green heathery foliage.

C. fastigiata. Himalaya. A congested, much-branched upright shrublet of 10"–12". Small nodding, solitary, open, bell-shaped white flowers. April–May.

D*C. hypnoides (*Harrimanella hypnoides*). N. Europe, Asia, America. A particularly finely growing small shrublet of about 2". The very narrow leaves are not so closely adpressed as in most other species, and the whole plant has the appearance of a fine, bright green moss. The bell-shaped flowers, white or faintly pink-tinged, though small, are conspicuous on their reddish-brown hair-like pedicels. This is a very difficult plant to keep in good health, even in the cool, damp, peaty site which it demands. When seen in perfect health and beauty it is an enchanting small plant. Early summer.

C. lycopodioides (*Andromeda lycopodioides*). N.E. Asia, America. Prostrate, and when not in flower resembling a lycopodium moss, with its fine much-branched almost prostrate stems covered with adpressed leaves. Small, white, bell-shaped flowers on 1" wiry stems. A rather sturdier form has been given a varietal name, *C. l.* var. *major* (*rigida*). 2"–3". April–May. (Pl. 7)

C. mertensiana. N. America. A taller evergreen shrublet of 10"–12", with rather larger white flowers. April–May.

*C. selaginoides. Himalaya, W. China. A tufted evergreen shrub, up to 10", with stiff narrow branches covered with tiny, lanceolate adpressed leaves. White bell-shaped flowers. April–May.

82

Castilleja, Ceanothus

D*C. **stelleriana** (*Harrimanella stelleriana*). N. America, N. Asia. This miniature prostrate shrub vies with *C. hypnoides* for pride of place as one of the most delightful of tiny shrublets, and is almost, but not quite as difficult to obtain and to grow. It forms a dense mat (when happy) of tiny, fine leaved shoots, tinged with reddish-brown, above which the pink-flushed bells dangle on inch-high stems. 1″. April–May.

C. tetragona. Northern areas throughout the N. Hemisphere. Here we return to the sturdier and more easily grown erect shrubs of up to 1 foot. This has dark green imbricated foliage and the usual white, or pink tinged, campanulate or urn-shaped flowers. April–May.

CASTILLEJA *Scrophulariaceae*

With one exception, this is a N. American genus. The species are upright growing perennials, and many are very spectacular by means of the brilliant bracts at the bases of the individual flowers, which are borne in close spikes well above the foliage. Although some are rather tall for the rock garden, the species range downwards to a few inches, but their beautiful spires of scarlet (*C. coccinea*, the Indian Paint Brush) crimson, pink, gold, or even purple are unfortunately beyond our reach, as the plants are parasitic and therefore, unless one can discover and provide the appropriate host, practically impossible to grow. Success has been achieved, as was shown by *C. hololeuca* (felted leaves and tawny-pink bracts and flowers), which gained the premier award at the International Rock Garden Conference in 1961, and was grown from seed, without a host plant. One can only hope that others of the tribe may sometime prove unexpectedly amenable. They would add gaiety to our gardens in colour and form. In general the seed germinates very freely, but the young plants die off when 1″–2″ high.

CEANOTHUS *Rhamnaceae*

Apart from the great tribe of Ericaceous plants, there are comparatively few shrubs sufficiently dwarf for the rock garden. Blue flowers are also in a minority. It is therefore a pity that the dwarf members of this delightful N. American genus are not very happy in cultivation, or long-lived.

C. prostratus. A spreading shrublet, only a few inches in height, but capable of extending several feet if it lives long enough. Its stout little holly-like leaves are thick on the congested branches, which terminate in clusters of small blue flowers. Barely hardy, especially when young. Summer.

C. thyrsiflorus var. **repens** (*C. repens*). A prostrate species for a sunny

83

well-drained site, with alternate toothed leaves and clusters of small, pale blue flowers. Early summer.

CELMISIA *Compositae*

This large genus is almost entirely endemic to New Zealand. The species are all characterized by handsome white daisy-like flowers, having more or less conspicuous golden discs. A few are shrubby, but most form rosettes with many radical leaves, usually covered beneath (and often on both surfaces) with silvery silky or woolly hairs, but occasionally tawny on the reverse. Hitherto they have been considered difficult in cultivation. This may partly be because seed seldôm ripens here, and imported seed, like most others from New Zealand, is capricious, to say the least, in germination. Consequently division and cuttings are the best means of propagation. Most of the woolly species appreciate overhead protection in winter, if only to preserve the beauty of the white or silvery foliage. Lately many more species have become available, and it is found they are by no means so intractable as they were reputed to be. They appreciate a soil rich in humus and, surprisingly considering their usually silky foliage, a rather damp situation. The following are a few of the really dwarf species.

*C. argentea. Mat-forming, with dense grey tufts of small, needle-like leaves. Stemless white flowers, singly at the apices of the shoots. Despite its name this is not so silvery as its near relation C. sessiliflora. 2″. Early summer.

C. bellidioides. A tiny mat-forming species, distinct in having completely smooth, shining, dark green leaves, small and narrowly ovate. A moisture lover. 1″. Early summer. (Pl. 7)

*C. coriacea. A most striking plant forming large rosettes of stiff, silver, pointed leaves and glistening solid daisies on stout stems. Up to a foot. Early summer. (Pl. 7)

C. glandulosa. A creeping plant for the scree; a mat of sticky leaves with the usual daisy flowers. Early summer.

*C. sessiliflora. Dense tufts of rigid needle-like leaves, silvery. Almost stemless white daisies. 1″. Early summer.

C. vernicosa. A densely tufted species from the Auckland Islands, unique in having purple disc florets. Damp situation. This interesting plant is barely in cultivation, unfortunately.

C. webbii. A small shrubby plant with short linear-oblong leaves of felted grey-green. 4″–8′. Summer.

84

Celsia, Centaurea, Centaurium, Cephalanthera,

CELSIA *Scrophulariaceae*

*C. acaulis. Greece. The only dwarf member of the genus is a delightful plant, forming a rosette of oblong, toothed leaves from which the many solitary yellow, mullein-like flowers, opening from attractive polished-mahogany buds, rise on 3″ stems. Seedlings are hardly ever true, as it crosses readily with *Verbascum phoeniceum*, the resultant plants bearing 6″–8″ spikes of flowers in unusual shades of mauve and bronze. *C. acaulis* flowers over a long period and makes a good pan for the alpine house. 3″–4″. Spring onwards. (Pl. 8)

CENTAUREA *Compositae*

The Cornflower family are mostly too tall and coarse for the rock garden, but use might be made of some of the better forms of *C. montana*, which may be found locally in the European Alps in a large flowered compact form with ray florets of a deep blue, though admittedly they are rather sparse. 6″–8″. Summer.

CENTAURIUM *Gentianaceae*

This genus, which is usually listed as *Erythraea*, under which name it was previously known, includes several dwarf species, not usually long-lived, which are very similar in appearance to a clear pink *Gentiana verna*.

C. scilloides (*Erythraea diffusa*). Europe, including Britain. A densely tufted plant with terminal inflorescence of deep clear rose-pink. A sunny well-drained situation suits it as it is a plant of the English Downlands. This is a very variable plant, and allied species are so near one another that they need not be considered here. Spring onwards. (Pl. 8)

CEPHALANTHERA *Orchidaceae*

D*C. rubra, the most distinguished European member of this genus and a rare British native, is one of the most lovely of the hardy orchids. Its large, rose-pink, spurless flowers are carried in a loose spike on one to two foot stems. It grows in open woodland and seems to prefer a limy soil. Early summer.

85

CERASTIUM *Caryophyllaceae*

The Mouse-ear Chickweeds include a few high alpine species, desirable either for their comparatively large white flowers or for their woolly foliage. Summer flowering.

C. alpinum. Alps of Europe (including Gt. Britain). A tufted plant with grey-green broadly lanceolate leaves and upright branched stems of 2″–4″ bearing a few white flowers with deeply cut petals. Usually grown in the form *C. a.* var. *lanatum*, which is much more compact and prostrate than the type, with crowded, smaller, wider leaves, hoary with many white hairs. Makes an interesting alpine house plant. Early summer.

C. glaciale. See **C. uniflorum.**

C. latifolium. High Alps. Mat-forming and variably hairy, with large, white, deeply-cleft flowers. This and the former species do well in a very gritty scree. 2″. Summer.

D***C. uniflorum** (*glaciale*). European Alps. An altogether smaller plant, with solitary, rather large flowers. Sometimes considered a variety of the foregoing. 1″–2″. Summer.

CERATOSTIGMA *Plumbaginaceae*

***C. plumbaginoides** (*Plumbago larpentae*). The only member of the genus which is dwarf enough for the rock garden. Easy in any reasonably good soil in sun or part shade. Valuable for its very late flowering (October–November), for its deep blue flowers and for its foliage, which takes reddish autumn tints. It spreads by rooting shoots, and is a useful and beautiful ground cover where it can be allowed to spread. The 8″–10″ leafy stems rise at the tips, bearing the inch-wide deep-blue Periwinkle-like flowers in the axils of the upper leaves.

CHAENACTIS *Compositae*

A genus of N. American plants, including several annuals, but at least one perennial provides a good foliage plant.

C. douglasii. A dense, almost shrubby plant, with very much cut, white, woolly foliage, and curious, rather attractive, sturdy tassel-like heads of grey-green, sometimes mauve or pink tinted. Recently brought into cultivation from seed collected in the Rocky Mountains. 6″–8″. Summer.

Cheiranthus, Cherleria, Chiastophyllum, Chimaphila

CHEIRANTHUS *Cruciferae*

The Wallflower family includes a few gay and good tempered dwarfs, easy in any sunny position, though not usually long-lived. They are generally at their best in their second year, and mostly after that become woody or straggling, tending literally to flower themselves to death. They can, however, be easily replaced from seed, which germinates readily. Most of the dwarf species have been removed to the nearly akin genus, Erysimum.

C. × allionii. Hybrid origin. The well-known fiery orange "Siberian Wallflower" is much used in bedding for its free-flowering and vivid colour. If introduced into the rock garden at all it should be used very sparingly or its strong colour will overshadow most other plants in its neighbourhood.

C. alpinus. See **Erysimum alpinum.**

C. helveticus. See **Erysimum dubium.**

C. linifolius. See **Erysimum linifolium.**

C. menziesii. See **Parrya menziesii.**

CHERLERIA. See MINUARTIA

CHIASTOPHYLLUM *Crassulaceae Monotypic*

C. oppositifolium. S. Africa. Better known, and usually found in catalogues, under its former names of *Cotyledon oppositifolia* or *Cotyledon simplicifolia* (Lamb's Tail). From basal, rounded, and coarsely-toothed rather succulent basal leaves rise 4″–6″ stems arching over with long catkin-like inflorescences of tiny yellow flowers. Summer.

CHIMAPHILA *Pyrolaceae*

A small genus of evergreen sub-shrubs, very near to Pyrola, mostly with whorled, leathery, dark green leaves, and few-flowered clusters of small five-petalled white or pink-flushed saucer-shaped flowers. They need a lime-free soil, rich in humus, in part shade. Not easy plants, and best propagated by seed.

C. japonica. Japan. Has toothed alternate leaves and white flowers. 4″–6″. Summer.

C. maculata., C. menzieii, and **C. umbellatus** are three very similar species from N. America, with whorls of lanceolate, often serrated, leaves and umbels of white flowers, often flushed with green or pink. 6″–10″. Summer.

CHIONODOXA *Liliaceae*

There is little variation between the few species of this genus. All are hardy bulbs and have strap-shaped leaves and sprays of six-petalled starry blue flowers, differing in appearance from Scilla by the flat open flower in contrast to the more campanulate form of the latter. Only two species are in general cultivation, and one of those only sparsely. They make attractive pans for the alpine house, although this is by no means necessary as a protection as they will naturalize and increase freely by seed or bulbils in the open garden. March–April.

*C. gigantea. Turkey. Very nearly akin to the following species, but with larger, more solid flowers, usually of a paler blue. 4″–5″. March–April.

*C. luciliae. Turkey. The 'Glory of the Snows' and the species universally grown. Each bulb produces two or three 3″–4″ sprays of flat, star-shaped flowers, blue shading to white in the centre. There are also a pale pink and a white form, but they are not so beautiful as the type. 3″–4″. March–April.

CHRYSANTHEMUM *Compositae*

*C. densum (*haradjanii hort.*). A recent introduction from Asia Minor, forming a spreading shrub of 6″–8″. The fern-like, much-cut leaves are like silver filigree. It is quite hardy and remains compact in a sunny, well-drained position. The yellow flowers are few and of less importance than the lovely foliage. Summer.

*C. hispanicum var. **sulphurem.** Spain. Sulphur-yellow daisies over much-cut silky leaves. 6″–8″. Summer.

*C. hosmariense. Morocco. Of shrubby growth, having much-cut silver-grey foliage and comparatively large clean-cut white daisies on slender stems of 2″–3″. Eventually 8″–10″. Early spring, or may even commence to flower during the winter.

*C. mawii. Morocco. Variable in height and may grow rather tall (15″–

A large summer-flowering genus of daisy-flowered species, usually with attractive much-cut foliage, which is often silvery or woolly. The alpine species will all keep more in character when grown in an open sunny spot, with well-drained soil which is not too rich.

D***C. alpinum.** This charming little plant is widespread throughout the European Alps and has neat white daisies on slender 3″–4″ stems above tufted narrowly divided deep-green foliage. It is not often seen in cultivation, but is not difficult to grow and to keep in character in stony scree mixture in full sun. 6″. Summer.

18″), but when the conditions of dry and stony ground keep it compact it is a charming plant, with the usual much-cut foliage and delightful pale pink daisies borne singly on slender stems. Coming from Morocco it is not reliably hardy in a severe winter, and hostages should be kept by taking cuttings. Summer.

CHRYSOGONUM *Compositae Monotypic*

C. virginianum. N. America. Forms mats of ovate, bluntly toothed leaves, with yellow daisy flowers on 5″–6″ stems. It is long flowering, and has value as a ground cover, but the ray florets are so few and so widely spaced as to give a meagre starry effect to the flower. May.

CISTUS *Cistaceae*

These lovely evergreen shrubs from the Mediterranean region are mainly too tall for the rock garden, and even the hardiest is not completely proof against an exceptionally severe winter. All are free-flowering, with delightful but fugacious flowers, like wild roses in white, often with central coloured blotches, or shades of pink. The following are nearly hardy.

p**C. crispus.** S.W. Europe. Sessile ovate, hairy leaves and clusters of purplish-red rose-like flowers. Eventually nearly 2 ft. Early Summer.

p**C. rosmarinifolius.** S.W. Europe. Linear, hairy leaves and inch-wide white flowers, shading to pale yellow in the centre. Up to 1 ft. Early summer.

p***C.** 'SILVER PINK'. Although rather taller and doubtfully hardy, must be mentioned for its extreme beauty of grey-green leaves and large (up to 3″) silver-pink salvers with centres of golden stamens. This *must* be preserved by over-wintering cuttings. Eventually 2 ft. Early summer.

CLAYTONIA *Portulacaceae*

These succulent little plants are interesting rather than conspicuous, and, like our native, the annual *C. perfoliata*, are likely to spread beyond bounds by self-sown seed. Summer.

C. australasica. Australasia. Makes spreading mats and bears almost stemless white-petalled flowers from June to August.

89

Clematis, Clintonia, Codonopsis

*C. nivalis. U.S.A. A small but charming plant with deep rose flowers on 1″–2″ stems, radiating from a rosette of linear, rather fleshy leaves. Scree treatment. Late spring.

C. caroliniana. E.N. America. A rosette of 1″–2″ narrowly spatulate leaves and deep pink flowers with cleft petals. 4″. Spring.

CLEMATIS *Ranunculaceae*

The only member of this genus which can be included here is the lovely ***C. alpina** (*Atragene alpina*) which may be seen in June–July throughout the European Alps, twining and wreathing low bushes in sparse woodland with its large pendent four-petalled flowers in shades of violet-blue to pure blue. It should be grown in the same way if introduced into the rock garden—that is, allowed to twine through some low shrub or among twigs specially placed for it. It is deciduous. Late spring.

CLINTONIA *Liliaceae*

A small genus, mainly from N. America, of woodland plants, nearly related to Trillium. The leaves are mostly clustered at the bases of the erect stems which bear long-stalked umbels of funnel-shaped flowers. Moist, sandy peat, in shade. Propagation by division in spring.

C. andrewsiana. California. May grow to a foot or more, but is very lovely, with heads of deep rose, lily-like flowers, followed by brilliant blue berries. Up to 1 ft. May–July.

C. umbellata. N. America. A more dwarf species with compact umbels of small, speckled greenish-white starry flowers. Black berries. 6″. Early summer.

C. uniflora. N. America. Narrow lanceolate leaves and solitary inch-long white flowers. Blue berries. Spring.

CODONOPSIS *Campanulaceae*

These Central Asian plants all have leafy, rather straggling stems, and in some cases need to hang over a rock face or to be supported by twigs or a dwarf shrub. Their flowers are loosely pendent and are large bells of muted greenish-blues and purples. They are often freckled or veined within, so need to be upturned to appreciate their

Colchicum

full beauty. Therefore they show to best advantage when planted on a high bank or walled bed, or so placed as to straggle amongst low branches. They are all summer flowerers and will grow well in gritty soil with plenty of humus.

C. clematidea. Mts. of Asia. One of the taller species, with large, very pale blue bells.

*C. convolvulacea. Himalaya, W. China. One of the twining species, and perhaps the most beautiful in flower as the open, almost saucer-shaped corollas are a good clear blue.

C. meleagris. Yunnan, China. Erect, 6"–12", with faint blue flowers, reticulated with chocolate markings, sometimes spotted with yellow within.

C. vinciflora. Asia. A semi-climber with salver-shaped blue flowers.

There are several other species on the fringes of cultivation, but as there is such a strong family likeness only the collector need hunt to obtain others than the above.

COLCHICUM *Liliaceae*

A family of beautiful bulbs, superficially rather like robust crocuses (and often wrongly called 'Autumn Crocus'), but readily distinguished from that genus by having six stamens (instead of three). In general, they are easy to grow, and liable to multiply, but they look more natural in a semi-woodland site, where, also, the very large sheath of lanceolate leaves (up to a foot or more) will not be out of place, but even rather handsome, when they appear in spring long after the naked flower stalks. Among grass, at the foot of a tree, makes a perfect setting, and the lush foliage must not be cut down until it begins to wither. A few of the most distinct are given below, and many other species can be found described in *Collins Guide to Bulbs*.

C. alpinum. Europe. The sturdy 'Autumn Crocus' which transforms the Alpine pastures in late summer. Pink. Curiously seldom grown in cultivation, and then not happy or permanent. 6". Autumn.

*C. autumnale. Europe. Altogether a smaller, more delicate flower. The type is pink, but there is a white form and also **C. a.** 'STRIATUM' which is white, striped pink. The foliage is finer than in most species, so that it might be used with discretion in the rock garden. 5"–6". Autumn.

*C. agrippinum. Origin unknown, possibly a hybrid. Another autumn flowerer with chequered petals of lilac purple. 7"–8".

Conandron, Convallaria, Convolvulus

*C. luteum. Afghanistan, Turkey. Notable as flowering in spring, and as having clear butter-yellow flowers. Rare in cultivation. 4″–6″. February, March.

*C. speciosum. Persia, Asia Minor, etc. Large, beautiful goblet-shaped flowers in autumn, followed by tall coarse foliage in spring. The type varies from deep purplish rose, *C. s.* 'ATRORUBENS' (Pl. 32) to white, and there are many forms selected for colour and size and named, and also a double rose-lilac, *C.* 'WATER LILY' and a rare double white. 8″–10″.

CONANDRON *Gesneriaceae Monotypic*

P***C. ramondioides.** Japan. As its name suggests, a near relation of the ramondas. Unlike them, however, it dies back completely in winter to "noses" of glossy, dark brown fur, but spring brings back its thick, very much corrugated, deep green leaves, from amongst which rise the 4″–6″ stems, each bearing six or more pale mauve, pointed-petalled ramonda-like flowers. It is reputed not to be reliably hardy, but will withstand most winters if kept fairly dry in an unheated alpine house. Propagation by seed, which needs care in the early stages, as it and the resulting seedlings are so minute. There is a scarce white form, **C. r.** var. **leucanthemum.** It is not an easy plant and requires rich leafy soil, and no lime. 5″–6″. Summer.

CONVALLARIA *Liliaceae*

The Lily of the Valley is too well known to need description, but both the type, *C. majalis,* and its pink form, *C. m.* 'ROSEA', have their welcome place in the outskirts of the shady rock garden. Both, however, and especially the former, can become very invasive if they are happy in their environment. 6″–8″. Spring.

CONVOLVULUS *Convolvulaceae*

A large genus, of which the following species are very desirable in the rock garden or alpine house. They vary from the distinctly difficult to the frankly invasive, but all these mentioned are beautiful.

C. althaeoides. S. Europe. This is perhaps the most beautiful (it has been

92

Coprosma

known as *C. elegantissima*), as it is certainly the most invasive when suited. It dies away completely in winter, and its first leaves are heart-shaped with scalloped edges, on long petioles. Its later leaves are deeply cut into long pedatifid sections, and are most attractive in shape and colour, being a silvery grey. They are a perfect foil to the many single inch-wide clear deep-pink trumpets. A hot stony position suits it, but it will ramp there. Prostrate. Summer.

p*C. cneorum. S. Europe. A small shrub of 1–2 ft., with many lanceolate silver-plated leaves and flowers which are pink on the outer folds of the buds, but open white. Not absolutely hardy, but will usually survive in a hot, sheltered position in very well-drained soil. May onwards.

p*C. incanus. America. Forms tufts of narrow silvery leaves with large trumpets of pale pearly-pink. Long flowering. Full sun and good drainage. 3″–4″. April onwards.

pC. lineatus. S. Europe. Makes close mats of silvery linear leaves, bearing rose-pink or white flowers. 6″. June.

p*C. mauritanicus. N. Africa. A prostrate spreading perennial, which breaks fresh ground by bearing over a long period in summer and early autumn a profusion of flatly-open trumpets of a most lovely clear blue. It is not rampant and is one of the most beautiful of plants, but it is only completely hardy in favoured spots. Propagation by cuttings, which should be over-wintered with protection.

pC. nitidus. Sierra Nevada, Spain. A rather rare species, forming cushions of small ovate, silvery, silky leaves and, but not freely, large rosy-white flowers in summer. 3″.

C. soldanelloides. If one could find the secret of pleasing it, our own native convolvulus, which flaunts its huge pink sessile trumpets at our feet among sand dunes by the coast, would vie with any of the foreign beauties. However, no one, I think, has yet discovered how to tame this beautiful creature. It probably needs to be able to probe a yard deep in pure sand.

C. incanus, lineatus, and *nitidus* make lovely pans for the alpine house, and are safer there.

COPROSMA *Rubiaceae*

Of this rather numerous genus from Australia and New Zealand, one or two dwarf species are grown on the rock garden. They make congested shrublets of 3″–4″ with inconspicuous flowers, but some bear showy berries of amethyst or blue.

C. petriei. New Zealand. The species most usually grown. This has curious translucent berries, suggestive of the eggs of a very large snail. Hardy in the south and west. Propagation by cuttings. 3″.

93

COPTIS *Ranunculaceae*

These are delicate little woodlanders from N. America and Japan, rather like fairy Wood Anemones. They are hardy and need a moist, leafy soil in part shade.

C. asplenifolia. N. America, Japan. Single, white anemone-like flowers over ferny foliage. 10″. Spring.

C. anemonifolia. N. America. Has particularly cut and saw-edged leaves, and rather smaller white flowers than the following. 4″–6″. Spring.

C. quinquefolia. Japan. Has five-lobed leaves, rather like a potentilla, and short-stemmed glistening white flowers. 4″–6″. Spring.

C. trifolia. N. Hemisphère. Three-parted leaves, bluntly toothed, and the usual white anemone flowers. 3″–5″. Spring.

COREOPSIS *Compositae*

Of this large genus the only one suitable and available for the rock garden is

C. rosea. E. United States. A perennial with branched stems and narrowly linear leaves, occasionally lobed, and many mauve-pink daisies with yellow centres. May grow to a foot or more. Summer.

CORNUS *Cornaceae*

Among this large family of trees and shrubs there are two very attractive miniatures.

*C. canadensis (*Chamaepericlymenum canadense*). N. America. An invaluable carpeter for moist woodland soil. The ovate leaves are crowded at the top of the 4″–6″ stems and the flowers, which are tiny and greenish-purple, are borne in dense little clusters which are made conspicuous by the four ovate white bracts which encircle them and give the appearance of a large four-petalled white flower. In the autumn the foliage takes bronze and red tints. The fruits form little bunches of bright red berries. 6″–8″. Early summer.

C. suecica. (*Chamaepericlymenum suecicum*). N. America and Europe (including Gt. Britain). Very similar, but the leaves are in pairs up the stem, and the bracts are yellowish. 6″–10″. Summer.

COROKIA *Cornaceae*

A small genus of New Zealand plants. Even *C. cotoneaster* eventually grows too large for the average rock garden, but it is slow growing

Coronilla, Cortusa, Corydalis

and for some years forms an attractive shrub for rock garden or pan culture, with its many wiry, contorted and congested branches with sparse, small, dark green, oval leaves, backed with white felt. The small star-shaped bright yellow flowers appear in May, followed by orange berries.

CORONILLA *Leguminosae*

These are attractive sun-loving shrubs with small very flat glaucous, pinnate leaves and terminal and lateral umbels of small bright-yellow pea-shaped flowers.

C. cappadocica. Asia Minor. A prostrate herbaceous perennial with pinnate leaves and large yellow flowers in tight umbels. 2″–3″. Summer.

*C. minima. S.W. Europe. A procumbent shrublet with glaucous curiously flat, pinnate leaves (short oval leaflets), and fragrant yellow flowers. Not absolutely hardy. 2″–3″. Early summer.

CORTUSA *Primulaceae*

A genus of two species, the following is in cultivation:

*C. matthioli. Mountains of Europe and Asia. A woodland plant (it flourishes on the banks of mountains streams, near the spray of water) with very much the habit of the primrose. The leaves are crinkled and softly hairy, more or less heart-shaped, with long petioles, and irregularly lobed. The flowers, in umbels on 6″–8″ stems are pendent, funnel-shaped, and of a reddish purple. There is a white form, *C. m.* 'ALBA'. Early summer.

CORYDALIS *Papaveraceae*

Natives of the temperate regions of the northern hemisphere, all have the narrow, lipped and horned flowers closely resembling their near relation the Common Fumitory, beautiful weed of cultivated spaces. They all have delicate finely-lobed glaucous foliage, and the genus is rather remarkable for the very varied colours of the different species.

C. bulbosa. See **C. solida.**

ᴅ*C. cashmeriana. The beauty of the family, but an intractable one. Above the usual attractive blue-green foliage rise erect spires of the typically shaped flowers of the genus, but of an indescribably brilliant clear blue with almost a hint of green in it. It demands a cool leafy, lime-free soil, and although it makes a lovely pan plant when well grown, it is really happier out of doors (where it is perfectly hardy, dying away below the surface during winter) if conditions can be found to suit it. Better specimens are seen in Scotland than further south. This native of Kashmir flowers in late spring or early summer, and may bear a few odd flowers later which are often of a poorer colour. 6". (Pl. 8)

*C. cava. Europe. A pleasant little woodlander which takes one unawares in early spring with its dense and stocky little spikes of flowers which are a curious smoky reddish-purple. The tuberous root is hollow. The whole plant quickly dies away, to reappear again the next February–March. 4"–6".

C. cheilanthifolia. China. Ferny foliage and erect spires of yellow flowers. Needs more sun than the foregoing. 8". Early summer.

C. glauca. N. America. Annual, with fine and fragile foliage and small pink and yellow flowers on slender erect 6" stems, which are quite attractive. Early summer.

C. lutea. Europe, including Britain. The well-known Yellow Corydalis which seeds itself freely, and is, quite surprisingly, hardy in spite of the fragile appearance of its delicate foliage, much cut into deep lobes. Although invasive (through seed) this is a beautiful and very long flowering plant and valuable for walls and rough corners, where it can easily be kept in check by weeding, as its roots are shallow and brittle. 6"–8". Almost continuous flowering.

C. rutifolia. Asia Minor, Europe. A pink-flowered species, whose foliage has large almost ovate lobes. Variable in tone to a good rose. 6"–8". April–May.

*C. solida (*bulbosa*). Europe (including Gt. Britain). Very like *C. cava* and enjoying the same woodland conditions, but having as root system a solid (not hollow) tuber, and bracts lobed, not entire. 4"–6". Early spring.

*C. wilsonii. China. A comparative newcomer, rather like a much more compact and solid edition of *C. lutea*, with erect spikes of large, deep yellow flowers, about an inch long. 6"–7". Late spring.

COTONEASTER *Rosaceae*

This very large and world-wide genus (with the exception of Japan) has a few dwarf and congested species that are of great value in the rock garden, being among the comparatively few small shrubs which

5

Aster alpinus
Aubrieta deltoidea variegata
Berberis corallina compacta

Astilbe chinensis
Bergenia schmidtii
Boykinia jamesii

6

Briggsia penlopii
Calceolaria darwinii
Campanula garganica 'Blue Diamond'

Calandrinia umbellata
Campanula arvatica
Campanula cochlearifolia var. alba

are almost indifferent to soil and position. The few described are prostrate and, being so good-tempered, may need pruning back to keep within desired bounds. The many quarter-inch flowers are white, tinged with pink, but their greater value is in the conspicuous and prolific display of bright red berries in the autumn.

C. adpressa. China. Inconspicuous flowers in spring, followed by $\frac{1}{4}$" red berries. Will follow contours of any rock. Deciduous. June.

C. congesta (*C. microphylla glacialis*). Himalaya. Very similar, but will form a close hummock, up to 1 ft., if there is no handy rock for it to clothe. June.

C. dammeri (*humifusa*). China. Of similar habit, but with larger (up to $\frac{1}{2}$") flowers, and coral-red fruits. There is a more compact form, *C. d.* var. *radicans.* June.

C. thymifolia. Himalaya. Perhaps the most congested of this rather homogeneous group, with thyme-like leaves and pinkish flowers, and smaller bright red fruits. May–June.

COTULA *Compositae*

A genus of perennials of spreading habit, mainly from New Zealand, with ferny foliage and, in some species recently introduced, striking pale pink or deep red rayless flower-heads on 2"–3" stems. These are more attractive than the well-known carpeter.

Cotula squalida, which has the characteristic deeply-cut, bronze-tinged foliage, but inconspicuous flowers.

COTYLEDON *Crassulaceae*

This South African genus, whose species all have succulent foliage, often in sempervivum-like rosettes, and many of which are not hardy, has recently been reclassified, removing the greater part of its members into a number of fresh genera. The three usually grown in the rock garden are:

C. chrysantha. Now *Rosularia pallida.*

C. oppositifolia (*simplicifolia*). Now *Chiastophyllum oppositifolium.*

C. spinosa. Now *Orostachys spinosus.*

These are all likely to be found in catalogues under their original name of Cotyledon.

CRASPEDIA *Compositae*

C. uniflora. Australia, Tasmania, New Zealand. The only species in cultivation. Rather thick club-shaped radical leaves of 3″–4″, grey-green with thick woolly hairs, and cream or pale yellow dense rayless heads of flowers. Summer.

> P**C. u.** var. **lanata** is quite white with woolly hairs, and makes an attractive foliage plant. The flowers are solitary pompoms of lemon yellow. July.

CRASSULA *Crassulaceae*

A large genus of succulent shrubs and herbs, many not hardy, from Africa, of which two are dwarf enough for the rock garden or alpine house.

> **C. milfordiae** (*sediformis*). Of recent introduction from Basutoland, this little plant makes mats or 2″ hummocks in the scree, and bears small heads of white flowers from crimson buds. The whole plant takes winter colours of bronze-red. July.

> P***C. sarcocaulis.** S. Africa. The hardiest of the crassulas, this will survive out of doors most winters in a sheltered spot, and makes an attractive alpine house plant. It is succulent-shrubby, forming a much branched "tree" of up to 10″ (usually less). The small, pointed leaves are deciduous, and the many clusters of tiny, pale pink flowers, crimson in the bud, make it a gay little plant in late summer. A hybrid has been raised between this plant and *C. milfordiae* which is, in effect, a neater version of *C. sarcocaulis*, smaller in all its parts. July–August.

CREMANTHODIUM *Compositae*

A little known and grown genus from N. India, Tibet, and China. Farrer wrote enthusiastically about the species, but few are in cultivation, and those not universally offered. They are graceful plants, with basal entire leaves, and single more or less pendent daisy-like heads, which do not fully open, on slender stems. Most have yellow flowers. Later expeditions have introduced or re-introduced a few species, so it is to be hoped that some may prove amenable to our conditions. Although coming from great heights, they prefer a cool, leafy soil, and not too dry a site. *C. delavayi, C. nobile,* and *C. reniforme,*

98

with yellow flowers are all rather tall for the average rock garden, but one or two dwarf species (about 6″) are offered by one grower, still under the collector's number. *C. pinnatum*, as described by Farrer, would seem to be a lovely plant, and departs from the family tradition in having pink flowers.

CREPIS *Compositae*

A wide genus, closely related to the Hawkweeds (*Hieracium*), most of which are too coarse and invasive for the rock garden, and are in fact weeds of the pastures.

C. aurea. European Alps. Appears an attractive little plant when seen in the mixed dwarf herbage of the high Alps, with single flower-heads like small dandelions on wiry 2″ stems, but of a rich coppery-orange. In the rock garden it is difficult to keep so small and compact, and tends to become weedy. Summer.

C. rosea (*incana*). Greece. This is a charming plant when kept compact in a rather meagre well-drained soil in full sun. It makes a clump of grey leaves, from which rise many branched stems, bearing a succession of pale pink dandelion-like flowers in summer. 7″–8″. (Pl. 8)

CROCUS *Iridaceae*

It is only possible here to make a small selection for continuous flowering from this large genus of small and most charming hardy bulbs. They differ mainly from the (usually) larger colchicums by having only three stamens whereas the latter genus has six. The following are chosen to give a succession of blooms from autumn to spring, but very many more species will be found described in *Collins Guide to Bulbs*.

AUTUMN FLOWERING

D***C. byzantinus.** E. Europe, Hungary. Not easy to get or keep but mentioned as it is one of the most distinct of the genus. The inner segments of the corolla are upright, pointed, and much smaller than the outer row, which, especially when the outer segments recurve a little, gives it a definitely iris-like appearance. This was emphasized in its former name of *C. iridiflorus*.

***C. kotschyanus** (*zonatus*, under which name it is usually offered). Asia Minor, Lebanon. A charming and prolific plant with rosy-lilac flowers

Crocus

having bright orange spots in the throat, which are conspicuous as the flower opens in the sun. Spreads freely, and is suitable for naturalizing.

*C. speciosus. E. Europe, Asia Minor, Caucasus, N.E. Persia. One of the best tempered and most valuable of the crocuses, with solid goblets varying from light mauve to purple, with conspicuous orange-red stigmata. Will colonize itself by seed and cormlets. Many of the colour forms are given varietal names in catalogues. One of the best is 'OXONIAN', a good luminous bluish-purple of lovely form.

C. zonatus. Now **C. kotschyanus** (q.v.).

WINTER AND VERY EARLY SPRING FLOWERING

*C. chrysanthus. Greece and Asia Minor. In all its many varieties the most beautiful and good-tempered of all the species. The type has medium-sized, rather globular flowers of deep yellow to orange, with fine brownish-purple veining on the outsides of the three outer petals. The seedlings vary from ivory-white to deep orange, and there is a lovely colour break into shades of silvery blue, probably the result of hybridization with *C. biflorus* var. *weldenii*. All the members of this species may be identified by the small black tips or barbs to the orange anthers. Dozens of forms have been propagated vegetatively by growing on the surrounding cormlets, and have been given varietal names. All are desirable and flower in early spring. A few of the most distinct colour forms are:

'BLUE BIRD'. Opening white, outer petals purplish-blue with a white margin.

'CREAM BEAUTY'. One of the best. Deep cream solid goblets with a golden throat. Very free-flowering and increases readily.

'E. A. BOWLES'. An earlier variety, named after the famous gardener, owner of Myddleton House and authority on crocus and other bulbs. A deep butter-yellow, globular flower, with bronze feathering at base of petals; not surpassed in beauty by any later forms.

'E. P. BOWLES'. Rather similar but deeper in colour and smaller in flower.

'MOONLIGHT'. A beautiful pale sulphur-yellow.

'SNOW BUNTING'. Raised by Mr. Bowles, who gave bird names to those of his own raising. White inner petals, outer creamy with dark lilac featherings.

'ZWANENBURG BRONZE'. Deep orange, with glossy mahogany reverse to the three outer petals. Very early.

*C. imperati. S. Italy. One of the most striking. The bud is buff coloured, veined with deep purple, and opens to a bluish-mauve flower, veined with deeper colour. Orange stigmata. Dry situation. January onward.

*C. laevigatus. Greece. As desirable as the last, with blue-mauve petals, strikingly feathered on the outside. Dry situation. May flower from early December to the end of January.

*C. tomasinianus. Dalmatia and E. shores of Adriatic. Spreads abundantly by seed and cormlets, and is quite distinct when its pale wraith-like spires appear in wide drifts. A burst of sun, however, expands them into unexpected glory. The type is clear mauve, but a wide range of colour will appear among the seedlings, varying to reddish-mauve and warm purple. Some of these have been propagated vegetatively, and given varietal names, but one is always likely to have a few good ones among the many self-sown seedlings.

'WHITEWELL PURPLE' is a good rich bluish-purple.
'TAPLOW RUBY' a deep reddish-purple.

SPRING FLOWERING (FEBRUARY–MARCH)

Among many delightful species, which make charming pans for the alpine house as well as filling little raised pockets in the rock garden are:

*C. balansae. W. Asia Minor. A small crocus but of a brilliant orange, feathered without in deep mahogany.

C. biflorus. Italy to Asia Minor. One of the later flowerers, usually obtained in one or two named varieties, of which the most attractive is:

*C. b. var. **weldenii,** large pale-blue flowers, with backs of outer segments almost pure blue. A lovely plant.

*C. sieberi. Attica, Mt. Parnassus. One of the most endearing of the crocuses, with sturdy, dwarf, rather globular flowers of a clear warm mauve, opening to show a golden throat. Variable, giving rise to several named varieties which are not, to me, so desirable as the type.

*C. susianus. S.W. Russia, Crimea. The 'Cloth of Gold' crocus. Small to medium flowers of brilliant orange, with outer featherings of mahogany.

C. vernus. Alps, Pyrenees. Drifts of these may be seen in the swampy patches right up to and in the edges of the melting snow throughout all the Alps in spring and in early summer, varying in form from thin, narrow petalled flowers to solid goblets, usually white (sometimes shaded or lined with blue) but among their pale companions small clumps may sometimes be found of mauve or even rich purple. This is not an easy plant to establish in the garden. Perhaps we never give it the boggy conditions in which it spends most of its year when in the wild. It has, however, in its varied forms given rise to the sturdy garden hybrids which are known collectively as Dutch crocuses.

CRUCIANELLA. See PHUOPSIS

CRYPTOGRAMMA *Polypodiaceae*

There is one species of this genus of ferns which has every right to a place among high alpines as it can be found growing profusely in the

Cyananthus

crannies of rocks at very high altitudes, e.g. above the Little St. Bernard Pass.

C. crispa. (*Allosorus crispus*). Parsley Fern. Arctic and N. Temperate regions, including Great Britain. This requires more moisture than most of the dwarf ferns, but when in good health is one of the most charming of them all. It produces thick bunches of very finely-cut bright green foliage on wiry stems of up to 6″. It dies away soon after its best moment, in early summer, but often puts up more foliage, although not so plentifully, later in the year.

CYANANTHUS *Campanulaceae*

A genus of attractive herbaceous perennials with procumbent wiry stems bearing single blue periwinkle-like flowers at their tips in August–September. Some of the species die back completely in autumn and do not re-appear until late spring. They all require damp, leafy, sandy soil, and perfect drainage. Propagation is most sure by seed or by cuttings in spring or early summer. It is best not to attempt division of an established plant.

C. delavayi (*barbatus*). Yunnan. A mat of downy foliage and deep blue flowers with tuft of hair at throat.

C. incanus. Sikkim. A smaller plant with lighter blue flowers. White hairs in throat.

C. integer of gardens. See **C. microphyllus.** The true *C. integer* has probably not yet been introduced.

C. lobatus. Himalaya. Short prostrate stems set with small oval leaves and many flowers of a deep purple-blue enclosed by large hairy calyces. This is a variable plant, and is offered in colour forms, including white, from selected seedlings or from seed collected in different localities.

C. longiflorus. Central Asia. A rare plant which has long (up to 2″) almost bell-shaped deep blue-mauve flowers.

*****C. microphyllus** (*integer* of gardens). N. India, Nepal. One of the most charming and the easiest of this genus, with narrowly elliptic, almost heath-like foliage and blue flowers in the autumn. (Pl. 8)

*****C. sherriffii.** Bhutan, S. Tibet. A softly hairy plant of great charm, but not too easy. Periwinkle-blue flowers.

Cyathodes, Cyclamen
CYATHODES *Epacridaceae*

A small genus of Australasian shrubs of which only two are hardy enough to grow out of doors, and even these are susceptible to a very severe winter, or late spring frosts cutting the new growth. Lime-free peaty soil. Plenty of water in the growing season, but keep fairly dry during winter. Safer in alpine house, where these conditions can be controlled.

C. colensoi. New Zealand. A neat twiggy shrublet with many blunt-topped linear blue-grey leaves. Clusters of small urn-shaped white flowers, followed by rose-red, or occasionally white berries. 6″–12″. Summer.

C. empetrifolia. New Zealand. A creeping heath-like shrublet with small, fragrant white flowers, followed by red or purple berries. 6″. May–June.

CYCLAMEN *Primulaceae*

One of the most delightful genera for the rock garden, and, for the most part, easy to satisfy in cool leafy well-drained soil. The leaves, all radical, ivy-shaped or rounded on long petioles, rise almost erect from the rounded, flattened corm, and are in most species so veined and mottled with silver and lighter green that they would be of value even without their charming shuttlecock flowers in every shade from deepest rose down to white. A succession of different species can give flowers from July until the spring. Dry corms sometimes take a while to re-establish, so, where possible, pot-grown plants should be obtained. They grow readily from the freely-produced seed if sown as soon as ripe. Otherwise germination may be delayed and spasmodic. All except *C. europaeum, orbiculatum* vars., *neapolitanum,* and possibly *cilicium* need at least alpine house or frame protection during the winter.

P**C. balearicum.** Balearic Is. A small-growing species with heart-shaped rounded, dull green, spotted leaves, and small white flowers with rose throat. Doubtfully hardy. 3″. Spring.

C. cilicium. S. Asia Minor. One of the most delightful, having roundish heart-shaped leaves with silvery markings, and neat little pale rose flowers, with deep rose spots at the base of the lobes. No auricles. 3″. Autumn.

C. coum. See **C. orbiculatum.**

*C. europaeum.** Woods of S.E. and Central Europe. This hearty looking plant with large dark green kidney-shaped leaves, more or less marked with

Cypripedium

silver, may flower at any time from July into the winter. Its leaves are almost evergreen and form a good foil to the deep carmine flowers. 4″–5″.

P*C. graecum. Greece and E. Mediterranean. Not entirely hardy except in very favoured spots, but a beautiful plant for the alpine house, as it can show the most outstanding of all leaf forms. Large, obcordate, with slightly dentate horny edges, they may be almost velvety in texture, and are quite distinct by means of conspicuous silver veining and light green or silvery patches. Flowers rose. 4″–5″. Autumn–winter.

DP*C. libanoticum. Lebanon. Perhaps the loveliest of the genus, with large, beautifully-shaped, fragrant flowers, held well above the rather large rounded heart-shaped leaves, which have a distinctive matt surface and are marked in shades of soft, dull green. White, with carmine marks at the mouth but flushing pink with age. Only hardy in very favoured districts. 4″–5″. Early spring.

*C. neapolitanum (*hederifolium*). S. Europe. This lovely plant is at its best when naturalized around and in the partial shade of trees, where it will spread by self-seeding. The leaves, which are roughly ivy-shaped, are beautifully veined and marked with silver in great variety. The flowers vary from pink to deep red, and there are white forms, the best of which have wide petals of good texture. Conspicuous auricles. Some forms are fragrant. 4″–5″. Autumn. (Pl. 8)

*C. orbiculatum. Europe. Under this name are now grouped as varieties or sub-species all those spring flowering cyclamen with rounded leaves, which were previously known as *C. atkinsii*, deep green leaves with silvery markings and pale rose flowers, *C. coum*, distinguished by having rounded dark green leaves entirely without markings, *C. vernum*, with leaves before the flowers, and others. These are all now considered to be varieties of *C. orbiculatum*, and all have white forms. They all have short dumpy flowers as compared with the elegance of the other species. 3″–4″. Spring.

C. persicum. E. Mediterranean. A taller, graceful species with large, narrow-petalled pale-pink flowers, and very variable leaves, often beautifully marked and veined. Not hardy except in alpine house. The forerunner of the cultivated house cyclamen. 5″–7″. Spring.

C. pseudibericum. E. Mediterranean. Large flowered, rose (or occasionally white). Rounded obcordate leaves, with silvery spots. 4″–5″. Winter and early spring.

C. repandum. S. France to Crete. A distinct species with thin-textured rather ivy-shaped leaves and long, narrow-petalled deep rose flowers, often with slightly spirally twisted petals. 4″–6″. Spring. (Pl. 9)

CYPRIPEDIUM *Orchidaceae*

The Slipper Orchids are rather tall for most rock gardens, but a small

Cystopteris, Cytisus

clump gives such character to a half-shady corner that a short description is given of a few of the most readily obtainable. They are quite hardy and appreciate a well-drained leafy soil in woodland conditions. They are herbaceous, dying away completely in the winter (and sometimes remaining dormant for a year), and all form leafy stems which bear one or more of the large characteristic orchid flowers with conspicuous inflated pouch. Early summer.

C. acaule (*humile*). N. America. Sepals and petals greenish, pouch rose, spotted purple. 10″–12″. Early summer.

*C. calceolus. High woods of Central Europe and a very rare British native. Narrow chocolate sepals and petals, pale yellow pouch. A handsome plant. 12″–14″. Summer. (Pl. 9)

*C. pubescens. N. America. One of the most easy to establish and one of the most attractive, with large yellow flowers, the long narrow petals, spirally twisted, drooping each side of the pouch. 12″. Early summer.

C. reginae. N. America. Leaves softly downy; showy flowers with white or pink-flushed sepals and petals and large rich rose pouch. 1′–2′. Early summer.

CYSTOPTERIS *Polypodiaceae*

The Bladder Ferns comprise a group of most delicate and elegant little plants, which take their name from the bladder-like shape of the little spore cases on the backs of the fronds. They are quite hardy, but develop latish in the spring, and die back almost immediately after they have arrived at their maximum beauty. A mixture of peat, leaf-mould, and loam suits them, with crumbled mortar or the like to ensure good drainage. The species are very similar, and the only one usually obtainable is:

C. fragilis. Temperate regions. A very delicate lacy fern, which is often grown in the alpine house owing to its brittle habit. 2″–4″.

CYTISUS *Leguminosae*

A genus of shrubs and small trees with simple or three-foliate leaves and small pea-shaped flowers, usually yellow. They are indifferent to soil, but do best in a sunny well-drained spot. They can be grown from seed, but established plants transplant badly.

*C. ardoini. Maritime Alps. A very useful rock garden shrub, deciduous,

Daboecia, Dalibarda, Daphne

with many 6″ arching stems with small three-foliate grey-green leaves and, in spring, masses of golden pea-shaped flowers. April–May.

C. decumbens (*prostratus*). S. France to Balkans. A prostrate close mat of tangled stems and minute simple leaves, covered in early summer with bright gold flowers. May–June.

*C. demissus (*hirsutus demissus*). S.E. Europe, Asia Minor. Another mat-forming miniature Broom, with tri-foliate hairy leaves and relatively large flowers, yellow usually stained with reddish brown. Makes a charming pan for the alpine house. May–June.

C. × **kewensis,** with delightful cascades of small creamy white flowers (Pl. 9), and **C. purpureus,** a rather muted mauve-pink, are both somewhat tall and spreading, except for a large rock garden. The former is one of the most beautiful of shrubs. Both flower in early summer.

DABOECIA *Ericaceae*

*D. azorica. St. Dabeoc's Heath. Azores. The only member of this small genus really suitable for the normal rock garden. It is a little open-branched heath-like shrub, with small, oval, pointed leaves and narrow 6″–10″ spires of a few, widely spaced, comparatively large urn-shaped flowers of a beautiful rosy-crimson. It is a lime-hater, and requires a peaty, sandy soil. It is doubtfully hardy in cold districts, especially the older plants. Early summer.

DALIBARDA *Rosaceae Monotypic*

D. repens (*Rubus dalibarda*). E.N. America. A tufted plant with long-stalked, heart-shaped leaves, and white five-petalled flowers with a boss of golden stamens. Peaty soil. 6″–8″. Early summer.

DAPHNE *Thymelaeaceae*

This is the most valuable of all genera in providing a number of quite delightful, usually fragrant, dwarf shrubby plants, which, although most thrive in a leafy, peaty soil, are, with about one exception, indifferent to lime and, in fact, certain species, such as *D. cneorum*, seem to prefer it. All enjoy a sunny site, but a cool root run which never becomes dry. This can be ensured by suitable use of large, flat stones around the plants and adequate watering in a dry season. The flowers are in tight clusters, and what appears to be the corolla (which is absent) is really the coloured calyx, which forms a slender tube opening out into four (rarely five) oval, pointed lobes, so that the inflorescence has the appearance of a cluster of little four-pointed

Daphne

stars. The stems are woody and the comparatively small leaves entire.

D. alpina. S. and Central Europe. Deciduous. Leaves lanceolate. Terminal heads of fragrant small white flowers, followed by reddish berries. 4″–18″. April–May.

*D. arbuscula. Hungary. A sturdy bushy shrublet, with dark green widely linear ¾″ leaves and few-flowered terminal clusters of deep rose flowers with tubes over half an inch in length. Evergreen. Fragrant. 6″–10″. June.

D. aurantiaca. China. Eventually too tall for the rock garden, but mentioned because of its unusual (in the genus) almost orange-yellow flowers. Temperamental. May.

*D. blagayana. Styria, Carniola. Has a spreading habit and its wandering branches should be weighted down with stones, both in order to keep it in shape and also to facilitate natural layering. Larger leaves than most (over 1″ by ½″–¾″) and large terminal clusters of fragrant creamy-white flowers. 8″–12″. April–May.

*D. cneorum. S. Central Europe to Russia, the Balkans. The Garland Flower, one of the best known and most grown. A low, procumbent shrub with many leafy twiggy branches; narrow oblong ¾″ leaves and dense terminal clusters of rosy, fragrant flowers. There are several named forms, of which **D. c.** var. **eximia** (Pl. 9) is the best, being a little larger and more robust than the type, and having larger clusters of rich rosy-red flowers. There is also a white form which is more frail than the type. Propagation by layering (lengthy) or cuttings. Plants so raised are longer lived than those grafted on to *D. mezereum*, but this species, even more than other Daphnes, can, and often does, die off suddenly from no apparent cause after years of healthy growth. 6″–8″. May–June.

*D. collina. Mediterranean regions. This and *D. sericea* are two very similar shrubs, very suitable for the alpine house, making well-shaped sturdy foot-high bushes, with silky young growth and heads of fragrant pink flowers. May–June. (Pl. 9)

DP***D. genkwa.** China. A beautiful shrub with slender wand-like branches with lateral clusters of small mauve lilac-like flowers. Small silky leaves and stems. Deciduous. Lime-free soil and part shade. Not easy. 12″–18″. April–May.

*D. giraldii. China. A deciduous bushy shrub, which eventually reaches 2 ft. It has small clusters of golden yellow flowers. May.

*D. mezereum. Europe, Asia Minor. A deciduous bush, whose bare upright branches are wreathed in early spring throughout their length with small clusters of fragrant flowers in all shades of pink to deep rich purple-rose. Later it bears many scarlet berries. There are white forms, some very good, and these have orange berries. All eventually grow too tall (4′–5′) for the normal rock garden, but they are mentioned because young plants form excellent stock for grafting other Daphnes upon, especially *D. petraea*. February–April, according to season.

Deinanthe, Delphinium

ᴾ***D. petraea*** (*rupestris*). N. Italy, near Lake Garda. This is perhaps the most beautiful of all the really dwarf shrubs, as evidenced at the Spring Shows of the Royal Horticultural Society, when it appears as a solid low bush of 4″–5″ in height and more across, completely covered with clusters of large, fragrant, pink flowers, of a delightful crystalline texture. It is not so easy to grow to such a height of perfection as the robustness of the specimens shown would suggest, but alpine house culture, in a leafy, limy, well-drained soil, never on any account being allowed to dry out, is the most suited for it. The form usually grown is *D. p.* 'GRANDIFLORA', with even larger flowers than the type.

D. rupestris. See **D. petraea.**

D. striata. Central and E. Europe. Like a frail, sparse-leaved *D. cneorum*, this little Daphne covers acres of ground with its procumbent, whippy stems, and suckers underground so that every apparent seedling seems to be traceable under soil and stone to parent plants a yard or more away. It makes a fragrant carpet with smaller heads of starry, pink flowers than *D. cneorum* (reputed to be streaked with deeper pink, hence *striata*) and *can* be established in very gritty leafy soil, where, if top dressed with sizable pieces of slate, it will sucker under them and reappear at a distance as it does at home. There is a good white form in the Savoy Alps. 3″–6″. Spring.

DEINANTHE *Saxifragaceae*

This is a genus of two species, of which

D. coerulea, China, is a beautiful and distinctive late-flowering plant for a cool shady corner. It has a few rather large, ovate, toothed leaves, and large, nodding, bowl-shaped flowers of an unusual dull violet-blue, with a boss of white or pale blue stamens. 10″–12″. July.

DELPHINIUM *Ranunculaceae*

D. chinense (*grandiflorum*). China. A delightful much-branched perennial, with bright blue flowers. Up to 1 foot. Not long-lived, but easy from seed. Early summer. (Pl. 9)

D. nudicaule. California. Variable in height, but may be under a foot. Slender spires of small, rather narrow red and yellow flowers. There is also an all yellow form. Early summer.

D. menziesii. N.E. America. A very variable plant, of which seed is sometimes available. Blue flowered and very attractive in its dwarf forms of about 6″, but in many localities it may reach 18″. Early summer.

D. muscosum. Himalaya. A really dwarf delphinium, making a bushy plant of much cut basal leaves, above which rise the hairy blue flowers, large

Dianthus

for the size of the plant. Two forms of this delightful plant were brought into cultivation some years ago, but it is now rarely seen. 5″–6″. Summer.

Other very dwarf delphiniums have been described, especially from Himalaya and western North America. They would be very welcome introductions to the garden.

DIANTHUS *Caryophyllaceae*

The majority of species of this large genus are ideally suited to the rock garden. They are compact growing, with low cushions of ever-green foliage, often attractively glaucous, and follow on with welcome colour in June, when the first spate of spring-flowering alpines is over. They include a number of exceedingly dwarf cushion plants, with almost sessile flowers which, for garden use, are very similar to each other. All grow readily from seed or cuttings. Early summer, except where otherwise stated.

*D. alpinus. Austrian Alps. This mat-forming plant is easily distinguished by its deep green (*not* glaucous), almost lush, narrowly strap-shaped leaves. Its large (1″ or more) attractive flowers are very variable in colour from deep rose down to white. *D. a.* 'ALBA' may have very good and solid flowers, but they are sometimes squinny. The flowers are backed with greenish-white, and have a central ring of deep purple spots. Not fragrant. 2″–3″. (Pl. 10)

*D. ×arvernensis (*monspessulanus* × *sylvaticus*). Central France. Symmetrical cushions of fine grey leaves sprayed in June with many 3″ arching stems of single pinks of a good rose.

*D. 'LA BOURBRILLE'. A neat little cushion plant with small pink flowers on 1″ stems. There is also a white form. A garden hybrid. Late spring. (Pl. 10)

*D. boydii. A garden hybrid with large pink flowers on 3″ stems.

*D. callizonus. Mts. of Central Europe. A beautiful mat-forming plant, which it is difficult to obtain true. Large dentate pink petals with a conspic-uous purple spotted zone around the centre. Leaves broadly linear. 3″–4″. Summer.

D. caesius. See **D. gratianopolitanus.**

D. carthusianorum. Central Europe. The typical pink cluster-head on disproportionately tall stalks of a foot or more, is too large and too ungainly for the rock garden (although one can, rarely, find forms of deepest velvety-crimson whose wonderful colour outweighs the small flowers and general gawkiness). In parts of the Valais, however, notably near Zermatt and Saas Fée, there is a delightful dwarf form (or possibly a natural hybrid with *D. sylvestris*) with few or even one-flowered heads on 2″–4″ stems.

109

Diapensia

D. deltoides. The Maiden Pink. Europe (including Gt. Britain). Slender spraying or prostrate stems with many grass-green linear to lanceolate leaves, and heads of small ($\frac{1}{4}''$) flowers opening in succession over a period from June to late summer. 6″–9″. Not fragrant. This is not a very distinguished plant, but selected forms are offered, including white, and there is a compact variety with dark reddish foliage and deep crimson flowers which is attractive. (Pl. 10)

*D. freynii. Hercegovina. A dense green or grey-green cushion, with small clear pink flowers on 1″–2″ stems. June.

D. gratianopolitanus (formerly *caesius*). Central Europe (including Gt. Britain). The Cheddar Pink has very fragrant single flowers of pale pink. 6″–8″. June.

D. knappii. Hungary, Bosnia. An ungainly late flowering plant, with deep green sparse foliage, but unique in cultivation in having small cluster heads of clear luminous yellow flowers. The floppiness of the 9″–10″ stems is not so conspicuous if they are grown among other spreading plants. July–September.

D. microlepis. Thrace. Hardly distinguishable from **D. freynii** (q.v.).

*D. 'MRS. CLARKE'. A charming garden hybrid with deep rose flowers. 4″. June. (Pl. 10)

*D. neglectus. S.W. Europe to Tyrol. One of the most delightful of the dwarf pinks. It forms a dense cushion of fine, green, rigid, linear foliage, often hardly distinguishable from grass when out of flower, above which rise on stems of 1″–4″ ample flowers of over an inch in diameter, usually a uniform deep clear rose, often with a rich blue centre. They are characterized by the light buff backs to the petals, and this feature appears in all hybrids with this species. June–July.

D. seguieri. Pyrenees, N. Italy. Another rather tall and lanky plant, with the habit of *D. knappii*, but useful because of its late flowering. Its purplish pink cluster-heads appear in July and August.

*D. subacaulis. Maritime Alps. Another dense cushion plant, with stiff linear leaves and almost sessile small pink flowers in summer.

*D. sylvestris (*frigidus, inodorus*). This graceful plant is found on rocky banks throughout the Alps (not in woods, despite its name). Its very fine stiff foliage forms clumps of silvery grey, from which the solitary flowers spray out on slender wiry stems of 4″–10″. They have a specially neat rounded outline (sometimes slightly dentate), and are of a clear luminous pink, with almost a touch of cream in it. Summer.

In addition to these, catalogues will give several hybrid dwarf pinks, some of considerable age, which are suitable for the rock garden.

DIAPENSIA *Diapensiaceae*

This is a difficult small genus of compact tufted evergreen shrublets. The only member which is even precariously in cultivation is:

D. lapponica var. **obovata.** Alpine-arctic regions throughout the northern hemisphere, including Scotland. Has many small oval, leathery, dark green leaves and solitary white flowers on 1″ stems, tubular, opening to five rounded lobes, about ¾″ across. A gritty peaty lime-free soil in part shade gives the best chance of succeeding with this interesting but difficult plant. A pink form has been reported from Japan. 2″–3″. Spring.

DICENTRA *Papaveraceae*

This most un-poppy-like genus has curious locket-shaped flowers, well typified by the well-known Bleeding Heart of the herbaceous border (*D. spectabilis*). There are, however, several small species which are very attractive for the rock garden, all with delightful delicate fernlike foliage, which dies down completely soon after flowering.

D. canadensis. Squirrel Corn. N. America. So named from the rounded corn-like tubers which form the root system. Among clumps of fern-like leaves rise 5″–6″ stems bearing whitish drooping tubular flowers, constricted at the mouth. April–May.

*****D. cucullaria.** Dutchman's Breeches. United States. Very similar in foliage and habit to the foregoing, but with thick scale-like root system and flowers with two blunt spurs, giving the characteristic breeches effect, although the soft creamy flowers, yellow-tipped, really more truly suggest a flight of small moths above the ferny foliage. 5″–6″. April–May. (Pl. 10)

D. eximia. United States. A rather taller, sturdier plant with pendent reddish-purple flowers. 7″–8″. May.

D. oregana. Oregon. Another of the delightful dwarf species with glaucous foliage and compact, spurred flowers, cream with purple tips. 6″. June.

DP*****D. peregrina** var. **pusilla.** Siberia, Japan. A very difficult species. which is only temporarily in cultivation from time to time, and seems almost impossible to raise from seed (perhaps it would have a better chance if seed were obtained by air and sown as soon as ripe), but it is the gem of a charming genus. It forms a small 2″ tuft of narrow, lobed silvery-grey leaves, and has comparatively large Bleeding Hearts of clear pink, dangling just above the foliage. 3″. Early summer.

DIGITALIS *Scrophulariaceae*

Most of the Foxgloves are too tall for the rock garden proper, but, in certain settings, an occasional group in the background of the slender-spired, pale yellow *D. lutea*, the larger flowered, but more dwarf deeper yellow *D. ambigua* or even any of the taller species from

Asia Minor, such as *D. ferruginea* or *orientalis* with their quaint, lipped flowers of buff and tawny shades with white lip, give great dignity and distinction. The only species even approximately within the desired size is:

D. dubia. Spain. This attractive little foxglove of 6″–9″ has a sturdy habit and downy leaves forming a rosette from which the leafy stem rises, bearing a few large, typical flowers of soft purplish-pink. Unfortunately, it is not entirely hardy, and is, in any case, not long lived. June.

DIMORPHOTHECA *Compositae*

Of this S. African genus, the only available species sufficiently dwarf for the rock garden is:

D. barberiae var. **compacta.** This plant's rather straggling growth is more than redeemed by the large and lovely purplish-pink daisy-like flowers, with blue-grey reverse and dark centres, which rise on slender stems above the clump of rather narrowly lanceolate foliage. It is necessary to obtain the dwarf form, as even this may be up to 9″, whereas the type species is well over a foot in height. Summer onwards. (Pl. 10)

DIONYSIA *Primulaceae*

This genus comprises the Persian and Afghanistan cousins of the high Alpine cushion androsaces, and was only brought (precariously) into cultivation at the beginning of the century. The genus differs from Androsace in having a long narrow tube to the corolla, often with a mid-swelling. Of those then introduced only two, *D. bryoides* and *D. curviflora*, two very dense cushion plants with almost sessile pink flowers, established even for a few years, and these have proved capricious in flowering, though occasionally there have been brought to the show bench symmetrical green cushions covered with the elegant long-tubed flowers. Recent expeditions to Persia have produced fresh seed, from which one species at least, *D. aretioides*, has germinated well and already produced its charming little golden flowers. This promises to be a much looser plant than the two foregoing species, with small hairy primrose-like leaves, crinkled and minutely scalloped at the edges persistent on the radiating branches which eventually form a loose cushion. It seems to appreciate a very gritty scree, with some humus, and plenty of water in the growing season. 1″. Spring and an occasional flower later.

Most of the thirty or more other species now identified seem likely to prove a challenge even to the expert for many years to come.

7

Campanula raineri
Carduncellus rhaponticoides
Celmisia bellidioides

Campanula waldsteiniana
Cassiope lycopodioides
Celmisia coriacea

8

Celsia acaulis
Corydalis cashmeriana
Cyananthus integer

Centaurium scilloides
Crepis rosea
Cyclamen neapolitanum

DIOSPHAERA. See TRACHELIUM

DODECATHEON *Primulaceae*

Shooting Stars. This N. American genus contains about thirty species, only a few of which are in cultivation in Gt. Britain, but there is a great family likeness between them so that a few can represent the whole. The habit of the plant is very like that of the genus Primula, consisting of a rosette of more or less erect leaves, smooth-surfaced and linear or rather narrowly spatulate. The flowers, borne (with one exception) in umbels, have reflexed petals and prominent stamens, which give them a cyclamen-like appearance. They are attractive easy-going plants in any partially shaded, rather moist spot.

DONDIA. See HACQUETIA

DORONICUM *Compositae*

The only Doronicum which it is safe to introduce into the rock garden is **D. cordatum,** and even this in congenial conditions is apt to become too rampant. If, however, it is grown in fairly poor soil it will not exceed 5″–6″, and its rather lush, cordate leaves will be hidden by the very large, golden, daisy-like flowers. A very showy plant if it can be kept compact. Early spring.

DOUGLASIA *Primulaceae*

This charming genus is the N. American (with one exception) counter-part of the European androsaces; from which it differs in having a longer corolla tube to the five-petalled flowers. The species are easily grown in well-drained gritty soil, with leaf-mould and/or peat, and make delightful pans for the alpine house. Late spring to summer.

D. biflora. Rocky Mts. Like most of the N. American douglasias, makes a cushion, then a mat, of rosettes of smooth, bright green, shortly lanceolate leaves. In spite of its name it is usually single-flowered, on 1″ stems or less. Bright pink. May–June.

ᴘ***D. dentata.** Rocky Mts. More stoloniferous in habit, with narrow, slightly toothed, finely downy leaves and violet ⅓″ flowers. 1″–2″. May–June.

ᴘ***D. laevigata.** Cascade Mts. Makes dense leafy tufts with two to four flowered clusters of bright pink ½″ flowers on 1″ stems. May–June. (Pl. 11)

D. montana. Cascade Mts. Rather like the foregoing, but rather larger flowers, singly or in pairs, just clear of the foliage. 2″. May–June.

D. nivalis. British Columbia. A loosely tufted plant, with slightly downy narrowly spoon shaped leaves, and almost sessile heads of three to six pale pink flowers. April–May.

***D. vitaliana.** (*Gregoria vitaliana, Androsace vitaliana*). Europe. A prostrate mat-forming species with half-opened flowers of clear yellow. In some forms difficult and loath to flower, but there is a compact, free-flowering form with more tufted grey-green foliage. 1″–2″. Early summer. (Pl. 11)

DRABA *Cruciferae*

This very large genus includes a number of dwarf cushion-forming plants which are superficially very much alike, forming very regular domes of packed rosettes varying in size of crowded pointed leaves from small to minute, and from glabrous to densely tomentose, which gives cushions from brilliant green to almost white. The flowers are borne in clusters, usually well above the congested, rounded pincushions, on thin wiry stems. They are, with few exceptions, bright yellow. The species are quite hardy, but, with the possible exception of *D. aizoides*, are grown in pans in the alpine house, where their very symmetrical growth and general floriferousness makes them attractive specimens, and the overhead protection in winter is welcome, especially for the more woolly species. All described are yellow flowered, except *D. dedeana*.

D. aizoides. Mts. of Middle Europe (including Gt. Britain). One of the larger, showier species, with rigid, bristle-tipped leaves and 2″–4″ stems bearing bunches of loose-petalled lemon-yellow flowers. Variable. April. (Pl. 11)

D. aizoon. E. Alps. A sturdier plant than the foregoing, but with smaller flowers on longer scapes. 4″–5″. April–May.

ᴘ***D. bryoides.** Caucasus. Very dense 2″ cushions with few flowers on wiry scapes. April.

D. b. var. **imbricata** is even smaller and denser, with 1″ cushions. April.

*D. dedeana. Pyrenees. An attractive little plant with white flowers held well above the grey-green mats of rosetted foliage. 3″. April.

D. imbricata. See **D. bryoides** var. **imbricata.**

ᴾ***D. polytricha.** Armenia. Very dense and dwarf with grey-white woolly tufts, a foil to the golden-yellow sprays of flowers. 2″. April.

D. pyrenaica. See *Petrocallis.*

D. rigida. Armenia. This rather larger plant (3″ cushions) has stiff bristly leaves and dense heads of golden yellow. 2″–3″. April.

Other very similar species are sometimes offered, such as *D. bruniifolia, D. hispanica, D. mollissima* (a densely hairy miniature) and others.

DRACOCEPHALUM *Labiatae*

The Dragon-heads are rather showy perennials, with upright stems and opposite leaves (often aromatic) and stiff spikes of many flowered whorls of lipped and hooded flowers. They are not fussy as to soil and situation, and are effective in the rock garden, although their size puts them on the borderline of suitability in the very small garden. They flower in summer, and may be propagated by cuttings, seed, or division of the roots. Among the dwarfer species are:

D. grandiflorum. Siberia. Needs a little more care than the others, with well-drained soil, kept fairly dry in winter. 3″ spikes of large violet-blue flowers, nearly 2″ in length. Cordate, long-stemmed leaves forming a rosette at base. 6″–9″. July.

D. purdomii. Central Asia. Very like the foregoing, but with smaller purple flowers. 8″. Summer.

D. tanguticum. China. A beautiful aromatic plant with much cut fern-like leaves, and 8″–12″ spikes of vivid blue flowers. Summer.

DROSERA *Droseraceae*

Those who have boggy patches adjoining their rock gardens may care to try two native species of these amusing and not unattractive little plants, or they may be grown in shallow pans standing in water. In either case, they need a very damp peaty soil and sphagnum moss, in a sunny spot. They form rosettes of long-stemmed leaves, like little salt spoons (*D. rotundifolia*) or narrowly spatulate (*D. longifolia*). In both cases the leaves are densely set, especially at the edges, with sturdy, reddish, glandular hairs, swollen at the tips, which gleam in the sunlight. The plants are insectivorous, and when the fly or other small insect alights on the leaf the glandular hairs close in on it, like a little fist, opening again when they have absorbed the nitrogenous matter they require. The small white flowers are in sprays on slender 3″–5″ stems above the rosettes, in late summer.

DRYAS *Rosaceae*

This genus contains three prostrate, evergreen, woody shrubs, which are invaluable in the rock garden, although they may have to be cut back a little if their spread becomes too great. All are densely branched, and have many small oak-like leaves, a dark shining green above and grey-green below. The eight-petalled flowers are of good substance, although the width of petal may vary. In the mountains, where it may carpet whole tracts of hillside, some have very noticeably wide and solid petals.

D. drummondii. N. America. Very similar to *D. octopetala* (below), but with creamish-white nodding flowers which do not open out into the clean open face of their European cousins. 3″–4″. Early summer.

*D. octopetala. The glory of the European Alps (and Gt. Britain, more rarely), and also found in N. America. A splendid and good-tempered rock plant with widely-open flowers 1½″ across. It layers itself and also can be grown from the feathery seeds. 3″–4″. Early summer. (Pl. 11)

D. o. var. **lanata.** Smaller than the type, and with softly downy leaves.

D. o. var. **minor.** Smaller and more compact in every way than the type.

D. tomentosa. A yellow flowered species from the Rocky Mts., with hairy oval leaves. 3″–4″. Summer.

ECHIUM *Boraginaceae*

Our native biennial Viper's Bugloss (*Echium vulgare*) *can* provide a welcome and rare note of intense deep blue, and *can*, in austere circumstances, raise its lovely spires only 8″–10″ above its hoary foliage, but it is difficult (although not impossible) to establish by seed in cultivation, and it might well get out of hand if well suited.

Edraianthus, Empetrum, Ephedra

EDRAIANTHUS *Campanulaceae*

This small genus from the Mediterranean regions is very nearly related botanically to Wahlenbergia, from which it differs in having its flowers in clusters instead of solitary, and in catalogues the individual species may well be found under either generic name. They are all prostrate herbs with showy, campanulate flowers of blue to purple, and although hardy are not always long-lived. They are summer flowering, and can be propagated by seed, or cuttings of non-flowering shoots.

E. caudatus (*dalmaticus*). Dalmatia. Rosettes of narrow, greyish-green leaves, and dense clusters of funnel-shaped purple flowers. 3″. Summer.

E. dalmaticus. See **E. caudatus.**

E. graminifolius. Dalmatia. Very similar to the foregoing, but with needle-shaped leaves and narrow purple bells. 3″. May-July.

*E. niveus. Bosnia, Yugoslavia. Makes a mat of deep green linear foliage with heads of pure white, bell-shaped flowers. Has been out of cultivation, but seems to be growing well from recent collecting. 2″–3″. Summer.

*E. pumilio. Dalmatia. Forms a compact clump of narrow silvery foliage. with heads of lavender flowers. 2″–3″. Summer.

EMPETRUM *Empetraceae*

Empetrum nigrum, the Crowberry, is a small heath-like plant widely distributed over high moorlands in the N. Temperate zone, and in the Andes. It forms mats of congested, wiry stems set with many stiff, dark green linear leaves of about ¼″ in length. It makes a good ground cover for moist, peaty soil (no lime), and will tolerate a dry, sunny position if well-drained. The small pink flowers with protruding stamens are scarce in cultivation, and, consequently, so are the brownish-black edible berries. 3″–6″. May.

EPHEDRA *Gnetaceae*

This curious genus from S. Temperate and tropical regions contains one hardy species which forms an unusual plant for the rock garden.

E. gerardiana. Himalaya, S.W. China. A very twiggy shrublet whose slender, erect, rigid branches suggest the Mare's Tail (Equisetum) as they are striated and jointed, and the leaves are quite inconspicuous, being merely pairs of tiny pointed scales, lying flatly on the stem at each node. It is attractive too if it can be induced to produce its small fleshy bead-like fruits of translucent orange. It will do well in a well-drained sunny position, and can be increased by cuttings or layers, as seeds are infrequently produced. 6″–8″. Summer.

Epigaea, Epilobium
EPIGAEA *Ericaceae*

This genus of two species, which was widely offered—and grown—
between the wars, seems undeservedly to have lost popularity of late
years. In the situation which suits them, woodland with peat and leaf-
mould (no lime), and shaded from direct sunlight, the species grow
freely and are among the most delightful and distinguished of ground
coverers. They are prostrate, with much branched hairy, rooting
stems, handsome evergreen leaves, and flowers in close terminal (rarely
axillary) clusters in late spring. Propagation by layers or seed.

*E. asiatica. Japan. This is rather more easy of cultivation than *E. repens*,
and has hairy, ovate leaves, 2″–3″ long, which tend to overshadow the bright
pink long-campanulate or urn-shaped flowers. Late spring.

*E. ×intertexta 'AURORA'. (*asiatica × repens*). This is intermediate between
its parents, with flowers shading from dog-rose pink to carmine, and less
obscured by foliage. Late spring.

*E. repens. N. America, especially Quebec. Trailing Arbutus, Mayflower,
Ground Laurel. Very free flowering when well established in well-drained
soil with plenty of leaf-mould, and the clusters of rather funnel-shaped
flowers, which vary in colour from white to deep pink, betray their presence
by their fragrance even when they are sometimes shaded by the large glossy
or slightly bristly dark green leaves. Late spring.

EPILOBIUM *Onagraceae*

The willow herbs, showy though they are, are mostly too large, too
rampant, or both, for the average rock garden, and their many seeds,
so easily airborne by means of the long silky hairs attached, and so
easy of germination, can soon populate the neighbourhood. There
are, however, one or two beautiful dwarf species which are safe to
introduce, and indeed very desirable. All are easily grown from seed.

E. dodonaei. (*fleischeri, halleri*). Europe. This is the creeping willow herb
of the high shingles, with flopping almost prostrate stems of 6″–8″ and large
deep rose flowers. Unlike its relations it is not too easy to establish, but likes
a very stony scree for its many stoloniferous branches to wander amongst.
Early summer.

*E. kai-koense. Japan. A very dwarf-growing species with opposite, rounded
leaves on 4″ stems, and a succession of rosy pink flowers through the summer.

*E. obcordatum. Nevada, California. Farrer is justified in considering this
the gem of the small willow herbs. It forms a spreading mass of wiry 4″

stems, with many bright light green, oval-pointed leaves, often tinged with red, and comparatively large terminal flowers of luminous, deep rose-pink with conspicuous protruding stigmas of dark red. Seed, or cuttings in August, or layering of the spraying branches by pegging down below soil at half their length. Summer flowering.

EPIMEDIUM   *Berberidaceae*

The genus of Barren-worts is distributed over the N. Temperate regions of Europe and Asia, including Japan. They are delightful and unusual plants as a ground cover for a semi-woodland position, with their almost evergreen attractive leaves, often veined, and, in late spring and early summer, airy sprays of pendent, slightly-spurred, cup-shaped flowers, rather suggestive of compact little Columbines, in white, yellow, pink, red, or violet—or sometimes parti-coloured. When out of flower, they are very similar in general appearance and habit, all having flat, bi- or tri-ternate leaves of a curious thin, stiff texture, on very slender petioles of 8″–12″.

E. alpinum. Central and S. Europe. The dwarfest of the genus. Small red and yellow flowers. 6″–9″. Spring.

E. grandiflorum. Japan, Manchuria. Flowers lavender to violet. 8″–12″. Spring to early summer.

E. g. 'ROSE QUEEN'. An attractive colour variant, has crimson-carmine flowers with white-tipped spurs.

E. g. 'VIOLACEUM' is more dwarf, with compact flowers of light violet.

E. pinnatum. Persia. Bi-ternate leaves with up to a dozen toothed leaflets, and small, bright yellow flowers with brown-purple spurs. 8″–12″. Early summer.

E. × rubrum. A hybrid of garden origin, with crimson and yellow flowers. 8″–10″. Early summer.

E. × warleyense. A hybrid originating in Miss Wilmott's famous garden at Warley. It has striking coppery red flowers. 8″–20″. April–May.

E. × youngianum ('NIVEUM'). Japan. Probably a hybrid. Has white, green-tinged flowers. There is a reddish-mauve variety, **E. × y.** 'ROSEUM'. 6″–10″. May–June.

EPIPACTIS   *Orchidaceae*

A small group of hardy orchids for shady woodland conditions in leafy soil, although they show no antipathy to lime. A few of the

European species are in cultivation. They have, in general, medium-sized flowers, rather widely spaced on spikes of 10"–12" or more. Summer flowering.

E. atrorubens. The Dark Red Helleborine. Europe (including Gt. Britain). Spikes of greenish-purple, dull red, or blackish-purple flowers, with a wide, pointed lip. Not to be confused with the more spectacular and larger flowered Red Helleborine, which is *Cephalanthera rubra*. 12"–14". June–July.

E. helleborine. Broad-leaved Helleborine. Europe (including Gt. Britain), N. Africa, and Himalaya. A very variable species with fairly large flowers in shades of green, shaded with yellow, pink, or purple. Summer.

E. palustris. Marsh Helleborine. Europe (including Gt. Britain), Siberia. This needs a sunny, marshy situation, and in such it forms large colonies which form a beautiful sight when seen in damp meadows in the Alps. There they appear as a forest of slender spikes of handsome, multicolour flowers of brown, green, purple, and white, rippling in the breeze. They seem definitely to prefer an alkaline soil. 10"–12". July.

ERANTHIS *Ranunculaceae*

In woodland soil these pleasant little plants will naturalize themselves and, after displaying in early spring their golden cups, held in a ruff of broadly linear, bright green leaves, they quickly lose their foliage, and disappear without trace until the following year. As with all Ranunculaceae, seed should be sown as soon as ripe, or may be left to self-sow round the plants, or propagation may be by division of the tubers.

*E. cilicica. Greece, Asia Minor. In early growth the leaves are copper-coloured, clasping the golden ball of the unopened flower. 2"–3". February–March.

E. hyemalis. W. Europe. Winter Aconite. The species most usually grown, and most readily naturalized. Bright yellow cups. 4". February–March. (Pl. 11)

*E. × tubergenii. Hybrid of the above two species, with larger flowers of deeper yellow. 4"–5". February–March.

ERICA *Ericaceae*

The heathers, long-flowering and hardy though they are, are most of them too free-growing and spreading for any but the large, landscape rock garden. There is, however, one notable exception:

Erigeron

E. carnea. S. and Central Europe. Most forms of this variable species are compact in growth (this is noticeably so in wild plants from the Central Alps), and they have the double advantage, rare in the genus, of tolerating lime and of winter-flowering. By choosing varieties from the long lists offered by specialist nurseries, one may have continuous flowers from December to April in an average season. Like all other winter flowerers their times vary from year to year quite considerably according to the occurrence of long periods of severe frosts. All remain in good condition for a considerable time. About 6″–8″.

E. c. 'ALBA'. White, early January.

E. c. 'ATRORUBRA'. Very deep pink. The latest to flower.

E. c. 'EILEEN PORTER'. Probably the best of all. A compact plant. with masses of rich pink flowers which last for three months or more. February–May, or even earlier in some districts.

*****E. c. 'JAMES BACKHOUSE'.** Very pale pink. Late spring.

E. c. 'KING GEORGE'. Dark red. Early.

E. c. 'QUEEN MARY'. Good rose-pink. January–February.

*****E. c. 'RUBY GLOW'.** A good, compact-growing variety with deep pink flowers and dark foliage. Early spring.

*****E. c. 'SPRINGWOOD PINK'** and **'SPRINGWOOD WHITE'.** (Pl. 12.) Two excellent varieties with crowded spikes of pink and white respectively. Vigorous and free-flowering plants. 8″–9″. January–March.

*****E. c. 'VIVELLII'.** Dark crimson flowers and dark foliage turning brownish-red in winter. February–March.

E. c. 'WINTER BEAUTY'. Deep pink. Very early, in flower by Christmas.

ERIGERON *Compositae*

This large genus, differing from the aster by having several series of ray florets to its daisy-like flowers instead of a single row, provides many compact little plants very suitable for the rock garden. They are completely hardy and indifferent to soil, but will remain more dwarf and in character in a sunny, well-drained position. In addition to those named below, new species are being introduced from N. America, mostly akin to *E. compositus* and *E. simplex*. Summer flowering.

E. alpinus. Alpine and Arctic regions (including Gt. Britain). A hairy plant, with lanceolate leaves and mauve ray florets with yellow disc. 6″–8″.

Erinacea

E. aurantiacus. Turkestan. Has solitary orange flowers on leafy foothigh stems. It is an effective colour, but a little coarse for the smaller rock garden.

*E. aureus. Western N. America. This very charming little plant forms clumps of spatulate leaves, and bears solitary bright gold daisies on 3″–4″ stems. The bracts containing the flower-head are densely hairy, and in some forms the long hairs are purplish-black, enclosing the bud in a conspicuous furry cup which is most attractive. 3″–4″.

*E. compositus. N.W. America. Solitary flower heads of white or pale mauve, with three-lobed leaves, again cut into three linear segments. 3″–4″. (Pl. 12)

E. glaucus. N. America. Grey-green spatulate leaves, and large flowerheads of purple daisies. 6″–10″.

E. leiomerus. Rocky Mts. Leaves mainly radical, spatulate. Flowerheads mauve. 4″.

E. mucronatus. Mexico. This well-known plant, with fragile, lanceolate leaves and many frail daisies on long wiry stems, is apt to be invasive, but when planted in rather arid conditions, such as a stone wall, nothing is more delightful than its sea of dancing daisy-like flowers, ranging from white or palest pink to deep rose according to age, and continuing over a long period. May–October. May be damaged by severe frost, but usually survives. About 6″, spreading.

*E. pinnatisectus. Rocky Mts. A charming foliage plant, with many radical, much dissected grey-green leaves and mauve daisies. 4″–6″.

*E. simplex. N.W. America. Forms a dense clump of lanceolate, greygreen radical leaves, and in early summer bears deep mauve daisies which unfold from darkly hairy buds. 4″–6″.

E. radicatus. N. America. A tiny plant of about 2″, with tufts of narrow leaves and mauve flowers.

E. uniflorus. Mountainous districts of Europe and N. America. This little plant is always attractive with its cluster of lanceolate or spatulate leaves, and sturdy little 2″ stems, each bearing a solitary flower in densely woolly purplish involucral bracts. The flowers are usually just off-white, but delightful pink shades and even mauve are not infrequently found. 2″–3″.

ERINACEA *Leguminosae Monotypic*

*E. pungens. (*Anthyllis erinacea*). Spain, N. Africa. An unusual and attractive shrub for the rock garden, flourishing in a sunny, well-drained position. It forms a low dense, intricately branched bush of grey-green spiny shoots, bearing only a few small fugitive leaves. The pea-shaped flowers are pale mauve, although darker forms are seen. It is difficult to propagate by cuttings, but the few seeds set germinate readily. It is long-lived, and will not reach more than a foot in height. May–June. (Pl. 12)

ERINUS *Scrophulariaceae*

The only species met with in the garden is the representative found in the mountains of W. Europe.

*E. alpinus. This delightful little plant makes tufts of almost fernlike leaves, narrowly spatulate with a deeply toothed margin, and little more than an inch in length. In early summer it produces a profusion of 3″ wiry stems bearing many small, bright pink, lipped flowers. It is not long-lived, but will keep going by self-sown seedlings. It is particularly suitable for crevices in walls. There is a white form, and deep crimson and clear pink forms have received varietal names, 'Dr. Hanele' and 'Mrs. Chas. Boyle' respectively. (Pl. 12, 31)

ERIOGONUM *Polygonaceae*

This large genus from ·N.W. America is not often seen in gardens, although it includes several very desirable sub-shrubs. The usual habit is to make loose bun-like cushions up to 10″ or so, with many small, tough, generally woolly, oblong, ovate, or rounded leaves, and crowded umbels of almost sessile small flowers, borne well above the foliage. They require full sun and a rich peaty soil to encourage them to flower well. Among those more readily procurable are

E. campanulatum. Close shrublets of leathery leaves, and pale lemon flowers. 4″–6″. Summer.

E. jamesii. Leaves in a basal rosette. Loose sprays rather than umbels of white to yellow flowers. Variable. 4″–8″. July.

*E. ovalifolium. The species most usually grown, with woolly white foliage and small close umbels of white or yellow. 3″–8″. Summer. (Pl. 12)

E. o. var. **purpureum** is a lovely variation with rose or purple flowers.

E. subalpinum and **E. umbellatum** are two very similar plants from British Columbia, with white fading to pale pink and yellow flowers respectively.

N. America has many other desirable species to offer, including at least one attractive red–flowered one. Collected seed is sometimes available, but the plants seem not too easy to establish.

ERIOPHYLLUM *Compositae*

This small genus from N. America has so far only produced one member for the rock garden.

*E. lanatum. Oregon Sunshine (*caespitosum, Bahia lanata*). A showy plant with masses of much-lobed green leaves (grey backed), which are hidden in summer by the prolific golden-yellow daisies. It is most attractive when meagre well-drained soil in full sunshine constrains it to compact growth and a low stature. 6″–8″. July onwards.

ERITRICHIUM *Boraginaceae*

When this genus is mentioned the most famed and romantic of alpine plants immediately springs to mind, *Eritrichium nanum*. There is, however, a very different and much easier member of the genus in cultivation. Early summer.

E. argenteum and **E. elongatum** are two N. American near relations of *E. nanum*, and at least as difficult to cultivate. The former has the same hairy rosettes, but rather smaller deep blue flowers; the latter has rather longer sprays, of 2″–3″, over close cushions. Collected seed is sometimes available, and should be sown as soon as possible. Germination then *may* be good, but it is not easy to grow the plants on to flowering stage—although Alpine Plant Shows have demonstrated that it can be done.

DP***E. nanum.** The King of the Alps (*terglouense*, and pictured in old Botanical books as *Myosotis caespitosa*, the stemless Forget-me-not). High mountains of northern hemisphere on non-lime rocks. This forms a dense, silvery, hairy cushion of rosettes of tiny, oval, pointed leaves, in crevices of the high granitic ranges of Central Europe, as compact as one of the Aretian androsaces, in summer covered with what appear to be large, sessile Forget-me-nots (they later elongate to an inch-high spray), of a bland, soft, matt-surfaced blue whose perfection can only be realized on seeing them as small blue pools in the grey or lichen covered rocks which are their natural home. The Germans call it The Eye of Heaven, and Farrer, in *The English Rock Garden*, finds five pages too little to convey the magic of its allure. It, too, *can* be grown from seed, if available, but collected plants are almost impossible to establish and, even if this is achieved, do not show here the prodigality of bloom or the indescribable blue of the mountain dwellers. For what it is worth, the best hope is to grow it in a double pot, in gritty, shaly soil, with the cushion raised slightly by pieces of stone, and kept dry, but not desiccated dry, in winter. To this end, watering can be between the two pot rims. (Pl. 12)

*E. rupestre var. **pectinatum** (*strictum*). Mountains of Asia. A very different plant, with upright stems of 8″–12″ having radical and stem leaves,

Erodium

narrowly lanceolate, of silvery, almost blue-grey, and sprays of solid pale blue forget-me-not flowers. It is comparatively easy of cultivation in the scree.

E. strictum. A synonym of *E. rupestre* var. *pectinatum*, and the name under which it is usually found in catalogues.

ERODIUM *Geraniaceae*

A genus very nearly akin to Geranium, but differing in having only five fertile stamens. It includes many compact-growing plants which are attractive whether in or out of flower by reason of their small woolly or much cut fern-like leaves. Being mainly dwellers of Asia Minor and the countries north and south of the Mediterranean, they prosper in a sunny, well-drained spot, but they are quite hardy.

*E. absinthoides. S.E. Europe, Asia Minor. One of the most attractive in flower, having loose heads of large violet-pink or white blossoms, over jagged, much cut foliage.

E. a. var. **amanum.** Syria. This is dwarfer and more slender than the type, with silvery, hairy foliage, and white flowers. It is usually offered in catalogues as *E. amanum*. 6″. Summer.

*E. chamaedryoides (*reichardii*). Majorca. A densely tufted small plant, with small cordate toothed leaves and rounded pink-veined white flowers on 1″–2″ stems. (Pl. 13)

E. c. var. **roseum** is the form usually grown, with clear pink flowers over a very long period. There is also an intermittently double form. All are useful, good tempered little plants, seldom without flower over a period of several months. 1″–3″. Summer.

*E. chrysanthum. Greece. This lovely plant makes a spraying tuft of graceful feathered leaves, silvery with adpressed hairs, and has 5″–6″ sprays of luminous pale yellow flowers. Summer.

E. corsicum. Corsica, Sardinia. Much the same mat-forming habit as *E. chamaedryoides*, but rather larger, having many oval, scalloped leaves with a surface like grey velvet. The flowers are rosy-pink with veins of deeper colour. It needs a warm, sunny position. 3″–4″. Summer.

E. gruinum. Sicily. Only annual or biennial, but mentioned because of its large showy flowers of violet, with a deeper eye on 4″–8″ stems above the frail, lobed leaves. Once obtained, it can easily be kept going by seed. Early summer.

E. guttatum. S.W. Europe. Almost a sub-shrub, with woody base. The many long, heart-shaped, lobed, and slightly scalloped leaves are softly downy, and the flowers are white, with a conspicuous dark blotch on the two upper petals. 3″–6″. Summer.

*E. macradenum. Pyrenees. Here the much-cut delicate, ferny foliage is green, and the veined pinkish-violet flowers which spray well above the foliage on wiry stems, are distinguished by a dark violet blotch on each of the two upper petals. 2″–6″. Early summer.

*E. supracanum. Pyrenees. Specially silvery twice-pinnate leaves of about 2″ (in length). Flowers on 4″–6″ stems, white veined red, or unveined clear pink. Summer.

ERYNGIUM *Umbelliferae*

A really dwarf Sea Holly suitable for the rock garden has yet to be introduced to cultivation, but

E. bourgatii. Pyrenees. Can be kept to a foot or under in meagre soil. It is an attractive plant, with the characteristic blue-grey, very spiny leaves and grey-blue spiny inflorescences. Summer.

E. vesiculosum. New Zealand. The only Sea Holly indigenous to New Zealand. From a central root stock radiate its creeping, rooting runners, with spiny, toothed inch-long grey-green leaves narrowing into 2″–3″ petioles. It would be an entrancing plant if only the leaves or the spiny inflorescences had at least some of the family suffusion of blue. But they have not, and their hardiness is not proof against a really hard winter. It makes an interesting pan for the alpine house. 2″. Late summer.

ERYSIMUM *Cruciferae*

The small Wallflowers provide a few welcome plants for the rock garden, and although they are not usually long-lived they are easily kept going by seed, and, indeed, usually perpetuate the species by self-sown seedlings. All are summer flowering.

E. alpinum. Scandinavia. Lanceolate leaves and heads of sulphur-yellow flowers. Fragrant. *E. a.* 'MOONLIGHT' has luminous primrose-yellow flowers. 6″. May.

E. asperum. California, Texas. Biennial. This has flowers of an attractive and unusual coppery-yellow. There are forms which are more perennial than the type. 6″–10″.

*E. capitatum. W. United States. A woody plant of about 8″–10″, with ample heads of large, clear pale yellow flowers.

*E. dubium (*helveticum*). Central Europe. A very useful little plant, short-lived, but self-seeding, which may be from 2″–10″ in height, and is seldom out of flower, even in the winter.

E. linifolium. Spain. This slender little wallflower of 6″–12″ is perennial, and bears dense heads of cool lilac flowers over a long period.

*E. pumilum. European Alps. This perennial plant makes clumps of upright, linear-lanceolate, slightly jagged, basal leaves which are hidden in early summer by the heads of comparatively large clear yellow flowers. Variable, but quite delightful in the high alpine forms of 2″ or so, which are quite covered by the large flowers.

E. rupestre. Asia Minor. Taller than the foregoing, with smaller flowers. Up to 8″. (Pl. 13)

ERYTHRAEA. See CENTAURIUM

ERYTHRONIUM *Liliaceae*

These delightful plants, with one exception (*E. dens-canis*) natives of N. America, are really more for the woodland than for the rock garden, except in the case of those of very large dimensions. Full descriptions of many species are to be found in *Collins Guide to Bulbs*, but the following are mentioned, with colour of their flowers, which may be borne singly or more, like small pendulous lilies, over (usually) ovate, radical leaves, often handsome with marblings of white, green, and sometimes brown. They take some time to flower, after moving, and therefore transplanting should be avoided where possible. Spring flowering.

E. californicum. White. 10″–12″.

E. citrinum. White, marked with yellow. 6″.

E. dens-canis. Rosy-purple, and *E. c.* var. *album.* White. Up to 6″. (Pl. 13)

E. grandiflorum. Yellow, and *E. g.* var. *candidum.* White. 6″–8″.

E. parviflorum. Yellow. 4″–10″.

E. revolutum. A group of late flowering Erythroniums, with named varieties, of white, pink, and deep rose. 10″–12″.

E. tuolumnense. Deep yellow, a good and easy plant. 10″–12″.

ESCALLONIA *Saxifragaceae*

This genus provides one useful little shrub in *Escallonia rubra* 'PYG-MAEA', Chile, which is a congested form of the red flowered *E. rubra*, not growing above 1–1½ ft. August.

EUNOMIA *Cruciferae*

A genus of two species from the mountains of Asia Minor.

E. oppositifolia (*Aethionema oppositifolia*). A pleasant little plant whose hardiness is slightly suspect. Its prostrate stems bear many pairs of small rounded, grey, rather succulent leaves and terminal clusters of pale to clear pink flowers in summer. Suitable for the alpine house. 4"–6". June.

EUONYMUS *Celastraceae*

E. farreri (Farrer sp. No. 708). China. The creeping Spindle-berry, a prostrate plant with long, slender, spraying branches bearing ½" linear leaves and many tiny green, star-like flowers, followed, if one is lucky, by the characteristic conspicuous bright pink, four-lobed fruits, splitting to show the enclosed orange seeds, which have small green cotyledons embedded in their hearts like tiny spoons. 4"–5". Spreading. Early summer.

EUPHORBIA *Euphorbiaceae*

Most of the Spurges are, by height and colouring (mainly green and yellow-green), only suitable for the woodland garden.

E. cyparissias. Cypress Spurge. Europe. The dwarf species found throughout the Alps may, in poor, dry soil develop shades of brilliant orange and scarlet and not exceed 4"–6". In richer conditions it may become invasive, and will not develop the colouring which makes its attraction. Summer.

E. myrsinites. S. Europe. Attractive when kept compact by a dry poor soil, bearing heads of tiny green flowers in conspicuous, rounded, yellow bracts, above rather succulent blue-grey foliage. 8"–10". Summer. (Pl. 13)

EURYOPS *Compositae*

This genus of African shrubs provides one outstanding plant for garden or alpine house.

*E. acraeus (*evansii*). A much branched bushlet of up to a foot, with upright stems closely set with blunt-tipped, linear leaves plated with brightest silver. The solitary flowers on 2"–3" stems are daisies of pure gold. It makes a handsome pan for the alpine house, but so treated tends to become leggy as the leaves die off on the lower stems. In the garden it usually keeps more compact. It is likely to put up welcome suckers around the parent plant, and is easily propagated by cuttings. Early summer. (Pl. 13)

128

9

Cyclamen repandum
Cytisus × kewensis
Daphne collina

Cypripedium calceolus
Daphne cneorum eximia
Delphinium chinense

10

Dianthus alpinus
(Above, *Viola saxatilis var. aetolica*)
Dianthus 'La Bourbrille'
Dicentra cucullaria

Dianthus deltoides
Dianthus 'Mrs. Clarke'
Dimorphotheca barberiae compacta

FELICIA *Compositae*

Were this African genus only slightly more hardy than it is, it would be invaluable for its delightful, clear blue, daisy-like flowers.

F. amelloides (*Agathaea coelestis, Aster rotundifolia*) is hardy in sea-coast rock gardens, where it forms a dense bushlet of a foot or so, covered for a long period in summer and autumn with its pure blue, yellow-centred flowers.

F. bergeriana, Kingfisher Daisy, is one of the few annuals which might be admitted for the sake of its deep azure flowers. 4″–6″. Summer.

F. pappei (*Aster pappei*). A small, much-branched bushlet, with spatulate, rather succulent leaves and clear blue daisy-like flowers. Beautiful, but not hardy except in some coastal districts. 10″–12″. Long flowering from July onwards.

FESTUCA *Gramineae*

F. glauca. Native of most of the cooler regions around the world; makes neat tufts of fine, blue-grey grass, which by colour and form add to the beauty of the rock garden when strategically placed. 6″–8″.

FICARIA

The Celandines are now included in RANUNCULUS.

FICUS *Moraceae*

The pygmy member of this vast genus forms a charming creeper in a sheltered warm position.

F. pumila var. **minima** has tiny veined, heart-shaped leaves, and is hardy in many districts. Flower inconspicuous.

FORSYTHIA *Oleaceae*

F. viridissima 'BRONXENSIS'. Garden origin. Of recent introduction, this promises to be a valuable addition to rock garden shrubs. Its congested woody branches are densely wreathed in spring with conspicuous pale yellow flowers. If it retains its dwarf stature of 1′–1½′ it will be a most useful plant. Probably in any case a little judicious pruning would keep it compact. Indifferent to soil. March.

Fragaria, Frankenia, Fritillaria

FRAGARIA *Rosaceae*

The wild strawberries are too invasive to admit to the rock garden, but lovers of the curious may like to find place in an odd corner for the Plymouth Strawberry, first mentioned (and figured) by Parkinson in 1629, and later described at length by E. A. Bowles in *My Garden in Spring*. Like a wild strawberry in which all floral parts have become leafy. The petals are bright green, and even the seeds (achenes) embedded in the typical red "berry" are minutely leafy. Ideal for miniature flower arrangements.

FRANKENIA *Frankeniaceae*

The Sea Heaths are pleasant small heather-like plants for a light sandy soil. They are mainly coast dwellers, and have clusters of tiny pink flowers at the tips and in the forks of their wiry prostrate branches.

F. laevis. Northern hemisphere (including Gt. Britain). Clustered linear leaves and flesh-coloured flowers. 2″–3″. July.

F. thymifolia. Spain. A grey, hairy, tufted plant with tiny, downy, triangular leaves along the procumbent wiry stems and clusters of very small rose-pink flowers. 3″. Summer.

FRITILLARIA *Liliaceae*

A genus closely related to the Lily family, whose species are very attractive in their grace of habit and (to many) in their quiet colours, generally of shaded or chequered greens and browns, but occasionally white or clear yellow, and, in one case, rarely seen in cultivation, bright red (*F. recurva*). They are found in the temperate regions of the northern hemisphere. The typical habit is of a few linear or narrowly lanceolate basal leaves and a single erect slender stem, usually with a few isolated leaves, and bearing terminal drooping bell-shaped or funnel-shaped flowers composed of six segments. Many are more suitable for frame or alpine house culture than out of doors. Propagation by seed, easy of germination, but often long in producing plants of flowering size, or from the bulblets which are in some species only too readily produced, reducing the parent bulb to non-flowering size for a while. Leafy, woodland, well-drained soil. The following are only a few of the more individual species. Many more are obtainable from time to time and species have lately been introduced, or reintroduced, from Asia Minor. Further descriptions will be found in *Collins Guide to Bulbs.*

*F. acmopetala. Syria, Cilicia, Cyprus. Stem up to a foot or more, large (1¼″) single pendent bells (occasionally two) of variable green, pale yellowish-green within. One of the more amenable to outdoor cultivation. Early April.

*F. camschatcensis. The Black Sarana. Japan, Kamchatka, Alaska, Oregon. Of great interest by reason of its very wide distribution, this species is also almost unique in the very dark maroon-purple, almost black, of its 1–3 or more nodding 1¼″ bells crowning an 8″–12″ erect stem which bears whorls of lanceolate leaves. Not difficult, but apt to lie dormant occasionally, probably while the parent bulb is gathering strength to flower size again after producing the many bulblets to which it is prone. Late flowering. May–June.

F. citrina. Greece, Taurus. Scattered narrow leaves and 8″–10″ stems bearing one or two pendent bells of clear yellow, green-flushed, but without definite markings. Alpine house. 6″. April.

F. delphinensis. See **F. tubiformis.**

*F. liliacea. California. A charming plant with erect branched inflorescence bearing several rather small, open bell-shaped white flowers, tinged with green. 6″–10″. April–May.

*F. meleagris. The Snake's Head Fritillary. Europe, including Gt. Britain. This rare native is one of the most attractive of the genus, with very slender, erect stems, each bearing a large, rather globose, single pendent bell, with six distinctive "shoulders", and of a deep dull purple, more or less prominently chequered with white or whitish mauve. There is a white variety, with green markings. This, curiously, seems more permanent in some gardens than the type. Can be naturalized (as in The Grove, Magdalen College, Oxford) when, if sited in sparse woodland among slender grasses, they will flourish and multiply. Variable, and some specially fine forms have been given varietal names. April.

*F. pallidiflora. S. Siberia. Very distinct, and one of the most beautiful. The flowers, 1–6 in the axils of the upper leaves, are large (1½″) globose bells of greenish yellow, becoming a pure, more luminous yellow as they age. 8″–12″. One of the easiest in cultivation. April–May.

*F. pudica. N.W. America. A charming plant for the alpine house, with one or two rather small pendent golden-yellow bells on wiry stems. 2″–4″. April.

*F. recurva. Scarlet Fritillary. California. Hard to obtain and to grow. It is rare to see a healthy, typical plant in cultivation, but it is mentioned because of its unique colour. The 3–6 funnel-shaped, lily-like 1″ flowers are borne singly on slender pedicels from the axils of the upper stem leaves, and are of a bright scarlet, flecked with orange. Seed, when obtainable, germinates well, but the resulting seedlings are difficult to keep until flowering stage. 10″–12″—up to 2 ft. in the wild. April.

*F. tubiformis (*delphinensis*). S.E. France, N. Italy. In effect a dwarfed *F. meleagris* with full-sized flowers on short erect wiry stems. A beautiful little plant with a distinct bloom on its fat, chequered bells. In nature found on high slopes of downland character. Not difficult in cultivation outside or, for the sake of its beauty and small stature, in the alpine house. It is a variable species and *F. t.* var. *moggridgei*, which is found spasmodically among the type plants, is a clear yellow. There are also hybrids between this and the type, with more or less yellow in evidence. 2″–3″. April.

*F. tuntasia. Greek Is. A very slender plant with 2–4 rather small funnel-shaped flowers to a stem, deep purplish-mahogany, with a greyish bloom. A very distinct species. 12″ April–May.

F. verticillata. Altai Mts. The 1′–2′ stems are leafy, with opposite or whorled narrowly lanceolate leaves and the few (1–5) white, pendent bells, with green markings, are borne singly in the axils of the upper leaves, which develop tendrils at the tips. The top flower is usually from the axil of a set of three tendrilled leaves, which gives the plant a very distinct appearance. April–May.

This is but a small selection, chosen as colour representatives or for some other distinct feature. For those to whom their quiet charm appeals, there are dozens more species available from time to time, sometimes after much search, all of which are desirable and attractive plants to the enthusiast.

FUCHSIA *Onagraceae*

There are a few dwarf forms in commerce of the typical shrubby fuchsia, under names such as 'PETER PAN', 'TOM THUMB', etc., which are delightful in the right setting, but difficult to mix harmoniously with alpines which are true species. They are also on the verge of hardiness in a severe winter.

DP***F. procumbens.** New Zealand. A curiously attractive little plant with many procumbent, long, wiry stems, set with small, rounded, heart-shaped leaves and flowers which, although not conspicuous, repay examining in detail. There is no corolla, but the calyx forms a ¾″ yellow tube, with four reflexed green and purple lobes, and protruding red stamens with blue anthers. This multi-colour flower is followed by persistent, bright red berries. Not quite hardy, but makes a delightful pan for the alpine house. Trailing. Summer onwards. (Pl. 19)

GAGEA *Liliaceae*

Gagea fistulosa (*liottardii*). Commonly met with in the European Alps, especially in the vicinity of cowsheds. It is a small bulbous plant of 3″–4″, with one or two linear, radical leaves and 1–4 bright gold, glossy, starlike flowers, green-backed. It is not easy to cultivate, and would seem to need damp, rich soil, in sun. Summer.

GALANTHUS *Amaryllidaceae*

The snowdrop family are so alike superficially that only the enthusiast will wish to explore the many species known and available (though sometimes rarely). Specialists are referred to *Collins Book of Bulbs*. A guide to the different species is provided by the arrangement of the leaves, which fall into three classes; Nivales, in which the leaves on emerging from the soil are placed quite flat against each other, Plicati, leaves flat, but with the edges rolled back, and Latifoliae, leaves wrapped round each other on emerging, also wider and, generally, brighter green than the foregoing. Transplant or divide immediately after flowering.

*G. elwesii (Latifoliae). Turkey, Greek Is. A handsome early-flowering snowdrop, with broad, erect, glaucous leaves of 6″–8″, and large, solid flowers with broad green markings at the base of the inner segments. January–February.

*G. nivalis (Nivales). Woods all over Europe from Spain to Russia. The ordinary English snowdrop will naturalize and form drifts at the edge of light woodland and is most floriferous and long lived. February–March. There are many varieties available, but few more lovely and airy than the type. They include:

G. n. 'FLAVESCENS' and G. n. 'LUTESCENS', both with yellow markings instead of green at the base of the inner petals.

G. n. 'SCHARLOKII', an amusing variant with the two little green linear bracts, which subtend the flower, elongated to nearly an inch and curved over, appearing like a pair of narrow hare's ears.

G. n. 'VIRIDAPICIS', in which the white outer segments of the flower are tipped with green.

G. n. 'STRAFFAN', a later flowering garden variant with beautifully shaped, solid flowers. Of medium size, but vigorous and free flowering.

*G. plicatus (Plicati). Crimea, Dobrudscha. Large, solid flowers with green marking along the scalloped tips (not the base) of the inner petals.

Gaultheria

Broad glaucous leaves (about 1″ wide) with rolled back edges. Likes a little shade. March.

There are double forms of *G. nivalis* and of *G. plicatus* but they are not so elegant as the types.

GAULTHERIA *Ericaceae*

This genus contains a large number of prostrate or dwarf shrubby plants of neat habit, attractive foliage, small but charming urn- or globe-shaped flowers and, in many cases, showy berries. They are hardy and require woodland conditions and a lime-free soil. Summer flowering.

G. adenothrix. Japan. Shrubby, zig-zag branches, with ovate, pointed leaves, pinkish-white flowers, hairy crimson fruits. 6″–12″.

*G. depressa. New Zealand. Small, cushion-like shrub, with little round crenulated leaves, bronzy in autumn. Pink and white flowers, globose scarlet fruits. 8″–10″.

*G. humifusa. British Columbia. Very dwarf and creeping, rounded serrated leaves, pinkish-white campanulate flowers. Scarlet fruits. 2″.

G. merilliana. Formosa. A recently introduced shrublet with lanceolate leaves on wiry stems of 4″–6″. White flowers and pinkish-white fruits.

*G. nummularioides. Himalaya, W. China. A densely hairy, prostrate shrublet with many interweaving branches closely set with small oval leaves. Small pink flowers and conspicuous blue-black fruits. Still smaller forms have been given the varietal names of *G. n.* 'MINOR' and *G. n.* 'MINUTA'.

G. procumbens. Creeping Wintergreen, Checkerberry. A good ground coverer with oval leaves of up to 1″ in length. Pinkish flowers followed by bright red, globose fruits. 3″–6″.

G. pyrolifolia (*pyroloides*). E. Himalaya. A tufted shrublet with rounded, reticulated bright green leaves and ¼″ pink, egg-shaped flowers. Blue-black fruits. 4″–6″.

*G. sinensis. Burma and neighbouring States. Compact shrub with oval, minutely bristly leaves, and small open-campanulate white flowers, followed by blue fruits. 6″.

*G. thymifolia (*thibetica*) and **G. trichophylla.** Himalaya, W. China. Two closely allied small shrubs with pale to deep pink campanulate flowers and blue fruits. 3″–5″.

Several other dwarf species may be found with nurseries specializing in ericaceous plants. Their neat habit and variety of coloured fruits give them great value in woodland conditions and lime-free soil.

GAYLUSSACIA *Ericaceae*

G. brachycera. Box Huckleberry. United States. This near relation of the vacciniums makes a leafy bush of up to a foot, with bright green glossy oval leaves, vivid crimson when young, and urn-shaped flowers of white, striped pink, and bluish, ½″ fruits. Shade and lime-free soil. Summer.

GENISTA *Leguminosae*

This genus provides several free-flowering dwarf shrubs which revel in a well-drained sunny spot on the rock garden, where the plants are hidden in early summer by the many golden pea-shaped blooms.

G. dalmatica. Dalmatia. Dense, spiny tufts of gorse-like branches, with linear leaves and spikes of bright yellow flowers. 6″.

G. delphinensis. See under **G. sagittalis.**

***G. humifusa.** Spain. A prostrate shrublet with densely interwoven silky-hairy branches and elliptical leaves. Terminal heads of rather small yellow flowers. 3″–10″. (Pl. 13)

G. sagittalis (*Cytisus sagittalis, Spartium sagittalis*). Central and S.E. Europe. A spreading sub-shrub with many radiating prostrate winged branches, narrowing at the nodes to give a jointed appearance. The winged branches appear like leaves. Actual leaves small, oval, pointed, and hairy when young. Erect spikes of yellow pea-shaped flowers. 4″–5″, spreading. June–July.

> ***G. s.** var. **delphinensis** (*G. delphinensis* of catalogues). S. France. An altogether smaller and neater edition, with few, very tiny leaves, and clusters of 2–3 relatively large bright yellow flowers. Prostrate, under 2″. July–August.

G. tinctoria. Dyer's Greenweed. Europe (including Gt. Britain), Asia. The type plant is a rather coarse shrub of up to 3 ft., but *G. t.* var. *humifusa*, a spreading prostrate form of up to 4″, and the double flowered *G. t.* 'FLORE PLENO' are both worth a place for their wealth of golden pea-flowers in full summer.

GENTIANA *Gentianaceae*

Of all flowers, the Gentian is perhaps the most evocative of the mountains, and, indeed, is often taken as the emblem of all mountain flora. Gentian Blue stands for that wonderfully deep and intense shade which is so characteristic, but, although the majority of the race are blue (with rare variations within a species to pale or white forms), certain species, especially some taller ones not described here, may be yellow or dull chocolate brown. All the New Zealand endemics are white, and from the Peruvian Andes come exciting dwarf species of clear, bright yellow, sometimes flashed with scarlet, which are scarcely yet in cultivation.

The species tend to fall mainly into two classes, that of the large five-pointed trumpet flowers, typified by the aggregate of species embraced by the general name of *G. acaulis* and that comprising species with starry flowers, having five pointed or more rounded petals opening flatly at the top of a narrow, cylindrical corolla tube. In each case, there are clusters of more or less fringed growths between the main petals, sometimes insignificant but in a few cases so large and sturdy as almost to suggest five extra petals. These are called plicae, and sometimes differentiate between the species by their size and shape.

In general, the European species flower in the spring, and the Asiatics in the autumn, when their rich colour and prodigality of bloom is most welcome.

The easiest to grow and flower are the Asiatic species, *provided* they are given suitable conditions. With few exceptions they are fiercely lime-hating, and will not exist at all if this is ignored, the first omen of demise being a yellowing of the foliage. In a lime-free soil, however, in a cool, leafy position, *G. sino-ornata*, for instance, will make a wide mat of fresh green linear foliage, almost hidden in September–October by the myriads of single, open trumpets, held upright at the ends of 6″–8″ prostrate stems and of a wonderfully deep, bright blue. These species die back after flowering, to a central resting tuft of rosettes of small, pointed leaves. These rosettes can readily be separated when dormant, each with its own system of thong-like roots, which gives a ready method of increase.

*G. acaulis. Trumpet Gentian, Gentianella. Europe. This name embraces several species whose superficial differences are of little garden importance. All form mats of sturdy, glossy, deep green, pointed, lanceolate or strap-shaped sessile opposite leaves, and bear the familiar trumpets of glorious and characteristic deep blue, often with green-freckled throats, and a prominent golden stigma. Colour variations are found in the wild, it is true, particularly in certain geographical localities where the blue is less pure and has a tinge of purple, and the rare odd plant may be found of etherial turquoise or even white (with freckled or green-shaded throat). The two main species met with in the Alps are **G. kochiana** (on igneous rocks), and **G. clusü**

Gentiana

(on limestone foundations), of which the former is usually the deeper, truer blue. *G. acaulis* is an easy plant to grow; its main requirements seem to be a rather heavy soil and *very* firm planting. But to make it flower freely, in all its breath-taking splendour, is a problem which is often debated but never decided. Soil, aspect, every known condition may seem to be alike in two adjoining gardens, but one patch may spray its glorious blue trumpets in every direction, while the other can, with difficulty, be coaxed to show one sulky bloom. I once had 25 blooms on an 8″ mat. This followed a dose of two Plantoids, broken and inserted round the plant, but whether it was effect or coincidence I cannot say, as the display was never repeated, after similar or any other treatment. 3″. Spring and spasmodically later. (Pl. 14)

D***G. alpina.** Locally on ranges throughout Europe. In effect, a miniature of *G. acaulis*, with close mats of short blunt leaves and sessile, upright, tubby trumpets with recurved petals. Lime-free, peaty soil. Not easy. 2″. Early summer.

G. asclepiadea. Willow Gentian. Europe. A graceful plant with slender stems set with narrow, willow-like leaves and bearing rather narrow, deep blue trumpets in late summer. Woodland conditions. May grow to 24″, but dwarfer forms of under a foot may be had.

D***G. bavarica.** Central Europe. A difficult but beautiful small gentian of 3″–8″ according to situation (taller and more robust in marshy places), with velvety deep blue tubular flowers with five spreading, rounded petal lobes and rosettes of small, lush, oval (not stiff and pointed as in *G. verna*) leaves in opposite pairs on the solitary flower stems, and smaller towards the base (the reverse in *G. verna*). If obtainable, a sunny but damp situation with plenty of humus would give it the best chance of survival. As seen in the wild, it is one of the most lovely of small gentians and has a high alpine form in *G. orbiculare* (*imbricata*) where the tiny, bright green, rounded leaves are congested into a dense mat of ¼″ in height, like a very miniature box edging, while the almost sessile deep blue flowers are almost as large as *G. bavarica*. Will stand a little lime.

***G. bellidifolia.** New Zealand. Forms a mat of glossy, dark green, narrowly spoon-shaped leaves, in rosettes. The flowers are borne on 4″–6″ stems and are white. They are more cup-shaped than the European species, and the rounded petals are divided almost to the base. There are no plicae. Quite hardy, and, having a long, stiff root, requires a deep, well-drained soil. No lime. August.

D***G. brachyphylla.** Europe. In effect, a high altitude form of *G. verna* (though they overlap). The leaves are rather narrower, greyer, and stiffer, and the petals more narrowly oval-pointed. Not an easy plant, but has been known to flourish and flower freely in a deep, well drained trough in gritty, leafy soil. 2″. Early summer and spasmodically.

D***G.** 'CAROLI' (*farreri* × *laurencei*). A small growing and rather frail plant, but with slender trumpets of piercing copper-sulphate blue. Acid soil. 2″. Autumn.

137

G. cashmerica. Kashmir. A pleasant little plant with prostrate stems and grey-green, oval pointed leaves. Mid-blue flowers, smaller than the other Asiatic species described. 3″–4″. Autumn.

G. clusii. See under **G. acaulis.**

*G. farreri. N.W. China, Tibet. Perhaps Reginald Farrer's most spectacular discovery, with radiating prostrate stems bearing many narrowly lanceolate leaves and terminal upturned trumpets of clear, luminous blue, spotted with greenish-blue and shading to white in the throat. It is best bought in flower, as since introduction several washed-out colour forms have occurred, which give no idea of the piercing, almost turquoise blue of the original plant. In well drained gritty soil with plenty of humus it will stand a little lime. Autumn. (Pl. 14)

*G. ×hascombensis. A useful hybrid between *G. lagodechiana* and *G. septemfida*, possessing the good qualities of both parents and flowering a little earlier. Although a hybrid, it sets seed, which comes reasonably true. 5″–6″. Autumn.

*G. hexaphylla. E. Tibet. Many prostrate radiating 4″–6″ stems, with terminal six-petalled, light blue, green-spotted trumpets. Acid soil. July.

G. kochiana. See under **G. acaulis.**

*G. lagodechiana. Caucasus. A good tempered free-flowering plant, with solitary flowers of deep blue at the end of semi-prostrate, radiating leafy stems. 5″–6″. Autumn.

*G. 'Macaulayi' (*farreri* × *sino-ornata*). One of the earliest hybrids and still one of the best. Procumbent stems and large deep blue trumpets. Acid soil. September–October.

ᴅG. nivalis. Mountains of Europe. One of the very few annuals from the high Alps. Makes one single stem or a much-branched bushlet, with a tiny star of piercing blue at the tip of each stem. A delight in the mountains but a challenge to growers which I believe has never yet been met, though seed is plentifully set. 2″–6″. Early summer.

G. orbiculare. See under **G. bavarica.**

G. parryi. N. America. Seldom grown, but mentioned as one of the few gentians from America. Not difficult, and in appearance very like *G. septemfida*. 10″. Autumn.

ᴅ*G. pyrenaica. Pyrenees and E. Europe (missing the Central Alps). This very beautiful, but difficult, little gentian forms tufts or mats of leafy shoots, some of which bear terminally the solitary flowers. They are of a very distinct, deep, velvety violet-blue, and the plicae are so large and rounded as to give the impression of a ten-petalled flower. A good open leafy soil, with no lime, fairly moist. A healthy plant of it is so valuable (and rare) that division should not be attempted. Propagation by seed, if obtainable. 3″. Early summer and spasmodically later.

*G. saxosa. New Zealand. Forms a dense mat of narrow, recurved, dark

Gentiana

green, glossy foliage, from which the 2″ stems rise bearing solitary white, cup-shaped flowers, very like those of *G. bellidifolia*. Hardy and free-flowering in any well drained soil or scree. Autumn. (Pl. 14)

G. scarlatina. Peruvian Andes. An unusual little plant which has been from time to time precariously in cultivation. It is about 4″ high, and bears solitary flowers which, in the form first introduced, were scarlet in bud, owing to the coloured reverses of the folds of the petals, but opened golden yellow with a scarlet and gold reverse. Quite attractive and interesting as being a distinct colour break.

D***G. schleicheri** (*terglouensis*). The very high altitude member of the *G. verna* group, forming a mat of tiny, closely-packed pointed leaves, from which rise the solitary deepest azure flowers on 1″ stems. Gritty scree, with lime. Summer and spasmodically.

*G. septemfida. Asia Minor to Persia. Very like *G. lagodechiana*, but with terminal *clusters* of flowers and a few in the axils of the leaves. Easy and floriferous, but should be chosen in flower as it is variable in colour to dull or purplish-blues, although the best forms are a good deep blue with lighter spots inside the trumpet. 6″. Autumn. (Pl. 14)

*G. sino-ornata. W. China, Tibet. This spectacular introduction by Forrest is the easiest and most prolific of all the Asiatics, *provided* it is given the completely lime-free leafy soil it demands. From central rosettes, which quickly multiply and are readily divisible, radiate the prostrate stems with narrow, linear leaves, each bearing an upturned trumpet of as pure a blue as *G. Farreri*, but deeper and fuller. Autumn.

*G. verna. The Spring Gentian. Europe (including Gt. Britain), Asia. A most lovely little flower, which may be seen throughout the Alps in early summer, sprinkling the close sward with millions of its deep blue five-petalled flowers, often singly but sometimes as a solid patch of colour over a close mat of the rather stiff, often slightly grey-green pointed leaves, which occur in pairs on the 2″–3″ flower stem. Colour variations occur in the wild, to turquoise and white (Pl. 14) and in the Dolomites there is a reddish-purple form. It is difficult to transplant, but will grow readily from seed (probably not germinating until the next March, whenever it is sown). It needs a very well-drained scree mixture, with plenty of humus, but is not long-lived, and should be reinforced with fresh seedlings from the seed which it sets copiously. The Irish native form appears to be sturdier and more permanent than importations from the Continent. (Pl. 14)

> **G. v.** var. **angulosa** is a particularly fine form with inflated and winged calyx.

This only touches the fringe of this wide and beautiful family. Many more Asiatic species and others may be found in catalogues, as well as notable hybrids, of which perhaps the most outstanding is:
G. 'INVERLEITH' (*farreri* × *veitchiorum*) with very large trumpets of deep and luminous blue.

Geranium

GERANIUM *Geraniaceae*

The Crane's-bill family furnish several delightful dwarf species whose foliage, usually palmately lobed or dissected within a roughly circular shape, on long slender petioles, make the bushy compact plants attractive at all times, and in some species takes autumn colourings. Summer flowering.

*G. argenteum. Europe. One of the most lovely, especially in the rose-pink form (it is sometimes paler) for which the brightly silver lobed leaves form a perfect foil. 6".

*G. cinereum. Pyrenees. Very similar to the foregoing, but with less silvery foliage and large pale, purplish flowers, beautifully veined with a darker shade. There are colour forms, including *G. c.* var. *album*, white, and *G. c.* var. *roseum*, deep rose.

*G. dalmaticum. Dalmatia. This recently introduced plant is one of the best, being very easy going and making dense cushions of the characteristic lobed leaves, glossy surfaced and showing tints of orange and red throughout the summer. The many flowers are of solid texture and a good clean pink. 6"–8". (Pl. 15)

G. farreri. See **G. napuligerum.**

*G. napuligerum (*farreri*). Yunnan. One of the best of Farrer's finds. Rather smaller growing than the foregoing, and the lobed leaves are more kidney-shaped. The clear, pale rose flowers are made conspicuous by the black anthers of the stamens. Not so prodigal of its seed as other species. 6".

G. pylzowianum. Kansu. A pleasant little plant, which runs about with finely clawed leaves on frail stems, here and there producing a large clear pink flower. 3".

G. sanguineum. Europe (including Gt. Britain) and Asia. The type plant is too tall for the rock garden, but a prostrate form, ***G. s.** var. **lancastriense,** originally from the coast of Lancashire, is a pleasant and good-tempered plant, forming mats of soft, lobed leaves, with inch-wide flowers of clear pink. 2".

G. stapfianum. A useful plant of similar habit to *G. cinereum*, with purple-pink flowers. 4"–6".

*G. subcaulescens. Balkans. A fairly recent introduction, sometimes considered a variety of *G. cinereum*. Very vivid carmine or deep rose flowers with almost black centres. 4"–6". (Pl. 15)

G. tuberosum. S. Europe. An unusual little tuberous-rooted plant, dying away completely during the winter, but producing linear-lobed leaves in early summer and purplish, or white, veined pink, flowers. 4".

Geum, Gilia, Gladiolus

GEUM *Rosaceae*

The following species are of great value in the rock garden, being, with the exception of the handsome *G. reptans*, easy in all soils and positions, and free with their ample, five-petalled golden flowers, like single roses.   Leaves radical, pinnate with irregular puckered leaflets, and the terminal leaflet always the largest.   Early summer flowering.

G. × borisii (*bulgaricum × reptans*).   Bulgaria.   A showy plant with bright orange flowers.   8″–10″.

***G. montanum.**   European Alps.   The short turf of the Alps, both below and above the tree-line, is made golden with the myriads of inch-wide golden blossoms of this plant, and it is equally free-flowering and good tempered in the garden.   2″–6″.

ᴅ***G. reptans.**   European Alps.   This glory of the high shingles is a magnified *G. montanum*, with huge golden suns, up to 1½″ across, larger, more upright leaves, and many conspicuous red runners from the central rosette.   This is not easy in cultivation.   Leafy acid soil, in full sun but with a plentiful water supply gives the best hope of pleasing it.   4″–6″.

G. rhaeticum.   This natural hybrid between *G. montanum* and *G. reptans*, found in the Engadine and elsewhere, is intermediate in size between its parents, but lacks the red runners of the latter, and is as easy of culture as the former.

GILIA *Polemoniaceae*

N.W. America and the Andes.   The majority of this striking genus are too tall for the rock garden, but

G. pungens forms a spreading mat of woody stems with many spiny leaves (sometimes a congested bushlet of 6″ or so) with variable phlox-like flowers of white to pale apricot.   Summer.

G. aggregata var. **bridgesii,** a dwarf form of the lovely *G. aggregata*, with its head of tiny, fiery stars reduced to a height of 6″ or so, exists, but is not, I think, in cultivation.   Its introduction would be welcome.

GLADIOLUS *Iridaceae*

The only species of this genus which is dwarf enough for the rock garden is:

G. alatus, the Wing-flowered Cornflag, from S. Africa, with slender stems bearing 1½″ tawny yellow, veined flowers, and even this may grow to a foot in height.   Sun, good drainage and lift the corms in winter.   8″–12″.   May–June.

Glaucidium, Globularia, Goodyera, Gregoria

GLAUCIDIUM *Podophyllaceae Monotypic*

*G. palmatum. Japan. This handsome woodlander, although seldom seen now, was by no means rare before the war. An upright stem of 8″–10″ bears two palmately-lobed, maple-shaped leaves, and one very large cup-shaped flower (rarely two), rather suggestive of a hellebore, with petalloid sepals of clear mauve. Woodland soil and conditions or alpine house. There is also a dwarf form of about 4″, and a white form. Late spring. (Pl. 15)

GLOBULARIA *Globulariaceae*

The mountain species of this genus are mainly mat-forming sub-shrubby plants of easy growth in any well drained sunny spot preferably in limy soil, but they are not always very free with their charming flowers, which resemble small powder-puffs in varying shades of soft grey-blue. Summer flowering.

*G. bellidifolia (*cordifolia* var. *nana*). S. Europe. Densely tufted with very many tiny, wedge-shaped leaves. Flowers, almost sessile heads of grey-blue. (Pl. 15) ˙

G. cordifolia. Europe, W. Asia. Rather larger than the above, with rounded, wedge-shaped leaves, and flower-heads on 2″ stems.

G. incanescens. Italy. Sub-shrubby, with sparse blue-grey spatulate leaves and heads of violet-blue flowers.

G. nudicaulis and **G. trichosantha** are two rather similar plants, from S. Europe, and Asia Minor respectively, with leafless herbaceous stems of 6″ or so, and rather large flower-heads of medium blue. A little coarse in growth compared with the foregoing species.

GOODYERA *Orchidaceae*

G. repens. Adder's Tongue. N. Temperate zone (including Gt. Britain). This charming tiny rhizomatous orchid is found deep in the shade of woods where it raises its small spike of yellowish-white flowers above evergreen dark green leaves. Where found it is abundant, in deep, damp moss usually under conifers. It is difficult to grow, but may be tried in similar conditions where available. 2″. Summer.

GREGORIA. See DOUGLASIA

GREVILLEA *Proteaceae*

ᴘ**Grevillea alpina,** Australia, is often offered, and grown, but it is on the fringe of hardiness, and, when happily placed, can reach 2 ft. or more, although it may be curbed by judicious pruning. It is an unusual and attractive shrub, with crowded downy leaves on hairy shoots, and the scarlet and yellow calyx (no petals) is tubular at the base, with prominent protruding stigma. April–May.

GYMNADENIA *Orchidaceae*

Three of this genus are among the small orchids most often seen in the Alps of Europe. All make basal rosettes of flattened, oval leaves, from which rise erect narrow spikes of rather small, very crowded, orchid flowers with three-lobed lips and very fine spurs. The lower part of the flower stem bears several lanceolate leaves.

G. albida (*Leucorchis albida*). Europe (including Gt. Britain). Has a close cylindrical spike of creamy-white flowers—otherwise resembles the following species. Fragrant. 6″. June–July.

*****G. conopsea.** Europe. N. Asia. Larger than the foregoing, and much more plentiful, with rather thicker spikes of bright pink. Fragrant. White forms are occasionally found. 8″–12″. June–July.

G. odoratissima. Europe. Very similar, but with a short narrow spike of pale pink, rarely white, flowers. Intensely fragrant. 3″–4″. June–July.

These small orchids may be grown in the garden, especially among a mixture of true alpines, such as an alpine lawn. They rarely increase, and are intermittent flowerers, sometimes remaining dormant for a year.

GYPSOPHILA *Caryophyllaceae*

A mainly European genus, with intricate wiry stems and opposite linear or lanceolate leaves and, usually, sprays of very many small five-petalled flowers. A few species are densely cushion-forming and are mainly grown for their neat symmetrical shape, as these are not, in general, free-flowering. All are easy to grow in well-drained, sunny positions, and the congested forms make attractive plants for the alpine house. Summer flowering.

G. aretioides. Mts. of Persia. One of the most striking cushion plants, making hard domes of tiny leaves and rarely showing its almost sessile pearl-white flowers. 2".

*G. cerastioides. Himalaya. Distinct from most of the genus, this makes tufts of stalked, spatulate or oval, greyish leaves, with many ½" flowers of white, strikingly veined with purple. 2"–3". May–October.

G. fratensis. See **G. repens.**

G. nana. Greece. A slow growing cushion or mat-forming plant, up to 2", with grey-green narrowly lanceolate leaves and pink or white flowers. Summer.

G. prostrata. See **G. repens.**

*G. repens (*prostrata* var. *fratensis*). European Alps. Forms a bunch of many, much branched, wiry stems of up to 8", which spray in all directions, with infrequent pairs of grey-green linear leaves and myriads of small flowers. Forms can be found from white to deep pink through every gradation in shade. Easy and most attractive plant. Excellent for crevices or the tops of walls. 3"–6". Summer.

HABERLEA *Gesneriaceae*

A genus of two very nearly allied species, related to the ramondas and succeeding in similar sites, i.e. preferably in upright crevices, facing north, in soil containing plenty of humus, or on shady banks.

*H. ferdinandi-coburgii. Balkans. Forms a rosette of thick-textured, narrowly spatulate, toothed leaves and umbels of 3–4 tubular flowers with five unequal petals which give them a slightly lipped appearance. Pale lilac, shaded. 4"–6". Spring.

*H. rhodopensis. Thrace. Very similar to the above, but rather smaller in all its parts. 4"–5". Spring. (Pl. 15)

H. r. 'Virginalis' is a very beautiful white form.

HACQUETIA *Umbelliferae Monotypic*

*H. epipactis (*Dondia epipactis*). A charming little herbaceous plant from E. Europe, with three-foliate radical leaves of very bright green and close umbels of tiny yellow flowers enclosed in large leafy bracts, which give the flower-heads the appearance of a small Victorian nosegay. A stiff soil in part shade suits it, and division, if necessary, should be made from established clumps in early spring before new growth begins, as it resents transplanting. 3"–4". March–April. (Pl. 15)

11

Dodecatheon meadia, dark form
Douglasia vitaliana
Dryas octopetala

Douglasia laevigata
Draba aizoides
Eranthis hyemalis

12

Erigeron compositus
Erinacea pungens
Eriogonum ovalifolium

Erica carnea 'Springwood White'
Erinus alpinus
Eritrichium nanum

HEBE *Scrophulariaceae*

The Hebes are the New Zealand counterparts of the European veronicas, and are often included in that genus, from which they only differ in small botanical detail. Most are medium-sized shrubs and of borderline hardiness, but are indifferent to soil and position.

H. bidwillii (*Veronica bidwillii*). A delightful miniature, with tiny box-like leaves on prostrate rooting sprays. White flowers, often with faint lilac veining. Summer.

***H. buch₁ nanii** 'MINOR' (*Veronica buchananii* 'MINOR'). An attractive congested shrublet making a bun-shaped cushion of dense wiry twigs set with stiff little oval, dull green leaves. The whitish flowers are not freely produced. 3″–4″. Summer.

***H. pinguifolia** 'PAGEI' (*Veronica* 'PAGEANA'). An attractive small shrub, probably a hybrid, with upright or semi-prostrate stems set with many small, oval, stiff, grey-green (almost silver-grey) leaves often tinged with red. Terminal spikes of small whitish flowers freely produced. 6″–12″. Summer.

HEDERA *Araliaceae*

The dwarf Ivies have their uses as foliage plants, and congested forms making dense-spreading bushlets of 6″ or so in height may be found among varieties of *H. helix*, the common Ivy, such as *H. h.* 'CONGLOMERATA MINIMA', etc.

HEDYSARUM *Leguminosae*

H. obscurum is a handsome herbaceous perennial from the European Alps. At the ends of slender stems with narrowly pinnate leaves, it bears conspicuous, narrowing spikes of rich red-violet pea flowers, followed by curious seed pods like a string of flat beads. It is difficult to establish, but once satisfied it grows and flowers well, but is apt to sucker in all directions. 6″–8″. Summer.

HELIANTHEMUM *Cistaceae*

The garden Rock Roses are all forms, rarely hybrids, of the species *H. chamaecistus* (*nummularium,*) and may be had in all shades from white, through every grade of yellow to deep orange, and through

Helichrysum

every shade of pink to scarlet and deep red, including fully double forms. The foliage is in many shades of green, and varying woolliness of surface to a silver-grey which is a delightful foil to the flowers and lovely when they are not there. They are all easy going, sun-loving plants, and rampant, and can provide a wonderful patchwork of colour in June. They do, however, require careful placing and are, in my opinion, best in a simple form of rockery devoted to a few species of easy, showy plants (see Introduction, page 17), as by their vigour and blaze of colour they are apt to swamp, literally and figuratively, the quieter, less rampageous inhabitants. They need cutting back drastically after flowering, and desirable forms are easily perpetuated by cuttings.

H. alpestre. Mts. of Central and S. Europe. A frail shrublet with hairy stems and small oval leaves. Bright yellow flowers. 3″–4″. June–July. (Pl. 16)

H. a. 'SERPYLLIFOLIUM' is even smaller in all its parts. 2″, prostrate. Early summer.

*H. chamaecistus (*nummularium, vulgare*). Europe (including Gt. Britain). The spreading shrubby Rock Rose, common on our chalk downs and all over Europe. The type plant has clear yellow flowers, but many garden forms have been raised in a large variety of colours. See above. (Pl. 16)

H. lunulatum. Italy. A dwarf shrubby species, with grey-green oval pointed leaves, and rather small yellow flowers, with a deeper mark at the base of each petal. 4″–8″. June–July.

H. nummularium. See **H. chamaecistus.**

H. vulgare. See **H. chamaecistus.**

HELICHRYSUM *Compositae*

The genus of Everlasting Flowers has this property (not absolute) by means of the dry, almost horny, bracts which enclose their flower-heads. A great many come from the warm temperate zones and are not hardy, but the following are attractive plants for the garden or alpine house, whose protection is often desirable by reason of the woolliness of the foliage which is generally present in lesser or greater degree.

H. bellidioides. New Zealand. A prostrate carpeter which can become rampant on a sunny bank. Long slender branches with small spatulate or oval white-woolly leaves and terminal flower-heads of tiny white florets in white bracts. Prostrate. Summer.

H. b. var. **prostratum** is a more congested form.

Helleborus

pH. **coralloides.** New Zealand. An upright branched shrublet of up to 10″. It makes a very attractive specimen plant, and although usually seen in a pan (probably because of its rarity) it seems to be hardy out of doors so far as it has been yet tested. Its sturdy whipcord branches are dark green with glossy adpressed leaves showing a narrow white edge, and the new growth is white-woolly. The flowers, which are seldom seen in England, are tiny white flower-heads, borne terminally.

pH. **frigidum.** Corsica. A tufted branched plant, prostrate in habit, with small, sessile, pointed leaves, the whole plant being silver with adpressed hairs. Compact silvery-white flower-heads, solitary and terminal, ½″ or more across. This seems to have become rare, but was popular as a foliage plant for the alpine house before the war. (Pl. 16)

pH. **lanatum.** S. Africa. A densely woolly sub-shrub, with oval leaves and bright yellow flower-heads. 12″ or more. A striking plant for its flannel-like leaves, but of borderline hardiness. (Pl. 16)

p*H. **marginatum.** S. Africa. A delightful mat-former with dense rosettes of small, silver, pointed leaves, and sessile russet-pink flower-heads. 1″–2″. Summer. Alpine house.

p*H. **orientale.** S.E. Europe. A shrubby plant with white felted, oval, pointed leaves of 1″ or more, and clusters of small "Everlastings" of clear yellow. Is quite hardy, but may suffer from excessive winter damp. 10″–12″. Summer. (Pl. 16)

pH. **selago.** New Zealand. An intricate wiry congested shrublet whose slender whipcord branches are dark green with the tiny adpressed leaves which completely clothe them almost resembling a cassiope. The tiny chaffy flower-heads are terminal and sessile. Makes a pleasant little pan, but is hardy, at any rate in the south of England.

p*H. **virgineum.** Balkans. A very similar plant in foliage to *H. orientale*, but the unopened buds are a beautiful silvery pink, to which the almost white leaves are a perfect foil. The flowers are eventually a creamy white. There is a hybrid between this and *H. orientale*, with pale coppery flowerheads. 8″–10″. Summer.

HELLEBORUS *Ranunculaceae*

The hellebores are too large for the average rock garden, but must be put on record, as they are invaluable as beautiful winter and early spring flowering plants where space and semi-woodland conditions can be provided.

*H. **niger.** The Christmas Rose. Central and S. Europe, and W. Asia. This lovely plant opens its solid white bowl-shaped flowers (rarely pink-tinged) with a boss of golden stamens, from Christmas onwards on sturdy 4″–8″ stems.

H. n. 'POTTER'S WHEEL' has enormous flowers of solid white.

H. n. 'LOUIS COBBETT' has shell-pink petals with a bright green base.

H. orientalis. Greece and Asia Minor. Considerably taller, up to foot or more, carries on the display until late Spring. From white through all shades of pink to deep purple-black.

There are also several other very distinct species available to the enthusiast, mainly with green flowers. All take time to re-establish after transplantation, but come readily from seed.

HELONIOPSIS *Liliaceae*

H. breviscapa and **H. japonica** are two charming Japanese plants with basal rosettes of evergreen, shining leaves, and clustered heads of little lily-like flowers of deep or paler pink, or striped. 8″. Summer. (Pl. 16)

HEMEROCALLIS *Liliaceae*

H. minor. E. Asia. An attractive miniature of the border Day Lily, having funnel-shaped flowers, few to a scape, of clear yellow, copper-backed or flushed copper. 7″–8″. Summer.

HEPATICA *Ranunculaceae*

Until recently this little group was included in the genus Anemone, where it is still found in many catalogues. They are all woodland plants, and their crisp entire leaves, on stiff wiry petioles of 4″–6″, are almost evergreen. By early spring they have shrivelled to reveal a stout resting bud, from which the new flowers begin to unfurl by the turn of the year, and slightly in advance of the new leaves which in their early stages are softly hairy. The blade of the leaf is roughly kidney-shaped, divided into 3 lobes (usually), which are either pointed or fluted according to the species. As with Anemone, the petalloid sepals take the place of petals. The flowers are solitary, and the distinguishing mark of the genus is the involucre of 3 small green leaves immediately below the flower. Propagation by seed, sown as soon as ripe (when it is still green). Large clumps may be divided, but one is loath to do so. These are some of the most delightful flowers of early spring, and appear in the new year as soon as there is a convenient mild spell.

H. acutiloba and **H. americana.** Two American species very like *A. triloba* (see below), of which the former has pointed lobes to the leaves and the latter more rounded. Rather smaller plants than *A. triloba* and with smaller pale blue, pale pink, and white flowers. 4″.

H. angulosa. See **H. transsilvanica.**

*H. × media 'BALLARD'S VAR'. This, which is the most magnificent of all the hepaticas, is said to be a cross between *H. triloba* and *H. transsilvanica*. The foliage is like a particularly sturdy *H. transsilvanica*, and the flowers have wider and more solid sepals than its parents, of a lovely and luminous mauve. 5″–6″. (Pl. 17)

*H. transsilvanica (*angulosa*). Roumania. Larger in all its parts than *H. triloba*, and slightly downy. The three-lobed leaves are fuller and rounder (not pointed), and inclined to pucker round the edges. The type flower is a palish mauve-blue, and there is also a pale pink variety. 5″.

*H. triloba. This is the hepatica of the high sparse woods of the Alps, and is also found across Europe, Russia, China, Japan and America. The leaves, which are sometimes mottled, are shallowly three-lobed, and the lobes are pointed. The sepals are oval or oblong, and in the type plant are mauve with white stamens (Pl. 17), although pink and white forms are readily found, one variety of the latter having pink stamens. There are selected colour forms, such as *H. t.* 'COERULEA', a really deep blue, and doubles, of which the pink is fairly readily obtained (Pl. 17), the blue much more scarce, and the white extremely rare in cultivation.

HESPEROCHIRON *Hydrophyllaceae*

This small W.N. American genus contains a couple of attractive species which should be amenable to cultivation in ordinary, well-drained soil, with ample water during their very short appearance above ground in spring. They form rosettes of small radical, rather succulent leaves, and bear solitary flowers of white, tinged or veined. That they are so seldom seen may be because they die back completely directly after flowering.

H. californicus. California. Beautiful white, veined flowers, suggestive of Grass of Parnassus, solitary on erect stems among upright, narrowly spatulate, bright green leaves. 3″–4″. Spring.

H. pumilus. Idaho to Oregon. A striking little plant with few, fat basal leaves, and wide, five-petalled saucer-shaped flowers on 2″ stems. 2″–3″. Spring.

Hieracium, Horminum, Hosta, Houstonia
HIERACIUM *Compositae*

The Hawkweeds of this very extensive genus, all with Dandelion-like flowers in shades of yellow, are mostly too coarse and invasive to admit to the rock garden, although a few species, for example *H. bombycinum* 6″, *H. villosum* and *H. waldsteinianum*, both 10″–12″, have attractive silvery or white-woolly leaves.

H. aurantiacum. Grim the Collier. Europe. Has flower-heads of an unusual rich shade of orange-red, but, by runners and its many airborne fluffy seeds, is apt to take possession of any neighbourhood to which it is introduced. 6″–8″. Summer.

HORMINUM *Labiatae*

H. pyrenaicum. Pyrenees to Tyrol. Attractive when its bluish-purple, slender spires of lipped flowers are seen in quantity among the geums and other small fry in the open sward between sparse woodlands throughout the Alps, but it is of little effect in the garden as its foliage, consisting of deeply scalloped radical leaves, is coarse and rough in texture and the flowers lack brilliance. 6″–8″. Summer.

HOSTA (FUNKIA) *Liliaceae*

The Plantain Lilies, although excellent foliage plants for half-shade in woodland conditions, with large tubular white to mauve flowers, are too large for the average rock garden, but a new comer,

*H. venusta, Yakushima, Japan, is a charming little plant with few small Funkia-like leaves and erect stems bearing two or three lily-like flowers of mauve. Up to 8″, though it is variable, and some forms flower at 2″–3″. Summer.

HOUSTONIA *Rubiaceae*

The only member of this N. American genus which is normally grown here is the delightful

*H. caerulea, known in its own country as Bluets. This forms a dense little clump, with many small radical spatulate leaves of light, bright green, and masses of small four-pointed stars of pale china-blue. A rather sturdier form with deeper coloured flowers is known as *H. c.* 'Millard's var.'. Although perennial it is usually treated as an annual or biennial as it is apt to impoverish itself by excessive flowering. It makes a charming pan for the alpine house. Propagation by seed or division after flowering. 2″–3″. Long flowering from June onwards.

HUTCHINSIA *Cruciferae*

Two of this genus are among the most typical plants to be found among the high screes of the N. Temperate regions. They are both appropriate to give character to a stone sink, among other true miniatures of like proportions from great heights.

H. alpina. A tufted perennial of about 2″, with a crowded rosette of small pinnatifid leaves, dark green, and fern-like. The dense clusters of tiny white four-petalled flowers are attractive at their best moment, but like most crucifers, look leggy when in fruit. Early summer.

H. brevicaulis is a dwarf edition of the foregoing, the whole tiny plant often being no more than 1″, although perfectly in proportion. It is only found at great heights, and usually upon granite. Early summer.

HYACINTHELLA. See HYACINTHUS

HYACINTHUS *Liliaceae*

H. orientalis, the species from which the florists' hyacinths have been derived, is, even in its more graceful original form, rather too tall for the rock garden, but a few of the smaller species are among the most delightful of the later spring bulbs (March–April). A well drained soil in full sun will suit them best.

H. amethystinus. Pyrenees. A charming plant with 6″–8″ tapering spikes of small six-petalled flowers of a delicate shade of Cambridge Blue, from rosettes of narrowly linear leaves. There is also a white form.

*H. azureus (*Hyacinthella azurea*). Mts. of Asia Minor. One of the most attractive small bulbs with clustered flower-heads like a miniature Grape Hyacinth, but differing from Muscari in that the individual flowers are not constricted at the mouth. Varying according to environment its bright clear azure spikes may be from 3″–6″. Increases readily by self-sown seed, and is one of the few bulbs small enough for troughs and sink gardens.

H. dalmaticus. Yugoslavia. A pleasant species with close, rather narrow heads of many small pale blue flowers. Up to 8″.

Hydrocotyle, Hylomecon, Hypericum

HYDROCOTYLE *Umbelliferae*

Two of this unspectacular genus are sometimes offered as ground coverers for shady spots, where their prostrate habit and neat little leaves form a pleasant carpet. These are *H. dissecta* with tiny palmately cut leaves, and *H. moschata* with small glossy leaves. The flowers are inconspicuous.

HYLOMECON *Papaveraceae Monotypic*

*H. japonicum. Japan, etc. A lovely and showy plant of about 8″–10″, with many four-petalled bowl-shaped flowers, up to 1½″ across, of a luminous golden yellow. Leaves, usually with two or three pairs of leaflets, are rather lush and of a bright green. Appreciates a rather rich soil with plenty of leaf-mould. April. (Pl. 17)

HYPERICUM *Hypericaceae*

This large genus, although varying extensively in size and habit, has the common characteristics of bright yellow five-petalled flowers enclosing a conspicuous boss of numerous spraying golden stamens. Among the many species are found some of the most beautiful and showy dwarf herbaceous plants, sub-shrubs, and prostrate herbs or shrublets. Coming, as most of them do, from hotter climates than our own, several species are not proof against an exceptionally severe winter, although the shrubby ones will often break again from the base when apparently dead. They will flourish in any soil, in a sunny open position. Summer flowering.

P**H. balearicum.** Balearic Is. One of the least hardy, but mentioned as being one of the most distinct. A dwarf shrub with erect branches, up to a foot, well-clothed with small, curiously puckered leaves, and solitary 1″ flowers.

P***H. coris.** S. Europe. A charming little heath-like plant, with wiry upright branches and whorls of narrow linear leaves. Flowers of golden yellow, striped red. 6″. Not hardy in a severe winter.

P***H. cuneatum.** Asia Minor, Syria. A tiny branching almost prostrate shrublet, with wiry 6″ red stems bearing wedge-shaped leaves and short spires of ¾″ flowers from scarlet buds. Barely hardy. (Pl. 17)

Hypsela

H. empetrifolium var. **prostratum.** S.E. Europe, Asia Minor. A dense mat of heath-like foliage and clusters of few golden ¾″ flowers. Not quite hardy.

H. fragile. S.E. Europe. A spraying shrublet with small oval leaves and 1″ flowers of paler gold than the foregoing.

*H. olympicum. S.E. Europe, Syria, Asia Minor. One of the most beautiful, with a forest of upright slender 8″–10″ stems with many sessile long-oval leaves. The terminal flowers are very large golden bowls of up to 2″ across. There is an even more lovely variety in *H. o.* 'Citrinum', with pale yellow flowers. (Pl. 17)

*H. polyphyllum. S.W. Asia Minor. One of the more hardy species, this makes a dense bunch of 6″ leafy shoots, hidden in summer by the clusters of 1½″ golden flowers, often marked with scarlet. A pale form is offered as *H. p. citrinum* or *H. p. sulphureum*.

H. repens. Asia Minor. A tufted herbaceous plant of up to 6″, with narrow leaves and golden yellow flowers.

*H. reptans. Sikkim. One of the loveliest of this attractive genus. Quite prostrate and best placed where its many stems with small oval leaves, often colouring in autumn, may hang over a wall or rock face. The fat scarlet buds are almost as decorative as the large deep golden suns, nearly 2″ across, which follow them.

H. rhodopeum (*origanifolium*). S.E. Europe, Asia Minor. A semi-prostrate sub-shrub with softly hairy oval leaves and many large golden flowers.

H. trichocaulon. Crete. A recent introduction, of prostrate habit, with 4″–5″ stems, bearing golden flowers which open from bronze-red buds.

HYPSELA *Campanulaceae*
(often wrongly spelt HYPSELLA)

A genus of four species occurring in such wide-spread localities as S. America (1), New Zealand (1), and Australia (2). Useful creeping plants with small, solitary lipped flowers on short stems from the axils of the alternate leaves. Peaty soil and a half-shaded position. Division in March.

H. reniformis (*longiflora*). S. America. A charming little carpeting plant for a pan in the alpine house, or for a sheltered position outside. Bright green round or kidney-shaped leaves and little lipped flowers, pale pink streaked with crimson. **H. longiflora** is a syn. of *H. reniformis*, but often listed as a separate species. May become invasive.

Iberis, Ilex, Incarvillea

IBERIS *Cruciferae*

The Candytufts include a few dwarf perennial species which are useful to provide densely bushy, very free-flowering shrublets which yet have a herbaceous appearance. Summer flowering.

I. gibraltarica. Gibraltar. An evergreen sub-shrub of up to a foot, with leathery, dark green, wedge-shaped leaves, and crowded flat heads of white flowers, sometimes tinged with pale pink or lilac. Needs a warm sunny position. Frequently offered but seldom obtained true to name.

I. saxatilis. Pyrenees to Sicily. A tiny evergreen shrublet of 3″–4″, with narrow, almost cylindrical dark green leaves, which gives the plant the appearance of a very small Yew. Flat terminal heads of small white flowers, sometimes tinged with mauve. (Pl. 1)

I. semperflorens. S. Europe. The parent of several named forms, and an invaluable free-flowering sub-shrub of 9″–10″, with numerous oblong, dark green, glossy leaves, hidden in late spring and early summer by the many flat, 1½″–2″ heads of pure white flowers. An even more compact form is offered as *I. s.* 'PYGMAEA', or *I. pygmaea*.

ILEX *Aquifoliaceae*

The Hollies provide a very un-holly-like congested shrub, **I. crenata** var. **nummularia** (*I. c.* var. *mariesii*), with small glossy round or broadly oval leaves on rigid twiggy branches. It is a rare plant, and very slow in growth (under 1″ a year), and makes a distinctive alpine house plant. When well established it produces black berries.

INCARVILLEA *Bignoniaceae*

A small genus of very showy plants from W. China. They are true perennials, and surprisingly hardy considering their lush appearance, although a light covering of bracken in winter is helpful, and they require a light but rich and well-drained soil in a sunny position. The brilliant flowers are suggestive of small Gloxinias. Summer.

I. delavayi. W. China, Tibet. A rosette of few, radical, twice-pinnate 8″–12″ leaves, with slashed margins, and huge trumpet flowers of bright rose-red, with tubes up to 3″ across, on stems of 1–2 ft. (Pl. 18)

I. grandiflora. W. China. A much dwarfer plant than the foregoing, with less cut leaves, but equally large trumpets of rich rose.

*I. younghusbandi. The best in cultivation. A more dwarf and compact plant with open, lipped trumpets of rich, deep rose.

INULA *Compositae*

Of this handsome genus there is one attractive pygmy, **I. acaulis,** from Asia Minor, which makes rosettes of 1½″ narrowly spatulate leaves, on which in early summer sit the stemless golden daisies, 1″ or more across.

IONOPSIDIUM *Cruciferae*

One of the very few annuals admissible, and indeed very welcome, to the stone sink or rock garden is the delightful ***I. acaule,** from Portugal. This makes a dense symmetrical tuffet of radical, rounded heart-shaped or spatulate leaves on slender petioles, and many small solitary cruciform lilac flowers just above the 1″ dome of light green foliage. It has a long flowering season from summer onwards. Seed sown in the open in spring, but freely self-seeds when once introduced.

IPHEION *Amaryllidaceae*

*I. uniflorum (*Milla uniflora, Triteleia uniflora*). S. America. A charming and free-growing bulb, comparable in habit with the scillas and chionodoxas, and suitable for similar positions, but distinct, with linear, grass-like foliage, 5″ stems bearing pale lavender-blue flowers, funnel-shaped at the base, opening into six-pointed stars, nearly 1″ across. The colour is variable, and deeper forms are sometimes given varietal names.

IRIS *Iridaceae*

The Iris family provides beauty in the rock garden and alpine house from winter to mid-June. Most species require full sun and good drainage, and a few need a complete baking in their resting season. Some of these last are so choice, and delicate in petal, as to ask for alpine house treatment in any case. They are then best in a container from which water is completely withheld from the dying down of the leaves in July until fresh growth begins to appear about October, the plants in the meantime being exposed to all the sun there is. A built-in bed on the staging is ideal for this. The species divide into two distinct groups, those with bulbs and those with rhizomes. The visible structure of the flower is common to both, consisting of three outer petals, called the falls, which are usually broad and reflexed,

Iris

often bearing a patch of coarse hairs at the centre (called the beard), and in some species veined or shaded; three inner petals, called the standards, which are erect and often wide and frilled to some extent, and the stigma (arising from the ovary) which is also petalloid, and curves outwards in three strap-shaped processes which lie back and along the bases of the three outer petals. The three stamens lie under the expanded stigma segments, and are not visible unless looked for.

BULBOUS IRISES

I. alata. S. Spain, N. Africa, Sicily, etc. (abundant on the slopes of Mt. Etna). Tempting by reason of its 1″–1½″ flowers of variable blue and blue-violet, but difficult to keep, requiring a long summer drought. Up to 1 ft. Winter flowering.

*I. bakeriana. Asia Minor, Mesopotamia. One of the most delightful small irises. Deep violet standards, white falls with violet markings and wide tips of inky blue velvet. Near **I. reticulata,** but smaller and having 8-sided leaves instead of square-sectioned. 4″–6″. January–February.

*I. danfordiae. Cicilian Taurus. 2″ flowers of clear bright yellow. Standards reduced to mere bristles. Lovely, but tends to split into dozens of wheat-like bulbs after flowering, which take years to attain flowering size, and are apt to be lost by the way. Bake in summer. 4″, but leaves eventually reach 1 ft. January–February.

*I. histrioides. Armenia. The most beautiful and good tempered of all the early spring bulbs. Comparatively large flowers of deep blue, shaded with blue-purple. Floriferous, and the individual flowers are long-lasting, even withstanding frozen snow on the petals. In a well-drained soil, with mortar rubble, will increase, dividing into few bulbs, some of which are large enough to flower the following year. The form usually offered is *I. h.* 'MAJOR'. 3″–4″. January–February.

ᴅ**I. persica.** Asia Minor to S. Persia. A scarce small iris which used to be obtainable in a lovely blue, shaded with sea-green. A wartime casualty, it has recently been reintroduced in other colour forms, mainly in buffs, with dull purple falls. It is likely to need care in cultivation or it would not have died out temporarily, as it was not scarce early in the century, and apparently grown extensively a hundred years ago. A very sunny well-drained position and a summer roasting seem to give the best hope of establishing its permanence. 2″–3″.

*I. reticulata. Caucasus, N.W. Persia. The best known of the spring bulbous irises and easy and permanent in any sunny, well-drained position. Makes an effective alpine house plant. The leaves are four-angled and the flowers in the type plant are a deep violet-purple, with conspicuous orange ridges on the falls. They are rather smaller, and the petals considerably narrower than

156

in *I. histrioides* 'MAJOR'. One of the oldest and most distinct varieties is *I. r.* 'CANTAB', Cambridge blue, deeper on the falls, which have a contrasting orange stripe. This is rather smaller in flower than the type. Among many other named varieties, selected seedlings or in some cases possibly hybrids with *I. histrioides*, are *I. r.* var. *krelagei*, reddish purple, *I. r.* 'ROYAL BLUE', one of the nearest to a deep pure blue, *I. r.* 'HERCULES', purplish red, etc. 4"–6", but leaves eventually 7"–8". February–March.

I. sisyrinchium. Mediterranean region to India. Not of much garden value as it is not easy, and its flowers, rather small, with short, broad, recurved falls, on slender 6"–8" stems, last individually only a day, but in its native habitat it is apt to astonish by painting a whole area sky blue overnight, the display disappearing again by the evening.

*I. winogradowii. W. Caucasus. A comparatively new introduction, and a showy, early flowering iris, with large very low-growing flowers of sulphur yellow, with orange markings on the falls. Has been called the yellow counterpart of *I. reticulata*, but falls and standards are both much wider and slightly frilled. 3"–4". Spring. (Pl. 18)

RHIZOMATOUS IRISES

These are, in effect, miniatures to a greater or lesser degree of the garden Flag Irises, and all have creeping rootstocks just under or in the surface of the soil, from the base of which depend the dense thong-like roots. They also have the long flat pointed leaves, enveloping the flowering stem at its base, which are characteristic of their cousins of the herbaceous border. Open, well-drained, sunny position.

I. attica See **I. pumila.**

I. chamaeiris. S. Europe. Often confused in gardens with *I. pumila*, from which it differs in having a longer stem and being practically evergreen. As each species is very variable confusion is more understandable, but for garden purposes it is immaterial. Four to six leaves in an upright tuft and relatively enormous flowers of blue, purple, yellow, or white. Varieties are offered in any catalogue under colours or descriptive varietal names. 4"–10". April–May.

I. cretensis. See under **I. unguicularis.**

*I. cristata. E. United States. Charming small iris, with well-proportioned flowers on thin, wiry 6" stems, pale mauve with deeper shading and deep yellow throat and crest of falls. More enchanting still is the small *I. cristata* var. *lacustris* (often given specific rank as *I. lacustris*), which is even more compact, with single, beautifully marked mauve flowers on 1"–2" pedicels. In spite of its name it does not insist on boggy conditions, and although both are hardy they are usually grown in pans in order to give protection to their lovely, though fugacious flowers. May. (Pl. 18)

Iris

*I. gracilipes. Japan. A fairy-like iris, with flat, rather rounded flowers on branched wiry stems from dense fans of typical flat spear-like foliage. There is an equally beautiful white variety. Usually grown in the alpine house because of its fragile appearance. 6″–8″. May.

*I. innominata. Oregon. A very variable species of 8″–10″, with many long narrow leaves and most attractive well-proportioned flowers in various shades, usually blue, mauve, yellow, and a golden bronze. Easy from seed, but like most American irises detests lime in the soil. Fairly permanent in a well-drained, sunny spot in leafy, sandy soil. May–June. (Pl. 18)

I. lacustris. See under **I. cristata.**

I. mellita, Malta. S.E. Europe. Again a miniature Flag Iris, even smaller than *I. pumila*, with pale smoky-brown petals, shaded and veined with reddish purple. The form *R. m.* 'RUBROMARGINATA' has a fine deep-red edge to the leaves. 3″–4″. April–May.

*I. pumila. Europe, Asia Minor. Resembles *I. chamaeiris*, but with almost stemless flowers, like a very dwarf Flag Iris, with disproportionately large flowers of purple, pale blue, yellow, and white. The Greek variant *I. p.* var. *attica* has usually straw to brownish-yellow flowers. 4″–5″. April.

I. ruthenica. Transylvania and Siberia to China. From a forest of 6″ narrow, grass-like leaves arise the wiry-stemmed single flowers of deep blue, veined and shaded lighter blue and white on the falls. They tend not to rise well above the foliage, but this defect is minimized in *I. r.* 'DYKE'S VARIETY'. May. An easy and attractive plant, but with a short flowering season.

*I. unguicularis, formerly *I. stylosa*, and as such often found in catalogues, Algeria, E. Mediterranean. This most welcome winter flowerer, when its surprising large and delicate bright lilac (occasionally white) flowers open successively for weeks from November onwards until the spring, is too tall, and too untidy in growth to admit to the rock garden, but *I. u.* var. *cretensis* of Crete is the type plant in miniature, with 6″ tussocks of grass-like foliage, and lovely mauve flowers with orange-crested falls, finely veined with violet. Needs a hot, well-drained position. April–May.

The Oncocyclus Group of rhizomatous irises is not described here individually as the few species hitherto in cultivation are too tall and, moreover, very difficult in cultivation. They are wonderfully beautiful, with showy flowers having intricate fine veining and conspicuous blotches, or even patches of dense, almost black "fur" on the falls. However, recent botanical expeditions to Turkey and Persia have resulted in the introduction of many new and dwarfer species and varieties of this lovely group. These will all require complete baking from the time their foliage dies back in July until growth starts again in October. This necessitates alpine house protection overhead—they seem quite impervious to cold. It is early yet to know how they will accept cultivation, but they are making a good start, and if they are amenable will afford a most distinguished addition to our late spring-flowering plants.

ISOPYRUM *Ranunculaceae*

I. thalictroides. Europe. A charming little plant for woodland soil in shade, with much divided leaves on wiry petioles, the leaflets being three-lobed, and very like the thalictrum from which the specific name is derived. Slender loose heads of few delicate white Anemone-like flowers. 4″–6″.

JANKAEA *Gesneriaceae Monotypic*

DP***J. heldreichii.** Mt. Olympus, Greece. Very like Ramonda in habit, forming a rosette of thick, ovate leaves from which the pale violet, campanulate or wider funnel-shaped flowers rise on 3″ stems, usually two to a stem. The whole plant is silver-plated with white adpressed hairs (reddish-brown on the backs of the leaves), and the flowers have an almost crystalline texture. It is a lovely little plant, but rare and very difficult to grow. It is quite hardy, but deeply resents winter wet. A very gritty peaty soil, in a crevice quite over-hung by rock, or a pan in the alpine house, shaded in summer and kept almost dry in winter would seem to give the best chance—if a plant is available. One must add that a collector of this plant waters copiously on the rosettes themselves, with great success. But this treatment in some other hands has proved fatal. 3″. Early spring.

JASIONE *Campanulaceae*

A genus of herbaceous plants with conspicuous heads of very small flowers, superficially rather like a phyteuma or scabious.

J. humilis. Pyrenees. Has a basal rosette of narrow leaves and bright blue flower-heads on 4″ stems. Summer.

J. jankae. Hungary. Taller than the foregoing, with lanceolate leaves on long wiry petioles, heads of blue flowers. Summer.

J. perennis. W. Europe, including Gt. Britain. Sheep's Bit Scabious is annual or biennial, but is a pretty little plant of about 10″, with globular heads of bright blue flowers. Summer.

Jasminum, Jeffersonia, Kalmia, Kalmiopsis, Kelseya
JASMINUM *Oleaceae*

The only really dwarf member of this genus provides one invaluable shrub for the rock garden or alpine house:

*J. parkeri. N.W. India. Forms a congested twiggy bush of up to a foot, with the characteristic small three-lobed dark green foliage, and, in June, many clear yellow Jasmine flowers, followed by black berries. Easy in any well-drained soil.

JEFFERSONIA. See PLAGIORHEGMA

KALMIA *Ericaceae*

This most beautiful genus has only one member small enough for the rock garden:

*K. polifolia var. **microphylla.** W.N. America. An evergreen creeping shrublet of 4″–6″, with small oval leaves and wiry stems bearing delightful pink saucer-shaped flowers with crimped edges. Requires a slightly moist, well-drained, lime-free soil in not too hot a position. Early summer.

KALMIOPSIS *Ericaceae Monotypic*

*K. leachiana. Oregon. Most attractive small evergreen shrub of up to a foot, intermediate between Kalmia and Rhododendron. The small leaves are oval and leathery. The beautiful rose-purple flowers are borne in loose heads and are shallowly saucer-shaped above a short funnel. It requires a dampish but well-drained lime-free soil in part shade, or makes a charming pan for the alpine house. Usually propagated by cuttings or layers. An even more compact form with deeper flowers, has recently been introduced. April.

KELSEYA *Rosaceae Monotypic*

ᴘ**K. uniflora.** Montana. Forms a mat or flat cushion of tiny erect leaved silvery silky rosettes peppered in early summer (if happily suited) with very small sessile chaffy flowers from reddish buds opening white. It is uncertain in flowering, but can be very floriferous. In any case, the silvery mats make attractive pans for the alpine house at all seasons, where it can be protected from overhead damp in winter. Gritty, well-drained soil. Propagation by division—or seed if available.

13

Erodium chamaedryoides
Erythronium dens-canis
Euryops evansii

Erysimum rupestre
(Above, *Penstemon scouleri alba*)
Euphorbia myrsinites
Genista humifusa

14

Gentiana acaulis
Gentiana saxosa
Gentiana verna

Gentiana farreri
Gentiana septemfida
Gentiana verna alba

LACTUCA *Compositae*

L. perennis. S. Europe (including Gt. Britain). When well grown is too large for the average rock garden, and if happily situated can become invasive, but in an arid starved soil which will stunt its growth it makes a lovely and unusual plant, with toothed pinnatifid leaves, and much branched stems bearing many 1″ wide dandelions of luminous blue. Summer.

LAMIUM *Labiatae*

The Dead Nettles provide one or two handsome ground coverers, but though useful and beautiful they are also very invasive and must be introduced with caution.

L. galeobdolon 'VARIEGATUM'. Europe. The creeping Yellow Archangel sends long sprays in every direction, with opposite nettle-shaped leaves, beautifully marked with silver, and very suggestive of a carpet of *Cyclamen neapolitanum* in leaf. In summer it produces spires of axillary clusters of yellow, lipped flowers, but its foliage is its chief attraction.

L. maculatum. Europe, N. Africa, W. Asia. Forms a carpet of 4″–6″ stems with opposite leaves, shaped like the Common Dead Nettle, but marked centrally with attractive silver patches. Purple-pink nettle flowers. Again invasive, but valuable in the appropriate place for its variegated foliage. There is also a golden variegated form, *L. m.* 'AUREUM'.

LAPEIROUSIA *Iridaceae*

A genus of graceful S. African plants, with somewhat the habit of Freesia. The only species which is reasonably hardy is valuable for its bright colouring and late flowering. It is most likely to be offered under its synonym, *Anomatheca cruenta*.

*L. laxa (*cruenta, Anomatheca cruenta*). Narrow, sword-like leaves and slender spires of six-petalled crimson-scarlet flowers with long, slender corolla-tubes. There is a rare white form, which is not so attractive as the type. Hardy in most districts, but may succumb to a particularly severe winter in an exposed position. The small corms may be lifted in the winter. 6″–12″. Summer onwards to November. (Pl. 32)

Lathraea, Lathyrus, Laurentia, Lavandula

LATHRAEA Orobanchaceae

For lovers of the curious, who can supply the appropriate host, the parasitic *L. clandestina*, from W. Europe, provides a beautiful and interesting early spring flowerer from February onwards. Where it is happy, as in the University Botanic Garden, Cambridge, it empurples the ground with its mats and outliers of sturdy 6″ spikes of crowded, violet, lipped flowers. Making no chlorophyll itself, it is parasitic on willows, poplars, or alders.

LATHYRUS *Leguminosae*

L. cyaneus. Caucasus. Although rather a coarse-looking plant for a choice spot, is invaluable for a quiet corner when in late spring its close bunches of 10″–12″ slender leafy stems are crowned by bright blue pea flowers. May–June.

L. vernus (*Orobus vernus*). Europe. Very similar with purple and blue flowers. They die down soon after flowering, and are easy in any soil or position. Early spring.

LAURENTIA *Campanulaceae*

L. tenella. S. Europe. This delightful little Lobelia-like species forms rosettes of delicate narrow leaves and fairy-like, china-blue, starry flowers singly on very slender stems, the whole plant being less than 2″. It prefers a damp soil, and a cool spot. Hardy, though not long-lived, and should be kept going by seed. Summer.

LAVANDULA *Labiatae*

The Common Lavender, *L. spica*, is too large for the average rock garden, but dwarf and congested forms are offered in commerce which might be acceptable.

L. stoechas. Spain, S. Europe. A more dwarf species, up to a foot, with equally fragrant, curiously crowded, four-angled spikes of deep purple. Summer.

Ledum, Leiophyllum, Leontopodium, Lepidium
LEDUM *Ericaceae*

L. groenlandicum var. **compactum.** N. America. A dwarf version of the Labrador Tea, forming a compact evergreen shrub, with oval, slightly hairy leaves, and terminal clusters of small fragrant white flowers in summer. Cool, woodland spot, and no lime. Up to one foot.

LEIOPHYLLUM *Ericaceae Monotypic*

*L. buxifolium var. **prostratum.** Eastern N. America. Makes a compact twiggy bush of less than a foot with small, evergreen, glossy, oval leaves, and in early summer many dense terminal clusters of tiny white flowers, pink in bud when they are even more attractive. A delightful little shrub, demanding leafy lime-free soil. May–June.

LEONTOPODIUM *Compositae*

The Edelweiss of the European Alps has an ill-deserved reputation for inaccessibility and difficulty. Certainly it is only found at high altitudes, but when there is likely to be among close turf, and difficult it is not, as it grows readily from seed, and is, surprisingly, happy and fairly permanent in any open well-drained site.

L. aloysiodorum, the scented Edelweiss. The name is invalid. See **L. haplophylloides.**

*L. alpinum. Edelweiss. European Alps. Many narrowly lanceolate radical leaves and a few on the 6″ stem bearing a close flat head composed of very small rayless Daisies, enclosed in many bracts, some long and linear, making an irregular star. The whole plant is enclosed in dense white woolly hairs. Geographical forms of the Flannel Flower, larger or smaller, and less or even more woolly are introduced from time to time, but have not generally proved permanent. Early summer. (Pl. 18)

pL. haplophylloides (*aloysiodorum*). The Lemon-scented Edelweiss. Kansu. Very similar to the foregoing, but a smaller, slenderer plant, and rather less woolly. Strongly scented like the Lemon Verbena. 8″. Early Summer.

LEPIDIUM *Cruciferae*

The Cress family provides one small plant of value for the alpine house in:

L. nanum. N. America. In the wild forms dense hard cushions of tiny dark green cress-like leaves, peppered with small heads of equally tiny white cruciform flowers. It is not easy to grow, and still less so to keep in the firm compactness of the wild plant. Seed. 2″–3″, more in the wild. Summer.

LEPTOSPERMUM *Myrtaceae*

The Leptospermums, mainly from Australia and New Zealand, form attractive, spraying, much branched, small leaved shrubs with sessile white or rose flowers, and are not entirely hardy in severe conditions. Accepting this, there is a delightful dwarf shrub.

P*L. scoparium 'NICHOLLSII'. New Zealand. Prostrate in habit, up to 8″–10″, with pale pink, or in one form rose-red, flowers, like tiny hawthorn blossoms. It requires leafy, well-drained lime-free soil, and alertness in protecting from severe winter weather, especially abrupt changes in temperature. May–June.

LEUCANTHEMUM. See CHRYSANTHEMUM

LEUCOGENES *Compositae*

The New Zealand counterparts of the Edelweiss of the European Alps. Both of these species are fully hardy only in our warmer counties, but make excellent pans for the alpine house.

P*L. grandiceps. A delightful silver-leaved bushlet of up to 6″, with crowded, overlapping small oval leaves, and flat 1″ silvery flower-heads, suggestive of small Edelweiss. (Pl. 19)

P*L. leontopodium. Rather taller, a 6″–8″ decumbent shrublet, covered with silvery felt, including the Edelweiss-like flower heads, which are enclosed in long narrow woolly bracts.

LEUCOJUM *Amaryllidaceae*

The Snowflakes might be more often grown than they are. There are spring and autumn species, hardy and easy in the rock garden, and a few which, for fragility rather than tenderness, are best grown

Leucopogon, Leucothoe

in the alpine house, where their quiet beauty may be more easily appreciated.

L. autumnale. Portugal, Morocco. A delicate looking, very slender-leaved plant with small dangling bells, by twos or threes from 3″–6″ stems. White, slightly flushed at base with pale pink. September.

p*****L. roseum.** Corsica. The most enchanting small bulb, flowering in autumn before the thread-like leaves. The tiny, ⅛″ bells, dangling singly from 2″–3″ fine stems are of a lovely pale pink, almost crystalline in texture. Can be grown from seed. Alpine house. September.

p**L. trichophyllum.** S. Spain, S. Portugal, Morocco. ½″ white flowers, tinged pink, up to 4 to a stem. Usually 3 leaves, very narrow, 6″–8″, produced with the flowers. Very early spring. Needs protection of alpine house. March–April.

*****L. vernum.** Central Europe. The Spring Snowflake has the largest flowers of the genus and is a beautiful and good-tempered plant which can be relied upon to flower freely in any open, fairly rich soil, from February onwards. The flowers are solitary and drooping, pure white with green-tipped segments, and rather suggestive of a very large and solid Snowdrop. Leaves linear, about 6″. Early spring.

LEUCOPOGON *Epacridaceae*

L. fraseri. New Zealand. This is a pleasant little creeping shrub, with dense erect shoots of 2″–3″, having many rigid pointed heath-like leaves, becoming bronze in the winter. Its ¼″–½″ five-lobed white flowers are followed by attractive translucent berries like little apricot beads. Hardy in most localities. Lime-free soil in half shade. June.

LEUCOTHOE *Ericaceae*

*****L. keiskei.** Japan. This is the only species dwarf enough for the average rock garden, and even so, when happy, it may spread considerably, although its height will rarely be above a foot. It is a lovely prostrate shrub, with slender zig-zag growths and thick pointed oval leaves of 2″–3″. The tubular white flowers, more than ½″ in length, are borne in terminal drooping clusters in July, and are the largest in the genus, but the most striking feature is the colour of the foliage, the young shoots in spring being a vivid red, and the whole plant taking deep crimson tones in autumn. Woodland soil in semi-shade and no lime. 9″–10″. July.

165

Lewisia

LEWISIA *Portulacaceae*

The genus is confined to N. America, and includes many showy plants
with flowers varying from white to deep rose, apricot, and orange.
They may be evergreen (marked E below), or may die down completely underground after flowering. They show a great tendency to
hybridize, and as a consequence some of the species are difficult to
obtain true—even collected seed has shown this trait. By selection
from seedlings, and intentional hybridization, a wonderful colour
range, sometimes of indeterminate parentage, has evolved, in shades
deepening to mulberry red and flaming scarlet. Some of these are in
commerce under varietal names. All form rosettes of rather succulent
leaves, varying from linear to long pointed ovate or even spatulate
and all like plenty of sun in a well drained rich soil, preferably lime-
free. They are usually wintered under glass, as the necks of their
thick carroty roots are susceptible to winter wet. Propagation is easy
by seed which, except for the hybrids, is usually freely produced.
Flowers in early summer with occasional odd blossoms in autumn.
(Pl. 18)

P***L. brachycalyx.** N.W. America. Rosettes of narrowly spatulate leaves
and solitary satiny-textured flowers, 1½″ wide, on 1″ stems. Usually white,
occasionally pink flushed. Dies down completely after flowering. April–
May.

PE**L. columbiana.** Columbia, Cascade Mts. Many narrowly spatulate
leaves forming a rosette about 3″ across, and heads of rather small magenta or
white flowers with red veins. Early summer.

E**L. cotyledon.** California. A dense 4″–5″ rosette of flat, fleshy, slightly
spatulate leaves, and 6″–7″ sprays of rather small flowers which may be white,
or pink with a deep central streak or even a dull reddish mauve. Early
summer.

  E**L. c.** var. **heckneri.** California. Seldom obtained true as it hybridizes
  so readily. The flat, fleshy, slightly spatulate leaves should be edged with
  an irregular close fringe of deep rose. Flowers pink to deep rose.

  L. nevadensis. Nevada. A miniature edition of *L. brachycalyx* with narrow,
  almost needle-shaped leaves and solitary, small white flowers, very rarely
  pink flushed. Dies completely down after flowering.

PE***L.** בֿ'PHYLLELLIA'. A delightful hybrid between *L. brachycalyx* and
L. cotyledon, almost perpetual flowering, with narrow succulent leaves and
flowers in shades of rose, deep rose, and crushed-strawberry, borne singly
on 1″ pedicles. 2″.

P**L. pygmea.** Rocky Mts. A charming little plant, too seldom grown, with

166

Lilium

a dense rosette of narrow 1½" leaves, often tinged with red, and solitary ¾" flowers of silvery pink on slender red stems. Rather later flowering than the

P*L. rediviva. Bitter root. United States. The gem of the deciduous Lewisias. After the rosette of reddish-green, very narrow succulent leaves dies back, the huge, solitary, wide-open flowers, 2" or more across, open on 1" stems like little white or clear rose-pink water-lilies.

PE*L. tweedyi. Washington and British Columbia. This, on the other hand, is the outstanding beauty of the evergreen Lewisias. It makes a loose rosette, less flat than most other species, of broadly lanceolate leaves, often tinged with red (richly so in the deeper coloured flower forms), and the large flowers, about 1½" across, are borne usually 2–3 on each 6" stem. They are of a lovely satiny texture, and can be had in forms from very pale pink, through creamy apricot, to a wonderful deep salmon rose, all deeper in colour when in bud. (Pl. 19)

LILIUM *Liliaceae*

This large genus has very few species which are really dwarf enough for the rock garden, but there are a few which, although a foot or a little more in height, are so beautiful and so graceful in habit that they add distinction in a way which no other plant can do, if an appropriate place can be found for them. The following are among the dwarfest, and, with one exception, are all of very slender, elegant growth. They all need well-drained, leafy soil, and protection from strong winds and drought. Those starting growth early in the year appreciate the shelter of low growing ground coverers. Propagation by division, by seed, or by scales, i.e. planting a few scales detached from the bulb, in the same manner as cuttings, when they will develop a new small plant at the base. Of course in this way there is the certainty of obtaining a plant exactly similar to the parent. A very detailed account, including an exhaustive selection of lilies, some others of which could be included in a really large rock garden, will be found in *Collins Guide to Bulbs*.

L. bulbiferum (*croceum*). Middle and S. Europe. A handsome lily, slightly variable in colour from the fiery tangerine-orange usually found in the wild, where it is usually from 1–2 ft. although it is apt to be taller in gardens. Many varieties form bulbils in the axils of the leaves, from which new plants may be grown. Under the name *L. croceum* is usually offered the variety without bulbils.

Limonium

L. croceum. See **L. bulbiferum.**

L. kikak. See under **L. × maculatum.**

*L. mackliniae. Manipur. A recently introduced lily which has affinities with Fritillaria and Nomocharis, and is a distinctive and quite delightful plant with drooping almost cup-shaped flowers, rose-purple in the bud, but fading to soft pale rose, with deeper shading, when the flowers are mature. This asks for half-shade, in rich, well-drained soil, and when happy may grow from 1–2 ft., but is always one of the loveliest of lilies. Summer.

L. × maculatum. Japan. These large erect-flowered lilies are probably hybrids of *L. dauricum* and *L. concolor,* and many varieties are in general cultivation, including some really dwarf forms of under 1 ft. Although for size one might think these the most suitable for the rock garden, the large upright flowers seem out of proportion to the plant, and give it a stocky look, without the elegance of the majority of the genus. However, they are showy plants, and the form usually offered is:

> **L. × m.** 'ALUTACEUM' ('KIKAK', under which name it is most often found). This is only 9″ or even less, with large golden apricot flowers with dark purple spots. Easy in any well-drained soil in full sun. Summer.
> There are several other varieties varying only in colour of flower, in shades of orange, mahogany, and crimson, which can be found under varietal names in catalogues of lily specialists.

*L. pomponium. N. Italy, S. France (Maritime Alps). This elegant little lily, with slender stems, usually between 1–2 ft., and many narrow, dark green leaves, has rather small flowers of such a vivid, glossy scarlet red that they stand out like little flames. It needs a sheltered, sunny spot and does not object to lime. Summer.

*L. pumilum (*tenuifolium,* under which name it is usually found). E. China, Siberia. An attractive small lily of a foot or a little more, with linear leaves and small, pendent bright scarlet flowers. Leafy soil and some sun. It is not an easy plant to establish and seed, if set, should be cherished and sown. Summer.

*L. rubellum. Japan. One of the most lovely of all lilies, usually between 1–2 ft., of slender habit, with few, spreading trumpet-shaped flowers of a luminous clear pink, almost crystalline in texture. Woodland soil and cool shade. Best without lime. Summer.

L. tenuifolium. See **L. pumilum.**

LIMONIUM (Statice) *Plumbaginaceae*

The many-hued statice with their small chaffy "everlasting" flowers provide at least a couple of species which form neat little clumps of congested linear-spatulate leaves with recurved margins, and sprays

168

Linaria

of long-flowering clusters of small membranaceous flowers on wiry stems above the crowded tuft of dull green foliage.

L. cosyrense. S. Europe. A huddled tuft of small leaves ½″–1″ long, with many crowded wiry stems bearing upright clusters of small mauve chaffy flowers. Any soil, in full sun. 4″. July onwards.

L. gougetianum. Italy. More bushy than the foregoing, with larger leaves (1″–2″) and lavender flower-spikes of 6″–10″. July–August.

LINARIA *Scrophulariaceae*

The well-known Toadflax genus has several delightful dwarf and creeping members. They are mainly fragile little plants with squat, lipped flowers, and are not long lived, but are easily kept going by the prolific seed. Not fussy as to soil, but they like a well-drained sunny position. When more than one species are grown they are very prone to hybridize.

L. aequitriloba. Corsica, Sardinia. A minute creeper of under 1″, with small rounded, three-lobed leaves, and tiny deep purple snapdragons in summer. Very good for crazy pavement.

*L. alpina. European Alps. This charming little species, met with widely in the screes in the High Alps, especially in calcareous districts, has frail flopping stems with many linear or narrowly spatulate leaves, almost succulent, and of a lovely blue-grey, as is the whole plant. It tends to form compact small mats, covered in summer and early autumn with fat little snapdragons of luminous mauve with two orange stripes on the lip. There is also a form lacking the orange markings, *L. a.* var. *faucicola*, which is often rather larger than the type. Short-lived, as it almost flowers or seeds itself to death, but will keep going by self-sown seedlings. Easy in any sunny scree. Summer, long flowering. (Pl. 19)

L. cymbalaria. S. Europe, and naturalized in Gt. Britain. The Ivy-leaved Toadflax is too well known to need description, and, although charming in itself, too invasive to introduce to the rock garden (although attractive colour forms, from white to pink, have a habit of cropping up), but there is a congested variety, *L. c.* var. *globosa* (often listed as *L. globosa*, or *L. globosa rosea*, the pink form) which makes a neat little green tuft of about 2″, in flower the summer through.

L. origanifolia. S.W. Europe. A 6″ bushlet with narrow-oval leaves and sprays of small violet flowers. Summer.

L. hepaticifolia (*Cymbalaria hepaticifolia*). Corsica. Another creeper, with slightly lobed, kidney shaped leaves, white-veined, and lilac-purple flowers. Summer.

L. supina. S.W. Europe. A more upright plant, up to 8″, with variable flowers of yellow shades to mahogany. Flowers all summer.

169

Linnaea, Linum

LINNAEA *Caprifoliaceae Monotypic*

The genus, which is found throughout the colder regions of the
northern hemisphere, is named in honour of the celebrated Swedish
botanist Carl Linné (Linnaeus).

L. borealis, the European type, is a delightful ground coverer, flinging
its many wiry stems of a foot or more, rather sparsely set with pairs of small
circular or fatly oval leaves, in every direction, making, where happy,
a wide mat of 2″–3″ in height. Here and there, from the axils of the leaves,
rise erect 2″–3″ stems, each bearing two pendent elegant slender bells of flesh
pink, shading from rose at the base and beautifully freaked with deep rose
within the bell. (Pl. 19)

L. b. var. **americana** from N. America is very similar, but slightly larger
in all its parts, and considered rather easier to grow. Both require a very
leafy woodland soil, in part shade, and are happy creeping among very
dwarf ericaceous shrubs. *L. canadensis* is the same as *L. b.* var. *americana*.
May–July or later.

LINUM *Linaceae*

The Flax family is one of the very few genera which produces species
with flowers in all three primary colours, clear blues and yellows and,
in the case of the showy annual, *L. grandiflorum*, bright crimson, as well
as white. They are all free-flowering, and not particular as to soil,
although they do best in a well-drained loam with added peat or leaf-
mould. They are reasonably hardy, but may succumb to an exceptionally severe winter in some cold districts. However, they are easily
raised from spring-sown seed, or propagated by firm wood cuttings
taken in summer. Summer flowering.

L. alpinum. European Alps. A fragile little plant of about 6″, with wiry
sprays bearing small, grey-green linear leaves and terminating in a few wide
five-petalled flowers of delicate pale sky-blue.

*L. arboreum. Crete, etc. A shrub of a foot in height more or less, according to position, with blunt leaves and many bunches of few large, golden
yellow flowers. 8″–10″. Summer.

ₚ**L. flavum.** Germany to Russia. A rather tender shrublet of a foot or so,
with dense, many flowered heads of clear yellow.

*L. × 'GEMMELL'S HYBRID' is one of the best dwarf linums and is a
spontaneous hybrid between **L. elegans** and **L. campanulatum.** It is more
compact than **L. arboreum** and has flowers of a deeper yellow. 6″–9″.
Summer.

Lippia, Liriope

p**L. monogynum.** New Zealand. A handsome plant with a forest of slender branching sprays, set with narrowly lanceolate leaves and bearing clouds of glistening 1″ wide white flowers. Graceful and attractive, but only suitable for the large rock garden as it attains 12″ or more. Slightly tender, needing a sunny, sheltered position. Summer.

***L. narbonense.** S. Europe. A most lovely plant with the habit of the foregoing, but with a long succession of 1″ wide luminous blue flowers. Also rather tall, 12″–15″.

L. perenne. Europe (including Gt. Britain). Mentioned because it is one of our own natives, but often as tall as the foregoing, and not as effective, being a frailer plant with fugacious flowers of a paler blue. Summer.

L. salsoloides. S.W. Europe. From a woody base radiate many slender semi-procumbent 6″ stems, bearing terminal sprays of large, pearly-white flowers. Usually grown in the prostrate variety,

> ***L. s.** var. **nanum** (*alpinum*), where the mat of wiry shoots, close-set with short, needle-shaped leaves, give it an almost heath-like appearance, and the many, rather smaller flowers are faintly flushed with opalescence. Summer. (Pl. 19)

There are many other Linums spasmodically in cultivation, but they are not often obtainable, and most are on the borderline of hardiness.

LIPPIA   *Verbenaceae*

The genus to which the Lemon-scented Verbena (*L. citriodorus*) belongs contains two attractive prostrate or slightly spraying low-growing plants which root from the nodes of their shoots, offering a ready means of propagation.

L. canescens (*repens* of gardens). S. America. Prostrate, spreading with small oblong or lanceolate leaves and heads of little lilac flowers with a yellow throat. 1″–2″. Summer.

L. nodiflora. S. United States. A rather larger plant, with spreading, wiry branches bearing toothed inch-long leaves and Verbena-like flowers of white to purple. 3″–4″. May–September.

LIRIOPE   *Liliaceae Monotypic*

L. graminifolia. China, Japan. A charming and unusual little plant, with linear-lanceolate radical leaves and clusters of small purple-blue funnel-shaped flowers on 6″–10″ stems. *L. g.* 'MINOR', 3″–6″, has fewer flowers to the cluster. Sandy soil and winter protection. Early summer.

LISTERA   *Orchidaceae*

The tiny **Listera cordata** with a pair of nearly opposite elongated heart-shaped leaves on the erect stem bearing short 2″ spikes of whitish green or reddish orchid flowers is, when found, plentiful in deep moss in woods in Europe and N. America, but is difficult to accommodate with suitable conditions in the rock garden or alpine house. 2″–3″. Summer. This charming little orchid is very like a miniature Twayblade (*L. ovata*), which is at least four times its size, with a single pair of oval, pointed leaves.

LITHOSPERMUM   *Boraginaceae*

This genus is usually represented in the rock garden by *Lithospermum diffusum* and its varieties, than which there is no more beautiful sub-shrub when seen in good health, forming a wide mat of rather rough, dark green foliage, covered with ½″ five-petalled flowers of intense gentian blue. It is, however, a lime hater, and will only be found in healthy growth, or, in fact, surviving at all for long, in sandy, lime-free soil, with peat or leaf-mould, in full sun. For the rock garden, these species are so similar that one is sufficient to represent the genus.

*L. diffusum. S. Europe. Spreading prostrate stems and many hairy oblong leaves about ½″ long. Deep blue.

> **L. d.** var. **album** is the white form; not an improvement as the wonderful intensity of colour is the chief attraction of the type.

> **L. d.** 'Grace Ward' is rather larger in flower, and possibly less exacting.

> **L. d.** 'Heavenly Blue' (often found in catalogues as *Lithospermum* 'Heavenly Blue') is the selected colour form usually grown. All flower in early summer and over a long period. 3″–4″.

> **L. graminifolium** (*Moltkia graminifolia, M. suffruticosa*). N. Italy. Tufts of long, narrow, grass-like leaves, and 6″–9″ sprays of drooping tubular bells of azure blue. Summer. (Pl. 20)

> **L. × intermedium.** See **Moltkia × intermedia.**

*L. oleifolium. Pyrenees. A pleasant twiggy shrub of 6″ or so, for the rock garden or alpine house. Its ½″ elliptic leaves are rather thick and covered with silky hairs, especially below, and the bunches of good-sized sky-blue flowers are borne in few flowered terminal clusters and are, like most of the genus, pink in the bud. There appear to be two forms, one distinctly larger in flower and of a better colour. Likes lime. Early summer. (Pl. 18)

L. purpureo-coeruleum. The Walking-Stick Plant. Europe (including Gt. Britain). This, for a short time in early summer, puts up 6″–7″ sparsely leafy stems which bear terminal twin racemes of most striking velvety, deep, intense blue flowers (red in the bud), ½″ across. But at other times the growth is rather coarse, as the short strap-shaped leaves are dark green and rough in texture, and the plant is apt to be invasive, as its habit is to make long arching sprays, up to a foot or more, which eventually bend over and root at the tips. It is, however, well worthwhile for the deep vividness of its flowers, so long as this propensity is allowed for.

LLOYDIA *Liliaceae*

Throughout the high alpine pastures of the northern hemisphere, including Gt. Britain, where it is a rarity, can be found drifts of the delightful little **Lloydia serotina,** with few narrow grass-like leaves and one (rarely two) upright small, tulip-shaped flowers of white, yellowish at the base and faintly red veined, on thread-like leafy 2″–3″ stems. Although a rare plant, it is plentiful locally, but is of little practical use in the garden as it is difficult to grow. A well-drained leafy soil, never parched, would seem to give the best chance.

LOBELIA *Campanulaceae*

The Lobelias in all their variety, from spectacular giants in the border to the ubiquitous and gay little bedding annuals, do contain one useful species for the rock garden, which flowers late and is valuable for that reason alone, although it is also a pleasant little plant although rather congested in habit.

L. syphilitica 'NANA'. E. United States. A sturdy dwarf plant of 6″–8″ with large pale blue lipped flowers, solitary in the leaf axils. Easy in any soil and autumn flowering.

LOISELEURIA *Ericaceae Monotypic*

D*L. procumbens** (*Azalea procumbens*). The delightful little creeping azalea, which is found in the alpine regions of N. America, Europe and Asia, where-ever there is lime-free soil. It makes a prostrate mat of many long slender woody stems, well set with sturdy little dark green oblong leaves, up to ¼″, and terminal clusters of two to five starry, campanulate flowers, which, although small, make the plant conspicuous in bloom by their colour, a warm vivid pink-to-red, and their number. It is not difficult to establish, in sunny but not parched positions, in a well-drained leafy soil and no lime, but not free-flowering in cultivation. July–August.

Lotus, Luetkea, Lupinus

LOTUS *Leguminosae*

L. corniculatus. Bird's-foot Trefoil. Northern hemisphere (including Gt. Britain). This pretty weed is too invasive to introduce, but the double-flowered variety, *L. c. fl. pl.*, is a gay little plant, long flowering and not invasive. Summer and autumn.

LUETKEA *Rosaceae Monotypic*

L. pectinata seems barely in cultivation in Gt. Britain, although it is reputed to be an easy plant, especially in rocky crevices. It is a N. American shrublet, from the timber-line parks and glacial screes, and makes a dense mat, up to 3″ in height, with three-cleft leaves, imitating one of the mossy saxifrages. The 6″–10″ spikes of Spirea-like flowers are white to pale yellow. Cool, leafy soil. Summer.

LUPINUS *Leguminosae*

An American writer says: "Of course the Lupins are always with us, from the Arctic to the Panama, but in ceaselessly changing varieties." Many are too tall for the rock garden, but there are several dwarf varieties already known which would be treasures to welcome to our gardens, and it is tantalizing to read from time to time of entrancing small species, often silver-foliaged, which have only found their way into cultivation spasmodically, if at all.

pL. **alopecuroides.** Near the snowline, Colombia and Ecuador. One of the most exciting to hope for, forming a sturdy little spike of small, bluish flowers, almost hidden in the thick white wool which envelops the whole plant. Its coat of cotton-wool would require alpine house protection. 6″–10″. Summer.

L. lepidus. W.N. America. A silky-hairy lupin of 6″ or so, with bright purple-blue flowers. August–September.

p*L. **lyallii.** W.N. America. A lovely little lupin of 3″ or so, with mats of silvery palmate leaves and clustered heads of blue flowers, brilliant in the wild, but often paler in cultivation. Well-drained light, gritty soil. When obtained should be kept going by seed, as, like most lupins, it is not long lived. Late summer.

p*L. **ornatus.** W.N. America. This is the species most usually seen, and is a beautiful plant, with silvery silky leaves and stems and short spikes of pale mauve-blue flowers. If it lives so long it may become rather large for the rock garden, up to 2 ft. or so, but it makes a lovely foliage plant for the alpine house, where growth is slower and can be kept in bounds. Summer.

LYCHNIS *Caryophyllaceae*

The two or three Lychnis which are sufficiently dwarf for the rock garden are mostly of such brilliant colouring that they need very careful placing in order not to overpower their more sober companions. They are summer-flowering plants, and do well in any open, sunny position.

*L. alpina (*Viscaria alpina*). Europe, Siberia, Labrador. Forms a tuffet of small, dark green linear leaves, from which rise the sturdy stems with a few pairs of opposite leaves, bearing close heads of many small five-petalled flowers of deep rose. The colour is variable and there is a white form. 2″–4″. Early summer.

L. ×haageana (*fulgens* ×*coronata*). A striking plant of up to a foot, with many scarlet five-petalled flowers, with lobed and slashed petals. Summer.

L. lagascae. See **Petrocoptis lagascae.**

LYSIMACHIA *Primulaceae*

L. nummularia. Our own pretty little native Creeping Jenny is one of the most charming ground coverers for a cool, rather damp spot, where it may be allowed to take possession. Its long, trailing, rooting stems have many rounded, fresh green, opposite leaves, and from their axils, $\frac{3}{4}$″–1″ golden cups held upright on fine stems of 1″ or less. *L. minutissima* is similar, but even smaller. Long flowering in summer.

MACROTOMIA. See ARNEBIA

MAHONIA *Berberidaceae*

M. repens. The only member of this genus suitable for the rock garden. N. America. This and its dwarf variety *nana*, are pleasant little ground coverers, with typical tough Mahonia leaves, dull, dark green, with two to four holly-like leaflets, often taking colour in autumn. The little bunches of globular, yellow flowers are followed by purple-black fruits. Summer.

MAIANTHEMUM *Liliaceae*

M. bifolium (*convallaria*). N. temperate regions (including Gt. Britain). A pleasant little plant for a cool shady position. An erect 6″–8″ stem, with two glossy heart-shaped leaves, bears a fluffy spike of tiny white flowers. Early summer.

MALVASTRUM *Malvaceae*

M. coccineum. United States. Provides an unusual colour note as its Mallow-like flowers are bright scarlet. The foliage is grey-green, and habit semi-prostrate or up to a foot. It is not, however, reliably hardy, and needs a hot, dry position. It is wiser to ensure its survival by cuttings, protected over winter. July–October.

MARGYRICARPUS *Rosaceae*

This small genus from the Andes includes **M. setosus,** a semi-prostrate shrublet of 6″–8″, with branched woody stems bearing many pinnate leaves, terminating in a short spine. The flowers are tiny, green, and inconspicuous, but they are followed by many white, pearl-like fruits, which are very attractive and long persistent.

MATTHIOLA *Cruciferae*

The stocks, so valuable in our borders, are mainly derived from the species *M. incana*, from the E. Mediterranean, which is itself too tall for the rock garden (up to 2 ft.). *M. tristis*, 8″–10″, is well worth growing for its scent. The foliage is grey-green, and the flowers a dull brownish colour. *M. pedemontana* and *M. vallesiaca* are very similar, with flowers of dull, indeterminate mauve. All are best kept going by seed, as the plants are not long-lived, and of suspect hardiness.

Geranium dalmaticum
Glaucidium palmatum
Haberlea rhodopensis

Geranium subcaulescens
Globularia bellidifolia
Hacquetia epipactis

16

Helianthemum alpestre
Helichrysum frigidum
Helichrysum orientale

Helianthemum, garden variety
Helichrysum lanatum
(Left, *Thymus serpyllum var. coccineus*)
Heloniopsis breviscapa

MAZUS *Scrophulariaceae*

This genus of small creeping herbs, with Mimulus-like flowers full large for the size of the plant, might well be seen more often. They are easy going in any sunny, well-drained position, and if they grow more straggling with the years they can easily be replaced by seed or cuttings.

M. pumilio. Australia, New Zealand. Tufts of 1″–3″ long spatulate leaves, and mauve and white, yellow-flecked flowers on 2″ stems in July and August.

M. radicans (*Mimulus radicans*). New Zealand. Another charming creeper, with ½″ musk flowers of white and gold.

*****M. reptans.** Himalaya. Perhaps the most delightful. Prostrate, with narrowly spatulate toothed leaves, and covered from June onwards with fat little snapdragons of blue-purple with gold-flecked lip. If grown in a pan this can vie in beauty with many of the rarer occupants of the alpine house.

MECONOPSIS *Papaveraceae*

This genus has become so associated in mind with the spectacular Blue Poppy, *M. betonicifolia* (formerly *M. baileyi*), that it is often overlooked that the species include, which is rare in one genus, clear yellow, white, and shades of red, as well as blue. Most of these are unfortunately too tall for the average rock garden, although where the taller species (not described here) can be accommodated, they add beauty and dignity in a way that very few other plants can do.

All require a cool leafy position, and although lime is not fatal to them, the blues are much more intense on an acid soil. Summer flowering.

D*****M. bella.** Nepal, Bhutan. This plant, if only it were more amenable, would be one of the finest gems of the alpine house or garden. From a tuft of pinnately-lobed basal leaves, almost fern-like, the solitary flowers rise on sturdy stems of 3″–5″, and are upright four-petalled bowls of clear blue, with a boss of pale golden stamens. It is difficult, and only spasmodically in cultivation, but it is mentioned in order that it may be kept in mind for when opportunity occurs to reintroduce this enchanting "Blue Papaver Alpina".

*****M. cambrica.** Welsh Poppy. W. Europe (including Gt. Britain). This is as easy as the foregoing is difficult. It is a lovely clear yellow (orange in var. *aurantiaca*) poppy, with tufted lobed foliage and solitary flower stalks up to a foot or more. Its only fault is its good temper, as, once introduced, it is likely to take possession and flaunt its undeniable beauty in swamping its neighbours.

*M. horridula. Nepal to W. China. In spite of its reputed 18″, there are dwarfer forms, well under a foot, of this entirely spiny plant with leafy spikes of flowers, variable from purple to purple-blue, according to soil. Woodland soil and no lime.

*M. quintuplinervia. Farrer's Harebell Poppy. Tibet, W. China. A lovely and unusual plant, forming a clump of 8″–10″ narrowly oval leaves tapering to a petiole, from which rise many 10″–12″ hairy stems, each bearing a solitary pendent poppy, a graceful half-open 1½″ bell of luminous mauve–blue, deepening to the base.

MELANDRIUM   *Caryophyllaceae*

This genus is so nearly akin to Silene that many of its members have had an uncertain career, alternating between the two genera. Even now the most spectacular species are as likely to be found in catalogues under the one generic name as the other. The following are now all allotted to the genus Silene, under which name they will be found: *M. elisabetha; M. hookeri; M. ingramii; M. virginica.*

MENTHA   *Labiatae*

The Mint family provides us with what must be the smallest of all alpine plants. This is:

M. requienii (*Menthella conica*). Corsica. A minute round-leaved carpeting plant, which quickly spreads in any soil and a not too dry position into a green film of no height at all, peppermint scented, and sprinkled in summer with very tiny lipped purple flowers. Excellent among paving-stones.

MENZIESIA   *Ericaceae*

The Menziesias are beautiful deciduous dwarf shrubs, nearly akin to the Daboecias, which have really only one member sufficiently small for the rock garden.

*M. ciliicalyx. Japan. A much branched woody shrublet with many oval, slightly hairy leaves, and, in May and June, nodding flowers in clusters at the end of the last year's shoots. The flowers are urn-shaped, ½″ or more in length, and variable in colour between soft pink and red, but of a most attractive waxy texture. In its earlier years a lovely pan for the alpine house.

M. multiflora (*M. ciliicalyx* var. *multiflora*). Japan. Only differing from the last in very small botanical details, but with a wider range of colouring from pinkish cream to purplish-pink.

MERENDERA   *Liliaceae*

These bulbs are closely related to Bulbocodium and Colchicum, but may be distinguished from the former by the fact that the three styles are free to the base, and from the latter by the long *pointed* segments of the perianth. They are also much dwarfer and the foliage, which also follows the flowers, is not so large or conspicuous.

M. bulbocodium (*Colchicum montanum*). See **M. montana.**

M. montana (usually offered under the above synonyms). Pyrenees, Spain, Portugal. The buds, like spear-heads, push up during the rainy season in autumn, opening widely into large narrow-petalled stars of varying shades of purplish-pink. The three linear leaves of 3″–4″ appear after the flower. This is the species usually grown, but others are described in *Collins Guide to Bulbs*.

MERTENSIA   *Boraginaceae*

Most of this genus, which belongs to the Forget-me-not family and is distinguished, like the rest of its members, by the crozier-like inflorescence, are very welcome in the rock garden, which is a good thing, as the nomenclature appears involved and under the same name from different sources one is apt to receive a variety of plants. With one exception, those described are 4″–6″ in height. They are hardy, although the choicer ones are not long-lived, and most die down completely in winter. Seed sown as soon as ripe, or division in autumn.

*M. coriacea. Rocky Mts. Dense heads of blue tubular flowers. 4″–8″.

*M. coventryana. Kashmir. There is confusion between this and the kindred, or it may be synonymic, species *M. echioides, elongata,* and *moltkioides*. All are tufted plants, with oblong to spatulate slightly downy leaves, and bright to deep true blue pendent flowers.

*M. longiflora (*oblongiflora, pulchella*). A small beauty from W.N. America, with two or three lovely blue-green rather fleshy leaves, and hanging clusters of light to deep blue flowers, pink in the bud.

ᴅ*M. maritima (*Pulmonaria maritima*). Northern sea shores (including Gt. Britain). The Oyster Plant is one of the most lovely of our native plants. It forms mats of ovate rather fleshy blue-grey leaves, and in July flings procumbent stems bearing large, flat flowers of opalescent shades of turquoise opening from buds of soft pink and mauve. It is difficult in cultivation, and in any case not long lived (keep going from seed and cuttings), but success has been achieved in ordinary rich loam, and a heap of spent ashes has also proved congenial to it. A well-flowered, healthy plant forms a beautiful picture. Summer.

M. primuloides. Himalaya. Quite a different plant, with roughish grey pointed oval leaves and 4″–6″ spires of deep velvety violet-blue flowers, developing from the usual pink and mauve-blue buds. Moraine treatment.

*M. virginica. N. America. The Virginian Cowslip should not be included, as it grows to a height of 1–2 ft., but it is so lovely, and so accommodating in dying down completely out of the way after flowering, that it could not be ignored. Like all the Mertensias it is variable (probably in most cases according to position and treatment), but at best its foliage on first appearance is of the most lovely amethyst-shaded green, and from its tall croziers dangle comfrey-like flowers of luminous sky-blue, set against the pink and mauve shades of the unopened buds. The whole plant has a stately and architectural beauty. Spring.

MIBORA *Gramineae*

M. minima (*verna*). A tiny annual grass with very fine 1″–2″ leaves. Useful in sinks, etc., where it can be used to good effect, and possibly helps by root association those small, very high alpines which are used to growing inextricably mixed with their equally diminutive neighbours.

MICROMERIA *Labiatae*

This genus of aromatic herbs or small shrubs is found in the temperate or warmer districts of the earth, and the species are happiest and most in character in very gritty soil in an open sunny position. They are neat growing, with a profusion of small lipped flowers in whorls or small spikes during late summer and early autumn. They are valuable, used sparingly, for their late flowering, fragrance, and compact, twiggy growth. Of the many rather similar possible species the following are representative and the most easily obtained.

M. corsica. Corsican maquis, Sardinia. An attractive little grey bushlet of 4″–6″, lavender-scented, and with small pink-lipped flowers. July–August. Actually an invalid name, but it is known and grown as such.

M. microphylla. Mediterranean basin. A delightful little intricately branched shrublet of 3″–4″, with pale pink flowers in late summer.

M. piperella (*Thymus piperella*). S.W. Mediterranean. A charming tiny shrub of about 3″, aromatic, and with many thyme-like leaves and rose flowers. Autumn.

MIMULUS *Scrophulariaceae*

The Monkey Flowers or Musks provide a range of colour in gold, orange, and flame which is rather rare in the rock garden, and, in its more flamboyant shades, needs careful placing. They mostly have bright green, thin but rather lush oval slightly toothed leaves in opposite pairs, and are happiest in a cool, rather moist spot. They can be propagated by seed or (very easily) by cuttings in moist sandy soil. Summer flowering.

M. alpinus. A variety of *M. luteus*.

M. × burnetii (*cupreus × luteus*). A tufted plant of about 6″, with many copper-yellow spotted trumpets. Will stand a drier position than most.

***M. cupreus.** Chile. Rather taller than the foregoing, 8″–10″, with yellow flowers ageing to copper colour. From this species have originated many striking colour forms which appear under varietal names in catalogues. Perhaps the most brilliant is 'WHITECROFT SCARLET', 4″–6″, with rather small flowers of an intense and glowing scarlet. (Pl. 21)

M. luteus. Monkey Musk. Alaska to New Mexico. Naturalized in Gt. Britain, for example in Dovedale. Large 1½″ yellow flowers, more or less spotted with brown. Damp places, where it is variable in height, but its rather flopping habit usually keeps it to under 6″–8″.

M. moschatus. British Columbia to California. This is the old-fashioned Scented Musk, a spreading plant with small oval slightly furry leaves, and pale yellow lipped flowers about ⅔″ long. Although one of the least showy of the genus, at the beginning of this century this was much grown for the sake of its strong odour of musk, but since then the scent has unaccountably been lost, and, although reports sometimes appear in the gardening press of a surviving scented plant, they never seem to have been followed up and verified. 2″–3″.

M. primuloides. Washington, California. A pleasant little plant with rosettes of ovate hairy foliage. It spreads by runners, and bears small solitary yellow flowers, spotted with red-brown, on slender stems of 3″–4″. Moist cool spot. (Pl. 21)

Minuartia, Mitchella

M. radicans. See **Mazus radicans.**

*M. repens. New Zealand, Australia, Tasmania. A delightful little carpeter, with white and lilac, golden-throated flowers nearly sessile on the mats of almost succulent oval leaves. Moist sheltered position.

MINUARTIA *Caryophyllaceae*

The following are neat prostrate or cushion-forming plants of almost no height at all, with dense small foliage and many tiny five-petalled flowers of white or, occasionally, green. They are very near Arenaria, and often found in catalogues as such—or even Alsine, a name no longer valid. Most are really only suitable for sinks and troughs, where their compact growth and small proportions are most appropriate. Early summer.

M. laricifolia. France to Roumania. Rather taller than the following, with loose mats of many linear grey-green leaves and few flowered umbels of white flowers over ½" across on 4"–6" stems.

M. imbricata. Caucasus. Tiny cushions of sharp pointed foliage, and 1" high stems bearing small white starry flowers.

M. saxifraga. S. Europe. A larger growing species with oval grey-green leaves, and large white blooms suggesting one of the high-alpine cerastiums. Very variable in size up to 6".

M. sedoides (*Cherleria sedoides*). Europe (including Scotland). Makes a mere scum of tiny green foliage, bearing in season many almost sessile tiny greenish flowers, sometimes apetalous. Only suitable for a sink or trough, where its size and neatness can give character.

M. verna (*Arenaria caespitosa, A. verna*). Europe (including Gt. Britain), Siberia. This variable little plant makes dense mats of small stiff, needle-like leaves, and in early summer is covered with the many pure white five-petalled flowers on wiry stems from 1"–3". In the best forms the petals are broadly oval, and it is a most attractive small plant. A completely double form has been found.

MITCHELLA *Rubiaceae*

There are only two members of this genus. They are both delightful trailers, with many branching stems, rooting at the nodes, and pairs of small, glossy, oval to heart-shaped leaves.

M. repens. N. America. In the Partridge Berry, the flowers, borne in pairs, are small and tubular, with four pointed petals, not unlike a Daphne, white and very fragrant. The fruits are conspicuous red berries.

M. undulata. Japan. This is of similar habit, but with bracts cupping the longer-tubed white flowers, which have fringed petals.

Both of these require shady woodland conditions in cool peaty soil, or make delightful pans for the alpine house when they display their scarlet berries persistently until the fresh flowers open in June–July.

MITELLA *Saxifragaceae*

These are small woodland plants from N. America, very like the Tiarellas. In fact, they are known locally as Mitrewort, and Tiarella as False Mitrewort. The species usually grown here is:

M. diphylla. Has Maple-shaped radical leaves, and slender 6″–8″ spires of very small white five-pointed stars, which, if examined closely, will be found to be delicately fringed. A pleasant little plant for the woodland which is its natural home. Other species of the genus are very similar, and all flower in late spring.

MOEHRINGIA *Caryophyllaceae*

These are minute moss-like plants, nearly related to Arenaria, and only suited for clefts and corners in troughs or sinks, where their tiny four-pointed white stars spangle the close green mat throughout the summer.

M. muscosa, from S. Europe, with creeping stems making a dense mat, is sometimes, but rarely, met in cultivation.

MOLTKIA *Boraginaceae*

A small genus of sub-shrubs with roughly hairy, dark green foliage, and the croziers of blue flowers so characteristic of the family. Will succeed in well-drained loam in open sunny positions, and are not averse to lime. They are nearly akin to Lithospermum, and are apt to be found under that name. Summer flowering.

M. × **froebelii** (*Lithospermum* × *froebelii*). A garden hybrid, shrubby, with narrow dark green hoary leaves and sprays of azure-blue flowers, on erect 6″ stems.

*****M.** × **intermedia** (*Lithospermum* × *intermedium*) (*M. petraea* × *M. suffruticosa*). A useful little shrublet of 8″–10″, with brilliant blue flowers in early summer. Easy and effective.

M. petraea (*Lithospermum petraeum*). Greece. A dense, woody shrublet, with pale green leaves, wider than in the other species, and profuse sprays of pinkish-blue flowers, deepening to blue-purple. 6″.

MONARDELLA *Labiatae*

This genus of miniature Bergamots contains one very desirable species, from S. California, which has, from time to time, been briefly in cultivation here:

*****M. macrantha.** A tufted perennial, spreading by a creeping rootstock. The leaves are oval, shortly stalked, and often tinted reddish-purple. The flowers, which are in close heads, form 1½″ scarlet tubes, emerging from purple or pinkish bracts. There seems no reason why this attractive plant should not be amenable and permanent in our gardens. 6″–8″. Summer.

A few less spectacular Monardellas from W.N. America, with light blue or whitish flowers, spasmodically in cultivation are *M. odoratissima* (blue) and *M. nana* (whitish or rose.)

MONESES *Pyrolaceae Monotypic*

The sole member of this genus has lately been removed thereto from Pyrola, with which it has near affinity, and total agreement in its choice of mossy woodland and leafy soil as its habitat. It differs from Pyrola in being single flowered, and in having two-horned anthers.

D*****M. uniflora** (*Pyrola uniflora*). N. and Central Europe (including Gt. Britain), Japan, N. America. This most delightful little woodlander spreads among deep moss by thread-like roots from the creeping stems set with round, almost sessile leaves of pale, clear green. The solitary flowers are borne on 2″ stems, well above the foliage, and are quite distinctive, with five slightly crimped, rounded, white petals of a solid, waxy texture, ¾″ across and fragrant. Difficult to establish unless one is lucky enough to possess the mossy woodland it requires. Summer.

MORISIA *Cruciferae Monotypic*

M. monantha (*hypogaea*, under which name it is more usually found). Sardinia and Corsica. A pleasant little crucifer, making a densely tufted rosette of much lacerated, glossy, dark green leaves, from the axils of which arise over a long period in spring, on very short stalks, conspicuous golden yellow, four-petalled flowers, ½″across. A valuable plant for sinks and troughs, or pans in the alpine house, or out of doors in poor sandy soil, fairly dry in the winter. Best propagated by seed, or root cuttings in sandy soil. 1″–2″. Spring onwards.

MUSCARI *Liliaceae*

The Grape Hyacinths are among the most useful and most beautiful bulbs for the rock garden. There is a strong family likeness among the species, which all form a crowded spike of small, almost globular flowers at the head of a leafless stalk, from a tuft of few, rather fleshy, linear, radical leaves. Mostly the flowers are in shades of intense blue, but in one or two rarer species they are yellow, usually shading to purple. They are showy and long flowering, March to April, and easy in every soil and position—in fact, a few species are apt to spread with almost too much vigour, although it is hard to discourage such a picture as they present in spring.

M. armeniacum. Asia Minor. Bright azure blue, with narrow white edge to incurved bells. Many selected forms have been given varietal names, the most popular being var. 'HEAVENLY BLUE'. Beautiful, but apt to spread very freely. 8″–10″.

M. azureum. See Hyacinthus azureus.

*M. botryoides. S. Europe. The Grape Hyacinth, less vigorous and invasive than the foregoing, and therefore more suitable to admit among small and choice plants in the rock garden. Deep sky blue. 6″–8″.

*M. latifolium. Asia Minor. A species with broader, fleshy leaves, and many dusky globes of purplish-indigo blue, the upper, sterile flowers paler bluish-purple. Height up to a foot.

M. luteum is a var. of M. moschatum.

*M. macrocarpum (Pl. 32) and M. moschatum, Asia Minor, are two very similar species. In fact the former is often listed as *M. moschatum* var. *flavum*. They are two sturdy yellow-flowered species, very fragrant, and by no means unattractive even when the pale or deeper yellow (var. *flavum*) shades to a dull, purplish, olive green at the apex. On the verge of hardiness, but well worth the small protection of an alpine house.

M. m. 'LUTEUM'.   A similar plant, dull yellow changing to waxy sulphur.

*M. paradoxum.   Caucasus.   A distinctive plant with almost blue-black flowers, slightly scented, on a purple stem.   About 6″–8″.

*M. tubergenianum.   N.W. Persia.   The 'Oxford and Cambridge Grape Hyacinth' is a delightful plant, with flowers shading from light to dark blue, from turquoise buds.   About 8″.   Not invasive.

Several other species are described in *Collins Guide to Bulbs*, but are mostly so similar to one or other of those described that only the specialist need consider adding them.

MYOSOTIS *Boraginaceae*

One usually considers the Forget-me-not and blue as being synonymous, but the New Zealand species are white-flowered, or even, in one or two cases, yellow.   Summer flowering.

*M. alpestris.   European Mts. (including Gt. Britain).   A variable little plant in height, inherently and/or by reason of its environment, but typically it is a tufted Forget-me-not of from 2″–3″, a charming plant, covered through the early summer with relatively large azure blue flowers with a yellowish eye. It is usually a not-very-long-lived perennial, but is easy from seed, which it is pleasantly apt to self-sow.   Ideal for trough gardens.

M. australis.   New Zealand.   A roughly hairy Forget-me-not, of very variable height from 6″ upwards, with yellow (occasionally white) flowers.

DP***M. azorica.**   Azores.   A striking little plant with large, deep blue flowers from reddish-purple buds.   Hardy in sheltered positions and well-drained gritty soil.   4″–6″.

*M. colensoi.   South Island, New Zealand.   One of the best of the N.Z. myosotis.   Prostrate leafy radiating stems with a single, comparatively large white flower in the axil of each leaf.   Long flowering, April–June.

M. explanata.   South Island, New Zealand.   A stout hairy little plant of up to 6″, with solid white flowers of ½″ or more across.

*M. rupicola.   European Alps.   Very similar to *M. alpestris*, from which it only seems to differ by being even more dwarfed and congested (up to 2″), and therefore suitable only for the moraine or trough.

M. saxosa.   New Zealand.   A small, white-flowered Forget-me-not, with rosettes of rough-surfaced lanceolate leaves.   2″–3″.

MYRTUS *Myrtaceae*

Among the hundred or so species of this aromatic genus, only one is a true dwarf, although in sheltered districts the small-leaved Myrtle, *M. communis* var. *tarentina*, may be kept in bounds as a lovely small shrub, in a strategic position.

Narcissus

p*M. nummularia. Straits of Magellan, Falkland Islands. A completely prostrate aromatic shrublet, making a tangled mat of wiry stems with many little rounded oval, dark green leaves and, in May, solitary flowers forming shallow white cups, ⅓″ across, filled with the very numerous white stamens. These are followed by conspicuous pink berries. Only hardy outdoors in sheltered positions in the south, but delightful for a pan in the alpine house. 1″–2″.

NARCISSUS *Amaryllidaceae*

The Daffodils number among them many entrancing pygmies, mainly from the Iberian peninsula, to enliven the rock garden and alpine house over a period of at least two months in spring. They are hardy, but are more intimately appreciated, and their beauty is protected from inclement weather, when grown in pans. Besides the numerous species, there is a wealth of delightful hybrids. For reasons of space, only the more distinct of the species are described here. For many other species and hybrids, see *Collins Guide to Bulbs*.

*N. asturiensis (*minimus*) Spain, Portugal. This variable species is an exact replica in miniature of the typical golden-trumpeted daffodil. In the most attractive forms, the stems are slender, and the flowers exactly in proportion, but in some the trumpets are rather larger and more sturdy. According to the variety and the position, height 2″–4″. Very early, late January–February.

*N. bulbocodium. France, Spain, Portugal, N. Africa. The Hoop-petticoat daffodil is distinguished by the large funnel-shaped corona, suggestive of a crinoline. The easiest and most often seen is:

N. b. var. conspicuus, deep yellow, about 4″, which naturalizes readily and is seen at its best from March onwards in the grassy slopes at the R.H.S. Gardens at Wisley, where it appears in myriads and includes many natural hybrids.

N. b. monophyllus is a very beautiful white form which is even earlier in flowering.

N. caniculatus. See N. tazetta.

*N. cyclamineus. The Cyclamen-flowered Daffodil. Portugal. In this very distinct plant the corona forms a long, narrow tube, and the narrow petals are sharply reflexed to lie back against the ovary. The height is from 4″ upwards (more in the shade), and the colour a bright self-yellow. Early flowering, from February.

*N. juncifolius. Spain, Portugal, S. France. The Jonquil group includes some of the daintiest of the genus. The wide, short petals stand at right

Nerine

angles (or very slightly reflexed) to the roundly cup-shaped corona. *N. juncifolius* itself is the most widely-grown, and bears two to four bright yellow 1″ flowers on slender 4″–6″ stems. Rather late flowering. March–April.

N. minor (*nanus*, *pumilus*). A sturdier, taller, and later flowering edition of *N. asturiensis*. 6″ or more.

N. pseudonarcissus. Plants from abroad under this name are seldom, if ever, true. The type plant is our own British wild daffodil, which may be seen occasionally, though abundant locally, in woodlands or open damp meadows from Devonshire to the north. It is not often grown in gardens, and is really only suitable for naturalizing. It is a very variable species, but approximates to a rather taller *N. minor*, less symmetrical in shape. 6″–9″.

*N. rupicola. Spain, Portugal. Very like *N. juncifolius*, but with solitary flowers, and in general rather more dwarf. 3″–4″.

N. tazetta. Spain, eastwards to Japan. The polyanthus section of Narcissus has one sturdy little dwarf in

    *N. t. var. **canaliculatus,** which bears four-to six-flowered heads of very fragrant flowers, with solid white petals and small lemon-yellow cups. Early flowering. 6″

*N. triandrus. Spain, Portugal. The Angel's Tears are a delightful group, but unfortunately not among the easiest to grow, and often impermanent. They are very distinct, having completely pendent flowers, with rather deep goblet-shaped cup and slightly reflexed petals. The type plant has pale lemon flowers. 6″–10″

    N. t. var. **albus,** the most properly called "Angel's Tears", is ivory-white, and very beautiful. It is also the easiest to grow of the species and varieties. April–May.

*N. watieri. Morocco. This enchanting species is, in effect, a pure white counterpart to *N. rupicola*. Excellent for a pan in the alpine house. 3″–4″

NERINE *Amaryllidaceae*

Only one of this valuable late-flowering South African genus is even doubtfully suitable for the rock garden, but

p***N. filifolia** is only about 12″ or less in height, and is very charming, with its tuft of very narrow leaves and umbel of 8–10 lily-like flowers with narrow freaked petals of a variable rose pink. On the borderland of hardiness, but excellent in the alpine house, where it can be kept dry after flowering. October.

Nertera, Nierembergia, Nigritella

NERTERA *Rubiaceae*

N. granadensis (usually found in catalogues as *N. depressa*), the Bead Plant, comes from S. America, New Zealand, and Australia, and forms a dense mat of no height at all, with very many fleshy, tiny round leaves and inconspicuous flowers. These are followed by conspicuous bright orange globose fruits in great profusion. A most distinct and attractive sight when in fruit. Not quite hardy, so best in alpine house.

NIEREMBERGIA *Solanaceae*

Two of this genus of the Potato family are welcome in the rock garden:

*****N. caerulea** (*hippomanica* of gardens). Argentine. This makes a close, bushy little plant of about 6″, covered with five-petalled, shallow bell-shaped deep mauve flowers. It has a long flowering season—June–September—and would be even more valuable if it were quite, completely hardy. (Pl. 20)

*****N. repens** (*rivularis*, under which name it was grown for many years). Argentine, Chile, Uruguay. This is a completely different plant, creeping and rooting to form a mat, with many upright, dark green, narrow leaves of 1″–2″, and a profusion of wide open, shallow cup-shaped flowers of pearly-white. Quite hardy, and easy in any position which is not parched. Not so often seen as it should be. Divide in spring as growth is beginning. 2″. July.

NIGRITELLA *Orchidaceae Monotypic,*

ᴅ*****N. nigra** (*angustifolia*). The Vanilla Orchid. Central and N. Europe. The close sward of the higher Alps is apt to be sprinkled with hundreds of this charming little vanilla-scented orchid, often mixed with Gymnadenia, with which it may hybridize. It forms a low sparse tuft of stiff, grass-like leaves, from which rises a 3″–6″ stem bearing a short crowded spike of small, dark red, almost black flowers.

N. n. var. **rubra** has flowers of rose or deep pink, shading to red, and the inflorescence is usually rather more lax. Early summer.

These are not easy in the garden, but planted in a raised scree bed among similar small fry may well survive, and even flower, although not every year.

189

NOMOCHARIS *Liliaceae*

This enchanting genus of bulbous plants from Himalaya, W. China, and Tibet, is so nearly allied to Fritillaria and Lilium, that newly-introduced species have at first often been placed among one or the other of these genera. They have, however, in general more delicate and attractive colourings than the former, and a more wiry fragile elegance than the latter. Their more or less open flowers are often freaked with deeper colour, and fringed. They are not easy plants in the south, but flourish in Scotland in cool, moist, well-drained leafy soil in part shade. Most are rather tall for the rock garden, but some dwarfs are available and those with conditions to suit these lovely plants should consult *Collins Guide to Bulbs* for further names and more detailed descriptions. Summer flowering.

D*N. aperta.** The easiest to grow, but may, when happy, be as much as 3 ft. Nodding pink flowers, spotted with maroon.

D**N. oxypetala.** Dwarf, 8″–10″. Solitary yellow flowers, purple stained.

N. o. PINK FORM. Has dusky pink flowers.

D**N. mairei.** Has 2–3 white flowers, spotted or flushed with rose purple. 1½–2½ft.

D**N. pardanthina.** The first discovered of the genus (1916), and a handsome plant, but again tall (up to 3 ft.), with several large flowers, pendulous and rather flat, pale rose spotted with crimson.

NOTOTHLASPI *Cruciferae*

One of the two species of this genus is a fascinating plant which has long been known but is seldom seen in cultivation.

DP*N. rosulatum.** The Penwiper Plant, from the Southern Alps of New Zealand. In the high shingles, it forms a very symmetrical flat rosette of many thick oval-pointed leaves with regularly pinked edges, white with hairs at first, then green. From the centre of the "Penwiper" rises a very stocky stem, so thickly set from the base with many rather large fragrant white flowers as to make a solid, round-topped cone or pyramid. Having a tap root it is almost impossible to transplant, so seeds seem the only hope for this odd, but attractive plant. Seeds from New Zealand are not usually easy of germination here, possibly due to the alternation of the seasons, but it is very well worth the effort if they can be obtained. 3″–6″. June–July.

NYMPHAEA *Nymphaeaceae*

Water-lilies are perhaps inappropriate in a list of alpine plants, but for a pool, even in a small rock garden, **N. pygmaea alba,** white, and **N.** × **helvola** (*mexicana* × *tetragona*), primrose yellow, both with goblet-shaped flowers about as big as a half-crown, are invaluable, and can be established in as little as 8″–9″ of water. Summer.

OENOTHERA *Onagraceae*

The Evening Primroses, with their rather lush, linear foliage, and large widely funnel-shaped flowers of white (sometimes fading to pink) or, more usually, of the clearest yellow, include a few species which are either actually dwarf or appear to be so by their flopping habit. They are valuable late-flowering showy plants, but their appearance prepares one for the fact that they are not usually long-lived. Propagation is easy by seed from most species; in others root cuttings may be taken. Summer-flowering.

O. acaulis (*taraxacifolia*). Chile. Large 2″–3″ flowers on short stems, white fading to pink, over the prostrate branches with 5″–6″ Dandelion-like leaves.

O. a. var. **aurea** (or *lutea*) is a form with yellow flowers.

O. caespitosa. W.N. America. An almost stemless species, with narrowly spatulate leaves and large white flowers, 2″–3″ across, fragrant, and flushing to pink with age. 3″–4″. (Pl. 20)

*O. c. var. **crinita** is an even more beautiful plant, with hoary leaves.

O. fruticosa. E.N. America. This and its variety, *O. f.* var. *angustifolia*, which has rather narrower lanceolate leaves, have deep yellow flowers. It is a variable species, and only in its dwarfer forms, 6″–12″, is it suitable for the rock garden.

O. linearis. See **O. fruticosa** var. **angustifolia.**

O. macrocarpa. See **O. missouriensis.**

O. mexicana rosea. See **O. speciosa** var. **childsii.**

O. missouriensis (*O. macrocarpa*). S. Central United States. A trailing species with huge yellow flowers, opening in the evening, over a long period in the summer.

O. perennis (*O. pumila, Kneiffia perennis*). E.N. America. A very distinct species, with small yellow flowers, less than 1″ across, in loose, leafy spikes above a mat of narrow lanceolate or narrow spatulate leaves. Almost the only member which does not tend to overshadow neighbours in the rock garden by its lushness and very large flowers. 6″.

O. pumila. See **O. perennis.**

*O. speciosa. The plant sometimes received from N. America as *O. mexicana* var. *rosea* appears to be the variety *childsii* of this species. It is an attractive little plant of 6″–8″ with flowers up to 1″ across, of clear rose.

O. taraxacifolia. See **O. acaulis.**

OMPHALODES *Boraginaceae*

The wild garden, the rock garden, and the choicest scree can find appropriate species of this lovely genus, with its characteristic blue Forget-me-not flowers.

O. cappadocica. Cappadocia. Mostly basal, long heart-shaped stalked leaves rise from the creeping rhizomes, and from June–August appear the loose, graceful sprays of delightful blue flowers. Half shade in leafy soil suits it best, but it is not temperamental. 4″–6″.

*O. luciliae. Greece, Asia Minor. This beautiful plant has narrowly oval leaves, and sprays of opalescent flowers, about $\frac{1}{2}$″ across, of a lovely soft blue, developing from pink buds. The whole plant, leaves and stems are of an indescribable almost blue-grey, which makes a perfect foil for the flowers. It is not too easy to keep in perfect health and beauty, but appears to prefer a sunny site in well-drained, moist, rich loam, with added mortar rubble. Summer, but odd flowers throughout the year. Lovely in the alpine house. 4″–6″. Summer. (Pl. 20)

*O. verna. Blue-eyed Mary. S. Europe. A lovely little woodlander for early spring flowering, where it will rapidly colonize by runners, and give plentifully of its wiry sprays of deep, clear blue flowers from March to May. 4″–5″

OMPHALOGRAMMA *Primulaceae*

This genus is a very near relation of the Primulas, and from the gardener's point of view is mainly distinguished from them by the irregular arrangement of the petals (the two upper ones more or less upstanding and the lower three outspread) of the solitary, conspicuous flower, which is held at right angles to the flower-stalk, or even slightly drooping. The species are not easy plants, especially in the southern counties, and have most chance of success in well-drained

17

Hepatica media ballardii
H. triloba, double pink form
Hypericum cuneatum

Hepatica triloba
Hylomecon japonicum
Hypericum olympicum

18

Incarvillea delavayi
Iris innominata
Leontopodium alpinum

Iris cristata, Lithospermum oleifolium
Iris winogradowii
Lewisia hybrid

leafy soil in semi-shade, or in pans in frame or alpine house, kept fairly dry when dormant in winter.

D*O. vinciflorum (*Primula vinciflora*). Yunnan. Of several rather similar species this is perhaps the most easily obtainable, and one of the most spectacular. From basal rosettes of wide, bluntly oval, hairy leaves rise 6″–8″ stems each bearing a lovely violet-purple flower, which in the best forms (it is a variable species) can be nearly 2″ across. Summer. (Pl. 21)

ONONIS *Leguminosae*

The fact that these charming alpine relations of our own native Rest Harrow are so seldom seen in cultivation may be because their customary tap roots make them almost impossible to transplant or divide. They come readily, however, from seed, when obtainable, or, in the shrubby species, from cuttings. Summer flowering.

D*O. cenisia. French Alps, S. Europe, N. Africa. This enchanting little species makes spreading mats of prostrate, almost woody stems, closely set with shortly stalked, trifoliate leaves, the whole plant being hidden in summer by the numerous solitary pea flowers of rich rose and pink, delicately veined. Deep, well-drained stony soil in full sun. 1″–2″.

O. natrix. Goat root. S. and Central Europe, E. Mediterranean, N.W. Africa. Although in certain situations liable to grow to over a foot in height, this attractive species can be kept to 8″ or so in poor, stony soil. It forms a much branched plant, shrubby at the base, with simple or trifoliate leaves and large single pea flowers of yellow, with conspicuously red-streaked standard, borne separately on short branchlets.

*O. rotundifolia. Central and S. Europe from Spain to Italy. A delightful sub-shrub, probably not long-lived, and, in any case, most beautiful during its first few years, making a rounded bushlet of a foot or less, with almost circular, shortly hairy, trifoliate leaflets, and, throughout the summer, comparatively large pea flowers of a clear rose, with red streaked standard, borne two or three together on axillary branches. Up to a foot or a little more.

ONOSMA *Boraginaceae*

The Onosmas are all stiff, hoary-leaved plants, with pendent tubular flowers, often scented. All do best in a hot, well-drained position, and can be grown from seed or cuttings.

Ophrys, Orchis

O. albo-pilosum. Asia Minor. Often offered as *O. alboroseum*. A downy leaved counterpart of *O. tauricum* below, with large, velvety bugles of nearly 1″ in length, opening white and gradually flushing to deep rose. Slightly tender and susceptible to winter wet. Safer in the alpine house. 6″–8″. Summer.

O. echioides. S. Europe. A coarsely hairy plant, with silvery, grey-green leaves, narrowly lanceolate or spatulate, and drooping croziers of pale yellow flowers. 6″–10″. June onwards.

*O. tauricum. Golden Drop. Very similar to the foregoing, and often offered in catalogues as a synonym of that species. Rather deeper yellow flowers on longer pedicels. A favourite and long flowering plant for a hot bank. 8″. Summer.

OPHRYS *Orchidaceae*

This genus of orchids includes several extraordinary mimics of the insect world. They are not easy to obtain, and almost impossible to grow, and are merely mentioned on account of their interest to alpine gardeners who may meet them in the wild. The most outstanding are *O. apifera*, the Bee Orchid, *O. bombyliflora*, the Humble-bee Orchid, *O. fuciflora*, the Late Spider Orchid, *O. insectifera*, the Fly Orchid, and *O. sphegodes*, the Early Spider Orchid.

ORCHIS *Orchidaceae*

Occasionally one or more species of the hardy orchids may be offered, and if grown in deep rich soil may survive for some years, flowering only spasmodically, but the tubers very rarely even produce a second shoot, and it is impossible to grow them from the plentiful seed set, except under special conditions provided by the orchid specialist. Those most likely to be met with in the wild are *O. latifolia*, the Marsh Orchis, with purple-red flowers in a spike from a sheath of widely lanceolate leaves, *O. maculata*, pale purple, with spotted leaves, *O. morio*, green and purple, and *O. sambucina*, a handsome species, found in two very distinct colour forms, often growing near by. The distinctive short, thick spikes of comparatively large flowers may be rosy purple or a clear yellow.

194

OREOCHARIS *Gesneriaceae*

These near relations of the Ramondas hail from China and Japan, and form basal rosettes of ovate or roughly heart-shaped, hairy leaves, and upstanding stems of up to 6″, bearing sprays of five-petalled, slightly lipped, tubular flowers. Most suitable for the alpine house, in well-drained leafy soil. No lime.

DP*O. forrestii* (*Roettlera forrestii*). Yunnan. An attractive plant with a rosette of solid, overlapping, coarsely toothed leaves and sprays of pale yellow flowers. 3″–8″. May.

ORIGANUM *Labiatae*

A genus of dense, much-branched, wiry-stemmed shrublets, usually aromatic, with close heads of small labiate flowers, often enclosed in pale green or coloured bracts, which give them an attractive hop-like appearance.

P*O. amanum.* One of the most distinctive and delightful of the genus, making a low growing mat of 2″–4″, with a dense thicket of slender stems closely set with opposite, tiny, apple-green leaves, and, in late summer, with many exquisite tiny flowers in deep rose, with very slender tubular corollas of more than 1″ in length, opening to the little lipped petals, with exserted stigma, like a galaxy of fairy trumpets. Recently introduced from Greece, it is safer in the alpine house until its hardiness has been fully proved.

DP*O. dictamnus.* Dittany of Crete. Perhaps the loveliest of this attractive genus, but definitely only safe with alpine house protection. It makes a rounded twiggy shrublet of 8″–10″, with opposite circular leaves, densely felted on both surfaces, on wiry stems, bearing in summer close terminal drooping heads of small pink labiate flowers, enclosed in large pinkish bracts, giving a hop-like appearance. 8″–10″. Long flowering. Summer.

O. hybridum. Levant. A much hardier plant, and, in effect, the counterpart of the foregoing without, or almost without, its attractive woolliness, although the basal leaves may be slightly downy. 8″. Long flowering. Summer.

O. laevigatum. Another recently-introduced plant, and a very valuable one, as for most of the year it forms a neat mat of 3″–4″ stems, closely set with small, dark green, oval-pointed leaves, and only in late summer does it erupt slender arching stems of a foot or more bearing airy sprays of tiny labiate flowers in great profusion, giving the impression of a red-purple mist. Hardy and easy. The 10″ arching stems do not rise above 5″–6″. August–September.

Ornithogalum, Orobus, Orostachys
ORNITHOGALUM   *Liliaceae*

The relations of the Star of Bethlehem have a strong family likeness, being all bulbous plants with white, green-striped flowers—rarely all white or yellowish. Several are admirable for the wild garden, where their invasive habit is an advantage, and of late years one or two really dwarf species, miniatures, in effect, of the Star of Bethlehem, have been introduced from Asia Minor, and adjoining districts, which are neat enough for the small rock garden, and have not yet shown the exuberance of *O. umbellatum*.

*O. nutans. S. Europe. In a quiet way, this is one of the loveliest of bulbs for leafy soil in half shade. The flower stem of 8"–10" bears half a dozen or so drooping six-petalled flowers, white within and green without, but of such a diaphanous texture that the effect is of ethereal grey-green pointed bells. Spring.

O. umbellatum. The well-known and invasive Star of Bethlehem, with green-striped white flowers so closely set as to appear as an umbel. 8"–10". Spring.

OROBUS is now included in LATHYRUS, though still appearing under the former name in most catalogues.

OROSTACHYS   *Crassulaceae*

A small summer-flowering genus which until recently has been included in Cotyledon or Sedum, under which names it is still usually found in catalogues. The species are rosette plants, suggestive of a rather succulent sempervivum, and are on the fringe of hardiness.

O. chanetii (*Sedum chanetii*). China, Kansu. An attractive plant with grey-green, pointed leaves in a flat rosette, and a large pyramidal inflorescence of many small pinkish flowers. Alpine house, not quite hardy. 8". Summer.

O. spinosum. (*Cotyledon spinosa, Umbilicus spinosus, Sedum spinosum*). N.E. and Central Asia. Very regular rosettes of thick, lanceolate leaves with spiny tips; the central leaves close up in winter to form a congested circle of small spines. Yellow flowers in a narrow spike. Hardier than the foregoing. 6". Summer.

Orphanidesia, Ourisia, Oxalis

ORPHANIDESIA *Ericaceae Monotypic*

ᴅ*O. gaultherioides.** E. Lazistan and adjoining Transcaucasia. A hand-some evergreen prostrate shrub, forming a mat, with many large oval leaves (up to 3″ long, nearly 2″ wide), tough and bristly. The large sessile flowers, five-petalled, and widely tubular, may be up to 2″ across, and are usually pale rose, although an even more beautiful deep rose form is known. Requires deep rich soil in woodland conditions, and is easier in the north than in the south, where it is usually grown in the alpine house. No lime. Propagation by seed, if available, ōr cuttings or layers. 4″–6″. March–April. (Pl. 21)

OURISIA *Scrophulariaceae*

A genus of low-growing plants from the southern hemisphere, spreading by creeping rhizomes, and hardy in moist, well-drained areas, not stagnant in winter. Only two are here described, but other desirable species from New Zealand are becoming more known, and should be attractive and useful plants.

O. coccinea. Andes of Chile. A creeping plant with stalked, rounded, dentate leaves, and from May–September erect stems of about 8″, each bearing a few long-trumpeted labiate flowers (over 1″ in length) of brilliant scarlet.

O. macrophylla. New Zealand. This is a taller plant with longer stalked, rounded dentate leaves, and 8″–10″ stems bearing irregular whorls of almost regular white flowers, about 1″ across, in July.

OXALIS *Oxalidaceae*

A very large genus with delicate five-petalled, slightly funnel-shaped, solitary flowers of white, yellow, pink, or mauve, carried well above the (usually) radical leaves, which are trefoil shaped (or sometimes with many leaflets) on slender petioles. Almost all are charming plants, but many are apt to be invasive, not only by the creeping runners of some species, but by the seed mechanism which, at ripeness, violently projects the seed in every direction at the slightest touch. Summer flowering.

O. acetosella. Wood Sorrel. N. temperate woods. A delightful little plant for a shady woodland corner, where it will naturalize. Pearly white flowers. 2″. March–April.

197

*O. adenophylla. Chile. From a fibre-coated bulb-like rhizome rise many radical leaves, each with up to a dozen leaflets on the 3″–4″ petiole, and widely funnel-shaped flowers of a deep satiny pink, often two or three to an inflorescence. Dies completely down in winter. 4″–5″. Late spring.

O. chrysantha. Brazil. A yellow flowered species, with trefoil leaves, spreading by runners. Hardy in warm districts, but safer in alpine house. 6″. June onwards.

O. deppei. Mexico. A low-growing species whose bulb-like roots are reputed to be edible. Showy flowers of almost brick-red. 8″–10″. Early summer.

O. depressa (*inops*). A comparative newcomer, with lush trefoil leaves and large bright pink flowers. 2″–3″. (Pl. 21)

*O. enneaphylla. Falkland Islands, Patagonia. From a dense rhizome, with thick, fleshy overlapping scales, rise the 2″–3″ petioles with (usually) nine deeply cleft leaflets, and solitary pearly-white funnel-shaped flowers. There is an equally lovely pink form (*O. e.* 'ROSEA'), and an attractive miniature (*O. e.* 'MINUTA') 1″–2″. Early summer. Long flowering.

O. floribunda. This is a name used in gardens for three or four very similar species. Is usually a rather rampant plant of up to 8″–10″, with many showy bright pink funnel-shaped flowers over a long period from summer onwards.

O. inops. see **O. depressa**

*O. laciniata. A newcomer from Patagonia, with slender trefoil leaves, and small wide trumpets which may vary from pink to deep mauve and almost blue. Dies down completely after flowering, to small scaly rhizomes rather like those of a miniature *O. enneaphylla.* 2″–4″. Early summer.

O. lobata. S. America. A charming little plant, whose bright green leaves appear in the spring and die away to reappear in autumn with the small butter-yellow flowers. 3″–4″. August–September. (Pl. 21)

O. oregana. W.N. America. A pleasant little plant, a pink edition of our own Wood Sorrel, *O. acetosella.*

There are many other delightful species rather similar to one or other of the above, but some are barely in cultivation, and most of doubtful hardiness in a severe winter.

OXYTROPIS *Leguminosae*

This is a large genus very nearly akin to Astragalus, having unequally pinnate leaves and close heads of pea-shaped flowers on long, wiry stems. Except for a few European species the nomenclature is far from clear, and several desirable species from N. America have been introduced under collector's numbers. They are attractive whether in or out of flower because of their often long, slender, pinnate leaves, which in many species are densely silvery or woolly. Propagation by seed, which germinates fairly well, but plants of the woolly species are not too easy to rear to flowering stage. Tap-rooted, so division is impossible and transplanting hazardous. Summer flowering.

O. campestris. Europe (including Gt. Britain). Erect 4″–5″ spikes of cream flowers, tinged with purple.

O. halleri. See **O. uralensis.**

D*O. lambertii.** Loco-weed. N. America. A handsome species, the whole plant silvery-white with adpressed hairs with 2″–3″ heads of rosy-carmine or blue-purple heads of flowers in inflated silvery calyces. 6″–8″. Not long-lived. Summer.

O. montana. European Alps. A delicate little plant with almost prostrate wiry branches carrying pinnate leaves with small, deep green leaflets. Heads of small pea-flowers, variable in colour from turquoise to reddish purple or purplish blue. A delightful little plant, seldom seen in cultivation. 3″–4″. April–May.

O. uralensis. (*halleri*) European Alps, Ural Mts. A sturdy plant, making a clump of radical pinnate leaves, grey with silvery hairs. Short stout stems bearing close heads of variable shades of purple. There is also a white form which is not so attractive. 6″–8″. April.

PAEDEROTA now included in VERONICA

PAEONIA *Ranunculaceae*

The only Paeony which is even doubtfully dwarf enough for the rock garden is **P. cambessedesii,** with single deep rose flowers and attractive cut and lobed foliage of deep green, strikingly purple-red on the backs of the leaves. It makes a beautiful pan plant in its younger stages, but will grow to 12″ or 18″ in the open garden. Early summer.

PAPAVER *Papaveraceae*

The small poppies are gay and delightful plants for the rock garden, but are not usually long-lived. Self-sown seed, which is abundant, seems more successful than that sown in boxes; and, in any case, all poppies are impatient of transplanting. Summer flowering.

*P. alpinum. Alpine Poppy. Alps, Carpathians. Delicate glaucous radical leaves, much lobed and divided, and white or orange-yellow poppies. 4″–6″. Early summer, long flowering. (Pl. 21)

P. nudicaule. Iceland Poppy. Northern sub-arctic regions. This variable species, from which the spectacular Iceland Poppies of gardens have been evolved, does contain a few local forms, only reaching 3″–6″, of which one, *P. n.* var. *radicatum,* can sometimes be obtained. It has comparatively large yellow or white flowers. Early summer, long flowering.

P. pyrenaicum. Pyrenees, Carpathians. Very like *P. alpinum,* but a rather sturdier plant and with greener leaves. 6″–8″. Early summer, long flowering.

    P. p. var. **rhaeticum** (*rhaeticum*) is a variant found in the Dolomites and elsewhere, with orange flowers.

PARAQUILEGIA   *Ranunculaceae*

These fragile little plants have an ethereal beauty, but are not easy to keep in health, or for long, in the south of England. As seen in some Scottish gardens, they are among the loveliest of plants, forming clumps of delicate fern-like foliage not unlike that of Corydalis, just above which hover luminous, almost opalescent, bowl-shaped flowers with pale yellow boss of stamens. Summer.

D***P. grandiflorum** (*Isopyrum grandiflorum*). China. The whole plant is no more than 6″–7″ in height. Flowers a diaphanous mauve-blue, less frequently white, solitary, 1″ or more across. April.

    P. microphyllum (*Isopyrum microphyllum*). N. India. Habit of *P. grandiflorum,* but smaller, white flowers. 4″–5″. April.

PARNASSIA   *Saxifragaceae*

There is a strong family likeness among the Parnassias, which may account for the fact that only one or two are in cultivation. They are, in general, lovers of a moist, peaty soil, or even a bog, although they may exist in a drier situation. They form clumps of slightly succulent bright green basal leaves, kidney-shaped on 1″–2″ petioles. The five-petalled, saucer-shaped flowers are white in most species, with delicate translucent veining. Division, or seed sown as soon as ripe. Summer.

P. fimbriata. N. America. White flowers, with rounded petals elegantly fringed at base. 6″.

P. nubicola. Himalaya. A taller species, with heart-shaped leaves and large white flowers, over 1″ across. 8″–12″.

P. palustris. Grass of Parnassus. Northern hemisphere (including Gt. Britain). White rounded petals beautifully veined. For boggy places. 4″–8″.

PAROCHETUS *Leguminosae Monotypic*

*****P. communis.** The cooler regions in the Himalayas, E. India, E. Africa. A prostrate plant like a rather lush clover, which, if happily suited in well-drained, rather moist soil in a mild district, rapidly covers the ground, rooting as it goes. It is a lovely thing, bearing erect in late summer, on 1″–2″ stems, many pea-shaped flowers of over ½″ in length and of a vivid blue which has almost a touch of green in it. Except in sheltered districts, it is of only borderline hardiness, although small bits here and there may survive. It is safer, however, to make sure of keeping this charming plant by taking rooted pieces in late summer, and keeping them potted up under glass through the winter. 1″–2″.

PARONYCHIA *Caryophyllaceae*

These Thyme-like carpeters, mainly from the Mediterranean regions, need a hot, dry position, but are quite hardy if protected from excessive damp. The flowers are tiny and inconspicuous, lacking petals, but the small clusters are surrounded by comparatively large, dry, translucent, white bracts, so that for a long period in summer the plant seems to glisten with myriads of small silvery scales. They make a good carpet for dwarf bulbs. Early summer.

P. capitata (*nivea*). This and *P. argentea*, both from the Mediterranean region, form neat compact mats, covered in summer with the shiny silvery bracts enclosing the tiny flower clusters. They only differ in small botanical details.

P. kapela. Mediterranean region. Makes a denser carpet of wiry shoots with blue-green leaves and even larger silvery bracts of up to ¼″ long.

P. serpyllifolia. S. Europe. Very like *P. capitata*, of which it is sometimes considered a variety. Slightly hairy tiny leaves.

Parrya, Patrinia, Pedicularis

PARRYA *Cruciferae*

These little plants, from N. America and the Arctic regions, are very similar to Erysimum and Cheiranthus, the dwarf Wallflowers. The one most usually met in cultivation is:

P. menziesii (*Cheiranthus menziesii*). Rocky Mts. From tufts of upright, narrowly lanceolate leaves, grey-green and slightly toothed, rise the 4″–6″ inflorescences of small purple wallflowers. Although hardy, it is not very long-lived, and should be kept going by seed and cuttings. Early summer.

PATRINIA *Valerianaceae*

These are easy-growing plants in any light, rich soil, and are, in appearance, like small yellow Valerians. Their chief value is their flowering season, which is August, when colour is scarce in the rock garden.

P. palmata. A synonym of *P. triloba,* and the name under which the latter is usually found in catalogues.

P. triloba (*palmata*). Japan. In effect, a dwarf valerian, with golden-yellow fragrant flowers in heads 3″–4″ across. July.

PEDICULARIS *Scrophulariaceae*

Perhaps these should not have a place here as they are practically impossible to grow in cultivation, owing to their parasitic habits which are not fully understood, but many of the species are such a conspicuous feature in all the higher European Alps that it seems impossible to ignore them completely. Many of them are very beautiful, not only for their heads of hooded and beaked flowers in cream, yellow, pink, brick red, and deep rose, but also for the sturdy fern-like foliage, which is often tinged with red. Of dwarf stature (3″–6″ or so).

P. foliosa, pale yellow.

P. oederi, clear yellow with burnt-orange "beak".

P. kerneri, very dwarf, deep, rich rose.

P. rostrata, with few large, deep red flowers.

P. verticillata, slightly taller, 6″–10″, with a close head of deep rose flowers.

These are pre-eminent among the many species seen among the turf of the Central European Alps.

202

Penstemon

PENSTEMON *Scrophulariaceae*

This large genus comes, for the most part, from the mountainous districts of W.N. America. Seeds of a great variety of species have been obtained from America, and almost all the dwarf forms are attractive plants for the rock garden, having comparatively large, tubular, more or less lipped flowers of pink, mauve, blue, purple, scarlet, or, rarely, white. Unfortunately, the species are not easily defined and, therefore, only a few of the most distinctive, and most easily obtainable, are described here, pending an authoritative investigation, which is long overdue. The complexity of the subject is shown by the fact that one American popular Flora lists over seventy species, and another writes of "over 150 species". Even the spelling of the generic name is debatable. Of Pentstemon and Penstemon the R.H.S. Dictionary says the latter "appears to have priority".

Although hardy in general, an unusually severe winter is likely to cause casualties, and it is safer to take a few cuttings each year, in August and September by choice, but they root easily at almost any season. They also come readily from seed sown in gentle heat in February or outdoors in June. Any open well-drained soil suits them, but excessive moisture is one of the causes of the occasional dying off, which seems to be a feature of the genus.

P. confertus (*procerus*). Rocky Mts. A very variable plant, and only small enough for the rock garden in its dwarf forms. Leaves lanceolate, flowers narrow, lipped, about ½″ in length, cream to sulphur-yellow, borne in slender spikes. 6″–20″. June, July.

P. crandallii. Colorado. A much-branched shrublet with linear leaves and large, open, blue flowers. 6″. July.

*****P. davidsonii.** California. Habit of *P. menziesii*, but with ruby-red flowers. 6″. June.

P. fruticosus. N.W. America. A sub-shrubby plant with large, single, reddish-purple flowers on short twigs. 6″–9″. August.

P. hallii. Colorado. A sub-shrub with medium, lipped flowers of a lurid brownish-purple. 6″–9″. July.

*****P. heterophyllus.** California. Makes a clump of narrow, lanceolate leaves, with graceful spires of many blue, pink-tinged flowers which open consecutively over a long period. The form offered as *P. h.* 'TRUE BLUE' has particularly beautiful azure flowers. Up to 12″. July–August.

P. menziesii. N.W. America. Erect or flopping in habit. Leaves small, oval, slightly toothed. Close sprays of large, 1″ long violet-blue to purple flowers. 6″–9″. June.

P. m. 'MICROPHYLLUS'. A miniature of the type. 3″–4″.

P. newberryi. W. United States. Similar habit to the foregoing, but with rosy-purple flowers. 9″–12″. July.

  P. n. forma **humilior** has more brilliant flowers and is the *P. roezlii* of gardens. q.v.

*P. pinifolius. N.W. America. A recent introduction of spreading habit with stems feathery with many ½″ needle-like leaves. Very narrow trumpets of bright scarlet. 4″–6″. June–August. (Pl. 21)

*P. roezlii (of gardens). N.W. America. The plant grown under this name in gardens is one of the most attractive of penstemons, making a low, rounded bush, hidden in early summer with myriads of rather narrow, tubular, lipped flowers of rich, glowing cherry red. It is correctly *P. newberryi* forma *humilior*. 6″–9″. May–June.

P. rupicola. Oregon and California. A prostrate shrub with small leathery leaves, and many clusters of rose-carmine flowers. This is very similar to the foregoing species, but the flowers are less vivid. 6″. May–June. (Pl. 22)

P. scouleri. N.W. America. A shrubby plant with large, tubular, lipped flowers, usually of a cool, luminous lilac, although colour is variable. Very floriferous. 9″–12″. July. *P. s.* 'ALBA' is a good white form. (Pl. 13)

P. 'SIX HILLS'. A good hybrid with erect spikes of purplish-pink flowers. 6″–9″. May–June.

PENTACHONDRA *Ericaceae*

P. pumila is a rare and interesting congested small evergreen shrublet from the N. Island of New Zealand. It has solitary white flowers in late spring, at the tips of its twiggy branches, which are set with small, glossy leaves with hairy edges. Conspicuous bright red berries in late summer. It needs a cool position in lime-free leafy soil. Propagation by green cuttings in June.

PEREZIA *Compositae*

This is a genus of S. American composites mainly from the mountainous districts of Peru. They are not much grown, but should be valuable as they provide, in their best forms, that rare colour in the rock garden, a deep, pure blue. Two, bearing rather small, Dandelion-like flowers, that are sometimes offered in catalogues are:

Pernettya, Petrocallis

P. linearis. A much-branched plant, somewhat suggestive of *Lactuca perennis*, which may be from 6″–12″, with brilliant blue flowers. Summer.

P. recurvata. Fuego and the Falkland Is. Makes a dense mat of stiff upright branches of 2″–3″, closely set with sessile, sharply-pointed, glossy, narrow, dark green leaves. It appears quite hardy, but is not very free with its flowers, which in the best forms are a pure, deep blue. Summer.

PERNETTYA *Ericaceae*

This decorative genus, mainly from S. America and New Zealand, is profuse flowering, bearing many small urn-shaped flowers in late spring, followed by a prolific crop of white, pink, purplish, or bright red berries. They must have well-drained, lime-free leafy soil, in a sheltered, but not too shady, spot.

P. nana. New Zealand (S. Island). A spreading sub-shrub with many wiry branches, more or less erect (up to 3″–4″) with tiny oval leaves and solitary white, campanulate flowers from the leaf axils. Reddish berries up to $\frac{1}{2}$″ across.

P. pumila. Magellan region and Falkland Is. A prostrate shrublet which will spread rapidly in congenial surroundings. White or pink fruits of over $\frac{1}{2}$″ diameter.

p***P. tasmanica.** Tasmania. Perhaps the most satisfactory of the dwarf species, this makes a dense cushion-like mat with creeping stems well set with tiny, glossy, pointed leaves, and many small, white, campanulate flowers from the leaf axils, followed by conspicuous bright red fruits, nearly $\frac{1}{2}$″ in diameter. Safer in the alpine house, where it makes a delightful pan.

PETROCALLIS *Cruciferae*

This very small genus provides us with one charming little plant which well deserves its name of Rock Beauty (Petros, Callis).

***P. pyrenaica** is to be found locally in the High Alps from the Pyrenees east to Carpathia. It makes a dense little cushion of under 2″, even when in flower. Its tiny, sessile, deeply three-cleft, wedge-shaped leaves are closely set on the little upright stems, giving it a moss-like appearance. The small heads of little cruciform lilac flowers are fragrant. Scree conditions or a pan in the alpine house. May. Seed, or cuttings by branches pulled off in late August.

Petrocoptis, Phacelia, Philesia, Phlox
PETROCOPTIS *Caryophyllaceae*

A very small genus from the Pyrenees, nearly akin to Lychnis, under which name it is usually found.

P. lagascae (*Lychnis lagascae*). A loosely tufted plant, up to 6″, with oblong leaves, and campion-like flowers of rich pink. Early summer.

P. pyrenaica. (*Lychnis pyrenaica*). A very similar plant, but with spatulate to cordate leaves, and white to pale pink flowers. Early summer.

PHACELIA *Hydrophyllaceae*

The majority of this genus are hardy annuals, of which the blue *P. campanularia* is the most distinguished example.

DP***P. sericea.** W.N. America, is a lovely, but difficult, biennial or perennial. It makes a spreading rosette of beautiful silvery, silky, much-lobed leaves, from the centre of which rise 6″ stems carrying long dense spikes of small blue-purple narrowly bell-shaped flowers. It is easy from seed, but difficult to keep healthy until its flowering stage. Its chief enemy seems to be winter damp. Safer in the alpine house. 6″. Spring.

PHILESIA *Liliaceae Monotypic*

P***P. magellanica** (*buxifolia*, under which name it is usually offered), is a very beautiful dwarf, evergreen shrub from Chile. In cultivation it is usually only from 6″ to 12″. It makes a much-branched bushlet with stiff stems bearing tough, narrowly oval, dark green, grey-backed leaves, and conspicuous tubular three-petalled, deep rose flowers, up to 2″ long, borne towards the end of the branches. It is only hardy in a sheltered district, but if well suited, in a moist but well-drained, leafy, lime-free soil, in part shade, it will spread by suckers. Propagation by division or rooted suckers treated as cuttings. June.

PHLOX *Polemoniaceae*

With one exception, not in cultivation, all the known Phlox are natives of N. America. The prostrate species are invaluable in the rock garden, providing, for the most part, mats of close, almost spiny foliage, covered in spring and early summer with myriads of wide,

Phlox

five-petalled flowers of up to $\frac{1}{2}''$ or more in diameter, in many shades of pink, mauve to purple, and white. They will do well in any well-drained open soil, in a sunny position, but not parched. Propagation is best by cuttings taken in July after flowering.

P. adsurgens. California, Oregon. One of the more upright Phlox, with slender stems of 6"–8", oval leaves, and few flowered heads of rather large white to pink flowers. May–June. (Pl. 22)

*P. amoena. S.E. United States. Another upright species, 6"–8", with slightly hairy, narrowly lanceolate leaves, and many-flowered heads of variable colour, the usual and most attractive being a reddish purple. May–June.

P***P. caespitosa.** W.N. America. The neatest and smallest of the phloxes, with dense, short, spiny leaves, and almost sessile flowers. In cultivation it never seems to achieve the completely tufted cushion that it shows in Nature, but makes a close mat, studded with the $\frac{3}{8}''$ or so flowers of white or palest moonlight blue. *P. c. bryoides* and *P. c. condensata* are even more congested than the type, and the latter has greyish green leaves.

*P. douglasii. W.N. America. A beautiful species, tufted, from 2"–4", with very neat round-petalled mauve flowers. There are many local forms, of which *P. d. diffusa*, a looser-habited plant from British Columbia and California, is one, and garden varieties, of which 'BOOTHMAN'S VAR.', rich mauve with vivid violet-purple centre, 'EVA', pink with crimson eye, and 'SNOW QUEEN', pure white, are outstanding.

P. mesoleuca. See **P. nana** var. **ensifolia.**

DP***P. nana** var. **ensifolia** (*mesoleuca*). Texas, New Mexico. Quite the most handsome of the group when well grown, but not easy, and safest when in the alpine house where conditions can be controlled. It has rather a sprawling habit from an almost woody central root stock, whence it flings its wiry branches with isolated pairs of opposite leaves, curved linear, and up to 2" long. The terminal flowers, on 1" stems, are very large, and of a peculiarly lovely, clean pink, with a white eye. It is best in a sunny position, in light, well-drained soil, with leaf-mould and sand, or in the alpine house. No lime. Propagation by root cuttings, or young tufts taken from the parent plant in May. Spring and early summer. (Pl. 22)

*P. nivalis. A compact plant very similar to *P. subulata*. Pale pink or pale mauve to white flowers as in *P. n.* 'GLADWYN'. (Pl. 22)

*P. subulata. Moss Phlox. E. United States. Amongst this lovely and easy-going species arise most of the colour forms and hybrids which form the stand-by for the rock garden, following the early spring flowering aubrietas and alyssums. They have a tufted growth, and in any sunny, well-drained spot, soon make hearty spreading mats of 2"–4" in height, covered over a long period in April and May with flowers of pink, mauve, or white. (Pl. 22)

A great variety, with their colours, may be found in the various alpine catalogues, but a few of those more universally offered are:

Phuopsis, Phyllodoce

'CAMLA' (Camlaensis), a large, salmon-pink flower, but not too robust.

'BETTY', very similar, but with a stronger constitution.

'G. F. WILSON', an old variety, somewhat ousted by brighter shades, but unrivalled in good temper, and the prodigality of its pale lavender flowers.

'TEMISCAMING', a comparatively new introduction, with masses of flowers of a piercing magenta crimson unmatched by any other in its spectacular effect.

'VIVID'. A dwarf and compact plant with rather small, neat flowers of a good deep pink. Not so robust as some, but a delightful form.

PHUOPSIS *Rubiaceae Monotypic*

P. stylosa (*Crucianella stylosa*, under which name it is usually found). Caucasus. A slender plant, very like the wild Woodruff in habit, having upright stems of 6″–8″, with whorls of narrowly lanceolate, almost spiny-pointed leaves, and flat heads of tiny pink flowers, tubular, with five pointed lobes. Early summer.

PHYLLODOCE *Ericaceae*

The species of this genus of small, evergreen, heath-like shrubs from sub-arctic regions of the northern hemisphere, have a very strong family likeness in their bushlets of rigid, woody branches, erect or slightly spreading, closely set with stiff little dark green leaves of about $\frac{1}{2}″$ in length, linear and with recurved edges, and terminating in clusters or spikes of charming urn-shaped or more open flowers of white, cream, pink, or purple. In the right situations they are easy and delightful little shrubs, but demand a lime-free soil, with plenty of humus, and part shade. Early summer. Most have at one time or another appeared as Andromeda, Bryanthus, Erica, or Menziesia.

P. aleutica. N.E. Asia, Alaska, and islands between. One of the more compact, 6″–8″, with few-flowered umbels of heather-like, small, greenish yellow flowers.

*P. breweri. California. More lax in growth with more spreading 6″–12″ branches, and a terminal spike of rather open, deep pink flowers with conspicuous stamens.

19

Lewisia tweedyi
Linaria alpina var.
(Below, *Fuchsia procumbens*)
Linum 'Gemmell's Hybrid'

Leucogynes grandiceps
Linnaea borealis
Linum salsoloides nanum

20

Lithospermum graminifolium
(Below, *Viola cornuta alba*)
Mimulus primuloides
Oenothera caespitosa

Mimulus cupreus vars.
Nierembergia caerulea
Omphalodes luciliae

P. caerulea. Alpine regions of N. Europe (including Scotland), Pyrenees, N. America, N. Asia. Rather a misleading name, as the urn-shaped corolla is of a pale or deeper purple. Flowers in loose umbels. 6″–9″.

P. empetriformis. W.N. America. A more spreading member of the genus, with purple, campanulate flowers in loose umbels. 6″–8″.

ᵏ**P. glanduliflora.** W.N. America. More erect than the foregoing, with urn-shaped corolla of pale greenish-yellow, usually described as plain yellow. 6″–8″.

P. × intermedia. Natural hybrid between *P. empetriformis* and *P. glanduliflora.* W.N. America. This is a useful group of compact, erect, or semi-procumbent shrublets variable between the two parents, and with flowers from mauve to purple, or yellowish pink. 6″–9″.

***P. nipponica.** N. Japan. A particularly neat little shrublet of dense upright branches and terminal loose umbels of campanulate white flowers. 5″–6″.

P. tsugifolia. N. Japan. Very similar to the foregoing, but with even denser, slightly larger, and coarser foliage. 5″–6″.

PHYLLOTHAMNUS *Ericaceae*

***Phyllothamnus erectus** is an extremely interesting intergeneric hybrid between *Phyllodoce empetriformis* and *Rhodothamnus chamaecistus*, and combines, in an attractive 8″ shrub, approximately the habit of Phyllodoce, with the larger, rosy, saucer-like flowers of Rhodothamnus. Requires the same conditions as Phyllodoce, but appears not to be so long-lived. Early summer.

PHYSARIA *Cruciferae*

A genus of small crucifers from N. America. The species are rather similar, and form rosettes of more or less silvery, broadly oval leaves, and 3″–4″ heads of yellow cruciform flowers. The attraction is mainly in the silvery rosettes, arching stems, and the large inflated seed pods, as the latter are often iridescent or pink-flushed. Seed is sometimes sent from America, but the genus seems short-lived in cultivation. The most attractive is

P. didymocarpa, Rocky Mts., which has particularly silvery leaves and silver, often pink flushed, inflated seed pods. Sandy soil in a sunny, well-drained position. 2″–3″. Early summer.

Phyteuma

PHYTEUMA *Campanulaceae*

Superficially the members of this European genus have little suggestion, other than the prevailing blue of their flowers, of the Campanulas as we envisage them, as the small, tubular flowers, with five-pointed, narrow-petalled corollas, joined at the petal tips, are crowded into dense neat heads or spikes, which appear almost fluffy by reason of the projecting two-pronged stigmas. There are several small species (2″-4″) to be found in the Higher Alps, and they are all charming little plants which might be much more often tried in the choicest screes or in the alpine house.

D*P. comosum. Dolomites, Dalmatia, etc. This is the most spectacular of the genus, making tufts of glossy, dark green, sharply-toothed leaves, and bearing in the summer many heads of comparatively large flowers of a most distinctive shape. The tips of the petals adhere, giving each flower a curious swollen appearance, and from each gathered tip protrudes a long and waving stigma. It has been compared by Farrer to a bunch of little soda-water bottles, shading from pale to deep purplish-blue, and is completely unlike any other species. It is not so difficult as has been reputed, in a well-drained rock crevice or in the alpine house. Slugs are its chief enemy. 2″-3″. Early summer. (Pl. 22)

The other small species of the higher alps and screes are very much alike in all having close heads of small, deep blue flowers, usually enclosed by green bracts, rising on slender 1″-3″ stems (depending on the species, but even more on the height and exposure of their site) from tufts of small, bright green leaves. Those most often met are

P. globulariifolium (*pauciflorum*, under which name it usually appears). Perhaps the most dwarf of all, with rosettes of short lanceolate leaves, rounded at the tips, and stocky little heads of few (3-7) deep blue flowers. 1″-2″.

P. hedraianthifolium (*carestiae*). Switzerland, etc. Characterized by very narrow grass-like leaves, and several very long, but unequal, needle-shaped bracts below the flower-head. 2″-3″.

P. hemisphaericum. European Alps. Linear leaves, and dense, globular flower-heads with small bracts. 2″-3″.

P. humile. Switzerland, etc. Dwarfer than the foregoing, with longer, pointed bracts. 1″-2″.

Taller than these, up to a foot or more, and only suitable for the large rock garden, are P. nigrum (dense, almost black spike), P. orbiculare, and P. scheuchzeri (both with round heads, deep blue), and P. spicatum (spikes of cream, white, or blue).

Pimelea, Pinguicula

PIMELEA *Thymelaeaceae*

This is a genus of over 100 species, confined to Australasia. The species are neat foliaged, twiggy shrubs, with clusters of small tubular flowers with four-pointed petals, nearly related to the Daphnes. Two species are charming little plants for a sheltered place in the rock garden or in the alpine house.

P. coarctata. New Zealand. A mat-forming plant with upright or spreading branches, closely set with small, oval, grey leaves, and terminal heads of small, white, fragrant flowers, followed by oval white berries. 2″–3″, May. (Pl. 23)

P. prostrata. New Zealand. More spreading than the last species, with very tiny grey-green oval leaves on prostrate, interlacing branches. Clusters of tiny white, fragrant flowers in the terminal axils of the twiggy stems, followed by glistening white berries. 2″–3″. May.

PINGUICULA *Lentibulariaceae*

The Butterworts are an insectivorous genus flourishing in boggy sites. Their leaves are densely glandular, exuding a sticky substance which holds the small insects alighting on it, and helps to digest them, thus providing nitrogenous matter which would otherwise be deficient owing to their position. They form a rosette of these entire, oval leaves, often with incurved edges, and the solitary lipped and spurred flowers are borne at right angles on slender 2″–3″ stems. Three species are met with fairly frequently in boggy spots in the Alps, and can be grown in similar surroundings if they can be provided:

P. alpina. Central and N. Europe. White, two-lipped flowers, with yellow throat. Short spur. 3″. May–June.

*P. grandiflora. W. Europe (including S.W. Ireland). This is more rare than the other two species described, and is a handsome plant with larger (nearly 1″) wide-open flowers of violet blue. 4″. Early summer.

P. vulgaris. Europe (including Gt. Britain). Forms flat rosettes of succulent leaves, incurved at the edges. Violet flowers on scapes of 3″–4″ or more, in boggy places. Early summer.

Plagiorhegma, Plantago, Platycodon

PLAGIORHEGMA   Berberidaceae

A genus of two dwarf woodlanders from widely distant habitats, which are generally offered under their old name of Jeffersonia. Both form clumps of very distinctive leaves on long wiry petioles, appearing in early spring, with or slightly later than the ethereal wood-anemone-like flowers on very slender stalks. Most delightful plants for woodland soil in part shade, or for a pan in the alpine house in sandy, peaty soil. Propagation best by seed, sown as soon as ripe, as it is rash to disturb a well-established plant.

P. diphylla (*Jeffersonia diphylla*). Tennessee. Leaves deeply cleft into two lobes and solitary white flowers up to 1″ across. 4″–6″. March–April.

*P. dubia (*Jeffersonia dubia*). Manchuria. An even more beautiful plant (and more easily obtainable) with large, blue, hepatica-like flowers of an almost crystalline texture, preceding (usually) the roughly kidney-shaped leaves, which are at first folded flat and flushed with a lovely metallic purple, on reddish petioles. Green on maturity. 3″–4″. March–April.

PLANTAGO   Plantaginaceae

The Plantains include one or two species which at least make interesting and unusual plants as specimens in the alpine house, although perhaps too suggestive of their humbler cousins to be popular in the garden.

P. major 'ROSULARIS.' Rose Plantain. Has the characteristic rosette of ribbed leaves, but the flower-spike is replaced by a rose-like rosette. This is sometimes grown as a curiosity, especially in the variety 'RUBRIFOLIA', which has purple-stained leaves. 4″–5″.

P. nivalis. Spain. Makes an attractive pan in the alpine house, having small rosettes, about 3″ across of very silvery hairy bluntly lanceolate leaves and small, globular green heads on 1″–2″ stems.

PLATYCODON   Campanulaceae Monotypic

P. grandiflorum. The Balloon Flower or Chinese Bell-flower, from China, Manchuria, and Japan, has two attractive dwarf forms. Each makes a small clump of upright slender stems, with broadly ovate, almost grey-green leaves, and large solitary flowers from the axils of the upper leaves. They open into wide shallowly bell-shaped flowers, 1½″–2″ across, but the tips of the petals remain adherent until the flower is fully developed, giving the large buds the

Pleione

typically balloon-shaped appearance. Easy in any well-drained soil in full sun. Summer.

P. g. var. **mariesii.** From 8″–10″, with deep purplish blue flowers. There is also a pinkish form of garden origin.

*****P. g.** 'APOYAMA' (*apoyama*). A newcomer, with even larger purplish-blue flowers on 4″–5″ stems.

PLEIONE *Orchidaceae*

This genus of showy Asiatic terrestrial orchids has only recently been recognized as possessing members which are so nearly hardy as to make spectacular pans for the alpine house, and even occasionally to survive out of doors in very well drained, warm spots where overhead protection from winter wet can be arranged. Individual flowers are long lasting, and the various species flower at different seasons so that it is possible to have one or another flowering over a long period. All grow from more or less flask-shaped pseudo-bulbs, which must be planted to only half their depth in an open spongy acid mixture with plenty of humus. A mixture of loam, leaf-mould, peat, coarse sand, and grit suits them, and some growers find the addition of old cow manure and chopped sphagnum beneficial, but the plants are not fussy about the exact proportions. Watering should be ample during growth, but very scant, if at all, during dormancy. Yearly repotting is advisable, preferably before flowering and before the fragile new roots appear. The pan may be surfaced with a small-textured, prostrate moss. Propagation is easy by means of the small, wheat-like bulblets formed around the parent pseudo-bulb.

All bear flamboyant orchid-like flowers, 2″–4″ across, with five outstanding petals at the back and a long and prominent tube with wide, fringed lip, beautifully streaked and spotted with red or purple. The nomenclature has not yet had time to become assured, and the first two species to be available have already changed names and may be found in some catalogues under either. At the moment work is being done on the whole tangled subject.

The two species most generally grown (and obtainable) are:

p*****P. formosana** (formerly *P. pricei*). Formosa. One of the easiest to grow. Very large flower of light rose-magenta, having a pale tip with fringed edge and few reddish markings. Deep green pseudo-bulb. 2″. Early spring.

Polemonium

p***P. pricei** (formerly *P. formosana*). Formosa. Very similar but with dark, almost black pseudo-bulbs. 2″. Early spring.

These two are so variable and have been so confused in nomenclature, at times having been considered as variations within one species, that they are given separately, out of their alphabetical order. Other species grown, distinct in appearance, and with very varying times of flowering, are

p**P. hookeriana.** Himalaya. A charming little plant with 2″ flowers of rose-purple with yellow-throated white lip, flecked with orange and red. Small, deep green pseudo-bulbs, one of the hardiest. 2″–3″. Late May.

p**P. humilis.** Nepal. The earliest, producing its 2½″ flowers in very early spring. Variable in colour from white to pale purple, the lip being flecked with purple, orange, or brown. 2″–3″. January onwards, but mainly March–April.

p***P. limprichtii.** W. China. One of the most beautiful, having a rose flower, with lighter lip, much fringed, and heavily marked with reddish brown. Flowers last 3–4 weeks. 3″–4″. April. (Pl. 23)

p**P. praecox.** Formosa. A late-flowering plant with very large flowers, variable in colour, but opening pale pink and gradually deepening to a uniform shade, usually reddish-purple. The pseudo-bulb is large, rather flattened, dark green with purple blotches. 3″–4″. September–November.

p**P. yunnanensis.** W. China. Smaller than the foregoing, and the deepest in colour of the group, being a vivid purplish-red. Small pseudo-bulbs of pale olive green.

POLEMONIUM   *Polemoniaceae*

The Jacob's Ladders are in general too tall, but there are a few of the American mountain species which are delightful small plants, with the long pinnate or closely-whorled leaves and close heads of five-petalled, comparatively large, shallowly tubular flowers. Easy in most well-drained soils, but probably at their best in their second or third years as they later tend to become woody and untidy in growth. Seed.

P. carneum. Western N. America. The typical pinnate leaves, and flesh-pink flowers. 6″–8″. Summer.

P. confertum. Colorado, Utah. An attractive species, with whorled leaflets, and the characteristic slightly mauve-blue flowers. 6″–8″. Early summer.

***P. brandegei.** Rocky Mts. A miniature species with frail whorled leaves and clusters of clear yellow flowers. About 6″. Late spring.

214

P. pauciflorum. Mexico. Few long, tubular, drooping, deep yellow flowers. 8″–10″. Summer.

*P. viscosum. Rocky Mts. Perhaps the most delightful, making a woody rootstock with many ample, whorled, sticky leaves and stems of 4″–5″, bearing loose heads of comparatively large flowers of a lovely clear blue. Late spring.

POLYGALA *Polygalaceae*

The dwarf hardy evergreen Milkworts provide some good-tempered twiggy prostrate shrubs which are happy almost everywhere, and especially so when planted on or in a retaining wall, where they will occupy the crevices by their creeping stolons. In spring the box-like growth of small, oval, dark green leaves is covered by the numerous butterfly-like flowers—two of the sepals forming conspicuous wing-like bracts—and odd flowers appear throughout the summer and autumn.

*P. calcarea. Europe (including Gt. Britain). A delightful little plant from high downlands, forming a mat of spreading branches from a rosette of small spatulate leaves. It is covered in summer with spikes of small but brilliant blue flowers. It appreciates a chalky soil, but is not usually long-lived, being inclined to flower itself to death. 2″–4″. Summer. (Pl. 23)

P. chamaebuxus. Bastard Box. Mts. of Europe. A prostrate shrublet with many, much-branched, woody stems, and oval, dark green, box-like leaves. The two most distinct forms are the type, yellow with golden brown wings, and

*P. c. var **purpurea** with brilliant deep rose or magenta-pink wings. A delightful, floriferous and long-lived small shrub. The stoloniferous stems creep under the soil, and are easily detached as rooted cuttings. 4″–6″. Early spring and spasmodically later.

*P. vayredae. Spain. Related to *P. chamaebuxus* var. *purpurea* but a smaller neater plant with linear leaves and flowers more predominantly brilliant reddish-purple. 2″–4″. May.

P. vulgaris. Common milkwort. Europe (including Gt. Britain). The ubiquitous milkwort of the South Downs and elsewhere, a smaller, frailer edition of *P. calcarea*, with sprays of tiny flowers in white, pinkish mauve, or blue. Not easy in cultivation and short lived. 2″. All summer.

POLYGONATUM *Liliaceae*

The Solomon's Seals are handsome herbaceous perennials, with graceful arching stems, bearing well-spaced paired or alternate leaves, from the axils of which dangle the narrowly-tubular bell-shaped flowers.

Easily grown in almost any soil. Early summer flowering. Other dwarf species from Central Asia to excite the imagination, have been described but the two in general cultivation are

*P. hookeri. W. Szechwan, Tibet, Sikkim. A very dwarf species which shows its rosy-mauve flowers as it breaks through the soil in late spring. The little stem lengthens to about 4″, better displaying the erect, solitary flowers from the leaf axils. A charming alpine house plant. May.

P. officinale. Wild Solomon's Seal. Europe, including Britain. A miniature of the Common Solomon's Seal, with pendent greeny-white narrow bells from the leaf axils. It can grow to a foot, but in a poor woodland soil remains only about half that height. Spring.

POLYGONUM *Polygonaceae*

The common Bistort (*P. bistorta*), which incarnadines the alpine meadows in early summer when its myriads of plantain-like rosy flower spikes on their tall slender stems shimmer with every breeze, is too tall and rampant for our use, but a few species are more restrained and provide most welcome colour in the autumn, when the main flowering season is over.

P. affine. Nepal. Slender lanceolate leaves, radical or on prostrate spreading stems, and erect 6″ stems bearing dense spikes of rosy red flowers. Autumn.

P. vacciniifolium. Himalaya. A mat-forming perennial with pointed oval leaves and many erect slender 6″ spikes of many ⅓″ bright red flowers. Long flowering and suggestive of a miniature heather. Autumn.

POTENTILLA *Rosaceae*

The Cinquefoils form a large genus of herbaceous and shrubby plants with five-petalled (rarely four-) rose-like flowers, usually yellow, but occasionally white, pink, or red. Divided leaves, which may be palmate and long petioled, pinnate or whorled. The several prostrate small yellow species found throughout the Alps are very similar to each other, and not always easily distinguished. All are easy growing in an open, well drained position. Long flowering throughout most of the summer.

P. alba. Central and S. Europe. Prostrate, spreading, leaves palmate with three to seven (usually five) leaflets on long petioles. Rather large white flowers, up to 1″ across. 2″.

Pratia

P. alpestris. See **P. crantzii.**

P. aurea. European Alps, Pyrenees. Much-branched creeping stems, leaves palmate with five wedge-shaped leaflets, toothed at the extremities. Deep yellow flowers. 2″.

P. brauniana (*minima*). S. France. A tiny, woody, prostrate shrublet, slightly hairy leaves with three leaflets. Small yellow flowers. 1″–2″.

P. crantzii (*alpestris*). N. America, Asia, Europe. Tufted plant, five leaflets, erect stems with broad-petalled yellow flowers. 2″–6″.

*P. eriocarpa. Himalaya. A comparatively recent introduction, and a valuable plant, easy going, and forming a mat of small woody stems with many palmate grey-green leaves and studded throughout the summer by almost sessile 1″ flowers of clear yellow. Excellent for troughs. 1″–2″.

P. fragiformis. N.E. Asia. A handsome plant with rather thick, ternate, softly downy, deep green leaves and large yellow flowers. If it kept to the 6″ allowed by the catalogues it would be invaluable, but in most gardens it eventually approaches twice that height.

ᴅ***P. frigida.** European Alps. A delightful tiny woody shrublet from 7,000 ft. or more, forming congested small mats of hairy ternate leaves, which often take yellow and reddish tints in autumn, and almost stemless pale yellow flowers. A gem for the sink garden. 1″–1½″. Flowers spasmodically through summer.

P. minima. See **P. brauniana.**

*P. nitida. S. Europe, especially the Dolomites. The outstanding beauty of a charming and easy family, forming spreading mats of much-branched woody stems, with many shortly-stalked palmate leaves of three-toothed leaflets, the whole plant being silvery with adpressed hairs. Large flowers, up to 1″, of clear, wild-rose pink, which can vary to deep rose or, occasionally, white. Likes lime and grows easily, but is sometimes rather temperamental about flowering in cultivation. 1″–2″. Early summer. (Pl. 23)

P. tonguei. A hybrid, probably natural, with dark green branching stems of up to 8″–10″, and striking flowers of apricot, with a crimson blotch. Long flowering.

P. verna. Temperate W. and Central Europe (including Gt. Britain). Mat forming, with stalked, palmate leaves (five to seven leaflets) and ½″ yellow flowers. Variable in size, and in the miniature *P. v.* forma *nana* charming for trough or sink. (Pl. 23)

PRATIA *Campanulaceae*

A genus of creeping plants allied to Lobelia, usually with inconspicuous flowers, but bearing coloured fruits.

Primula

P. angulata. New Zealand. A mat of slender, pinkish, branching stems with alternate, almost round leaves, and with white purple-streaked starry flowers of about ½″. Purple berries. 1″–2″. Spring.

P. treadwellii of gardens appears to be a good selected form of the last plant, with larger flowers and brighter berries, and should be **P. a.** 'TREADWELLII'.

P. repens. Falkland Is. Very similar to the foregoing, but with kidney-shaped leaves. Flowers white, tinged violet; purple fruits. 1″–2″. June–October.

PRIMULA *Primulaceae*

This immense genus of over 500 species, in addition to many hybrids, both natural and man-made, has been divided botanically into no less than thirty sections. Most of the species are hardy, and these are almost without exception very desirable in the rock garden or alpine house. All have flowers on the plan of the native wild primrose, *P. vulgaris* (*acaulis*), with five-rounded (sometimes indented) petals spreading at right angles to the corolla tube, which rises above the five-cleft green calyx. The flowers are on single scapes (as in the Primrose), or in simple umbels (as in the cowslip, *P. elatior*), or in rising tiers of umbels as in the Candelabra section (*P. aurantiaca*). Partly for the convenience of the many who spend their holidays in the European Alps, and partly because cultural needs tend to be so divided, it has seemed most useful to give representative selections divided into European primulas, Asiatic primulas, and American primulas.

EUROPEAN PRIMULAS

These are, without exception, hardy, and most will succeed in any well-drained gritty soil with plenty of humus. Except in a few noted cases, they will tolerate lime, even welcome it. All are spring flowering. With few exceptions (notably *P. auricula, marginata, rubra,* and *viscosa,* which are almost invariably found in crowded rosettes along rock crevices) they are plants of the dense fine sward above the tree line, where their roots, with those of the dwarf grasses and other small plants, make a close fibrous mat. Although most prefer an open, sunny position, they must be protected from becoming dried out in

218

Primula

summer, and one isolated day of burning sunshine taking us unawares is enough to scorch to death even the accommodating *P. rubra*.

ᴘ***P. allionii.*** French and Italian Maritime Alps. Rare in nature, but a beautiful and popular plant for the alpine house as, although quite hardy, it seems to resent winter damp on its close rosettes of 1″ long, broadly spatulate, slightly sticky leaves. The flowers are large, 1″ across, on very short scapes, and a healthy cushion may be completely hidden by the clear pink blossoms. In cultivation there is much variation, in shade from the typical full pink down to white, and in size of flower. Gritty soil with lime and humus, appropriately wedged between pieces of rock. 1″–2″. March–April. (Pl. 23)

P. altaica. Various early pink primroses are grown under this name in gardens, especially *P. amoena*.

P. amoena. Caucasus, N.E. Turkey. One of the earliest and best-tempered species, with crinkled leaves and mauve-pink "Primroses". Very early flowering (February–March). Vigorous anywhere, but appreciates leaf-mould and half-shade. 5″–6″. (Pl. 24)

P. auricula. European Alps. The wild Auricula is widespread, usually being found in rocky crevices, making flat rosettes of 2″–4″ oval leaves, narrowing into the petiole, of solid texture, and, with few local exceptions, heavily powdered with farina. Although there are very distinct geographical variations in the species, the flowers, in 2″–6″ umbels, are always clear yellow. Spring.

> ***P. a.*** var. **balbisii,** from the Dolomites, is a small version, having leaves without farina, and 1″–3″ umbels of rather bell-shaped flowers of a deeper yellow.

> ***P. a.*** 'Blairside Yellow' is a charming miniature, a small neat plant of 2″.

The well-known old garden Auriculas, the Yellow and Red Dusty Millers, both sturdy plants with heavily-powdered foliage, and full-flowered umbels of clear yellow and rusty-red respectively, have obviously *P. auricula* in their long ancestry.

P. × berninae (*rubra × viscosa*). A lovely natural hybrid, found where the two species overlap, especially in the district around the Bernina Pass. Combines the best points of both parents, having large, deep rose flowers over neat, sturdy rosettes. Usually offered in the selected form *P. × b.* 'Windrush' 2″–3″. Early spring.

P. × bilekii (*minima × rubra*). Forms a mat or low cushion of rounded, toothed leaves, in 1″ wide rosettes, and bears many large, almost sessile, deep pink flowers. 2″. April.

P. carniolica. Alps of Carinthia and Carniola. 2″–3″ wide rosettes of glossy widely-oval, sometimes bluntly-pointed leaves and umbels (usually

Primula

few-flowered) of rosy-purple, rather flat flowers, with a white throat. 3″–4″. Spring and summer.

*P. clusiana. Tyrol. A rosette of more upstanding 2″–3″ leaves, broadly lanceolate, and often with wavy or slightly incurved edges. Rosy-mauve flowers, rather large, usually only 2–3 in an umbel. 3″–4″. Early summer.

P. farinosa. All European countries except Greece and Ireland, and having very near relations in most of the rest of the temperate parts of the northern hemisphere, especially Japan and N. America; also found in the Andes. The little Bird's Eye Primula is a plant of the high downlands, inextricably mixed with the fine alpine turf and often at its finest in slightly marshy positions. Lovely in all forms, with its rosettes of lanceolate leaves, rounded at the tips and heavily powdered beneath, and erect powdered 2″–6″ stalk with its umbel of clear, clean pink, with a yellow eye. It is variable, according to position and locality, in its height, and the size and depth of colour of its flowers. Although not usually very long-lived, it makes a delightful plant for the stony scree or deep sink (with added humus). In winter dies back to a resting bud. 2″–6″. March–April. (Pl. 24)

P. frondosa. Balkans. In effect a sturdier edition of *P. farinosa*, and rather more permanent. 5″–7″. March–April.

P. glutinosa. Tyrol and Central Alps. Fiercely lime-hating, this little species, with upright 1″–2″ dark green, glossy, strap-shaped leaves, may be found in the close turf in non-lime districts. It is almost impossible to grow in cultivation, and not very free-flowering in nature, but its umbels of semi-drooping small, rather bell-shaped flowers are the nearest to a deep true blue of any of the European primulas. 2″–3″. May.

P. halleri (*longiflora*). Switzerland, N. Italy, etc. In habit like a taller *P. farinosa*, with larger leaves and flowers, but distinguished by the abnormally long corolla tube. Variable in height from 3″–6″, and in colour from clear pink to a beautiful deep rose. April–May.

P. hirsuta. *See* **P. rubra** (p. 222).

P. integrifolia. Pyrenees, Switzerland. Another small mat-former, with 1″–1½″ strap-shaped, glossy leaves, and large, almost sessile, rosy-purple flowers. Usually abundant when found, as in the Engadine where high slopes are purple with it in season. 1″–2″. April–May.

P. juliae. Caucasus. This delightful small primrose was only introduced into cultivation during the early years of this century, and is now almost completely overshadowed by its many hybrids with *P. vulgaris* (*P.* 'JULIANA', *P.* 'WANDA', etc.) which, easy and floriferous though they are, lack the charm of *P. juliae* itself, which makes flat mats of creeping, woody stems with many neat, dark green, round or kidney-shaped leaves, and bears solitary red-purple flowers with a yellow eye. Rather damp position. 1″–1½″. March–April. (Pl. 24)

*P. marginata. Maritime and Cottian Alps. Though having only a small distribution in nature, this species, in one or other of its many forms, is one of the most valued primulas for rock garden or alpine house. In common they

Primula

have heavily-powdered oval leaves, narrowing to the petiole, and more or less widely or closely serrated at the edges, so that they are most welcome for the beauty of their leaves alone, the perfect foil for the flowers, which are in shades of cool bluish-mauve. Several leaf forms and some plants with deeper mauve-blue flowers have been given varietal names.

P. m. 'LINDA POPE', an old plant of unknown origin, but probably a marginata hybrid, has perhaps more than any other the combination of lovely jagged silvery leaf with large rounded flowers of a particularly bland and luminous mauve.

All are easy in any limy scree, and appreciate mortar rubble. They do not increase very rapidly, but seed germinates well and may give an acceptable variation from the parent. So-called white forms have hitherto hardly justified the name or had squinny flowers, but nothing can be more beautiful than the mauve of the type. Among other beautiful named forms **P.m.** 'DRAKES FORM' (Pl. 24) has particularly lovely foliage and **P.m.** 'COERULEA', good, almost blue flowers; **P.m.** 'HOLDEN CLOUGH' is a particularly neat form with small, regularly serrated powdered leaves.

P. × marven (*venusta × marginata*). A beautiful but not always very robust hybrid, with rather mealy, more or less serrated foliage and umbels of deep blue-purple flowers with a conspicuous white eye. Limy scree, with humus. Lovely in the alpine house. 6″–7″. April–May.

P. minima. Central Europe, especially the Dolomites. A very distinct tiny primula of the high alpine turf, indifferent to lime in the soil, and forming rosettes of glossy 1″–1½″ strap- or wedge-shaped leaves, sharply serrated into three or four points across the blunt end. Large (1″) flowers of a good rose-pink, with petals so deeply indented as almost to appear double in number. Sink, or crevice, in scree with plenty of humus. Not free-flowering in cultivation. 1″–1½″. April–May.

P. palinuri. S. Italy. Interesting by reason of its colour, a rich deep yellow, but the several flowers in the umbel are funnel-shaped, and seem small in proportion to the sturdy scape, which rises from a rosette of long (6″ or more) narrowly spatulate leaves with serrated edge, and without farina. Best in the alpine house. 6″–8″. April.

*P. × pubescens. The comprehensive name given to a wide variety of primulas, hybrids of *P. auricula*, usually with *P. rubra*, but occasionally with *P. viscosa*. Some are natural hybrids, and some of garden origin. They are extremely variable in size, and in the amount of farina on the leaves, and may occur in almost any colour. The following are old-established plants, but still vie with any later introductions, which may be found in quantity in catalogues. All flower in early spring.

'ALBA' (sometimes offered as *nivalis*). A very compact plant with globular heads of many pure white flowers. 3″–4″.

'FALDONSIDE'. A neat growing plant with full umbels of bright crimson flowers. Rich scree. Not too permanent. 4″. (Pl. 25)

221

Primula

'MRS. J. H. WILSON'. An old favourite, very free-flowering and of a good constitution. Violet. 4″–5″.

'RUFUS'. A striking plant, of sturdy habit, with rich, almost brick-red flowers. 4″–5″.

'THE GENERAL'. Beautiful velvety terra-cotta flowers. Rather scarce.

With the exception of one or two of the deep reds, they are all easygoing plants in any well-drained gritty soil, and are all very floriferous. They add beauty and colour to the rock garden or alpine house over a considerable period in spring.

P. rubra (*hirsuta*). Central Alps, Pyrenees. One of the most delightful and free flowering, as it is the commonest primula of the Alps, where it fills the rocky crevices, especially on granitic formations. Curiously seldom seen in gardens, as it is good-tempered and free-flowering, although slow to increase except by seed. Tightly-packed rosettes of slightly sticky, long-oval or spatulate leaves of 1″–3″, and many umbels of clear pink flowers, varying in size and depth of colour, and often with a distinct white eye. Early flowering—in the Alps before the main display in late June, and therefore sometimes missed in its full splendour. 2″–4″. March–April.

P. scotica. N. Scotland. In effect a miniature *P. farinosa*, with umbels of small, but well-rounded, flowers of deep purple, with a yellow or white eye. An enchanting little plant, but not easy. A cool, but not sunless, position in leafy scree suits it. Although not long-lived, it is easy from seed. 2″. Late spring.

P. spectabilis. E. Alps. From a rosette of rather fleshy, long-oval leaves with a cartilaginous edge, up to 4″ long, rise the scapes of few-flowered umbels of 1″ wide, flat, pink flowers. 2″–5″. May.

P. tyrolensis. S. Tyrol. A very local small primula, making neat rosettes of small, round, glandular leaves, slightly serrated. Comparatively large pink flowers, singly or in pairs on ¾″ scapes. 1″. April–May.

P. × venusta (*auricula × carniolica*). Variable, with flowers of crimson, purple, or brownish-red, and slightly farinose leaves. In its best forms a good, compact, free-flowering plant. 3″–4″. May.

P. viscosa. Pyrenees, Savoy, Switzerland. Always found on granitic formations, this makes a rather lax rosette of long-oval leaves, of a dull, dark green, and slightly sticky, up to 6″ long. The deep violet, rather funnel-shaped flowers are borne in a one-sided umbel, which is very characteristic of the species. 5″–8″. May.

P. vulgaris (*acaulis*). W. and S. Europe (including Gt. Britain). Our own wild primrose, with solitary pale sulphur-yellow flowers with a deep golden-orange eye. One of the most lovely of all primulas and the earliest, a stray flower or two often opening by the turn of the year. When allowed to naturalize in leafy, cool soil around the rock garden, it will produce white hybrids with an even deeper eye, or various shades of pale pink, but none excel

Primula

the type. Its foliage is apt to make a rather dishevelled clump later in the year, otherwise it would be welcome among the choicest plants. 4″–5″. From winter into spring.

ASIATIC PRIMULAS

During the last hundred years, and particularly the first third of the twentieth century, a spate of fresh introductions has reached us through the plant-collecting expeditions of Lowndes, Kingdon-Ward, Ludlow and Sheriff, Stainton, Sykes and Williams, and others, in the Himalaya and Central China. The Candelabra section are hardly mentioned here, as they are mostly too tall, especially when growing in their favourite position of moist, part-shaded sparse woodland glens, when their graceful spires of tier-upon-tier of yellow, buff, pink, copper, and red flowers may rise from 1–2 ft. or even more. Perhaps the most notable additions have been among the near relations of what was grown for many years as *P. winteri* (now *edgeworthii*), until this century the only one of its section (Petiolares) in cultivation. These are very beautiful, rosette-forming plants with widely-oval leaves, narrowing to the petiole, often of somewhat thin texture, and with more or less serrated edges. They die back to a resting bud in winter, as do most of the other rosette-forming species from these areas. These all require overhead protection in winter, except where otherwise noted. It is only possible to give a small selection from the scores which have been, if only temporarily, in cultivation, and which include several enchanting miniatures of exacting temperaments. They require a well-drained, gritty soil, with plenty of humus, and a cool, half-shady position. Most are difficult to keep in good health in the south, but are much more amenable to cultivation in Scotland and the north of England, where they not only may flourish out of doors, but are larger and sturdier plants. Propagation by division and by seed, which in the Petiolares section should be sown as soon as ripe, even when still green in the capsule.

*P. aurantiaca. Yunnan. One of the most dwarf of the Candelabra group, with rosettes of narrowly-oval, slightly-toothed leaves and two to six whorls of rather small flowers of reddish-orange. Sometimes forms adventitious growths on the whorls of flowers, from which it may be propagated, or by seed. 8″–12″. July.

ᴅ**P. aureata.** Sikkim. Petiolares Section. A rather crumpled rosette of densely farinose oval or broadly spatulate leaves and short umbels of velvety

223

Primula

pale yellow flowers deeply flushed with orange from the centre half-way up the corolla lobes. 3″. Spring.

D***P. a.** forma, more lately introduced, has a better constitution, and is rather similar, but with paler, cream, orange-flushed flowers. 2″-3″. Spring.

P***P. bhutanica.** Bhutan. Perhaps the most lovely of the Petiolares group, with ample, irregularly-toothed leaves and flowers which are near an ice-blue, with a green eye. 3″-4″. March–April.

P***P. bracteosa.** Bhutan. Another Petiolarid, with cordate or spatulate, serrated leaves, and pale lilac flowers, with a yellow eye. After flowering, bracts form on a short scape, and if pegged down will form new plants. 3″-4″. March.

***P. capitata.** Sikkim, S.E. Tibet, Bhutan. Forms a crowded globular head of violet flowers above a rosette of oblong-lanceolate leaves, slightly farinose above, white backed. The best form is *sub.-sp. mooreana*, with rather deeper, more open flowers. Easy in well-drained soil in part shade, and a handsome plant. 6″-12″. July–October. Useful as a later flowerer.

P. chionantha. Yunnan. Rather tall (variable up to 12″ or more if in congenial moist conditions), but a fine plant, with bluntly-pointed oval leaves, narrowing to the petiole and slightly farinose, and heads of large, fragrant, white flowers.

***P. clarkei.** Kashmir. A delightful small primula of recent introduction, whose bright, rose-pink flowers are produced, singly or in very short umbels, before the leaves. These are glossy and deep green, circular to broadly ovate, cordate at the base. Half shade (or alpine house) in leafy, well-drained soil. 1″-1½″. Early March–April.

***P. denticulata.** Himalaya. Very well known, but not so often grown as its floriferousness and hearty good nature warrant. From rosettes of long-ovate or spatulate leaves rise many sturdy stems bearing large globular heads of light mauve flowers. The whole plant is powdered with farina. 4″-10″. Long-flowering, March-May. (Pl. 24.) Many shades from white to deep purple have appeared, and also pink forms up to a glowing ruby, 'PRITCHARD'S RUBY'. These appear in catalogues under self-explanatory varietal names.

P. d. var. **cachemiriana** has deep purple flowers, and is rather later.

***P. edgeworthii.** W. Himalaya. One of the most lovely of the Petiolares group, and the longest in cultivation (as *P. winteri*). The well-powdered, rather broadly spatulate leaves have wavy, dentate edges. The large flowers, in full umbels only just above the foliage, have slightly-serrated petals, which shade to a white eye. The type is a rather variable mauve—a beautiful cool blue-mauve at best—and there is a white form, variable in texture, but at its best the petals are like thick, white kid. One of the easier of the Petiolarids, in cool, leafy, well-drained soil, or in a crevice in the alpine house. In any situation, the fat resting buds require overhead protection from damp in winter. 3″. Very early flowering, from January onwards.

P. erratica (*loczii, sertulum*). Kansu, Szechwan. Rarely now seen, but

21

Omphalogramma vinciflorum
Oxalis inops
Papaver alpinum

Orphanidesia gaultherioides
Oxalis lobata
Penstemon pinifolius
(Centre, *Veronica teucrium var.*)

22

Penstemon rupicola
Phlox nana var. ensifolia
Phlox subulata

Phlox adsurgens
Phlox nivalis 'Gladwyn'
Phyteuma comosum

Primula

grown fairly widely earlier in the century. Rather like a coarser and somewhat anaemic *P. farinosa*, but interesting because spreading by leafy stolons of 4″–6″ from the axils of the leaves. 3″–4″. Early summer, often starting in April.

P. fauriae. Japan. Like a neat, compact *P. farinosa*, but with golden farina. 1″–3″. Early summer.

P. forrestii. N.W. Yunnan. A plant with almost woody rhizomes and very wrinkled leaves, covered with glandular hairs, bluntly-pointed oval on 4″ petioles. The flowers, in one-sided umbels, are a deep yellow with an orange eye. It seems to prefer a rocky crevice, in limestone, where there is perfect drainage, but is not easy. 6″–9″. May–June.

p*****P. gracilipes.** Sikkim. Another of the Petiolares group, with leaves without farina, and wavy serrated edges. Flowers pale pink. 3″. Spring. (Pl. 24)

P. heucherifolia. W. Szechwan. A leafy plant, superficially rather like Cortusa, with crumpled, rather hairy leaves on 2″–5″ petioles, and umbels of pinkish-mauve to deep purple flowers. 6″–12″. Early summer.

*****P. hyacintha.** A sturdy garden hybrid, with *P. marginata* in its parentage, and not to be confused with the species *P. hyacinthina*. Large, deep green, smooth leaves without farina, and umbels of large and solid flowers of a deep purple-blue. A handsome plant. 6″–8″. Spring.

P. hyacinthina. S.E. Tibet. Rosettes of upright oblong leaves and small violet flowers on disproportionately long pedicels (up to 12″). Difficult and impermanent, and only mentioned to avoid confusion with the foregoing.

P. melanops. S.W. Szechwan. Like a smaller *P. chionantha*, with long, narrow, powdered leaves, and umbels of pointed-petalled flowers of rich purple, with an almost black eye. 8″. May–June.

p*****P. nutans.** Yunnan, Szechwan. One of the most beautiful of Primulas, but not usually long-lived, although it is not actually monocarpic as was originally thought. From a basal rosette of rather upright, softly-hairy leaves rise the tall pedicels bearing umbels of rather pendent, funnel-shaped flowers nearly 1″ across, and of a lovely, luminous bluish-mauve, the whole inflorescence suggesting an aetherial pagoda. Not difficult in cool, well-drained soil, with plenty of humus. Seed usually sets and germinates well, although not all the seedlings survive. 8″–12″. June.

p*****P. ×'PANDORA'.** Of the various hybrids made between members of the Petiolares group, this (*P. scapigera* × *P. edgeworthii*) is one of the most attractive and permanent. It is intermediate between its parents, and rather more freely growing than either. The flowers are a pinkish-mauve. 3″–4″. March.

dp*****P. pusilla.** Nepal, Sikkim, Bhutan. A delightful tiny Primula, making mats and mounds of rosettes of slightly hairy, bluntly-pointed, lanceolate leaves of 1″ or little more, with large (for the size of the plant) pale violet-blue flowers with white hairs in the throat, borne singly or in pairs. Rather a damp, but well-drained soil, with overhead protection from winter wet, or alpine house in a partly-shaded position. 1″–2″. Early summer.

Primula

P. pycnoloba. W. Szechwan. An oddity among Primulas, with coarse, hairy leaves, almost suggesting a small burdock, and drooping umbels of curious flowers having remarkable calyces with five pointed, fringed lobes, much longer than the small enclosed reddish corollas. Woodland conditions. 6″–8″. June–July.

P. reidii. N.W. Himalaya. A very lovely plant, with primrose-like leaves, but softly furry with long hairs. The fragrant, semi-pendent, ivory-white flowers, in few-flowered umbels, are large, and widely bell-shaped. 3″. May.

p*P. r. var. **williamsii.** A later introduction, and even more beautiful, being larger in all its parts, and having even more fragrant flowers in soft shades of blue. 5″–6″.

p*P. **reinii.** Japan. A small charmer with sparse rosettes of round or kidney-shaped velvety leaves on 1″–2″ petioles and few-flowered umbels of large rose or pale lilac flowers, with a yellow eye, held on slender pedicels well above the foliage. Scree with plenty of humus, and part shade. Dies down in winter and, although hardy, is safer in the alpine house. 4″. Early spring.

dP. **reptans.** Kashmir. The tiniest of all primulas, making rhizomatous mats of almost sessile, round, deeply-serrated deep green leaves only ¼″ across, and bearing, not profusely even in nature, still less in gardens, solitary, stemless mauve to purple flowers. Very gritty leaf-mould, or peaty scree, and a cool position in summer. When not in flower of no height at all. Rare and difficult. Summer.

*P. **rosea.** N.W. Himalaya. When grown in the cool, damp site it appreciates, such as the margin of a pond, this is one of the most showy of all Primulas when, in early spring, its startlingly deep carmine-rose flowers begin to unfold from their winter resting-buds. Of sturdy habit, each bud produces a forest of tall, loose-flowered umbels. After flowering, which commences at 2″–3″, the flower stems elongate and the smooth, blunt-tipped, lanceolate leaves eventually lengthen to 8″ or so. Increases in moist leafy soil, and is easily divided. Easy from seed which gives some small variations. Selected forms have been given varietal names, of which the best known is *P. r.* 'VISSER DE GEER' ('DELIGHT') with flowers of extra size and depth of colour. Eventually 6″–8″. Flowers from April over a long period.

p*P. **scapigera.** W. Himalaya. Another of the Petiolares group, a more robust plant than most, with wide, dentate leaves without farina, and mauve-pink flowers. Nearly as early flowering as *P. edgeworthii.* 2″–3″. February onwards.

*P. **sieboldii.** Japan. An old-established plant, which has suffered an undeserved lull in popularity. With softly-crinkled, scalloped oval leaves on long petioles, and loose-flowered umbels of large fringed, pure white to deep rose flowers, at sight it suggests greenhouse treatment. It is actually quite hardy, dying down completely in winter. Leafy, well-drained soil in a cool position. 6″–8″. Early summer.

dP*P. **sonchifolia.** Yunnan, Tibet, N.W. Burma. One of the most spectacular of the Petiolares group, forming a huge, bulb-like resting bud which

226

Primula

may be 1″ across. It is a difficult plant to keep in the south, but where suited, in well-drained but rather rich soil, and with overhead protection in winter for the resting crown, it forms a very sturdy plant, with short umbels of large, almost blue flowers with a yellow eye. Eventually the long, oval leaves, crinkled and dentate at the edges, elongate to 10″ or so. Seed sown as soon as ripe, while still green in the capsule. Flowers at 3″–4″. February–March.

P. strumosa. Bhutan, Nepal, N.E. Tibet. Neither easy nor widely procurable, but mentioned as being one of the few Petiolares primulas with yellow flowers. It has the general habit of the group, and requires the same conditions, but the lanceolate, slightly farinose leaves are small compared with the 6″–8″ umbel of 1″ wide yellow flowers with a deeper eye. June.

P. vialii (*littoniana*). N.W. Yunnan, S.W. Szechwan. Tall, usually over a foot, but mentioned as one of the most distinctive of all primulas, resembling an elegant Red Hot Poker, with narrow spires of small, lavender, pointed-petalled flowers, scarlet in the unopened buds at the tip of the spike, arising from tufts of erect narrow lanceolate leaves. Light rich soil. Early summer.

AMERICAN PRIMULAS

Compared with the inexhaustible wealth of Central Asia, the American mountain primulas are sparse indeed. There are, however, a few which are near kindred of the Bird's Eye Primula (*P. farinosa*), a few tiny species which are attractive miniatures, but difficult in cultivation, and one unique in the genus by being almost shrubby. Although, with the exception of the last, they are at present barely grown in this country, a few are described to show what fresh fields are opening up with the recent introductions of American seed, mainly collected in the Rocky Mountains. All are safest in well-drained scree, with plenty of humus in the shape of leaf-mould and/or peat, and protected from scorching and drought. Although hardy, overhead protection from damp is advisable in winter. Seed germinates fairly well, but the small species need constant care to preserve until flowering size.

P. angustifolia. Rocky Mts. Narrow strap-shaped rather glossy leaves of less than 1″, a few purplish-pink flowers borne just above them. Mat-forming if it lives long enough. Alpine house because of its small size. 1″. Summer.

ᴅ***P. ellisiae.** N.W. America. A sturdy plant with fleshy, rather narrow leaves, sometimes slightly farinose, and stout scapes bearing umbels of mauve flowers with a deeper eye. In nature prefers a rather damp spot. Makes an attractive pan for the alpine house, where it requires plenty of water during the growing season. Sometimes considered a sub-species of the very similar *P. rusbyi* from New Mexico. 6″–7″. May–June.

P. mistassinica. Newfoundland to Alaska. The smallest of the American

Bird's Eye Primulas, like a tiny *P. farinosa*, and with the same habit of dying back to a resting bud in winter. Slightly and variably farinose. Has the habit of producing new plants at intervals along its shallow fibrous roots. Pale pink flowers. 2″–4″.

P. parryi. Colorado. Scarce in cultivation, but quite a striking primula, with the narrow, deep green, smooth leaves and general habit of a Dodecatheon. Deep magenta-pink flowers in umbels on 6″–12″ pedicels. Not easy, but most hopeful in a deep, well-drained mixture of loam, leaf-mould, and sand, in a cool position. May.

P. rusbyi. See **P. ellisiae.**

P. specuicola. Rocky Mts. Another of the Farinosa group, but larger and stouter than *P. mistassinica.* and farinose throughout. Very near the European *P. frondosa.* 6″. Early summer.

*P. suffrutescens. California. Almost shrubby, making stiff, semi-prostrate branches, closely set (especially towards the tips) with 1″ long, narrowly spoon-shaped leaves, serrated at the tips. Umbels of deep rose flowers, ¾″ across, with yellow throat and tube. A beautiful plant, and not difficult in sandy, peaty scree. 4″. June–July.

PRUNELLA *Labiatae*

The Self-heals, often still known by the pre-Linnean name of Brunella, are all really variants of the well-known native weed, *P. vulgaris,* which, considered dispassionately, is an attractive little plant, with its oval leaves and close sturdy 4″ spikes of whorled, hooded flowers of blue-purple, but is disqualified by its invasive character especially in damp sites where it quickly takes possession, by seed, and even more by tough rooting stolons. Colour forms of pink, mauve, and white are offered which are claimed to be more restrained, and these are pleasant and useful when they are kept in control.

P. grandiflora. Europe. Much the habit of *P. vulgaris,* but with larger flowers (over 1″ long) of purple-violet. Colour forms are 'PINK LOVELINESS' and 'WHITE LOVELINESS'.

PRUNUS *Rosaceae*

Only two of this large genus are sufficiently dwarf to be considered here.

*P. prostrata. E. Mediterranean. This very attractive twiggy shrub has

Pteridophyllum, Pterocephalus, Ptilotrichum, Pulmonaria

small ovate toothed leaves and, in late spring, many small clear pink flowers. The small red fruits are seldom produced in cultivation. On the rock garden it needs a sunny position in well-drained soil. It makes a delightful pan for the alpine house. Up to 12".

P. tenella (*nana, Amygdalus nana*). This very polymorphic shrub, which may in some cases reach 3 ft. or more, is, in its dwarf forms of 12" or so, a delightful plant in late spring, when its slender, wand-like branches are wreathed with bunches of small bright pink flowers for most of their length. It is, however, invasive by means of underground stolons. Fruit rarely formed in cultivation. May.

PTERIDOPHYLLUM *Papaveraceae Monotypic*

P. racemosum. Japan. This is a delightful woodlander, making a rosette of fern-like leaves, with many oval, pinnate leaflets. The small white, four-petalled, cup-shaped flowers are freely borne on branched spikes. Shady woodland soil. 6". May.

PTEROCEPHALUS *Dipsaceae*

These Scabious-like plants include one of the most attractive and easygoing later flowering plants for the rock garden.

*P. parnassi (*Scabiosa pterocephalus*). Greece. A tufted plant with short, prostrate stems and velvety grey, widely club-shaped toothed leaves, with 1" wide scabious-like flower-heads of pinkish-mauve. 3"–4". Summer onwards over a long period.

PTILOTRICHUM *Cruciferae*

P. spinosum (*Alyssum spinosum*). S. Europe. A spiny bushlet of dense, much-branched, wiry stems with many small, hoary, pointed-oval leaves, and small Alyssum-like heads of tiny white flowers. 6"–9". June–July.

*P. s. 'Roseum' (*Alyssum spinosum* 'Roseum'). Should, if possible, be seen in flower before introducing, as most forms are a very pale pink; but it can be had in a really deep rose, when the contrast with the congested grey stems and foliage makes it a charming small shrublet for sink or garden. (Pl. 2)

PULMONARIA *Boraginaceae*

The Lungworts, although their coarse bristly foliage debars them from the choicer parts of the rock garden, are useful in odd half-shady

229

Pulsatilla

corners by reason of their dependability in providing their drooping clusters of tubular flowers in early spring. The different species are very similar, and hybridize readily, but the colour forms at least are distinct.

P. angustifolia (*azurea*). Central Europe. The narrowly elliptic leaves are unspotted, and the flowers bright blue, from pink buds. 'MAWSON'S VAR.', has particularly rich blue flowers. 5"–7". February–March.

P. officinalis. Lungwort, Soldiers and Sailors. Europe. Basal leaves, cordate and wider than the foregoing, coarsely bristled and irregularly spotted with white. Flowers pink, becoming purple and then blue. 5"–7". February–March.

P. rubra. Carpathians, Balkan Peninsula. Softly hairy green leaves, flowers a very distinct brick-red. Rather later than the foregoing. 6"–7". March–April.

PULSATILLA *Ranunculaceae*

A lovely genus closely related to Anemone, under which name most of the species have until recently been included. As in Anemone, the flowers have petalloid sepals, the petals being absent. They all have more or less hairy, stiff, ferny foliage which, with the exception of *P. vernalis*, dies down during the winter. Easy from seed, especially when sown as soon as ripe, but most species take some years to attain flowering size. An open position and well-drained soil with humus suits them. Here they will be long-lived when once well established.

D***P. alpina** (*Anemone alpina*). Mts. of Europe from Spain to the Caucasus. A sturdy plant with stiff, hairy, carrot-like basal leaves, and a whorl of similar leaves about two-thirds of the way up each stout stem bearing a solitary, pure white flower up to 2" across, with six or more widely-opened sepals and a central boss of golden stamens. Difficult to transplant owing to its tough rootstock, and takes long to attain flowering size from seed. This is probably why this lovely plant is seldom seen in gardens. 5"–12". May.

D***P. a. var. sulphurea** (*sulphurea, Anemone sulphurea*). Mts. of Central Europe. The yellow counterpart of the foregoing and until lately considered a separate species. One of the most handsome of all anemones, especially when it is seen dappling a mountainside with its flowers, 2" or more across, of a luminous, deep sulphur yellow. Variable in height with position and altitude. A little later than *P. alpina*. 3"–12". May–June.

P. caucasica. Caucasus. Like a very miniature *P. a.* var. *sulphurea*, but variable in size and shade of flower from good to meagre. 3"–4". May.

***P. halleri** (*Anemone halleri*). Switzerland, Austria. The Continental near

Puschkinia

relation of our native Pasque Flower (*P. vulgaris*), but rather larger flowers of a deeper purple. 5″–8″. May–June.

*P. hirsutissima. United States and Siberia. Very similar to our own *P. vulgaris*, but larger and rather bushier, and with even longer, silkier hairs. Flowers light to medium purple. 4″–9″. April.

P. occidentalis (*Anemone occidentalis*). W.N. America. An American counterpart of *P. alpina*, with smaller, more cup-shaped flowers of white or pinkish. 4″–12″. June.

*P. vernalis (*Anemone vernalis*). Mts. of Europe. One of the loveliest of all alpine flowers. From the almost prostrate rosette of harsh, hairy, lacinated leaves rises the short, sturdy stem, with a whorl of almost linear leaves 1″ or so below the single, chalice-like flower, 2″ or more across, pure, solid white (or sometimes pink-flushed) with central boss of golden stamens. It is almost as beautiful (and very photogenic) when in bud, as stem-leaves and outer calyx (which has opalescent hues of bluish-mauve) are all silvery with long silky hairs. 3″–4″. In the wild, as soon as the snow melts. In gardens, April–May. (Pl. 25)

*P. vulgaris (*Anemone pulsatilla*). Pasque Flower. Europe (including Gt. Britain). As seen on the chalky downs in England, where it is still locally to be found, this is a small plant with roughly hairy, lacinated leaves in single (or more rarely two or three) rosettes and whorl of leafy bracts on 1″ stems under a charming, wide open starry flower with six widely or more narrowly oval petals of rich purple, the height at flowering being only 2″–3″, although the stem elongates to 5″–6″ as the seeds are ripening. The cultivated forms, however, make sturdy bushy clumps of many rosettes, from which rise one or two dozen, or even more, 10″–12″ stems of showy, purple, more cup-shaped flowers. (Pl. 25.) This is a very good-tempered, long-lived, and beautiful plant, with cultivated forms varying from deep red, 'RUBRA', to pale shell pink, 'MRS VAN DER ELST' and white. Easy from seed, sown as soon as possible, but seedlings from named forms will vary in colour. April–May.

A magnificent pulsatilla which obtained a First Class Certificate at an R.H.S. Show in 1963, under the name of *P. vulgaris* 'BUDA PEST', bears very many large cup-shaped flowers of a luminous, almost opalescent pale blue. This was later identified at Kew as a form of *P. halleri*, but has also been known as *P. grandis*, and has been offered as *P.* 'BUDA PEST'. It *is* variable, however, and should be chosen in flower if one hopes to obtain anything like the breathtaking beauty of the plant shown.

PUSCHKINIA *Liliaceae*

A very small genus of dwarf bulbs closely related to Scilla, and having similar pendent bell-shaped five-petalled flowers. The only species in cultivation is the pleasant little *P. scilloides*, with 3″–5″ stems bearing five or six flowers of palest blue, with a greenish-blue stripe down the middle of each petal. March.

PYROLA *Pyrolaceae*

The Wintergreens are attractive plants which revel in mossy, shady positions in light woodland. They are all impatient of disturbance, but the tough, smooth foliage is so persistent that it is often a year or more before one discovers that the move has been fatal. The species are very similar in general appearance, having rounded basal leaves on long petioles and sturdy erect stems bearing spikes of almost globular five-petalled flowers, which persist for a long time, and suggest a very solid Lily of the Valley. The more usual species, in the wild and in cultivation, are:

P. minor. Europe (including Gt. Britain), N. America. A charming little plant, the smallest of the genus, with little spikes of pendent globes, white tinged pink. 4″–6″. June–August.

P. rotundifolia. Europe (including Gt. Britain), N. America. The most robust species, which, in favourable circumstances, can produce handsome spikes of up to a foot in height. White, tubby, bell-shaped pendent flowers. Summer.

P. secunda. Europe (including Gt. Britain), W. Asia, W. America. Intermediate between the two foregoing, and distinguished by its one-sided inflorescence. July.

P. uliginosa. N. America. Very similar to *P. rotundifolia*, but with larger flowers (up to ¾″) of rose or red-purple. Summer.

P. uniflora. See *Moneses uniflora*.

RAMONDA *Gesneriaceae*

A genus of three species, which have a curious geographical distribution across S. Europe. *R. myconi* is found locally in the Pyrenees, especially in the great Cirques, such as at Gavarnie. The genus is not found again until one meets the two E. European species, *R. nathaliae* and *R. serbica*, in the Balkans. All form basal rosettes of dark green, roughly spatulate, corrugated hairy leaves, and bear attractive four- to six-petalled flowers (usually five), predominantly mauve, but occasionally white. They stand conspicuously, one to three or four on leafless scapes, well above the foliage. The species are very long-lived, and easy of culture in a soil rich in leaf-mould, if they are inserted in a north-facing bank or rock wall, where moisture cannot settle in the rosettes. It is best to give them a soaking occasionally in a very hot season, when they will miraculously recover, even after the leaves have shrivelled. The seeds are numerous and very minute. Germination is easy and profuse, but care is needed in dealing with the seedlings as they are tiny, and very slow growing in the early stages. All the species make attractive pans for the alpine house in spring.

*R. myconi (*pyrenaica*). Pyrenees. The species most usually met with in gardens. Rosettes of large, dark green, rough-surfaced leaves, with close copper-coloured hairs on the under surfaces. Flowers five-petalled, variable in size, and shade of mauve, and rather suggestive of the potato flower by reason of the projecting cone of conspicuous rich golden stamens. (Pl. 25) Especially fine forms have been given the varietal names 'GRANDIFLORA', 'COERULEA', etc., and *R. myconi* 'ALBA' should be a pure white. *R. myconi* 'ROSEA' is usually a pale but clear pink, but a form has occurred with a very beautiful flower of deep, rich rose. 4″–6″. April–May.

*R. nathaliae. Bulgaria, Serbia. A neater plant than *R. myconi*, with more oval leaves of a lighter, more glossy green, more regularly seamed, and having a dense fringe of hairs. Flowers usually four-petalled, although this is not an invariable characteristic. The bright gold anthers are as conspicuous as in the previous species. There is a good white variety. 3″–4″. April–May.

R. pyrenaica. See **R. myconi.**

*R. serbica. Balkans. The rosette leaves follow more the shape of *R. myconi*, but are slightly smaller, and have a more glossy surface. This species can, however, always be distinguished from the two foregoing by its purple (not yellow) anthers. Also, the flower is distinctly campanulate and this, with the dark anthers, gives it a curious similarity to the flower of its near relative, *Jankaea heldreichii*, once known as *Ramonda heldreichii*. There is also a white form of *R. serbica*. 3″–4″. April–May.

RANUNCULUS *Ranunculaceae*

The Alpine Buttercups include both easy and difficult species, with flowers of yellow, white, and, rarely, pink. All require a gritty, well-drained soil, and plenty of moisture, especially in summer, and all come readily from seed, *if sown immediately it is ripe*. Otherwise germination may be delayed, spasmodic, or not at all.

*R. alpestris. European Alps. This charming little plant, which is so wide-spread over the Alps, has much-lobed, glossy green foliage on petioles of 1″ or

Ranunculus

so, and shining white solitary "Buttercups", often with crimped petals, on 2″–3″ stems. In the wild, like others of this genus, it is very variable, but in its good forms is delightful, and should be more often grown. Very suitable for trough gardens, but requires plenty of water in the growing season. If grown in pans this may be ensured by standing them in shallow water during the summer. April–July.

R. amplexicaulis. Pyrenees. Slender, pointed lanceolate leaves, some stem clasping, and 6″ scapes bearing three to six large white flowers. April–May.

*R. × arendsii. A beautiful hybrid between the foregoing and *R. gramineus*, giving a long succession of large flowers of pale sulphur-yellow on 6″–8″ stems. Late spring and summer.

*R. calandrinioides. Morocco. The very handsome almost blue-grey, wavy-edged, broadly lanceolate leaves appear above the ground in early autumn, to be followed by the large flowers, usually in sprays of two, at a height of 6″ or so. The petals have a crêpe-like texture, and are white, flushed pink, appearing in succession from January onwards according to the season. Hardy out of doors, but usually grown in an alpine house, where its beauty is protected from rough weather. 5″–7″. December–February, according to the weather.

R. crenatus. Hungary, Macedonia. In size and general appearance very like *R. alpestris*, but with rounded heart-shaped leaves, toothed at the edges. 3″–4″. June.

R. ficaria. Lesser Celandine. Europe (including Gt. Britain). Were it not so invasive one could not have a more attractive plant for early spring than our native celandine, with its petals of burnished gold and flat rosette of glossy, angled, heart-shaped leaves, mottled with silver and mahogany. There are, however, one or two less invasive, but not more beautiful colour forms in *R. f.* 'Albus', white, *R. f.* 'Primrose', creamy-yellow, and *R. f.* 'Cupreus', copper-coloured. 2″–3″. March–May.

R. glacialis. European Mts., Greenland, Iceland. This most distinctive plant is such a feature of the damp screes and shingles throughout the lime-free regions of the High Alps (it is one of the highest recorded plants) that it must be mentioned, but it is almost impossible to grow, and even more so to flower in cultivation. It is plentiful among the damp stones, sometimes sprawling and sometimes making dense tufts of its almost succulent, very deeply lobed, almost metallic dark green or purplish foliage, covered with ample flowers 1″ across, with central golden boss of stamens, usually white, but sometimes pale pink, fading with time to deep red. The only chance of keeping it is in very open, pebbly scree, incorporating leaf-mould and peat, with underground water throughout the summer. In a pot, in a similar mixture, it may be kept, but seldom flowered, if stood through the summer in a saucer of water. No lime. 2″–3″. Spring and an occasional odd flower through the summer.

*R. gramineus. S.W. Europe. A pleasant plant when young, with fresh

Ranzania

green grass-like leaves, and slender stems with golden buttercups, but inclined to become tall and lank with age (up to 12"). Long-flowering. Summer. (Pl. 25)

R. hybridus. See **R. phthora.**

D*R. **parnassifolius.** Alps, Pyrenees. In its best form one of the most delightful of the small buttercups, but should be seen before purchasing, as it is very variable, and in the wild squinny and apetalous forms predominate. It *should* show a rosette of short-stalked, solid, deep green, heart-shaped leaves, and 2"–3" sprays of very beautiful white flowers, pink flushed at the back of the petals, and the usual boss of golden stamens. Sunny, fairly moist scree. 3". Spring.

R. ×phthora (*hybridus*). Austrian Alps. A little curiosity, pushing its golden fists of buds through the soil in early spring, to be followed by the few, stalked, widely kidney-shaped leaves with shallow serrations. Long flowering. About 3". March onwards.

R. pyrenaeus. Alps, Pyrenees. Perhaps the predominant buttercup of the Alps, where the high pastures are so closely bespangled with it in late spring as to appear at a distance like snowfields. Seldom seen in cultivation, but should not be too difficult in scree with ample watering. Upright sprays of slender stems bearing one to many white flowers, from tufts of lanceolate, almost grass-like leaves. Very variable, from small, thin, and irregular petals to ample pure white flowers of 1" across, and often partially double. 2"–8". Spring.

R. seguieri. Alps. The limestone counterpart of *R. glacialis*, and a much more amenable plant, persisting in a well-drained scree, and flowering regularly. It is smaller in all its parts, and the equally deeply lobed leaves are grey-green and often slightly hairy. The charming flowers, which often have slightly crimped petals, are pure white. 2"–3". Spring.

RANZANIA   *Berberidaceae Monotypic*

P*R. **japonica.** Japan. A delightful semi-woodland plant which was grown by enthusiasts before the war, although it was always somewhat rare in cultivation. It was one of the war casualties of our rock gardens, but has reappeared spasmodically, and one hopes this heralds its more general distribution. In growth it is somewhat suggestive of Podophyllum, although botanically it is nearer Epimedium. The flowering stems are thrust up in April, and the solid six-petalled, pale mauve flowers centred by a ring of pale yellow stamens open before the leaves, which develop later in a whorl of two or three on the same stem, 1"–2" below the flowers. It makes a charming and unusual alpine house plant, but is quite hardy. 6"–8". May.

RAOULIA *Compositae*

This genus, which is confined to Australia and New Zealand, provides several very distinctive plants, composed of neat little rosettes of tiny foliage, in dense spreading mats or close cushions or hummocks which, in the wild, may spread to some feet across. In cultivation a plant of 1″–2″ diameter of the rarest species is a matter for pride. The flowers are almost sessile, white or pale yellow, enclosed in translucent bracts and resembling small Helichrysums. Until recently, only a handful of the 22 known species were attempted, but latterly a few more are creeping into cultivation, possibly as a result of the increased familiarity with these charming little plants which has followed the spate of photographs of them in the wild. Like most New Zealand seeds, they are not easy in germination. Rooted pieces from an established plant form the best hope—if one is lucky enough to have access to an established plant.

R. australis. New Zealand. Leaves up to ⅛″ long, densely tomentose, making a silvery carpet of less than ½″. Flowers pale sulphur yellow. Summer.

P*R. eximia.** S. Island, New Zealand. This, the most famous and one of the rarest in cultivation, is the species known as the Vegetable Sheep. The tiny rosettes of minute woolly leaves are tightly pressed together to form, in their native habitat, irregular rounded mounds several feet across, so closely packed as to be hard to the touch, but of a velvety silvery whiteness which suggests from a distance a flock of recumbent sheep. In cultivation, if obtainable, this species forms very regular hemispherical cushions of tiny, woolly, silvery-white rosettes, with, rarely, a few small sessile "everlasting" flowers. Very few specimens are in cultivation, and those only small pot-grown plants in the alpine house.

R. glabra. New Zealand. This differs from most of the species in having tiny glabrous leaves, thus forming a green carpet. White flowers about ¼″ across. Summer.

R. grandiflora. New Zealand. This is more lax in growth than the foregoing, and is rather suggestive of the smaller silver saxifrages, such as *S. caesia*. The flowers are quite conspicuous, as neat white daisies about ½″ across. 2″–3″. Summer.

R. lutescens. New Zealand. One of the easiest to grow, making a close, almost lichen-like carpet of minute greyish leaves, well sprinkled in summer with tiny sessile lemon-yellow flowers. (Pl. 25)

RHAMNUS *Rhamnaceae*

The Buckthorns provide one prostrate and congested shrublet which is locally abundant in many mountain localities.

R. pumila. Dwarf Buckthorn. Alps of Europe. From crevices at high altitude, this forms knarled woody mats, following the contours of the rocks. The pale green flowers are small and inconspicuous, but they are followed by globose blue-black fruits. Deciduous.

RHODODENDRON *Ericaceae*

This huge genus of spectacular free-flowering shrubs now numbers well over 500 species, only a handful of which were in cultivation before the last decade of the nineteenth century. From then onwards a spate of seed under name or (more often) number has been sent back from Central Asia by various collectors. In many cases, different numbers from the same collector were found to be the same species, and from a single packet the resulting plants often showed great variation in colour (especially) and habit. Consequently, the nomenclature is even yet not firmly established in many cases. All are branched, woody shrubs, usually evergreen and generally very floriferous. Among the dwarf species are many enchanting shrubs for the rock garden, *provided* the local soil is lime-free. Only one species, the European *R. hirsutum*, will tolerate and even flourish on a limy soil.

They all require a light, leafy, or peaty soil, and, although they are surface-rooting, very good drainage. At first it was thought that shade was necessary, but it has been found that they will tolerate a fair amount of sun (although not a scorched position) and, in fact, the dwarf species will remain more compact and flower more freely in a comparatively open situation. They must never, however, be allowed to dry out, and watering (with rainwater) is necessary in a dry season. If and when the rainwater supply gives out, it is a help to add a very small amount of one of the 'Sequestrene' preparations to the domestic water supply. Propagation may be by seed, cuttings, or layering of young wood (very slow). Seeds, which are very small, should be sown thinly on the surface of fine peat and sand (more peat than sand), and barely covered, if at all, with a film of silver sand. The pots should be covered with a glass, to minimize evaporation, and watered with a

Rhododendron

very fine spray or, better, stood, when necessary, in a tray of water. The seedlings should be pricked out, when large enough to handle, 1″–2″ apart, into boxes of fine leaf-mould, peat, sand, and a little loam. Cuttings of the small, alpine species root fairly easily when taken half-ripe, and set in sand and peat, in July if heat is available, or in December in a cold frame. Being surface rooting, rhododendrons transplant easily at any time, but preferably between October and mid-April, given firm (but not deep) planting and a generous watering. The genus offers a wonderful variety of foliage and flower. The leaves are always entire and vary from broadly oval to narrow. The flowers, usually with five petals, but occasionally six to ten, may be very small and neat or wide and flamboyant, and vary in colour from white through mauve-pink to shades of purple, through clear pink to scarlet, and even deeper red, and through sulphur to clear yellow and apricot.

From the many attractive species suitable for the rock garden, there follow two lists. The first is of very dwarf, or completely prostrate species, which are unlikely to reach a height of more than about 10″. The second, and longer, list is a selection, chosen to give a wide choice of habit and colour, from among the dozens of species available from specialists in ericaceous plants, which may grow to 12″, and some which will, in time, reach as much as 2 ft., but which flower while they are still quite small, and form delightful shrubs for the rock garden or pan in the alpine house for several years before outgrowing their surroundings. Those whose soil contains chalk may yet enjoy these very varied and delightful shrubs by growing them in peaty soil, in pans sunk outside in ash beds, preferably raised. Watering must be by rainwater or, in default, with small additions of 'Sequestrene' to the domestic supply.

Species usually growing to less than 12″ in height (evergreen except where otherwise noted).

*R. camtschaticum. N.E. Asia, N.W. America. Deciduous. One of the most beautiful, with 1½″ shallow, pure pink saucers borne well above the oval, fresh green leaves. 4″–8″. May.

R. forrestii. China, Tibet. A sturdy creeping shrub with broadly oval 1″ leaves stained with purple on the under surface, and large red to crimson funnel-shaped flowers, solitary or in pairs. 6″. April–May.

*R. impeditum. China. A very dense, twiggy shrub, with small leaves and short tubular flowers with five spreading lobes. Very variable. Even more compact pygmy forms are available, and the flowers may be mauve or

Rhododendron

purplish blue, or, in some forms, the nearest to a true blue of any in the genus. 6″–18″. May.

R. imperator. Burma. Aromatic, narrowly elliptic leaves and narrowly funnel-shaped flowers in various shades of pinkish-purple, produced on very young plants. 6″. May. *R. patulum* is almost identical.

R. intricatum. China. Intricately branched shoots and small oval grey-green leaves spangled with rusty scales. Smallish flowers in many open clusters, violet in the bud, opening to lavender blue. 6″–12″. April–May.

*R. keleticum. Tibet. A charming plant for garden or alpine house, forming in time a shapely spreading little tree, with bright green, oval leaves, and wide, open flowers of clear pink, held on 1″ pedicels. 6″–12″. June.

R. lowndesii. Nepal. Deciduous. A delightful little plant with fresh green, oval leaves, and shallow pale yellow saucers, spotted deeper yellow, on 1½″ pedicels. Unfortunately not completely hardy, but makes a very attractive pan in the alpine house. 6″–8″. April.

*R. microleucum. Central Asia. An unusual little shrub with small oval leaves and clusters of small, pure white flowers. 6″–12″. April–May.

R. myrtilloides. N.E. Burma. Makes a tufted bush with oval, ½″ glossy leaves, and delightful thimble-shaped flowers of an indescribable purplish crushed-strawberry colour, with a beautiful "bloom". Variable in colour. 6″–12″. May.

R. patulum. Assam Frontier. See **R. imperator.**

*R. pemakoense. Tibet, Tsangpo Gorge. Very free-flowering, with oval leaves nearly 1″ long, and wide, trumpet-shaped flowers of purplish-pink. Unique in its habit of suckering. 10″–12″. Apt to be caught by frost as it is so early flowering. April.

R. prostratum. China, up to limit of vegetation. Quite prostrate, making a much-branched woody mat. Leaves ½″, oval; flowers open flatly, pinkish purple, with purple stamens. 4″. April.

R. radicans. Tibet. Somewhat similar to the foregoing, but even more prostrate and congested, especially the earlier form, introduced by Forrest. Tapered, dark green, glossy leaves and solitary purple flowers borne singly on 1″ pedicels. A charming pygmy. 3″–4″. May.

R. repens. China, Tibet. Almost identical with *R. forrestii* (q.v.), and often classed as *R. forrestii* var. *repens*. The only obvious difference is that in this species the backs of the leaves are green. Not very free flowering. 6″. April–May. (Pl. 26).

Species usually reaching a height of 1′–2′, but flowering at an early stage and remaining dwarf enough for rock garden or alpine house for several years. All evergreen.

R. aperantum. Burma. A prostrate plant with dark green, oval-pointed leaves and very large, solid trumpet-shaped flowers of white, pink or deep

Rhododendron

rose. Takes some years to attain flowering size, and then does not flower freely in cultivation. A most striking and beautiful plant in the wild. 6″–18″. May.

R. calostrotum. Burma. Oval grey-green leaves about 1″ long. Wide, showy flowers of shades of rose. About 12″. May–June.

***R. campylogynum.** China, Tibet, Burma. A delightful species, with 1″ long glossy, dark green leaves with recurved edges, growing on the twiggy stems in bunches from which rise the 1″–2″ pedicels, each bearing a nodding, thimble-shaped flower with a lovely "bloom" upon it. Variable shades of soft unusual, almost brownish reds, and rarely dull yellow. *R. myrtilloides* is sometimes considered a variety of this species. 12″–18″. May.

***R. caloxanthum.** Burma. Eventually 3′–4′, but included because of its beauty, and the fact that it flowers when young and grows slowly so that it will not outgrow rock garden or alpine house for several years. The new leaves in spring, 1½″ roundish oval, are a wonderful bluish jade green, unfolding from glistening, long, narrow, deep pink bracts, and the large flowers are almost scarlet in bud, paling through shades of apricot to open clear yellow. April–May.

R. charitopes. Burma. An attractive free-flowering shrub, with 1″ wide clear pink flowers, speckled with deeper pink, in few-flowered trusses. 1½′–3′. April–May.

R. chryseum. China. A yellow counterpart of *R. fastigiatum*, with ¾″–1″ flowers of bright yellow. 1½′–2′. May.

R. didymum. Tibet. Oval leaves 1″–2″ long, but notable for the colour of its very solid 1″, bell-shaped flowers, which are of a lurid, very dark purplish-red, almost black, in clusters on 1″ pedicels. 1′–3′. June–July.

R. fastigiatum. Yunnan, W. China. A very twiggy bush akin to *R. impeditum*, but more erect in habit. ½″ light purple flowers. Up to 3′. April–May.

***R. ferrugineum.** Alpine Rose. Central Europe, on lime-free formations. The ubiquitous rhododendron of the Alps, whose open spaces it often covers like heather, where it reddens the hillsides in July or August according to altitude. Forms close bushes with many small oval leaves, often with recurved edges, and rusty at the back with brown tomentum. The ½″ campanulate flowers, rose to deep scarlet-rose, are borne in dense clusters. 1′–2′. July–August.

***R. hirsutum.** Central Europe. The limestone counterpart of the last and very similar, except that the leaves have less substance, have hairs around the edge, and *green* backs. Both of these, in their appropriate soils, make attractive plants in the garden and are long-lived, and thoroughly in character. The only rhododendron to thrive in a limy soil. 1′–2′. July–August.

***R. leucaspis.** Tibet. One of the loveliest, but prone to be caught by late frosts owing to its early flowering. Spreading habit, with oval glaucous leaves of 1″–2″, and large wide-open 2″ flowers of pure solid white. 1′–2′. February–April.

240

23

Pimelea coarctata
Polygala calcarea
Potentilla verna forma nana

Pleione limprichtii
Potentilla nitida rubra
Primula allionii

24

Primula amoena
Primula farinosa
Primula juliae

Primula denticulata
Primula gracilipes
Primula marginata 'Drake's Form'

Rhodohypoxis

*R. megeratum. Himalaya. Another twiggy small shrub, with 1″ leaves, and delightful bell-shaped flowers of bright yellow, with brown anthers. 1′–2′. March–April.

R. racemosum. China. One of the earliest dwarf introductions and an attractive shrub which has been collected in many variations. Forrest's form (No. 19404) is the most compact, remaining under 2′. Very free-flowering with terminal and axillary clusters of bright pink flowers. April–May.

R. radinum. China. A twiggy shrub with narrow ⅓″ scaly leaves and terminal clusters of rather small pink flowers which, in the best forms, much resemble *Daphne cneorum*. *R. ledoides* and *R. tricostomum* are very similar. Up to 4ft. May.

R. russatum. China. Another twiggy shrub, with dark green, oval 1″ leaves, rusty beneath, and close clusters of deep blue-purple flowers with white throats. A very distinctive colour. 2′–4′. Late April.

*R. sargentianum. China. A close, aromatic shrublet with ⅓″ glossy, oval leaves, and clusters of rather small (¼″) flowers of sulphur-yellow. Up to 2ft. May.

*R. williamsianum. China. One of the most handsome and distinct, with round leaves, cordate at the base, attractively bronze-coloured when young, and very large lily-like flowers of soft pink. The flower buds are apt to be cut by spring frosts, but this contributes to the rounded compactness of the bush as below each blighted bud three dormant leafy shoots develop. Very floriferous when the flower buds survive the winter. Remains small enough for pan or rock garden for many years. Eventually 3′. April.

RHODOHYPOXIS *Hypoxidaceae*

These charming little plants were introduced from S. Africa towards the end of the last century, but only within the last thirty years or so have been extensively grown. The original species, ***R. baurii**, forms bunches of erect, radical leaves, narrowly lanceolate and silkily hairy, and many solitary rose-red flowers of a very distinctive shape, the six petals being arranged in two overlapping sets of three. This is still to many one of the most beautiful, but a large number of other colour forms have since occurred, many of which have been given varietal names. These include variations from pale to dark rose, and a beautiful large-flowered white of solid texture and great purity, and also miniature forms. A sunny, well drained but not arid, position suits it, but it is intolerant of winter damp. It makes a most attractive pan for the alpine house, where its long flowering period, from April through-out the summer, is most valuable. 1″–3″. April onwards. (Pl. 26)

Rhodothamnus, Ricotia, Romanzoffia

RHODOTHAMNUS Ericaceae Monotypic

*R. chamaecistus. E. European Alps (especially the Dolomites), E. Siberia. One of the most delightful dwarf shrubs for the rock garden. It forms densely twiggy 6″ evergreen bushlets, with many tiny oval leaves, hairy at the edges, and in spring its beautifully clear-cut pale pink flowers open as shallow bowls 1″ wide, the deep pink stamens showing prominently against the five rounded petals. It is locally abundant in the Dolomites, but is also found in E. Siberia. It is not easy to establish, although it seems indifferent to soil, but once having settled down it is long-lived. A sunny position where the roots are protected by rock or low growing vegetation seems the most promising situation. One should not tempt fortune by attempting to move a healthy specimen of this charming plant. Seed. Early summer. (Pl. 26)

RICOTIA Cruciferae

In the 1930s Dr. Peter Davis introduced from Asia Minor a new species of this genus:

R. davisii. It is doubtful if many of the original seedlings now survive, but if not it is to be hoped this species may be reintroduced, as it is a most distinctive small crucifer, with surprising, almost succulent, greyish trefoil leaves, and comparatively large clear pink cruciform flowers. An unusual and attractive plant, which will have to be perpetuated by seed (when obtained) as it is not in general long lived. 3″. Spring.

ROMANZOFFIA Hydrophyllaceae

This genus closely resembles the moisture-loving meadow saxifrages of the granulata group, and all four of its species are easy and charming in a similar damp and shady spot, in leafy or peaty soil. They are all natives of N.E. Asia or W.N. America. The species most usually found in cultivation is:

R. californica (*sitchensis*). Mist Maidens. N.W. America. A small tufted plant of up to 6″, with solid kidney-shaped stalked leaves, with many rounded lobes. The five-petalled creamy-white flowers are borne in airy sprays well above the leaves, and their velvety texture, enhanced by the pale gold stamens, helps to make this an attractive little spring-flowering plant for a woodland setting. 2″–6″. April.

Romulea, Rosa, Roscoea

ROMULEA *Iridaceae*

This genus contains about 50 species, but few are in general cultivation. They are delightful little plants, rather suggestive of a slender crocus, with, at maturity, spreading tips to the petals. The colour is usually mauve-blue, often with a golden throat. Unfortunately, the individual flowers are short-lived, and only open in sunshine. Propagation by seed or offset. Those in cultivation are mainly from S. Europe, N. Africa, and Asia Minor, and of these the most hardy is:

R. bulbocodium. S. Europe. Small, cup-shaped flowers of violet with a yellow base. Hardy in a well-drained sunny spot, and very attractive in a pan in the alpine house where the delicate flowers have overhead protection. 5"–6". March.

Other romuleas, including the less hardy species from S. Africa, will be found described in detail in *Collins Guide to Bulbs*.

ROSA *Rosaceae*

Of this very large genus the only species really suitable for the rock garden is **R. pendulina** (*alpina*), the (usually) thornless Wild Rose of the Alps. This, in appearance very like our own Dog Rose, forms a thicket of woody, upright stems, up to 3 ft. or so, but more dwarf forms have been collected which may be trusted not to exceed 12". *R. pendulina* 'ELLIOTT'S VAR.' is a well known and reliable one. The single, deep pink roses are succeeded by showy flask-shaped hips. It is an easy and attractive plant, but where well suited (and it is not fastidious) it is apt to sucker around freely.

The large and increasing number of miniature roses (of which the forerunner was *R. rouletii*, more correctly *R. chinensis* var. *minima*, the Fairy Rose) are delightful small replicas of the old Monthly Rose and others, and can now be obtained in many shades of red, pink, yellow, and white, but, charming as they are individually, they do not seem to consort happily with the other inhabitants of the rock garden.

ROSCOEA *Zingiberaceae*

These handsome plants from Central Asia form sturdy upright sheaths of widely lanceolate leaves, from which emerge the spikes of showy, lipped flowers, rather like very solid orchids. If planted deeply (at least 6″) in soil rich in humus the following should be reasonably hardy. Division. Summer flowering.

R. alpina. Himalaya. The most dwarf of those described. The solitary pinkish-purple flowers are almost sessile. 4″–8″.

*R. cautleoides. China. Perhaps the most lovely, producing a spike of six to seven flowers of a luminous soft yellow. It may, however, grow to over a foot when happily suited.

R. humeana. W. China. The same habit, but bearing four to six large and showy violet-purple flowers. About 8″ or less when flowering, but the leaves develop later to nearly 12″.

*R. purpurea. Kumaon and Sikkim. Rather tall for the rock garden, reaching 12″ or more. Two to four purple flowers. (Pl. 26)

ROSMARINUS *Labiatae*

S. Europe, Asia Minor. Usually regarded as monotypic, although sometimes divided into four species.

R. officinalis. S. Europe, Asia Minor. The well-known Rosemary has a dwarf, prostrate form, *R. o.* var. *prostratus* (*lavandulaceus*) which makes a shrublet of attractive habit, with small, dark green, glossy leaves (white-downy beneath), and few, small pale-violet, lipped flowers in the axils of the leaves, but unfortunately it is not quite hardy and demands winter protection. 2″. Spreading. May.

ROSULARIA *Crassulaceae*

These succulent, rosette-forming plants, in habit resembling semper-vivums, have often been included in *Cotyledon*. They are on the verge of hardiness, and most require a little protection in winter, from overhead damp as well as from severe frost.

R. pallida. (*Cotyledon chrysantha, Umbilicus chrysanthus*). Asia Minor. Forms a rosette of small, hairy-edged leaves, with a spike of upright, comparatively large, white or cream, bell-shaped flowers. 6″–8″. Summer.

RUBUS *Rosaceae*

The Brambles include a few miniature or prostrate forms which have a charm of their own and are not seen as often as they should be,

Rupicapnos, Rydbergia, Sagina

especially as they are among the few really dwarf shrublets which do not object to lime. Also they flower in June–July, after the spring pageant has waned. The following die down completely in winter.

R. arcticus. N. hemisphere. A small thicket of frail brambles, with three-foliate, toothed leaves, and solitary rose flowers $\frac{3}{4}''$ across. Fruit, spare amber "blackberries". 4″–6″. June.

R. chamaemorus. N. Europe (including Scotland). About the same height, but with pure white flowers, followed by edible amber-coloured "blackberries", at any rate in the wild. Widespread in Scandinavia, where it is valued for its fruits. 3″–8″. June.

*R. illecebrosus. Japan. The Strawberry Raspberry. Although as dwarf as the foregoing, it is much more sturdy in growth, and the foliage takes tinges of red, which suffuse it towards the autumn. This, with the abnormally large and solid fruits, suggestive of the mulberry in colour and size, make it an unusual and attractive little shrublet. 6″. July.

RUPICAPNOS *Papaveraceae*

Like its near relation, Fumitory, which it much resembles, this is totally different in flower from the Poppy clan.

p**R. africana.** N.W. Africa. Makes a tufted plant of many slenderly cut, glaucous grey, fern-like leaves, with sprays of delicate, narrow, spurred flowers of variable colour, but usually rose-tinted white, hardy but not long lived. Seed. 4″–6″. Summer.

RYDBERGIA. See ACTINELLA

SAGINA *Caryophyllaceae*

The Pearlworts are small tufted plants, closely related to Minuartia and Arenaria. They make close green 1″ carpets or cushions of narrow, pointed leaves, spangled in early summer with tiny, white, five-pointed flowers.

S. boydii. Scotland. A rare, very slow-growing cushion plant, with congested, tiny, dark green foliage. Useful for sinks.

S. glabra. W. Alps, Scotland. A slightly larger, more creeping moss-like plant, with bright green narrowly linear leaves. The golden foliaged form, *S. g.* 'AUREA', is attractive as a carpeting plant.

245

Salix

SALIX *Salicaceae*

The Willow genus contains a number of members most suitable and desirable for the rock garden, where they are easy and long-lived in any not too dry position, and provide in time the most delightful dwarf and often gnarled bushlets, bearing in spring the more or less showy catkins of their male forms, down to the minute high alpine varieties which become sprinkled with a million points of gold. In the European Alps great variation of the prostrate species may be found, with catkins in every shade through yellow and deep orange to red and almost purple. They are completely deciduous and most are readily increased by cuttings.

S. apoda (male form). Europe. A most spectacular sight in spring, when its 1½″ silky catkins become enveloped in gold to orange stamens. An effective plant when curbed in a pan, but outside when happy will spread to 1½ ft. in height, and 2 ft. or more in breadth.

S. arbuscula. Europe (including Scotland). Rather gnarled bushes with thin grey catkins—up to 2 ft. in time, but very variable in size. The truly dwarf forms from the high Central Alps are more in character with their surroundings.

S. herbacea. N. hemisphere (including Gt. Britain). A completely creeping plant, with its network of woody stems often under the surface. It makes a carpet of rounded, glossy leaves, about ½″ across, which in spring is densely sprinkled with the gold dust of its stamens.

*S. lanata and vars. Europe (including Scotland), N. Asia. This perhaps should not be mentioned as it forms a sturdy branching shrub up to 3 ft., but where there is room for it there is hardly any other plant which becomes so plated with silver by its silky woolly, widely oval leaves each spring.

*S. reticulata. Europe (including Scotland), W. Asia. Perhaps the most beautiful of all the dwarf willows, forming in the mountains wide patches of densely branching prostrate woody stems, which in spring put forth solid, roundly oval leaves, about ½″ across, plated with the purest silver of the long adpressed hairs. From the intricate gnarled branches rise the golden catkins like little candles. Later the hairs disappear, and the leaf surface shows as glossy deep green, with the conspicuous indented fine network which gives it its specific name. Slow growing and never likely to spread more than one would wish.

*S. myrsinites. Europe. A very variable species but a dwarf variety, *S. myrsinites* var. *jacquinii*, forms a delightfully twiggy bush of under a foot, bearing in spring short upright catkins of deep ruby-red.

S. retusa. Central and E. Europe. A prostrate shrublet, much branched, which follows the contours of the rocks. Many small glossy oval leaves, about

246

$\frac{1}{2}''$ long, and small upright catkins of various shades of yellow and burnt orange.

S. serpyllifolia. European Alps. Often considered to be a variety of the foregoing, which it resembles in every way in miniature, with even smaller leaves (about $\frac{1}{4}''$) and even more congested gnarled woody prostrate branches. In the mountainous parts where they are abundant, there seem to be numerous gradations between this species and the foregoing.

SANGUINARIA *Papaveraceae Monotypic*

*S. canadensis. N. America. A delightful herbaceous plant which dies away completely during the winter, and in spring put up "fists" of rather solid, rounded, deeply lobed leaves of grey green. From them unfold the solitary anemone-like flowers, nearly 2″ across, of purest white with central bosses of golden stamens. Longer-lived in the flower, although not more beautiful, is the completely double form, *S. c.* 'FLORE PLENO'. Shortly after flowering the whole plant dies away until the next spring. It takes its name from the reddish sap which exudes if the roots are damaged. Propagation by division in August. Almost any position, but is at home in partial shade in leafy, sandy soil. 3″. April. (Pl. 26)

SANTOLINA *Compositae*

The Lavender Cottons are mostly too tall, too invasive or both for the rock garden but:

S. chamaecyparissus (*incana*), S. Europe, is an aromatic shrub with many twiggy branches, closely crowded with deeply pinnatisect leaves, almost plume-like by means of the dense white tomentum with which they are felted. The small rayless flowers are borne in slender spikes. *S. c.* 'NANA' (usually found as *S. incana* 'NANA') is a delightful and effective dwarf form of under 12″. July-August.

SAPONARIA *Caryophyllaceae*

The Soapworts include several prostrate forms which are useful as late flowering plants. The genus is very near Silene and the nomenclature is often confused between the two.

247

Sarcocapnos

*S. 'Bressingham Hybrid'. A good plant with the habit of *S. pumila* but easier to grow and flower. Many large clear pink flowers. 3″–4″. Early summer. (Pl. 26)

S. caespitosa. Pyrenees. An attractive tufted plant with many rather fleshy upright linear leaves, and sprays of pink, five-petalled flowers, opening from dark velvety buds. On the borderline of hardiness. 4″. Summer.

S. lutea. W. Alps. An interesting but not very showy little plant with sprays of smallish flowers, dull cream rather than yellow, but relieved by conspicuous dark stamens. 3″–4″. Summer.

*S. ocymoides. Alps and Jura. Locally the glory of shingle banks at medium heights, where it forms prostrate mats a foot or more across, completely covered in summer with myriads of neat pink flowers, about ½″ across. Very variable in nature, and in seeding itself in the garden, where particularly solid flowers of a rich deep shade may be found. Invaluable for colour and complete ease of growth in any open situation. Not long-lived, but self-seeds copiously. 2″. Early summer onwards.

S. o. 'Rubra Compacta' is a selected form of congested growth with particularly deep rose flowers.

*S. ×'Olivana' (*pumila × caespitosa*). A most attractive hybrid from the Continent, with the mat-forming habit of its parents, but more easy to grow than either of them, and much more prodigal of its 1″ wide bright pink flowers, well distributed, instead of being mainly on the fringes of the mats as in *S. pumila*. 2″. Summer.

D*S. pumila (*Silene pumila, Silene pumilio*). Alps, particularly locally in the Dolomites. This is the most lovely of the genus, forming close mats of rather fleshy linear leaves from much branched prostrate stems, and in summer producing many almost sessile brilliant rose flowers, with five widely separated, deeply cleft petals, almost suggesting a clarkia flower. This plant abhors lime, and is shy flowering in captivity. From the gardener's point of view, the foregoing hybrid is the more satisfactory plant, owing to its comparative ease of cultivation. 2″. Summer.

S. pulvinaris. Lebanon, Anatólia. A congested tuffet of narrow linear leaves, bearing short-stemmed flowers of bright rose. 1″. Summer.

SARCOCAPNOS *Papaveraceae*

Like Rupicapnos, this genus bears a strong resemblance to the fumitories, having similar spurred narrow flowers rising from fragile, almost succulent, much branched ferny foliage.

PS. enneaphylla. S. Europe, N. Africa. A rather short-lived perennial, forming a loose tuft of elegantly cut foliage, and having loose spikes of narrow yellow flowers, marked with purple. Easy from seed, which should be kept as a hostage. 4″–5″. Early summer.

Sarcococca, Satureia, Saussurea, Saxifraga

SARCOCOCCA *Buxaceae*

Easy-growing small evergreen shrubs from E. Asia, of which the hardiest of the dwarf species is:

S. humilis. China. Dense tufted growth with narrowly elliptic, glossy, oval leaves, 1″ or more long, and clusters of small, white, very fragrant flowers in the axils of the leaves, followed by black globose fruits. Valuable for its early flowering and its fragrance. Up to 12″. January–March.

Other nearly related species are sometimes offered, including *S. repanda*, even more dwarf (about 3″) with white flowers.

SATUREIA *Labiatae*

A genus of intricately branched wiry shrublets, with one exception from the Mediterranean region. Their thyme-like leaves are strongly aromatic, and the clusters of small, lipped flowers are borne in late summer in the axils of the leaves.

S. montana. S. Europe. This has a miniature variety, *S. m.* 'PYGMAEA', which is particularly neat and delightful, with small, deep mauve flowers. 6″. June.

SAUSSUREA *Compositae*

This race of rather thistle-like plants, with a wide distribution over the world, are very little in cultivation, but some of the more congested forms are becoming available, and have a curious attraction for the lover of the unusual plant. Indifferent to soil, but need good drainage, and full sun.

S. stella. Tibet. Occasionally available, this forms a very flat rosette of linear, dark green leaves, purplish red at the base, at the centre of which sits a thistle-like head of blue-purple, encircled by straw-coloured bristles, the whole having an exotic star-fish effect. 2″. Summer.

One or two attractively woolly forms are known from Yunnan, but have only been spasmodically in cultivation.

SAXIFRAGA *Saxifragaceae*

A genus which, with the genera Campanula, Dianthus, and Primula, provides perhaps the largest numbers of species and varieties suitable

Saxifraga

for the rock garden or alpine house. It comprises over 300 species, almost all of which are suitable for these positions, and, in addition, a very great number of delightful hybrids, especially in the Kabschia–Engleria section. So varied are they that they are divided into no less than 16 sections, but the most important for the alpine garden, and the most numerous, are the Aizoons, the Kabschias, and the Englerias. The last two have so much in common and hybridize so readily that they are here grouped together, and the genus is described alphabetically under the three heads—Aizoon Saxifrages, Kabschia and Engleria Saxifrages, and Other Saxifrages.

AIZOON SECTION
(*Encrusted Saxifrages*)

The type plant of this section is the very variable *S. aizoon* itself, which is, in one or other of its forms and varieties, one of the most common of the saxatile saxifrages of the European Alps. Basically the species form rosettes, flat or slightly incurving, of widely or narrowly strap-shaped leaves, almost invariably grey-green, and often beautifully encrusted with dots of lime, especially around the edges, and bear sprays of many, rather small but solid-textured, five-petalled, often spotted, white flowers. Mat-forming by means of short stolons. Well-drained limestone scree, in an open position, except where noted otherwise. All are quite hardy. May–June flowering.

*S. aizoon. Europe, N. America. Rosettes of rather narrow tongue-shaped leaves, minutely scalloped at the tips, grey-green and often regularly pitted with chalk. Sprays of white flowers on rather solid, slightly leafy pedicels. Very variable, but attractive in all forms. 3″–6″. June. A few of the more distinct named forms are:

  S. a. var. **baldensis.** Mt. Baldo. Italy. The smallest in the section. Silvery rosettes ½″ across. White flowers. 2″.

  S. a. 'LAGRAVEANA'. La Grave. French Alps. Dense ½″–¾″ cushions and white flowers with many rounded teeth. 3″.

  S. a. 'LUTEA'. Of sturdy habit, with 2″ rosettes and lemon-yellow flowers. 6″–8″.

  S. a. 'REX'. Collected by Reginald Farrer on the Dossenhorn, Bernese Oberland. A handsome form with very silvery leaves and mahogany red stems bearing creamy-white, unspotted flowers. 4″–6″.

  S. a. 'ROSEA'. Bulgaria. Rosettes of strap-shaped leaves, with silvery margins. Sprays of pink flowers, deep rose in the bud. 6″–10″.

Saxifraga

S. × canis-dalmatica (*aizoon* var. *balcana* × *cotyledon*). Of *aizoon* habit, but sprays of white flowers very heavily spotted with purple. 10″–12″.

S. cochlearis. Maritime Alps. Humped masses of 1″ wide encrusted rosettes with slightly recurved leaves. White flowers. 6″. *S. c.* 'MINOR' is a miniature version, making a hard, dense cushion of ½″ rosettes. A very attractive and good tempered plant for the alpine house. 3″.

*S. cotyledon. S.W. Alps (Pyrenees), north to Lapland and Iceland. A very handsome plant, especially as seen in the wild, spraying from crevices in high rock faces. Large for the normal rock garden, as its rosettes of broad leaves, lime-encrusted at the edges, erupt into huge 1½′–2′ plumes branched almost to the base, of myriads of solid white flowers. June–August. Several selected forms and hybrids are also offered, one of the most striking being *S. c.* 'SOUTHSIDE SEEDLING' with solid flowers heavily spotted with bright red. 12″ (Pl. 28).

S. crustata. E. Alps. A beautiful foliage plant, with dense mats of narrow, strap-shaped leaves, encrusted round the edges, but the sprays of rather small, off-white flowers do not quite live up to the promise of the sturdy, often red-tinted stems. Always found on limestone. 4″–6″. June–July.

DP**S. florulenta.** S.W. and Maritime Alps. An almost fabulous saxifrage, rare in nature, difficult to grow, and very distinct in appearance. It forms very symmetrical rosettes of narrow, sharply-pointed, sombre, dark green leaves, of almost glossy texture, which gradually increase for many years until a compact, branched 18″ spray of rather dingy pink flowers is produced. After this the plant, being monocarpic, dies. It rarely lives to produce flowers, but its beauty is in the rosette, unmistakable among saxifrages. Its chance of survival, if obtainable, is in a crevice backing to deep, rich scree. Water settling in the rosette is fatal, and so too is any damage to the leaves.

*S. kolenatiana. Caucasus. Related to *S. aizoon*, but with more pointed leaves, and attractive sprays of good rose-pink flowers. 6″–9″.

S. lingulata. W. and Maritime Alps. Very distinct, with large tumbled rosettes of very numerous, long narrow leaves, iron-grey, with a fine edge of silver beading, and slightly swollen and recurved at the tips. A rather one-sided full plume of innumerable rather starry white flowers. Tall and requiring a high crevice where its 12″–18″ plumes have room to spray. Early summer. Several local forms have varietal names, but are not sufficiently different from the type to note here.

*S. longifolia. Pyrenees. Like the foregoing, produces a flowering truss which may extend to 18″, but is one of the handsomest of all saxifrages. The rather flat rosette, up to 6″ across, of very numerous linear or strap-shaped greyish leaves narrowing to acute points, is very beautiful in itself, and eventually produces a thick spire of copious white flowers, unique in extending right down to the base. It probably will not flower for some years, and, having done so, dies, being monocarpic. It will, however, set copious seed, most of which will produce hybrids with one or other saxifrages in the garden. Especially fine forms or hybrids have been named, two of the best known being

251

Saxifraga

S. l. 'FRANCIS CADE', with particularly lovely silver rosettes, and *S. l.* 'TUMBLING WATERS', with a wonderful cascade of blossom, less erect than the type. June.

S. valdensis. French Alps. Even smaller than *S. cochlearis* 'MINOR', with hard congested tufts of dull grey-green, recurved tiny leaves and clustered heads of rounded white flowers on stout red stems. Rare in nature. 2″–3″. Early summer.

ENGLERIAS AND KABSCHIAS

These two sections have much in common. Both form rosettes of stiff, pointed leaves, usually silvery, and often pitted with lime, especially around the edges. These group themselves to form dense, low, symmetrical cushions. They are both very free flowering, the Kabschias bearing open, round, five-petalled flowers, either solitary or few to a spray. The Englerias are usually taller, and the flowers, several to a spray, are more or less pendent and are enclosed in coloured, often fluffy, inflated calyces. The leaves in the Kabschias are smaller, and on the whole narrower, more pointed, and more upright in the rosettes. Because in their extreme forms they approach so nearly (Engleria is considered by some as a subsection of Kabschia), and because they hybridize so readily, the two sections, including some of their many hybrids, are here included in a single list. They are among the most beautiful of all the early flowering plants, and all make delightful pans for the alpine house, where their lovely cushions, silvery in the majority of cases, would justify their inclusion, even if they did not so abundantly display, from January to March or later, according to the species and the season, their symmetrical, round-petalled flowers of white, yellow, pink, or red. Although completely hardy, there are two hazards in the open garden which may prove fatal. A single day's scorching sun may blanch a healthy cushion to a pale ghost of itself, from which there is no recovery, or prolonged autumn rains may cause rotting. In the latter case, the plant may be saved if the affected parts are cut away, the healthy part pressed together and made compact by a top dressing of limestone chips, and the saxifrage placed under cover or in the alpine house. All do well in a well-drained soil, a mixture of loam, leaf-mould, and chippings (of limestone, with one exception), and a good top dressing of limestone chippings pushed well under the edges of the cushion. Or the cushion may be planted in a hole in tufa, or set in a pan between small pieces

Saxifraga

of rock. Propagation by seed, which may produce hybrids, or by single-rosette cuttings, which will root readily in a mixture of peat and sand, if kept close in a frame or under a bell glass.

It is only possible to give a few of the very numerous hybrids offered by alpine nurseries, but all are beautiful and suitable plants, as will be seen from the selection illustrated in Pl. 27.

$E.$ = Engleria $K.$ = Kabschia

K. **S.** × **apiculata.** Probably the first hybrid grown of the Kabschia section, and one of the few with deep green foliage. It spreads rapidly into a wide mat of dense shoots of sharply-pointed leaves, and does well out of doors. The type has primrose-yellow flowers, and there is a white variety. 3″. March–April. (Pl. 27)

*K. **S.** × **arco-valleyi.** Small, neat foliage and soft pink flowers. 1″. March.

*K. **S.** × **borisii.** Distinct, with blue-grey rosettes, and few, large, pale yellow flowers on reddish stems. 3″. March–April. (Pl. 27)

*K. **S.** × **boydii.** For some reason more difficult to satisfy than most, but a beautiful plant with blue-grey needle-like leaves and red stems and buds. The few flowers, two or three to a spray, are large and citron-yellow. 2″–3″. April.

*K. **S. burseriana.** E. Alps on limestone, especially the Dolomites, very local. The transcendent beauty of a lovely race. Forms dense, spiny, rather flat cushions of rigid, blue-grey, pointed leaves, and bears, on 2″ reddish stems, solitary round-petalled white flowers of solid texture. (Pl. 27.) There are several local and selected forms, and this species is a parent of many good hybrids.

***S. b.** 'BROOKSIDE' and **S. b.** 'GLORIA' are selected forms with particularly large flowers of nearly 1″ across.

***S. b.** 'CRENATA'. A compact plant with smaller flowers having delicately fluted and neatly scalloped petals. (Pl. 27)

***S. b.** 'HIS MAJESTY'. Large flowers, faintly pink-flushed. Probably a hybrid. (Pl. 27)

***S. b.** var. **major** 'LUTEA'. Large, clear pale yellow flowers, probably a hybrid. (Pl. 27)

***S. b.** var. **minor.** A smaller version of the type plant, from the Karawanken Mt.

***S. b.** 'SULPHUREA'. As the type, but with soft yellow flowers, probably a hybrid. (Pl. 27)

***S. b.** var. **tridentina.** A specially robust plant from Laentino, Italy, from which some of the named large-flowered varieties have been selected.

*K. **S.** 'BUTTERCUP'. Neatly rounded, dark green spiny rosettes. Deep yellow flowers. 2″. March–April. (Pl. 27)

Saxifraga

*K. S. caesia.** Pyrenees to E. Alps. Widespread in nature, forming cushions and mats of small ($\frac{1}{4}''$–$\frac{1}{3}''$) rosettes of tiny recurved leaves, basically dark blue-green, but varying in appearance to light grey-green, and even white, according to the density of their limy glands. Loose, few-flowered sprays of small, rounded white flowers on wiry stems. A charming little plant and easy in open, well-drained limy scree, or rock crevice. May–June.

*K. S. 'CHRISTINE'.** Cherry-red flowers over cushions of dark green, silver-edged rosettes. March–April. (Pl. 27)

*K. ×E. S. 'CHRYSTALAE'.** A delightful hybrid, with handsome silvery rosettes and arching sprays of small pink flowers in purple-red calyces on hairy reddish stems. 4″–6″. March–April. (Pl. 27)

*K. S. 'CRANBOURNE'.** One of the best tempered and most attractive hybrids, forming wide, rather flat cushions of grey-green blunt leaves and bearing many large, solid rose flowers on 1″ stems. 1″–1$\frac{1}{2}$″. March onwards.

*K. S. diapensioides.** European Alps. Forms a hard cushion of rosettes of very tiny blunt leaves, very closely impacted, and looking, and feeling, like some grey-green lichen, hard and unyielding to the touch. One to two milk-white flowers on each 1″ stem. May–June.

*S. d.** var. **lutea** (*aretioides* var. *primulina*). A pale yellow form, or possibly a hybrid.

*K. ×E. S. 'EDITHAE'.** A pleasant hybrid with grey-green leaves and soft pink flowers. 2″–3″. March–April.

*K. S. 'ELIZABETHAE'.** One of the *burseriana* hybrids. A good and easy plant, with grey-green cushions and prolific heads of soft yellow. 2″–3″. March–April.

*K. S. 'FALDONSIDE'.** An old hybrid and one of the best yellows, with beautiful grey-green spiny rosettes and large, solid, citron-yellow flowers. 2″–2$\frac{1}{2}$″. March–April. (Pl. 27)

S. ferdinandi-coburgii. Bulgaria. Dense silver-grey cushions and bright yellow flowers from red buds.

*E. S. ×frederici-augusti.** The name given in gardens to what is possibly a hybrid of *S. porophylla*. Rosettes of narrow, tiny leaves, and arching sprays of small pink flowers in large, furry, claret coloured calyces. 6″. April–May.

*K. S. 'GEUDERI'.** Small, dense cushions, and 2″–3″ heads of deep yellow flowers in early spring. (Pl. 27)

*E. S. grisebachii.** Mts. of Macedonia, Greece, Albania. A very handsome Engleria with wide flat rosettes, deeply encrusted in lime, and tall arching sprays of small pink flowers, hidden in the baggy calyces which, like the whole flower stalk, are covered with deep red, glandular hairs, giving the appearance of crimson fur. Beautiful over a long period, while the inflorescence is lengthening and unfolding. 6″–9″. March–April. (Pl. 27)

*S. g.** 'WISLEY VAR.' is a particularly fine form which was first seen at Wisley but was later found in the wild, on Mt. Tsukala, Albania.

Saxifraga

K. **S.** 'HAAGII'. A good-tempered hybrid which does well out of doors, with rather lax mats of dark green, pointed foliage and rather small, starry, bright yellow flowers in small clusters. Prolific flowerer. 2″–3″. March–April. (Pl. 27)

*K. **S.** 'IRVINGII' and **S.* 'JENKINSIAE'. Two very similar, free-flowering hybrids, probably of the same parentage (*burseriana* × *lilacina*), forming dense, rather flat cushions of small, blue-grey leaves, with solitary, pale pink, sessile or almost sessile flowers, the latter hybrid being slightly larger in all its parts. Very free-flowering. 1″–1½″. March–April. (Pl. 27)

K. × *E.* **S.** 'IRIS PRICHARD'. Habit of *S. burseriana*, with flowers of an unusual shade of pale buff-apricot. 3″. March–April. (Pl. 27)

K. **S.** **juniperifolia.** Caucasus. Smells of juniper when crushed and, oddly, the whole plant suggests a prostrate, huddled juniper, as its tumbled cushions are composed of dense or sprawling shoots closely set with dark green spiny leaves. Small clusters of narrow-petalled yellow flowers, with prominent stamens. 2″. Summer.

*K. × *E.* **S.** × **kellereri.** The earliest of all to flower, from early January onwards, according to the season. Rosettes of grey-green pointed leaves and sprays of rather small but charming soft pink flowers. 3″–4″.

*K. × *E.* **S.** 'KEWENSIS'. Beautiful spiny grey-green rosettes, and graceful sprays of pink medium-sized flowers. 3″–4″. March–April.

K. **S.** **lilacina.** W. Himalaya. Forms a dense cushion of small, rather flat, dull-green rosettes, with solitary flowers of reddish-amethyst. A parent of most of the pink and red hybrids. Prefers a rather shady position, and, uniquely for this section, hates lime. 1″–1½″. March–April.

*K.*S. **macedonica.** In cultivation, the name given to a form of *S. juniperifolia*, with wider petalled flowers of a richer yellow. (Pl. 27)

*K. **S.** **marginata.** Italy. A variable species, forming mats of irregular hummocks of leathery, blunt-tipped leaves, green with a marginal band of lime pittings. Sprays of large, pure white flowers of good texture. 2″–3″. Early spring.

*K. × *E.* **S.** 'MARIAE THERESIAE'. A very distinct hybrid between *S. burseriana* and *S. griesbachii*, with small rosettes of short, grey-green, very pointed leaves and sprays of rather small pink flowers on red stems. An attractive neat plant whose buds first appear as bright crimson hearts deep in the centres of the rosettes. 3″. Early spring.

*E. **S.** **media.** Pyrenees. A typical Engleria, with narrow, pointed, silver-grey leaves, and leafy stems bearing pendent small pink flowers, almost hidden by the inflated red, hairy calyx. 4″–5″. Early.

*K. **S.** 'MEGASEIFLORA'. The habit of *S. burseriana*, but with large, rose flowers, shading to a deeper centre, with ample petals well separated, as in Megasea. 2″–3″. March–April. (Pl. 27)

*K. **S.** 'MOTHER OF PEARL'. A hybrid of unknown parentage with large flowers of soft, shaded shell-pink. 2″–3″. March–April. (Pl. 27)

255

Saxifraga

*K. S. 'Obristii' (*burseriana* × *marginata*). Larger rosettes than *S. burseriana*, and large white flowers from red buds. 2″–3″. March–April. (Pl. 27)

S. 'Parcevalis' ('Myra' × *aizoides*). A hybrid with greener rosettes than most, and clusters of small flowers of the nearest shade to orange since the delightful *S.* 'E. D. Doncaster', which seems to have been a casualty of the war. Not a very striking plant, but an interesting colour break. 3″–4″. April.

*K. S. 'Paulinae'. Another yellow hybrid, rivalling *S.* 'Faldonside', and of a stronger constitution. Solid, well-rounded, clear yellow flowers in sprays above the tight cushions of silvery-green rosettes. 2″. March.

*E. S. porophylla. Appenines, Abruzzi Mts., Italy. Rosettes of grey-green, sharply pointed leaves and glandular, leafy stems, with clusters of small pink flowers in inflated, fluffy, purple-red calyces. This, and the nearly akin *S. thessalica*, are two early flowering saxifrages which are attractive over a long period, by reason of their coloured stems and buds. 4″–6″. March–April. (Pl. 27)

K. × E. S. 'Prosenii'. Parentage unknown, but an interesting plant as the rather crowded clusters of small flowers are reddish-orange. Rosettes small, and greener than most in the section. Flowers over a long period. 2″–3″. March–May.

*K. S. 'Riverslea'. A charming small hybrid, with comparatively large, purple-rose flowers over close silvery mounds. 2″. April. (Pl. 27)

K. S. 'Salomonii'. Silver-grey, spiny rosettes and sprays of few, large white flowers, red in the bud. Not very free-flowering. 3″–4″. April.

K. S. sancta. Greece, Asia Minor. A good-tempered mat-former, quite happy out of doors in almost any soil. Dark green, pointed leaves and sprays of deep yellow flowers. Most free-flowering in poor soil. 2″. March–April.

*K. S. scardica. Macedonia. Dense tufts of small, bristly, blue-grey leaves, and rather flat heads of large, white, vase-shaped flowers, sometimes slightly flushed pink. *S. s.* var. *erythrantha*, Kyllene, Greece, has large flowers which fade to pink, but is reputed in the wild to have deep rose-purple flowers. 4″. June.

K. × E. S. 'Schleicheri'. A very early flowering *burseriana* hybrid, with pale pink flowers on stout reddish stems. 2″–3″. January–February. (Pl. 27)

*K. S. squarrosa. Dolomites, Carpathians, and Karawanken ranges. The smallest of the group, with miniature rosettes of upright $\frac{1}{6}$″ narrow leaves, varying from green to silver-grey, crowded densely to form a slightly humped mat of tiny points, hard as a lichen. Loose sprays of small, round-petalled white flowers on wiry stems. Very gritty scree. A charming little plant, and easy when established, but very slow-growing at first. 1″–2″. Summer.

E. S. stribrnyi. Rhodope Mts., Bulgaria. Handsome rosettes of silver-grey leaves, wide sprays of small pink flowers in inflated, fluffy purple calyces. 3″–4″. Early summer.

*K. S. 'Suendermannii'. Grey, spine-tipped rosettes and solitary large

256

25

Primula pubescens 'Faldonside'
Pulsatilla vulgaris
Ranunculus gramineus

Pulsatilla vernalis
Ramonda myconi
Raoulia lutescens

26

Rhododendron repens
Rhodothamnus chamaecistus
Sanguinaria canadensis

Rhodohypoxis baurii, pink and white forms
Roscoea purpurea
Saponaria 'Bressingham Hybrid'

white flowers. **S.* 'MAJOR' in pale pink (Pl. 27), and *S.* 'PURPUREA' a handsome plant with rich, deep rose flowers. 2″. March–April.

*E. S. **thessalica.** Greece. A handsome Engleria, almost indistinguishable from *S. porophylla*, of which it is often considered to be a form, having the same grey-green to silver-grey, sharply pointed leaves, and sprays of small pink flowers in fluffy purple inflated calyces. 4″–5″. March–April. (Pl. 27)

*K. S. **tombeanensis.** S. Tyrol, very local. A quite distinct small saxifrage, with short, creeping shoots, very densely set with tiny blunt leaves, and so tightly packed upon each other that the slightly humpy green to grey-green cushion feels hard to the touch. Comparatively large pure white flowers on wiry, glandular stems. 2″. Early summer.

*K. S. 'VALERIE FINNIS'. An attractive modern hybrid, possibly of *S. burseriana*, with large, clear yellow flowers of good substance. 2″–3″. March. (Pl. 27)

*K. ×E. S. 'VALERIE KEEVIL' (*godroniana × lilacina*). An early hybrid with very close silver-grey rosettes and deep rose-pink flowers. 2″. March–April. (Pl. 27)

*K. S. 'WINIFRED'. An excellent modern hybrid with close, dark grey-green rosettes, and comparatively large flowers of rich, deep rose. 2″. March–April. (Pl. 27)

OTHER SECTIONS

These vary to such extremes, both in appearance and requirements, that no general comment will cover them.

S. aizoides. Alpine and Arctic Europe (including Gt. Britain), Asia. A mat-forming plant with long, leafy prostrate stems, the individual leaves being fleshy, narrow, almost cylindrical, ½″ long. Flowers starry, bright rich yellow, varying in some districts to orange or rich mahogany red. Moist situation (often found at stream sides), but will persist, though not so lushly, in ordinary scree with plenty of humus, in sun. Summer.

S. androsacea. Alps. Insignificant, except for sink or trough, but found often in non-lime districts up to nearly 10,000 ft. Mimics the high androsaces in the close sward by forming slightly hairy, 1″ rosettes, bearing few-flowered sprays of white flowers. Non-lime scree, not easy or permanent. 1″–2″. Early summer.

S. aspera. European Alps. Forms either tufted cushions or spreading mats of long prostrate shoots, closely set with stiff, narrow, pointed bristly leaves. Sprays of pale yellow, orange-freckled flowers on thin, wiry stems. *S. a.* var. *bryoides* (sometimes reckoned as a separate species, *S. bryoides*) is its high alpine development, with more congested little hummocks, and slightly larger flowers borne *singly*. Scree. 2″–3″. Early summer.

S. biflora. Central Alps. A very high alpine from moraines up to 13,000 ft. Like a more succulent *S. oppositifolia*, with almost metallic foliage and flowers

257

Saxifraga

in shades of blood-red. Attractive, despite Farrer. Difficult in cultivation. Summer.

*S. brunoniana. Sikkim, Himalaya. A very distinct plant, forming loose mats of bright green, bristly margined, pointed leaves in 1″ wide rosettes. In summer, dozens of hair-like runners, several inches long, spray in every direction. These are bright red, and glisten in the sun like spun glass. Each bears at its tip a minute new growth bud, which will root wherever it touches soil. Sprays of rather large, rich yellow flowers in late summer. Easy in any rather moist open soil, and stands all but the most severe winter. 3″.

S. bryoides. See under **S. aspera.**

*S. cebennensis. Cevennes, France. Of the mossy group, this forms symmetrical, hemispherical cushions of close, three-pronged leaves, and bears many rounded white flowers on 2″ stems. Alpine house. Spring. (Pl. 28)

S. cernua. Europe (including Gt. Britain), America. A small but interesting plant with rather succulent, kidney-shaped leaves, slightly scalloped, and erect stems with solitary, rather drooping terminal white flowers. Distinctive by the scarlet bulbils in the axils of the stem leaves. Moist but not stagnant position, but not easy. 3″–4″, or more when suited. Summer.

S. conifera. Pyrenees, Spain. Makes ⅓″ rosettes of slightly hairy three-lobed leaves, and has few-flowered sprays of rounded white flowers fading to pale rose. After flowering the rosettes die back into their resting condition, when they resemble tiny light-brown, green-centred cones. Mat forming. 2″–3″. Summer.

S. cymbalaria. Caucasus to Persia. One of the few annuals suitable for the sink or rock garden. Forms compact branched tufts with rather succulent, bright green leaves up to ½″ across, round or kidney-shaped, slightly lobed, very like our native Ivy-leaved Toadflax (*Linaria cymbalaria*). Very variable in size up to 2″–3″, according to the soil, but even a ½″ tuffet in an arid spot will cover itself with starry, golden-yellow flowers. Seeds itself copiously, but can easily be controlled. A gay and good tempered little plant. May–July. (Pl. 31)

S. decipiens. Very variable and of wide distribution. A parent of many of the named garden mossy saxifrages with various coloured flowers. 4″6–″. Early summer.

S. exarata. Alps, east to Persia. A very variable plant of the mossy group, but as usually grown forms a compact dome of rosettes composed of little three-lobed (sometimes again divided) leaves. Creamy-white flowers. When not in flower very similar to *S. iratiana*. 3″. Spring.

S. flagellaris. Arctic and Sub-Arctic. Very similar to *S. brunoniana*, but rather larger in all its parts and fewer, stouter and less spectacular runners. 3″. Late summer.

S. geum. S.W. Europe (including Ireland and Scotland). Like a small London Pride, but with rounded leaves on long footstalks. Sprays of small white flowers, often spotted red. Cool, rather damp spot.

Saxifraga

S. g. var. **minor** is a dwarf variety of only 3″. Type, 8″–10″. Early summer.

S. granulata. Fair Maids of France, Meadow Saxifrage. Europe (including Gt. Britain, e.g. Dovedale). A deciduous, tufted plant, with rather thick, kidney-shaped, lobed leaves, and slender leafy stems bearing large, pure white flowers. Moist situation. *S. g.* 'FLORE PLENO', with fully double 1″ wide flowers, is more popular in gardens. 6″–10″. Early summer.

S. hypnoides. Dovedale Moss. W. Europe (including Gt. Britain), N. America. A very variable Mossy, which in the native form quickly forms wide dense mats of fresh green mossy foliage, the little leaves, on ½″ pedicels, being so deeply lacinated as almost to be palmate. The flowers are pure white, few to a spray, on wiry stems. 3″. Early summer.

S. iratiana. Spain. Forms a dense cushion of deeply three-cleft leaves, very similar in appearance to *S. exarata*, but the solitary white flowers are almost or completely sessile in the hearts of the rosettes. 2″–3″. Flowers on and off all summer and autumn.

S. latepetiolata. Spain. Basal and stem leaves bright green, hairy, rather succulent, palmately lobed on long petioles. Much branched sprays of clear white round-petalled flowers. Not long-lived, but easy from seed. 9″. Summer.

S. moschata. Pyrenees to Caucasus. The little carpeting mossy saxifrage found in engaging tuffets throughout the Alps, with dense three-cleft leaves and wiry erect stems with sprays of creamy-white or dull yellow, sometimes varying into a dull pink or brownish-red. Seldom grown in the wild form, but delightful in sinks among other small fry of the mountains. 1″–1½″. Early summer.

S. muscoides. High Alps, usually in moist crevices or shingle beds. Often confused with the foregoing, but differs in having undivided linear, bluntly pointed leaves. Flowers white or yellow, very variable, but most attractive in some of the high altitude forms, where they are well-rounded and of solid texture. Choice fine scree, or sink. 1″–1½″. Early summer.

*S. oppositifolia. Widely distributed over Europe (local in Gt. Britain), N. Asia, N. America. Makes dense spreading mats or low cushions of many interlacing prostrate wiry shoots, closely set with tiny, rigid, sessile triangular dark green leaves. Terminal flowers (up to ½″) on main and lateral shoots, of shades from pale purplish-rose up to a deep intense crimson (but usually a rosy heather-colour), and with petals varying from amply-rounded to rather squinny and pointed. The occasional white form is usually of poor constitution. Many varietal names will be found in lists. Among the more distinct are *S. o.* var. *latina*, with rather silver foliage and compact growth, large purple flowers, *S. o.* 'SPLENDENS', with dark green mats and ample deep rose sessile flowers, rather easier and more permanent than most, and *S. o.* 'W. A. CLARK', of neat habit, with good crimson flowers. All require good, open, sunny scree, with plenty of humus, enough water in the growing season

259

Scabiosa

and protection from sudden and abnormal scorching in summer. 1″. Early summer and odd flowers spasmodically. (Pl. 28)

S. 'PRIMULAIZE' (*aizoides* var. *aurantia* × *umbrosa* 'PRIMULOIDES'). A rather surprising hybrid, producing, in effect, a miniature London Pride, with narrower leaves and flowers of red, salmon, or carmine. 3″. Summer.

S. primuloides. See under **S. umbrosa.**

D***S. retusa.** Pyrenees to Bulgaria. Like a smaller, and often more congested, *S. oppositifolia,* with many tiny leathery oval leaves along prostrate wiry shoots, bearing terminally clusters of up to five bright ruby-red, pointed-petalled flowers (not singly as in *S. oppositifolia,* and not as fully open as in that species). A delightful little plant for scree or sink. 1″. Summer.

S. sedoides and **S. seguieri** are two insignificant little plants of no horticultural value, except possibly in a trough garden, but are mentioned as their neat green mats and cushions, closely covered in June–July with tiny greenish yellow flowers, have charm among the other very small fry at great heights. 1″.

S. umbrosa. London Pride. Very widespread in mountain woods. A useful plant for part-shade in any rough corner or border, or will even thrive in the smoke of towns, where it will form masses of long-stalked, leathery, dark green spoon-shaped leaves and, in summer, erupt into foot-high clouds of tiny pink starry blossoms. *S. u.* 'PRIMULOIDES' is a dwarf edition of the type, of neat and not invasive habit, with 7″–8″ sprays of pink flowers. *S. u.* P. 'ELLIOTT'S FORM' is even smaller and a delightful little plant with neat, glossy foliage, and a cloud of small, deep rose flowers on 4″–6″ stems. Early summer.

SCABIOSA *Dipsaceae*

Of the two Scabious most widely grown, one has now been assigned to the genus Pterocephalus. All are valuable for their ease of cultivation in any open site, their long life and their late and prolonged flowering.

S. columbaria. Europe (including Gt. Britain). The very variable blue-purple scabious, which is such a lovely feature of the South Downs and elsewhere, usually reaches 1½′–2′, but in the European Alps dwarf forms may be found, in which the basal leaves are prostrate and the flowering stalks only from 2″–5″. When obtainable these are delightful plants for poor stony soil, and for pans in the alpine house, giving a series of neat blue-purple heads of flower over a long period. July to late autumn.

S. graminifolia. S. Europe. Makes a loose mat of spreading linear leaves, silvery with adpressed hairs, from which rise throughout the summer 6″–8″

heads of pinkish lavender. It appreciates a sheltered well-drained sunny spot and a limy soil.

S. parnassi. See **Pterocephalus parnassi.**

S. pterocephalus. See **Pterocephalus parnassi.**

SCHIVERECKIA *Cruciferae*

This genus of two species is nearly related to Alyssum, under which name it is often found.

S. doerfleri. Balkans, Asia Minor. A tiny plant with neat little silvery rosettes and many small white flowers. 2″. Spring.

S. podolica (*Alyssum podolicum*). S. Europe. Makes a silvery rosette of narrow leaves, forked at the tips, from which rise 6″ sprays of small white cruciform flowers. Late spring.

SCHIZOCODON *Diapensiaceae*

These beautiful evergreen plants from Japan form spreading mats of tough, glossy, oval or rounded toothed leaves on 1″–2″ wiry stems. The flowers, in clusters of four to six, form beautifully fringed bells of shaded pink, rather similar in shape to Soldanella. The foliage takes autumn tints of rich to dark red. They require cool woodland conditions in leafy lime-free soil, but the autumn colouring is less pronounced in deep shade. Seed. 4″–5″. Spring.

Catalogues sometimes list two or three species, but these are all considered to be varieties of the single species ***S. soldanelloides,** of which the type plant is described above.

S. s. var. **alpinus** is smaller and more compact in all its parts.

S. s. ilicifolius has smaller leaves with fewer teeth, giving them a holly-like appearance. *S. s.* 'MAGNUS' has larger leaves edged with small teeth, and deep rose fringed flowers.

SCHIZOSTYLIS *Iridaceae*

The Kaffir Lilies are welcome subjects for their gaiety and late flowering period, September–November. They are hardy in a warm sunny border, and although they can rise to 2 ft. they are usually considerably

261

Scilla

less in a dry, meagre situation. The elegant sprays of star-shaped flowers, in habit like slender gladioli, are in clear shades of scarlet and pink above narrow iris-like foliage. The only species in cultivation is:

*S. coccinea. S. Africa. This has brilliant scarlet flowers. There are two colour variations, *S. c.* 'MRS. HEGARTY', a beautiful rose pink, and *S. c.* 'VISCOUNTESS BYNG', a paler pink.

SCILLA *Liliaceae*

The Squills or Wild Hyacinths mainly flower in the early spring when their ease of cultivation and unfailing wealth of flowers make them welcome and almost indispensable. They do, however, increase freely and seed themselves widely in almost any soil or position. This may be counted an advantage or a fault, according to circumstances. Of the many hardy species described fully in *Collins Guide to Bulbs*, the following are a representative sample:

S. autumnalis. Europe, N. Africa. Found in Gt. Britain, especially amongst short turf in the W. coastal districts, this has rather narrow bell-shaped flowers of reddish-purple. Autumn flowering. 4″–5″.

S. bifolia. Mediterranean region. Linear rather lush leaves (generally only a pair) like most of the genus, and sprays of rather small, pendent flowers which may be blue, pinkish, or even almost white. 4″–8″. Spring.

*S. peruviana. Mediterranean region. The so-called Cuban Lily has no connection with Cuba or Peru. It is a handsome plant with a rosette of 1″ wide glaucous, purple-suffused leaves from which emerges a stout stem bearing a large, dense, conical head up to 5″ across, of many small, star-like flowers, variable in colour but usually of a deep purplish blue, which is the most attractive form. Hardy in a sunny sheltered spot, or makes a striking plant for the alpine house. Early summer flowering. 10″–12″.

*S. siberica. E. Russia, Siberia. The Spring Beauty or Siberian Squill, produces in early spring its sprays of slightly pendent, bell-shaped flowers with the utmost prodigality. With very little variation, they are of a rich and brilliant pure blue, and several flowering stems are produced from each bulb. Freely self-seeding. 4″–6″.

*S. tubergeniana. N.W. Persia. An invaluable, very early flowering plant, introduced accidentally amongst imported *Puschkinia scilloides*. This resembles the foregoing in habit, but has a much larger bulb and flowers of a clear pale blue, with streak of deeper blue, rather suggesting a solid, deeper coloured Puschkinia. Flowering begins as the buds emerge from the ground, and continues over a long period, the succeeding flower-stalks lengthening until eventually they attain 6″ or more. Increases well, but seldom produces seed. March–April.

*S. verna. Europe (including cliff edges in Gt. Britain). A most delightful miniature, rarely seen in cultivation. Small star-shaped mauve-blue fragrant flowers on 2″–3″ slender stems. Mid-spring.

SCUTELLARIA *Labiatae*

The Skull-caps are of easy culture in any open, well-drained position. They have hooded and lipped flowers, usually with a relatively long and narrow corolla tube, either from the axils of the leaves or as a close terminal spike. They flower in late summer and early autumn.

S. alpina. Europe, Central Asia. A procumbent plant with whorled heads of purple, hooded flowers with cream lips. Variable, but handsome in its best forms. 8″. July–August.

S. indica var. **japonica.** Japan. A bushy little plant with many small, grey-green, slightly toothed leaves, and many blue-purple skull-caps in mid-summer. 5″–6″. Summer.

S. orientalis. S. Europe, Central Asia. A rather charming low plant with small hoary leaves and 1″ long yellow and brown flowers. 2″–6″. July–August.

S. scordiifolia. Korea. A comparative newcomer, making a tangled bushlet of up to 6″, with many narrow, lipped, flowers of an almost pure deep blue. Long flowering throughout the summer.

SEDUM *Crassulaceae*

This genus of about 300 species is often neglected, sometimes undeservedly. It must be confessed that many of its members lack any air of distinction, but almost all are doggedly good-tempered plants which will grow on most unpropitious sites. There are, moreover, a few species, including the two monocarpics, *S. pilosum* and *S. sempervivoides*, which can take their place with the choicest alpines. Most are of mat-forming or sprawling habit, with stout semi-prostrate stems (often self-rooting) plentifully set with rather succulent small leaves, in some species narrowly cylindrical, and in some almost circular or rounded triangles. The flowers, which may be solitary but are more often in flat inflorescences, are five-petalled and starry in outline. In the mass they are showy, as they are borne in abundance. Propagation is almost too easy by seed or self-layering, and in many of the more succulent species any small leaf accidentally broken off will form

263

Sedum

roots and develop a new plant in the soil on which it falls. Summer flowering. Of the very many obtainable, some of the more distinct are here described.

S. acre. Stonecrop. Gt. Britain to Persia, Norway to Morocco. The little native stonecrop of our country walls is not to be despised as it will grow and flower abundantly where little else will survive. Covered in summer with its bright yellow stars. 1″–2″.

S. a. 'AUREUM' is a variety in which the little leafy shoots are tipped bright golden-yellow in spring. 1″–2″. Summer.

S. album. Europe (including Gt. Britain), Siberia, W. Asia, N. Africa. Creeping and mat-forming, with many ½″ narrowly cylindrical grey-green leaves, and much-branched inflorescences of white starry flowers on pinkish stems. Useful for the odd corner, but invasive. 3″–4″. Summer.

S. anglicum. W. Europe (including Gt. Britain). A tiny charmer with fat, long-ovoid, often red-tinted leaves and white, sometimes pink-flushed ½″ stars. 1″–2″. Summer.

S. atratum. Mts. of Europe. Only an annual, but attractive as seen in the mountains, with 1″ high stems crowded with tiny, sausage-like leaves, often suffused with rich, deep red. Reddish or greenish-white flowers. Attractive in a sink, where it will seed itself, but likely to need aridity to produce its richest colouring. 1″. Summer.

*S. brevifolium. S.W. Europe, Morocco. Very like a small, powdery *S. dasyphyllum*, of which it is sometimes considered a sub-species. A tiny creeper with small ovoid leaves crowded in 4 rows along the stems. The whole plant is densely mealy and slightly suffused with pink. White flowers. 1″–1½″. May–June.

S. b. var. **quinquefolium** is similar, but with leaves in five ranks. Both need perfect drainage, and make attractive pans in the alpine house. 1″.

*S. coeruleum. S. Europe, Algeria. Only an annual, but most attractive when its branched stems, with rather sparse fat little leaves, erupt into clouds of tiny, pale blue, starry flowers. Easy from seed. 2″–3″. Summer onwards according to when sown.

*S. cauticola. Japan. Very similar to the old-established and better-known *S. sieboldii*, but differing in having pairs of opposite leaves on its arching, radiating stems. Rather variable, but in its more compact forms an attractive late-flowering plant with large heads of crimson flowers. Spreading. September. (Pl. 28)

*S. dasyphyllum. S. Europe (including Gt. Britain). Forms dense mats of leafy, upright stems, densely set with small egg-shaped leaves of a lovely soft grey-green. Starry flowers of palest pink, or sometimes pure white. One of the most attractive, at all seasons, of the easy sedums. 1″–2″. June.

S. ewersii. W. Himalaya to Mongolia. Quite a pleasant plant, but may ramp. Long trailing stems with pairs of rounded leaves, blue-grey in tone. Heads of pink to ruby flowers. August–September.

Sedum

S. hispanicum. Caucasus and Asia Minor westwards to Italy. A curious plant, forming a carpet of short, quite prostrate stems, very leafy with small, grey-blue adpressed pointed leaves, and white flowers. Dies back to a tangled mat of dried twigs but revives after a period of dormancy. 1″–2″. June.

*S. hobsonii. Tibet. Introduced in the early part of this century as *S. praegerianum*, this is one of the more attractive sedums. It has completely prostrate growth, its 4″–6″ stems radiating like the spokes of a wheel, with narrow fleshy leaves, dark green and often red-tipped. The rather large, bluish-rose flowers, in appearance like heather bells, are borne in few-flowered clusters towards the ends of the shoots. Quite hardy, but makes a good pan for the alpine house. Dies down completely in winter. July.

DP***S. humifusum.** Mexico. A delightful plant when in good health, forming thick, tumbled mats of short-creeping shoots, densely set with tiny, fleshy leaves, red tinted when old. The solitary terminal flowers are bright yellow. Requires plenty of water in the growing season, and must be grown in the alpine house, where it makes a very attractive pan, as it will not stand severe frost. Should be kept almost dry through the winter. 1″–2″. April–June.

S. kamschaticum. N. China, Kamchatka, E. Siberia. An easygoing plant with dark green fleshy spatulate leaves and yellow flowers. 4″. June–September.

S. k. 'VARIEGATUM', whose leaves have a white margin, is the form usually grown.

S. lydium. W. Asia Minor. Forms a mat of short, rooting stems, with many ¼″ narrowly cylindrical leaves, the whole plant usually red-tinged. Dense heads of small white flowers with pink-tipped sepals. 2″–3″. June.

S. oreganum. W. N. America. One of several rather similar species forming mats of loose rosettes of flat, fleshy, spatulate leaves, in this case often red-tinged. Flat heads of yellow flowers. 2″–3″. July–August.

*S. pilosum. Persia, Caucasus, Asia Minor. The beauty of the genus, forming dense, softly hairy, tubby rosettes very suggestive of a closely-packed sempervivum of the *ciliosum* group. It is monocarpic, and may flower at any period from its second year onwards, so that a succession can be kept going from seed. The short, dense, flower clusters, 1″–3″ across may well hide the · plant when it is in flower, and suggest giant heads of a five-petalled *Daphne cneorum*. A lovely pan for the alpine house. Easy from seed. 2″–3″. May–June.

*S. populifolium. Siberia. A very distinct, shrubby sedum, with slender, branched, erect stems, with ¾″ almost holly-shaped succulent leaves, and much branched inflorescences of white or pink-flushed flowers, with a distinct hawthorn scent. Not proof against very severe frost, which makes it difficult to place, as it tends to become rather leggy for the alpine house. 8″–15″. August.

S. praegerianum. See **S. hobsonii.**

*S. primuloides. Yunnan. In general appearance very like *S. hobsonii*, but

265

Sedum

with a few central evergreen, barren rosettes, and greenish-white narrow bell-shaped flowers, equally large, but fewer to each trailing shoot. 2″–3″. August.

*S. 'Schorbusser Blut'. A modern introduction, possibly a variety or hybrid of *S. spurium*, with deep purple-red foliage, and rich crimson flowers. Best in a hot, dry spot. Prostrate or up to 4″. August. (Pl. 28)

*S. sempervivoides. Asia Minor, Caucasus. A spectacular little plant but biennial, which is probably why it is so seldom seen, as it is not difficult from seed. Sempervivum-like rosettes of thick, dark green, widely-oval, pointed leaves, softly downy and stained dark red. Ample heads of rather small flowers of a brilliant, fiery scarlet. Alpine house. 4″–8″. June–July.

*S. sieboldii. Japan. Often seen in hanging baskets indoors, but almost hardy, dying back to a cluster of resting buds in the winter. Long spraying shoots with little grey-green succulent, slightly serrated, rounded leaves, grouped in sets of three along the stems (in contrast to pairs in the case of *S. cauticola*, which otherwise it much resembles). Terminal heads of numerous pinky flowers, but its chief beauty is in the foliage, which at different seasons is opalescent or suffused with rose and lemon. October.

S. s. 'Variegatum' has handsome variegated foliage.

S. spathulifolium. W. N. America. One of the most attractive for the open garden, making dense mats of overlapping flat rosettes of 1″ or more across, with fleshy spoon-shaped leaves, recurved at the tip. Evergreen and often red-tinged. Flowers yellow, in a flat head 2″–3″ across.

*S. s. 'Capablanca' (Cape Blanco, S. Oregon) is attractive by means of its grey, almost white, foliage, for whose protection an alpine house is indicated.

*S. s. var. **purpureum** is a handsome plant with larger rosettes and leaves which are wine coloured when young and later white with meal. 3″–5″. Summer. (Pl. 28)

S. spurium. N. Persia. Caucasus. One of the most commonly grown, forming mats of tangled shoots with opposite, widely-oval leaves, slightly serrate, and variable flowers of white through rather muted shades of pink. Easy in all soils, and even under trees.

S. stahlii. Mexico. Should perhaps not be mentioned as it is definitely only suitable for the alpine house at most, but it is one of the most attractive in foliage, the upright stems bearing glossy, sausage-shaped leaves which flush from bronze to a glowing orange, like strings of almost translucent berries. Flowers yellow. 4″–8″. August–September.

S. tatarinowii. N. China. Representative of a small group which make many annual erect or arching stems from a perennial rootstock, alternate ½″–1″ narrow leaves, hemispherical in section, with heads of pinkish-white flowers. 4″–6″. July–August.

p***S. winkleri.** S. Spain, Gibraltar. Perhaps the most attractive of the perennial sedums, but not proof against the severest frosts. Mat forming, with softly hairy, rather fleshy sempervivum-like rosettes and few-flowered sprays of beautiful, solid, white, green-veined flowers—½″ or more across. Worth care in preserving. Summer.

This list includes the most desirable species as well as some more usually found in gardens, but the latter category can be enlarged almost indefinitely with others of equal merit, from any alpine specialist's catalogue.

SEMIAQUILEGIA *Ranunculaceae*

Until recently the members of this genus were included in Aquilegia, which they much resemble, differing in having the spurs absent or only rudimentary. The only species in general cultivation is:

S. ecalcarata (*Aquilegia ecalcarata*). W. China. Of habit like a slender aquilegia, with rather small brownish-red (almost chocolate) spurless flowers. A charming little plant, and easy in any soil or position. Up to 12″. Early summer.

SEMPERVIVELLA *Crassulaceae*

This small genus from N. India has one member of the greatest charm which is also valuable for its late flowering:

*S. alba. Himalaya. Forms a close mat or cushion of sempervivum-like rosettes of small, red-tinted, succulent leaves, from which rise in August–September short 2″ sprays of comparatively large, very solid-petalled, star-shaped flowers of a deep cream. Hardy without protection in all but exceptional winters. Very free from seed. Autumn. (Pl. 29)

SEMPERVIVUM *Crassulaceae*

The R.H.S. Dictionary mercifully restricts this genus to about 25 species, but the list of those in cultivation, including synonyms, varieties, and innumerable hybrids, either natural or man-made, runs into hundreds. In fact, one nursery alone offers a collection of 50 different named varieties. All form symmetrical rosettes of thick, succulent, pointed leaves, producing young plants from the leaf-axils,

267

Sempervivum

usually on runners but occasionally sessile. The stout flower-stalk, generally leafy to a greater or lesser degree, emerges from the centre of a rosette, which thereafter dies. It bears a flat head of star-shaped flowers, with from 6 to 20 petals, usually in dull shades of reddish- or greenish-brown, but occasionally yellow, or bright rose. Some species are not free-flowering, but this is not always a matter of regret as the genus owes most of its appeal to the satisfying cushions or mats of its rosettes, which may be glossy or downy, green or parti-coloured, or white with wool. Most are content in dry, exposed positions, provided there is some humus in the soil, although some of the larger-rosetted species appreciate a richer diet. All except the most long-suffering species are better for overhead covering from too much winter rain. They will fill large pans with a tightly-packed mat of rosettes (achieved by careful removal of stalks after flowering) but look more in character when allowed to run along rock crevices if this can be con- trived. Any individual species is very variable in size, shape, colour, and hairiness of rosettes according to the season and the conditions in which it is grown. This, with the fact that some flower infrequently, often makes exact identification difficult between nearly allied species. The following list selects representatives with the most distinct and recognizable features. All are summer-flowering, and spasmodically at other times.

S. allionii. S. Alps, France to Tyrol. Distinguished by its pale green rosettes, which are about 1″ across and very finely hairy. Greenish-white flowers. 2″–3″.

*S. arachnoideum. The Cobweb-Houseleek. Pyrenees to Carpathians. Tightly packed, rather spherical rosettes, flattened across the top, with the tips of the leaves connected by cobweb-like hairs. Variable in size from less than ½″ rosettes to 1″ or more, and in degree of woolliness, some forms, with a little protection from excessive damp, appearing as packed balls of white cotton-wool. Flowers a bright rose-red, the best of the genus. A very lovely little plant when seen truly in character. 3″–4″. (Pl. 29)

S. arenarium. E. Alps. An attractive little species with small (¼″–¾″) almost globular rosettes of pointed, incurving leaves, often tipped with brown- ish-red. Offsets minute, on short, very slender stems. Flowers (infrequent) pale green with upright petals. One of the smallest sempervivums.

*S × calcaratum. Probably a hybrid with *S. tectorum* as one parent. A hand- some plant with wide rosettes of up to 6″. Leaves glaucous, crimson at the base and occasionally at the tips, or, in some forms, of a uniform glaucous purple. Branched inflorescences, up to 6″ across, of reddish-purple flowers on stout stems with many reddish leaves. Up to 12″.

Sempervivum

S. ciliosum. Bulgaria. A very distinct species, with slightly flattened, globose, 1″–2″ rosettes of grey-green incurving leaves with very many long, stiff, translucent hairs, lying flatly to enclose the rosette. Offsets on slender, finely leafy runners. Flowers greenish-yellow to yellow.

*S. c. forma **borisii** has an even hairier, and, if anything, more compact rosette.

*S. c. 'MALI HAT' is smaller still, with denser hairs through which the red-flushed rosettes give a very lovely colour effect. One of the most delightful sempervivums.

*S. erythraeum. Bulgaria. Rather open rosettes of a lovely glaucous grey-green, softly flushed with pinkish mauve. There are two distinct forms, one with noticeably wide, oval pointed leaves, and the other with narrower leaves extremely symmetrically arranged. Both are among the most beautiful of the genus by reason of their lovely texture and colouring. Red-purple flowers on very leafy stems. Offsets on short, thick runners. 5″–6″.

*S. heuffelii. S.E. Europe. Distinctive by its method of increase. The parent rosette splits symmetrically into two or more equal rosettes (or very occasionally produces sessile shoots among the lateral leaves) but never makes stolons. 1″–5″ flattish rosettes, leaves green, sometimes with a purple tip, finely hairy. Flowers pale yellow or yellowish-white. 4″–6″.

S. kosaninii. Macedonia. Large, flat, dense rosettes, 2″–3″ across of very fleshy, purple-tipped leaves and strong offsets on leafy stems up to 5″. Red flowers. (*S. kindigeri, S. leucanthum, S. pittonii, S. ruthenicum* are very similar in rosette but have yellow flowers.) 6″–8″.

S. montanum. Pyrenees, Corsica, Alps, Carpathians. The species most universally met with in the Alps (and in gardens), but extremely variable. The comparatively small rosettes ($\frac{1}{2}$″–1$\frac{1}{2}$″) are of a rather sombre dark green, and very finely hairy. Flowers violet-purple, but colour variations are occasionally reported. It very readily crosses with other species in the vicinity, especially with *S. arachnoideum, S. tectorum,* and *S. wulfenii*. Many offsets, on slender leafy stems. 3″–4″.

S. octopodes. Balkans. A distinct species with 1″ rosettes of rather upright downy leaves, and many conspicuous radiating stolons set with tiny leaves. Flowers greenish-yellow. 3″–4″.

S. o. var. **apetalum** is without petals but has numerous sepals and more numerous, narrower leaves. It is also more permanent in cultivation. 3″–4″.

S. pumilum. Caucasus. One of the tiniest sempervivums, with $\frac{1}{2}$″–$\frac{3}{4}$″ rosettes, like a miniature *S. montanum*. Flowers rosy-purple with a pale margin. 1$\frac{1}{2}$″–4″.

S. schlehanii (*marmoreum*). Hungary to Greece. The type plant is very like the ordinary Houseleek, *S. tectorum*, but *S. s.* var. *rubrifolium* (*rubicundum* of gardens) is a handsome plant which has crimson leaves with green tips. A specially brilliant colour form, with strong demarcation between the bright

269

Senecio

crimson main portion and the sea-green tip, has been given the name *S.
'ORNATUM', and is possibly a hybrid between S. schlehanii and S. tectorum.
This is the most spectacular of all Sempervivums, and not so often seen now
as before 1939. Flowers whitish, with broad crimson medium band. 5″-6″.

S. soboliferum. Hen and Chickens Houseleek. N. Europe, Asia. Crowded,
globose, incurved, bright green rosettes and very many globular offsets, often
from among the middle leaves, which easily detach themselves from their
frail stolons, and scatter in all directions. Greenish-yellow flowers. 4″-6″.

S. tectorum. Houseleek. Pyrenees, Alps, Appenines, naturalized in Gt.
Britain. This, the commonest and largest of all the sempervivums, is so
variable that during its many centuries of cultivation it has, according to
Dr. Praeger's exhaustive monograph, accumulated no less than 67 synonyms.
To this day it has, in Central Europe, a reputation for healing, and its
presence on a roof has long been believed to protect against lightning. Its
large rosettes, usually 2″-3″, but occasionally up to 8″, are rather flat and
open, the leaves smooth, wide, and pointed, usually with a large purple tip.
Flowers (infrequent) are a purplish colour. Catalogues list many varieties,
of which the two most attractive are S. t. var. calcareum, with very glaucous
leaves with brown-purple tips, and S. t. 'TRISTE', with reddish-brown tips
to the rosettes and reddish-brown stem leaves. This last name is also given to
other forms with leaves suffused with purplish-brown. The species hybridizes
readily, especially with S. arachnoideum and S. montanum. Stem 8″-12″, shaggy
with white hairs and many overlapping hairy, lanceolate leaves.

S. wulfenii. Austrian and Swiss Alps. An attractive species with large
rosettes (up to 3″) of grey-green glaucous leaves shading to a soft reddish-
purple at the base. Distinctive by the erect conical shape of the centre of the
rosette when the young leaves are forming, and by being the only smooth-
leaved species to have yellow flowers (in this case with purple base to the
petals). Few offsets, on short thick stolons. One of the easiest to identify in
the Alps, though rather rare, but not widely grown in cultivation. 6″-7″.

SENECIO   Compositae

The Groundsels form probably the largest genus in the vegetable
kingdom, and the majority are as weedy as their common prototype,
or too large for our purpose. There are to be seen, however, in the
European Alps, a few species which are not only compact and slow
of increase, but which are delightful as foliage plants alone and, in a
few cases, for their flowers also. The high mountain forms require
very gritty, well-drained soil, in a sunny position.

S. abrotanifolius. Central Europe. Around the tree limit in the Eastern
Alps, this handsome plant makes stiff 10″-12″ stems with many carrot-like
leaves of crisp, glossy dark green, and sprays of daisy-like flowers of fiery

Serapias, Serratula

almost orange-yellow. A more compact form found in the Dolomites is often given varietal or even specific name (*S. a.* var. *tiroliensis* or *S. tiroliensis*). Good peaty soil. Summer.

*S. incanus. European Alps. A small tufted perennial with silvery foliage almost white with adpressed hairs. The leaves are deeply, but very variably, lobed. A delightful little foliage plant, not really enhanced by the narrow spires of tiny tufted sessile golden buttons in August. 2″–4″.

S. i. var. **carniolicus** is very similar, as variable in leaf shape, not quite as woolly-white as the type plant, and with rather larger flower-heads.

*S. uniflorus. European Alps, especially on high granitic formations. This is one of the most charming high alpines, with its small rosettes (up to 4″) of more or less deeply lobed, finely woolly, white leaves, and single daisy-like heads of purest gold. Not easy to keep for long in cultivation. Needs a well-drained gritty acid soil, in sun but not parched. Very variable in leaf form and flower, but always delightful. 2″–4″. Spring and early summer.

SERAPIAS *Orchidaceae*

These handsome orchids are being introduced more widely into cultivation, but although a few prove hardy out of doors in some districts it is safer to grow them in pots, with possible protection in a hard winter. The flowers, two to ten, are borne at the top of a 7″–12″ stalk, and are spurless. Each emerges horizontally from an upright, pointed, parallel-veined sheath, and shows a very large, pendent, tongue-like lip under an arched hood. Stony, damp, woodland soil with plenty of humus. Summer.

S. vomeracea (*longipetala*). The Long-lipped Serapias is common throughout the Mediterranean region, and the only species found in Switzerland. The flowers are large and handsome, the hood being pale red, with deeper red parallel veins, and the lip reddish-brown, with a central yellow zone.

S. parviflora, the Small-flowered Serapias and **S. cordigera,** the Heart-flowered Orchid, from all countries surrounding the Mediterranean, are dwarfer and less robust plants, with the same general pattern of flower.

SERRATULA *Compositae*

S. 'SHAWII'. Europe. Useful for its late flowering season, as the rather stocky cornflower-like heads of purplish-red do not appear until October. 8″–9″.

271

SHORTIA *Diapensiaceae*

The two species of this genus which are in cultivation are among the most beautiful of our spring-flowering sub-shrubs, when happy in their conditions. They require a cool, moist, well-drained site, in neutral or acid soil (with peat and/or leaf-mould). The evergreen leaves, which are all radical, and are held on thin, stiff petioles, have a glossy, deep green surface which is suffused, more or less, according to position and the time of year, with deep red. They are quite hardy but their attractive appearance at all times makes them welcome in pans in the alpine house. Seed is occasionally set. Propagation may be by seed or very careful division.

1 Saxifraga burseriana 'His Majesty'
2 S. 'Obristii'
3 S. × borisii
4 S. burseriana 'Crenata'
5 S. 'Buttercup'
6 S. oppositifolia var. alba
7 S. burseriana 'His Majesty'
8 S. 'Haagii'
9 S. × apiculata 'Alba'
10 S. burseriana 'Gloria'
11 S. 'Geuderii'
12 S. burseriana major 'Lutea'
13 S. 'Faldonside'
14 S. juniperifolia var. macedonica
15 S. 'Valerie Finnis'
16 S. ferdinandi-coburgii 'Radislavovii'
17 S. 'Valerie Finnis'
18 S. burseriana 'Sulphurea'
19 S. oppositifolia 'W. A. Clark'
20 S. 'Suendermanii Major'
21 S. porophylla
22 S. 'Hocker Edge'
23 S. 'Iris Pritchard'
24 S. 'Irvingii'
25 S. burseriana var. minor
26 S. 'Biasolettii Chrystalie'
27 S. grisebachii
28 S. oppositifolia 'Splendens'
29 S. 'Megasiflora'
30 S. 'Christine'
31 S. 'Jenkinsae'
32 S. 'Schleicheri'
33 S. 'Winifred'
34 S. oppositifolia var. latina
35 S. 'Mother of Pearl'
36 S. thessalica 'Waterperry'
37 S. 'Winifred'
38 S. 'Riverslea'

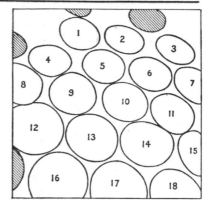

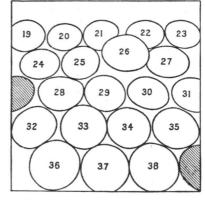

Kabschia saxifrages in pots: below, *pink
and red;* above, *yellow and white*

Saxifraga cebennensis
Saxifraga 'Southside Seedling'
Sedum 'Schorbusser Blut'

Saxifraga oppositifolia
Sedum cauticola
Sedum spathulifolium purpureum

Sieversia, Silene

*S. galacifolia. N. Carolina. Has almost round leaves on long slender petioles, and solitary 1″ white flowers, becoming faintly pink-tinged. The five petals, slightly crenate at the edges, form a shallow funnel. 5″–6″. Spring and early summer.

*S. uniflora. Japan. A rather dwarfer, sturdier plant, with widely heart-shaped leaves with dentate edges, on shorter petioles. The larger, more widely open flowers of white to pale pink have rounded petals, more deeply crenate and on shorter pedicels. Unless grown in dense shade the glossy leaves are richly suffused with red throughout the year. A most beautiful plant, of which colour forms in different shades of pure pink have at times been given varietal names. 3″–4″. Spring.

> **S. u.** var. **grandiflora** is even more free-flowering than the type, and has larger flowers, up to 1½″ across. (Pl. 29)

SIEVERSIA. See GEUM

SILENE *Caryophyllaceae*

The Catchfly or Campion genus extends throughout the northern hemisphere, and varies from the 1″ high Moss Campion to species of 12″ or more, which are too tall for the rock garden, and from good-tempered, rather ordinary plants, valued for their floriferousness and late flowering, to flamboyant beauties from N. America, more tempera-mental and exacting. Several of the more exotic members have alternated between the genera Silene and Melandrium, and may be found in catalogues under either name. Members of the Pink family, they are mostly perennial herbs, making tufts of linear to lanceolate foliage, with spraying stems, characteristically swollen at the nodes by the opposite leaves, with conspicuous five-petalled flowers, often in brilliant reds or bright pinks. Best increased by seed, which is usually but not always in some American species, prolific. The rarer and more spectacular ones are not usually long-lived, nor easy to procure, so, when obtainable, seed should be sown to ensure a continuance of stock. Well-drained soil with humus.

S. acaulis. Northern hemisphere, as far south as Spain (including Gt. Britain). Moss Campion, Cushion Pink. Densely mat-forming with narrow, pointed, glossy green leaves of about ½″. Common throughout the European Alps, where its wide cushions are covered with small, five-petalled, vivid pink, almost sessile flowers. Easy to grow in cultivation, but shy flowering. Poor soil or scree treatment, in an open sunny position, gives the best hope of obtaining flowers. Variable in shade through paler pinks to white.

273

Silene

S. a. 'ALBA'. White, not so attractive as the type plant.

S. a. var. **exscapa.** Has very small flowers almost lost in the dense cushion of tiny upright leaves.

S. alpestris. Central Alps. A tufted rambling plant with wiry sprays of many white, starry flowers. Good for walls or cliffs. There is an attractive double form, *S. a.* 'FLORE PLENO', with densely-rosetted flowers which are more long-lasting than the type. Summer.

S. armeria. Europe, naturalized in Gt. Britain. An annual, with narrow, blue-grey, pointed foliage, and sprays of small, vivid pink Campion flowers. Height 4″–12″, according to position. Once grown it will continue by self-seeding, but not so freely as to become a nuisance. Summer.

DP***S. californica.** California. A striking plant by reason of its unusual, almost brick-red flowers. Light green, lanceolate foliage which dies back in winter. Not an easy plant, but perennial in a light, well-drained soil. 6″–10″. Summer.

DP***S. elisabetha** (*Melandrium elisabetha*). Southern Alps. Perhaps the outstanding beauty of the family, with very narrow glossy leaves and huge Ragged Robin flowers of magenta-rose, on downy, purplish stems. 3″–6″. Likes lime.

S. elongata. Central Alps. Distinct from *S. acaulis* by its larger, looser mats, and larger flowers on stems of 1″ or more.

S. e. 'CORREVONIANA' is a double form of this species. 2″. Summer.

DP***S. hookeri.** California. A rare and spectacular plant making tufts of pointed oval leaves, greyish with soft hairs, and large flowers, 2″ across, with petals so deeply lobed as to appear to be double in number, of a clear, soft, almost chalky pink, white streaked at the centre. Needs a sunny, very well-drained site, or alpine house. 2″–3″. May–July.

S. ingramii (*Melandrium ingramii*). W. N. America. Barely in cultivation, and where it has been grown it has hardly lived up to its reputation of being an *improved* version of *S. hookeri*.

S. keiskei 'MINOR'. Japan. A comparative newcomer, this flowers in late summer, when its more compact tufts of bronzy green leaves and shorter, neater heads of bright pink flowers make it an improvement on *S. schafta* for autumn colour. 3″. July–August.

S. maritima. W. Europe (including Gt. Britain). The well-known Bladder Campion can, in poor soil, make a symphony of grey-blue narrow tufted foliage and pale opalescent flowers with inflated pale green calyces, veined with soft purple, but is in general too straggling a plant for the rock garden.

S. m. 'FLORE PLENO', the double-flowered form, is more compact and suitable.

S. m. 'ROSEA' is a pink form of the type.

S. nutans. Europe. This, although locally common near the tree limit of the Alps, is seldom seen in gardens, although its slender habit (up to 12″) and

Sisyrinchium

pendent small Campion flowers of shades of muted pink have a quiet charm of their own. Summer.

S. schafta. Caucasus. This 6" tufted plant is happy in any situation, where it will make wide masses of tufted oval-pointed foliage, and produce many 4"–6" sprays of magenta-pink flowers over a long period. It is invaluable for its happy disposition and long and late flowering, but somehow manages to look more like a border edging than a characteristic dweller in the rock garden. July–October. (Pl. 29)

S. vallesia. Cottian and Maritime Alps, Piedmont, etc. A local species, making a loose mat of oval-pointed, grey-green leaves from which rise lax sprays of flowers, ½"–¾" across, with long tubular, striped calyces and cleft pale pink petals, incurving at the tips to show a scarlet reverse. Summer.

*S. virginica. (*Melandrium virginicum.*) W. N. America. The Fire Pink well deserves its local name, as from the tuft of lanceolate or narrowly spatulate deep green leaves 6"–7" stems bear sprays of 1" wide flowers, of the most intense and fiery red, each petal being cleft into two points, more flame-like than any flower I know. Seed is not freely set, at any rate in cultivation. Very careful detaching of an outlying shoot can give a successful cutting. Long-flowering in summer and again in the autumn.

SISYRINCHIUM *Iridaceae*

When not in flower the members of this American genus look like pygmy irises, spreading by creeping rhizomes among the paving-stones or similar crevices which seem their most appropriate home. The foliage is flat and narrowly strap-shaped, and in the summer, and over a long period many of the "leaves" show themselves to be leafy stalks, which erupt at the tips into small satiny six-petalled flowers, usually blue (hence the common name for some species, Blue-eyed Grass), but occasionally yellow and sometimes white. Most are very easy of culture and self-seed, as well as being readily divisible. Flowering from early summer.

*S. angustifolium. N. America. Shares the name of Blue-eyed Grass with the following species. Dense tufts of iris-like linear leaves and bright blue flowers. 6"–7". Summer.

S. bermudiana. Bermuda. Rather taller, up to 10", with satiny, violet-blue flowers, yellow at base. Summer. (Pl. 29)

*S. brachypus. N. America. A comparative newcomer, rather sturdier than *S. angustifolium*, and with clear, bright yellow flowers. 6"–7". Summer.

S. douglasii (*grandiflorum*). N. America. From among rush-like leaves appear the two-flowered sprays of pendent, shimmering purple bells, $\frac{1}{2}"–\frac{3}{4}"$ in depth. Dies down completely after flowering. 8"–10". Summer.

*S. filifolium. Falkland Is. A most ethereal beauty with pendent flowers like translucent fairy goblets—diaphanous white, most delicately veined with pale purplish-red. 6"–8". May.

S. grandiflorum. See **S. douglasii.**

Other species similar to one or other of the above have been spasmodically in cultivation. All are desirable for their neat leafage at all times, and the charm of their delicate flowers, but the small blueflowered species are apt to be invasive and should therefore be judiciously placed where they will not become a nuisance, e.g. among paving-stones.

SOLDANELLA *Primulaceae*

A charming group from the mountain regions of Europe, with a very strong family likeness between the species, which may account for the fact that they hybridize readily when growing in proximity. They are all neat plants, with more or less circular, dark green, glossy, leathery, basal leaves on petioles long in comparison with the blade. The flowers, singly or in loose heads of one to three, are bell- or funnelshaped, with the five petals (shades of violet down to pale lavender and white) fringed more or less, according to the species. All appreciate a moist, cool position, and flowering is more certain when protection is given from overhead winter wet, and from slugs. They are among the most typical flowers of the high Alps and flower with the melting of the snow, the fringes of which they pierce with their little carillons of mauve.

*S. alpina. Alps from Pyrenees to Tyrol. Roundish kidney-shaped leaves and funnel-shaped flowers (one to three) of deep mauve, freaked inside with crimson. 3". Spring.

S. minima. E. Alps. A tiny beauty with little circular leaves on wiry petioles, and single flowers, tubular but fringing outwards at the rim. Pale lilac. 1"–2". Spring.

*S. montana. Throughout the European Alps, in light woodland rather than the higher altitudes of the other species. This is the largest and most showy of the species, making robust clumps from which rise a forest of stout stems, each bearing several (up to ten) wide, fringed, funnel-shaped flowers of bluish-amethyst. Easier and more reliable in flowering than the mountain species in a suitable position in leafy, cool soil, although not so often seen in cultivation. Up to 6″–8″. Spring.

S. pindicola. N. Greece, Albania. Even more sturdy than the foregoing, with dull green leaves, ashy-blue below. Flowers pinkish lilac. 3″–4″. Spring.

*S. pusilla. European Alps. Another small charmer, a little larger than *P. minima*, with singly-borne, narrow, straightly tubular flowers, slightly fringed at the mouth. Pale lavender. Rarer than the foregoing and usually found on high acid formations where it rings its little bells by the million over the close sward on the melting of the snow. 2″–3″. Spring.

S. villosa. Pyrenees. Really a hairy counterpart of *S. montana*, of the same general habit and size, but coarser in appearance. 4″–5″. Spring.

The many natural hybrids between the above species are so variable towards one or other parent as to present no easily distinguishable characteristics.

SOLIDAGO *Compositae*

The Wild Golden Rod, *S. virgaurea*, found throughout Europe, including Gt. Britain, is immensely variable, up to 2 ft., but in the mountains congested forms are found which have been grouped loosely as *S. v.* var. *minuta* or *S. v.* var. *alpestris*. These, although not among the aristocrats of the rock garden, are valuable for their dependable perennial nature, and their summer flowering. They may be depended on to produce bushy little clumps of 4″–8″, with close heads of deep golden flower-heads from July onwards.

SORBUS *Rosaceae*

Really dwarf shrubs, apart from ericaceous plants, are far too few, so a pygmy Mountain Ash is very welcome.

*S. reducta. W. China, Burma. This makes a sturdy woody bush of 6″–12″ or a little more, but is very slow growing, with characteristic pinnate leaves and flat heads of white flowers, ½″ across, followed by conspicuous crimson-pink berries. Seed. Summer.

SPIRAEA *Rosaceae*

The woody Spiraeas provide a few densely twiggy shrublets of under
12″, which are long-lasting and indifferent to soil, although the
growth will be more compact in a sunny position.

S. × bullata. Japan. This forms an intricate bush of rusty stems bearing many
small dull-surfaced, dark green oval leaves, puckered and with toothed edges.
From July onwards it produces flat heads of small, deep rose flowers. Upright
growth to about 12″.

S. hendersonii. Rocky Mts. A compact, narrow-leaved plant with many
inch-long cream "bottle-brushes" on arching stems. 3″–4″. Early summer.
(Pl. 29)

S. caespitosa. See **Petrophytum caespitosum.**

*S. × bumalda 'NANA'. A prostrate dense twiggy plant, with many spraying
branches of small, light green, toothed, oval, pointed leaves and many heads
of small bright rose flowers. 4″–6″, spreading. June–July.

The first and last are invaluable for their compact, twiggy habit and
gay, although individually small, flowers, but to have them at their
attractive best it is really necessary to remove all the dead wood,
including flower-heads of the previous year, as soon as the new growth
is sufficiently advanced.

SPIRANTHES *Orchidaceae*

The Ladies' Tresses are delightful small orchids with the tiny sessile
flowers arranged spirally up the slender spike. They can be naturalized
in turfy loam, and can do well and multiply in fine lawn turf which
is left uncut during the short growing and flowering season.

S. aestivalis. W. Europe (including Gt. Britain). Similar to, but rather
larger than, the commoner *S. spiralis* (q.v.), and a little earlier flowering.
Prefers a damp situation.

S. autumnalis. See **S. spiralis.**

S. spiralis (*autumnalis*). Europe (including Gt. Britain). The flat rosettes
of small pointed leaves are formed in autumn and die away as the flower stalk
arises in August or September. The slender spike of spirally-arranged tiny,
greenish-white flowers is fragrant. Found in dry, short turf, often in chalky
districts. 3″–4″.

Spraguea, Stachys, Statice, Stellera, Sternbergia
SPRAGUEA *Portulacaceae*

S. multiceps. California, especially the high volcanic-ash ridges of the Cascade Mts. Known locally as Pussy Paws, this neat little plant is seldom seen here in cultivation, but when in character it forms a small flat rosette of evergreen fleshy leaves, tinted with dull red or bronze, with oval blades narrowing into short petioles. The flower-stems also radiate, almost horizontally, bearing woolly, pinkish heads of close-packed tiny flowers, carried well outside the leaf rosette. It is sometimes considered a variety of:

S. umbellata, which grows at lower altitudes, and is a larger, less succulent plant.

STACHYS *Labiatae*

Of a race of rather coarse Hedge Nettles two are pleasant and good-tempered plants for the rock garden, in any well-drained sunny spot.

S. corsica. Mediterranean region. A neat plant quickly spreading into a close mat of blunt, oval leaves of a bright, shining green, with myriads of creamy-pink lipped flowers. 1″–2″. Summer.

S. lavandulifolia. Armenia. A more upright plant, with creeping rooting stems and spires of purplish-red flowers in whorls, to which the grey-green velvety leaves make a good foil. 10″–12″. Summer.

STATICE. See LIMONIUM

STELLERA *Thymaeleaceae*

S. chamaejasme. Central Asia. Forms a small thicket of erect slender stems, with many narrowly arrow-shaped leaves and terminal, almost globular, heads of small white flowers, pink-tinged by the reddish corolla tubes. Up to 12″. June.

STERNBERGIA *Amaryllidaceae*

The species of this small genus superficially resemble golden-yellow crocuses when in flower, but actually belong to another Natural Order,

Stokesia, Stylidium, Swertia

a readily recognizable feature being their six stamens (three in crocus). The leaves are strap-shaped, and of a deep glossy green, elongating after flowering time. They are not difficult to grow, but are sometimes capricious in flowering. When established leave undisturbed. Propagation by the splitting of the bulbs. Only two species are in general cultivation:

*S. fischeriana. Caucasus. A valuable and attractive spring bulb, with rich golden-yellow flowers, two or three to a bulb. 6″. March.

*S. lutea. E. Mediterranean to Turkey and Persia. A very valuable autumn-flowering bulb, with solid, glistening, crocus-like flowers of bright golden-yellow, appearing above the deep green, strap-shaped leaves, which elongate later. A good summer ripening helps to encourage free-flowering, but where it is happy it is prolific with its golden chalices. Variable in nature, some geographical forms have been given varietal names. 3″–4″. Late August–October.

STOKESIA *Compositae Monotypic*

S. laevis (*cyanea*). N. America. This is tall for the rock garden, as its normal height is 12″ or more, but the earlier-flowering *S. l.* 'PRAECOX' can be curbed to well below this height by planting in full sun and light, poor soil, and is welcome for its late flowering. A variable plant in size and colour of its Knapweed or sturdy Cornflower-like heads, attractive forms are offered in mauve or almost-blue. 8″–9″. August.

STYLIDIUM *Stylidiaceae*

Of this large genus from Australasia many are not hardy, but one species is attractive for a warm corner or alpine house.

S. graminifolium. Trigger Plant. Tasmania. Forms a perennial tuft of 6″ rigid, grass-like leaves, and produces a slender spike of delightful pink flowers in spring. Sunny, well-drained position or alpine house. Seed or division. 6″–12″.

SWERTIA *Gentianaceae*

A large and very varied genus, of which the widespread *S. perennis* of the alpine regions throughout the northern hemisphere (America,

Symphyandra, Synthyris

Europe, and Asia) is the best known. This forms a spike of wide, star-shaped dull purple flowers, $\frac{3}{4}''$ across, arising on a leafy stem from a basal rosette of elliptical leaves. Boggy conditions. $6''-12''$. Summer.

SYMPHYANDRA *Campanulaceae*

This genus, very nearly akin to Campanula, provides three distinguished plants whose individual flowers merit close examination to appreciate their beauty. Therefore, a position near or even above eye-level is an advantage. Their large, rather solid bells have a wonderful, almost translucent texture, and in a rich sandy loam they bloom freely throughout the late summer.

S. hoffmannii. Bosnia. The flowering stems bearing many white, $1''-1\frac{1}{2}''$ flowers, although $12''$ or more in length, arch gracefully so that the total height is much less.

S. pendula. Caucasus. Velvety, ovate leaves, and cascades of leafy stems, with many beautiful translucent bells of pale greenish yellow. $1'-2'$, but arching stems.

S. wanneri (*Campanula wanneri*). Roumania and Transylvania. A more dwarf plant with branched stems bearing many sharply-toothed leaves and beautiful bells of Tyrian purple in late summer. $6''$.

SYNTHYRIS *Scrophulariaceae*

This genus is the N. American counterpart of the European Wulfenia, bearing close spikes of small labiate flowers in shades of blue-purple in early spring. Seed, or careful division of the green-leaved species. The woolly-leaved members are so temperamental in any case that it is most unwise to disturb an established plant. Woodland soil, not summer-baked.

S. alpina. See **Besseya alpina.**

DP***S. lanuginosa.** Olympic Mts. A very lovely but difficult plant with much cut, feathery foliage, white with adpressed hairs, and $6''-8''$ spikes of blue flowers. Avoid winter wet. A delightful subject for the alpine house. Spring.

S. reniformis (*rotundifolia*). Washington, Oregon, California. Makes a compact clump of basal leaves, kidney-shaped to orbicular, bluntly toothed, with many short stout spikes of small, purplish-blue flowers in March–April.

281

Syringa, Talinum, Tanacetum

One of the earliest Dicotyledons to flower and a beautiful little plant when growing robustly. 4″–6″.

S. r. var. **cordata** (*reniformis*, or *rotundifolia* var. *sweetseri*, or *sweetseri*) is even better than the type, with heart-shaped leaves and darker blue-purple flowers.

SYRINGA   *Oleaceae*

The miniature lilacs, *S. microphylla* (Pl. 30) (China) and *S. velutina* (*palibiniana*) (Korea), are two very similar dwarf shrubs for the rock garden. Each makes a twiggy bush, and flowers freely in early summer, with many small oval leaves and panicles of small purple flowers. They are delightful when small, in the rock garden or alpine house, but, growing freely, they will, in time, attain several feet, and this must be remembered in placing them.

TALINUM   *Portulacaceae*

The Talinums are a race of small, succulent plants, mainly from Central America, of which only one hardy member is in general cultivation. Seed.

T. spinescens. N.W. America. Forms a close bushlet with many rather succulent, linear leaves like fat little pine needles. The flowers, borne in 4″ sprays on wiry stems, are saucer-shaped, and of a vivid magenta with bright yellow stamens. Hardy, but perhaps safer in the alpine house. Summer.

TANACETUM   *Compositae*

The widespread Tansy genus is mainly too tall and rank for the rock garden, but a recent introduction from America provides a charming silver-leafed addition to rock garden or alpine house.

ᴘ**T. compactum.** Rocky Mts. Forms a low mound of very silvery much cut foliage, suggestive of the high mountain Artemisias, from which arise, in early summer, white 3″–4″ stems bearing three or four small Tansy-like rayless pale golden heads. Seed or cuttings.

Tanakaea, Tecophilaea, Tetragonolobus, Teucrium

TANAKAEA Saxifragaceae Monotypic

T. radicans. Japan. A delightful and easy little woodlander, with deep green, serrated leaves, and short clusters of white Spiraea-like flowers. Peaty soil in half shade. Seed or runners. 4″. Summer. (Pl. 30)

TECOPHILAEA Amaryllidaceae

One of the two species comprising this genus is perhaps the most breath-taking of dwarf bulbs or corms—as it is certainly one of the most difficult to keep permanently in good health, or, indeed, at all.
DP***T. cyanocrocus.** Chile. Though of a different Natural Order this has the superficial appearance of a rather large crocus, but is one of the most brilliant and piercing blues of the plant world. From a small corm arise, in early spring, the narrow linear leaves from which comes the single spectacular flower (occasionally two). A compost of rich, sandy loam, very well drained, is needed, and it has been grown successfully out of doors, in a sun-baked position under a wall, in some favoured gardens, but it is safest in the frame or alpine house, where a certain amount of protection can be given in very early spring when it starts into growth. Seed (when obtainable). 3″–5″. March–April. (Pl. 32)

DP***T. c.** var. **leichtlinii** is a slightly easier form, and almost as beautiful, with the blue petals suffused with white, especially towards the throat.

T. c. var. **violacea.** Chile, Peru, S. Brazil. A smaller and less conspicuous plant, with blue-purple flowers.

TETRAGONOLOBUS Leguminosae

One member of this genus **T. maritimus** (*siliquosus*) may be found locally throughout the Alps, and is worth growing as a perennial trailer, making a low mound of oblong, light green, hairy leaves on sprawling stems bearing comparatively large, pale yellow pea-shaped flowers, with brown veinings on the standards. It takes its name from the curious seed pod, which is four-winged.

TEUCRIUM Labiatae

The Teucriums are natives of the temperate and warmer regions and are often aromatic. They include several useful, late-flowering,

Thalictrum

twiggy little bushlets, with narrow, hooded flowers in pairs in the axils of the leaves. In general, those named are hardy, but there may be casualties in an exceptionally hard winter. These make delightful pans for the alpine house and flower in later summer. Cuttings or seed. Light soil in a well-drained, sunny position.

P*T. ackermannii. Asia Minor. A dwarf mat-forming sub-shrubby plant with narrow grey-green foliage and terminal heads of lipped flowers of soft rose-crimson. 4″–6″. July.

P*T. aroanum. Greece. This little bushlet with woolly grey-green leaves bears many crowded heads of a curious purplish-grey. Up to 4″. Late summer.

T. chamaedrys. Europe. The Wall Germander is a good tempered, half-shrubby plant, with much-branched stems bearing many little oak-like leaves and numerous small spikes of lipped pink flowers. In poor soil may be kept fairly compact. 6″–9″. Summer.

T. montanum. S. Europe, W. Asia. Forms a spreading bushlet of 4″ or so, with many short heads of white and yellow flowers. Summer.

T. polium. Europe, W. Asia. A small evergreen woolly-leaved shrublet, with whorls of yellow or white flowers. 5″–6″. Summer.

T. pyrenaicum. S. Europe. A trailing plant with woolly leaves and rather larger, hooded flowers of mauve and cream in few flowered heads. 2″–3″. June–August.

P*T. subspinosum. Asia Minor. This delightful little shrublet makes a dense spiny bush, eventually, but slowly, reaching 8″ or so, with many tiny crinkled grey-green leaves, and in summer is covered with narrow, bright pink, labiate flowers. Safer in the alpine house, although it will survive normal winters outside. Summer.

THALICTRUM *Ranunculaceae*

The Meadow Rues are all graceful perennial plants with much cut and lobed basal leaves, usually glaucous, on long wiry petioles, and tall sprays of four- or five-petalled flowers, individually small but usually conspicuous by reason of the tassel of stamens, or, in a few cases, by the colour of the petals. Many are too tall for the average rock garden, but are nevertheless admitted (especially some of the later introductions from Himalaya) for their elegant foliage and flower sprays. All like a leafy woodland soil, and most appreciate half-shade. Seed or division.

T. alpinum. Europe (including Gt. Britain), N. Asia, N. America. The

284

Alpine Meadow Rue has very dainty grey-green foliage, almost suggestive of a fine-leaved Maidenhair Fern, and heads of small yellowish tassels. July–August. 6″.

T. coreanum. Korea. Delicate, bronze-tinted foliage, and few flowered sprays of rose-pink flowers. 6″. Summer.

*T. kiusianum. S. Japan. A dainty plant, which spreads mildly—but never too much— with fluffy mauve-pink flowers. 4″. Early summer.

T. chelidonii, Central and E. Himalaya, and **T. diffusiflorum,** S.E. Tibet, are usually too tall, but are very variable, and dwarfer forms (under 12″) are welcome for their beautiful mauve to violet flowers.

THLASPI *Cruciferae*

The Alpine members of this genus are well known, and very characteristic of the Central European Alps from heights from 7,000 to 10,000 feet, where they sprawl or make low 3″ clumps among the shingles. A very porous, stony soil, in full sun, but with ample water in the spring, suits them, but they are not long-lived plants, and best kept going by seed, sown as soon as ripe, or cuttings. Early summer. The species most often met, the loveliest and perhaps the easiest to grow is:

T. rotundifolium. European Alps. This makes patches or tufts in the high screes with little stalked rounded leaves, almost succulent and of a metallic greyish-green. The many Iberis-like heads of varying shades of warm, pinkish-mauve are almost globular and very fragrant. White forms are found, but are not as beautiful as the type. 3″. Spring to summer.

THYMUS *Labiatae*

A genus of aromatic shrublets varying from entirely prostrate to 12″ in height. Besides the creeping Thymes there are a few of upright or shrubby growth which add usefully to the comparatively few shrubs dwarf enough for the rock garden. Of the mat-forming species there is a great variety, which may be found in any catalogue, but, invaluable and attractive though they are, they need placing with care (e.g. among crazy-paving or as a thyme carpet for a pathway) as they are most of them apt to become invasive. It is hardly possible to bring any small plant from the mountains without a gate-crasher of seed or sprig of some form of *T. serpyllum*—a fact which makes itself only too

285

obvious in a year or two. They are indifferent as to soil, but the more freely-growing species need an open, sunny position, and even judicious clipping back after flowering, to prevent their becoming straggly. Summer flowering, but wild forms, collected on purpose or inadvertently, vary in hue, habit, and flowering time, giving a natural succession of bloom.

T. caespititius (*micans*). Spain, Portugal. A particularly neat and compact little plant of the *T. serpyllum* habit.

T. cilicicus. Asia Minor. An attractive bushlet with many deep green pointed leaves, forming characteristic dense, four-angled shoots. Terminal hemispherical heads of small, pale pink flowers. 4″–6″. Summer.

T. × citriodorus (*pulegioides × vulgaris*). The lemon-scented Thyme, a bushlet of 6″–9″, has two varieties: golden foliaged, *T. c.* 'AUREUS', and silver variegated, *T. c.* 'SILVER QUEEN'.

T. hirsutus. Crimea, Balkan Peninsula. A mat-forming species, the whole plant grey with dense hairs. Hemispherical heads of deep pink flowers. The variety usually available is *T. h.* var. *doerfleri* (*doerfleri*) from the Balkans.

P***T. membranaceus.** Spain. A very attractive little shrub of up to 10″. The dense, twiggy upright branches bear from June–August, heads of narrow-tubular, pale lilac flowers, each nearly ½″ long, with large, papery bracts, whitish usually but in some forms delightfully pink-flushed. Full sun and a very well-drained soil, but safest in the alpine house. (Pl. 30)

T. micans. See **T. caespititius.**

T. lanuginosus. A name given to various species of very hairy Thymes, usually varieties of *T. serpyllum.*

T. serpyllum. Europe (including Gt. Britain). A prostrate species, forming dense mats of thread-like branches, with many tiny oval leaves, barely stalked, and hemispherical ½″ heads of tiny flowers, so numerous as to make a continuous carpet of colour. Even from one locality there are variations, from light to deep pink, in size and compactness of plant, and in flowering time, and the leaves may have any surface from glabrous to conspicuously hairy. Alpine catalogues list selected forms which carry these individual characters. The most distinct are:

T. s. 'ALBUS', light green foliage, white flowers.

T. s. 'ANNIE HALL', very pale pink.

T. s. 'COCCINEUS', deep red. (Pl. 16)

T. s. var. **lanuginosus,** grey woolly foliage, pink flowers.

T. s. 'MINUS', very small and compact, useful for troughs.

T. s. 'PINK CHINTZ', rich rose flowers.

T. s. 'SILVER QUEEN', silver and green variegated foliage. (Pl. 1)

Tiarella, Tofieldia, Townsendia

TIARELLA *Saxifragaceae*

These woodland plants are nearly akin to Heuchera, and the one most usually grown is:

T. cordifolia. E. N. America. The Foam Flower spreads happily by stolons in a very cool leafy soil, and produces in June its airy, fluffy spires of small white starry flowers, above slender-stalked three to five-lobed leaves which take autumn tints of reddish brown. 10″. Summer.

TOFIELDIA *Liliaceae*

The small Bog Asphodels are not showy, but have a quiet charm for a cool, moist corner in well-drained soil.

T. calyculata. Mid-Europe. From a few radical, linear leaves rises a slender spire of small greenish-yellow flowers in July. 6″. *T. alpina* is even smaller, and is often considered as a diminutive form of *T. calyculata*. 4″.

TOWNSENDIA *Compositae*

This genus from W. N. America has conspicuous Aster-like flowers over a close mat of upright linear or spatulate leaves. They are gay plants for a sunny, well-drained spot, but, although perennial, are often short-lived. Kindred attractive species await introduction, but those most easily obtained are:

T. exscapa (*sericea, wilcoxiana*). W.N. America. The large (¾″) flower-heads of white or pale pink are almost sessile among the slightly silky leaves. May–June.

T. formosa. New Mexico. The smaller, lilac flowers are borne above narrow, thin-textured foliage, rather like a dwarf *Aster alpinus*. 3″. Summer.

*T. grandiflora. S.W. United States. A handsome plant with large (1½″) violet flower-heads on 5″–10″ stems. Summer.

TRACHELIUM *Campanulaceae*

A Mediterranean genus, valuable for its late flowering. The species are delightful subjects for the alpine house.

p***T. asperuloides.** Greece. Forms a dense cushion of light green sessile leaves, from which emerge shoots with terminal clusters of one to five tiny lilac flowers, deeply lobed. The whole plant is under 2″, and makes a charming pan for the alpine house. August–September.

***T. rumelianum** (*Diosphaera dubia*). Bulgaria, Greece. A taller plant, with graceful sprays, well furnished with oval-pointed, toothed leaves, and bearing terminating dense, rounded heads of small blue-lilac flowers. This thrives on the open rock garden, in limy soil, but appreciates overhead protection during a very wet winter, and makes a delightful pan. 6″. August–September.

TRICHINIUM *Amaranthaceae*

There is much discussion as to whether even one member of this genus is sufficiently hardy for inclusion, but its beauty merits giving it the benefit of the doubt, and its survival is vouched for in several unheated alpine houses.

DP***T. manglesii.** S.W. Australia. Leaves irregularly oval, pointed, mainly radical. The 2″ flower-heads, on 6″–8″ stems with few small leaves, are roughly ovoid, and present a soft dense cluster of long white hairs, from which emerge, well spaced, the rose-pink flowers, looking like narrow tassels, except for the brief period when they spread their five very narrow petals. An unusual and delightful plant which needs sun, a rich soil, and little water after flowering. Propagation by root cuttings, with bottom heat.

TRICYRTIS *Liliaceae*

The Toad Lilies, natives of E. Asia, are plants for lovers of the curious. They require a woodland position in sandy loam and peat—sheltered because they are so late in flowering as otherwise they tend to be caught by early autumn frosts.

T. hirta. Japan. The Japanese Toad Lily. This bears six to twelve inch-long curious purple-spotted white, lily-like flowers from the axils of the slightly hairy, oblong, pointed stem leaves. 10″–12″. August–September.

29

Sempervivella alba
Shortia uniflora grandiflora
Sisyrinchium bermudianum

Sempervivum arachnoideum
Silene schafta
Spiraea hendersonii

30

Syringa microphylla
Thymus membranaceus
Trollius pumilus

Tanakaea radicans
Trillium grandiflorum
Tropaeolum polyphyllum

Trientalis, Trifolium, Trillium
TRIENTALIS *Primulaceae*

This genus has only two very similar species, from the New and Old World respectively. Both are dainty little plants, with a superficial resemblance to the Wood Anemone. The erect single stems each bear a whorl of oval-pointed leaves, from which rise two or more five to nine-petalled $\frac{1}{2}''$ white flowers in early summer. Shady situation with leaf-mould.

T. europaea. Europe (including Gt. Britain). 4"–8". June–July.

T. borealis. The Star Flower of N.W. America is similar, but rather larger, and tends to carry more flowers from each whorl. 9". May.

TRIFOLIUM *Leguminosae*

The very large genus of Clovers includes a few members welcome in the rock garden. All have pea-shaped flowers, often in a terminal cluster, usually purple, red, or white. They are easy growing, and often attractive, but their colour lacks the brilliance of a real deep rose or red.

T. alpinum. European Alps. A more or less prostrate plant with heads of comparatively few, long narrow flowers of variable pink, good in some forms. 3"–6".

T. badium. S. Europe (including Gt. Britain). The Hop Clover has close ovoid heads of yellow, turning golden brown with age. This small plant might have its use in the rock garden, but is rarely seen there. 4"–6". Summer.

*T. macrocephalum. N.W. America. One of several American mountain species which might prove welcome acquisitions to the rock garden. It has large clover-heads of deep rose-pink, bright in comparison with the muted tones of other members of the genus. 2"–3". Summer.

T. uniflorum. Greece, Syria, etc. A completely prostrate plant forming almost woody radiating stems, with long-stemmed, trefoil leaves, and solitary, short-stemmed, rather narrow pea flowers of rose-pink. There is also a white form. 1". Summer.

TRILLIUM *Liliaceae*

The Wake-Robins are very distinctive and beautiful woodland plants, the species in cultivation being natives of N. America. All have a stout central stem bearing a whorl of three leaves, sometimes mottled or spotted, from which rises a single, stalked, three-sepalled, three-petalled, lily-like flower. A leafy, well-drained soil in part shade suits these plants, of which all are beautiful but some are rather tall for the average rock garden. A few of the dwarfer species are:

T. erectum. Eastern N. America. The Red Trillium grows up to 12″, with brownish, pointed sepals, and petals of variable brownish or reddish purple. May.

*T. grandiflorum. N.E. America. Although rather tall, this must be mentioned as it is the most handsome of the genus, with single, 2″, solid, white-petalled, long-lasting flowers, tending to blush pink with age. 10″–12″. April–June. (Pl. 30)

T. luteum. E. United States. A dwarf species with mottled leaves and sessile greenish-yellow flowers which hardly unfold. 6″. June.

*T. nivale. Dwarf White Trillium. S.E. United States. A charming little plant of 6″ or so, with 1″ almost sessile white flowers. One of the earliest to flower. March–April.

T. sessile. United States. Leaves often a mottled green, flowers sessile, purple petals. 6″–10″. March–April.

TRIPTILION *Compositae*

T. spinosum. Chile. One of the hardiest of the genus but needs a sunny well-drained sheltered spot. Very narrowly divided pinnate leaves, the lobes ending in a short spine. Heads of charming small blue daisy-like flowers. 6″. July.

TROLLIUS *Ranunculaceae*

The handsome Trollius of the European Alps, *T. europaeus*, is too tall a plant for any but the largest rock garden, but its dwarfer Eastern cousins, although lacking its luminosity and globe-like form, are easygoing, pleasant perennials in any open, rather moist and heavy soil. Seed may be slow germinating unless sown immediately after ripening. Summer flowering.

T. patulus. See **T. ranunculinus.**

T. pumilus. N. India, W. China. A free-flowering plant with solitary flatly open golden flowers of 1″ or more, above leaves having five three-lobed segments. Up to 12″. June–July. (Pl. 30)

Tropaeolum, Tsusiophyllum, Tulipa

T. ranunculinus (*patulus*). Caucasus, Armenia. Rather similar to the foregoing, but compact forms down to 3″ or so can be found. Leaves radical, palmately cut. Flowers golden yellow, flat, 1½″ wide. June–July.

TROPAEOLUM *Tropaeolaceae*

Most of this gay and showy genus climb, usually by twining leaf-stalks, but there is one beautiful and distinctive prostrate species which, planted on a slope, will spill streams of clear, yellow, nasturtium-like flowers in wide swathes, at a time when the main alpine pageant is diminishing.

*T. polyphyllum. Chile, Argentine. Forms long, prostrate trails of deeply-lobed, grey-green leaves, erupting into wide cascades of many rather small, clear yellow, nasturtium-like flowers. Excellent for a high spot on the rock garden whence it casts its rivulets of luminous yellow. It dies away completely after flowering, to very deep rhizomes, and the new shoots in spring are likely to appear in unexpected, widely-distant spots. Seed is rarely, if ever, set. Propagation by division of the rhizomes, which may in time be 12″ below the soil. Prefers a sunny position, preferably in peaty or leafy sandy soil. Summer. (Pl. 30)

TSUSIOPHYLLUM *Ericaceae Monotypic*

*T. tanakae. Japan. One of the most attractive of the really dwarf shrubs, forming a rounded bushlet or miniature tree with many, much-branched, woody twigs bearing small (⅓″) oval, pointed, deep green leaves, hairy at the edges and almost evergreen. The many small, white, five-petalled, tubular flowers are borne in pairs. The twin buds are at first enclosed in a copper-coloured chaffy cap. When this is released the buds spring apart, and the flowers open. Leafy woodland, lime-free soil in part shade. Propagation by seed (as for Rhododendron) or cuttings. A long-lived and delightful shrublet which has the appearance of a small Bonzai tree. Up to 10″. Summer.

TULIPA *Liliaceae*

Most of the tulip species are too tall for any but the very large-scale rock garden, and many, especially those of brilliant shades of scarlet, too flamboyant to mix well with the exquisite small bulbs of early spring. All, however, make excellent pans to give early gaiety to the

Tulipa

alpine house, where they may be positioned to avoid unwanted competition. Out of doors they require an open, sunny, well-drained position. The few described below are either really dwarf (up to 6″) or have the charm of slender, graceful habit, and comparatively small flowers. For the many other species available, consult *Collins Guide to Bulbs*.

*T. aucheriana. Persia, Syria. One of the most delightful, with rather small, wide-open, starry flowers of an unusual softly glowing, almost crushed-strawberry pink, with a yellow base. 3″. April.

T. australis. See under **T. silvestris.**

*T. batalinii. Turkestan. An egg-shaped flower of luminous pale yellow, with olive-tinted base to petals. Often described as the yellow counterpart of *T. linifolia,* but the latter has a narrower, more pointed-petalled flower. 6″–8″. May.

T. biflora. Caspian and Caucasus regions. A small-flowered species with up to five blooms to each slender stem. Outer segments stained green and crimson, opening to a flat, starry flower, white with a yellow base. 5″–10″. February–March.

T. celsiana. See **T. silvestris.**

*T. cretica. Crete. A delightful tiny tulip, sometimes considered a sub-species of *T. saxatilis,* with slender white flowers, backs of petals tinged pink and green. Best in the alpine house. 3″–4″. April.

*T. clusiana. The Lady Tulip. Persia, Afghanistan to Kashmir (naturalized in some Mediterranean countries, e.g. S. France). One of the most charming and one of the longest in cultivation. Narrow, slightly glaucous leaves and slender stems bearing solitary, elegantly-shaped starry white flowers, with a small purple basal blotch, stained deep red on the outer segments, so that the buds are bright crimson. 6″–12″. April–May.

T. dasystemon of gardens is *T. tarda.*

*T. humilis (N.W. Persia, N.E. Turkey), **T. pulchella** (Asia Minor), and **T. violacea** (N. Persia, Kurdistan) are nearly allied, and usually considered as one aggregate. They are among the earliest and the most dwarf of all tulips, and commence to flower in February–March, when their stocky, egg-shaped buds emerge from the leaves almost at ground level. All are very variable, but, in general, *T. humilis* is in shades of pink, sometimes verging on magenta, with olive-green, yellow-edged (sometimes all yellow) basal blotch, *T. pulchella* light crimson to purple, with deep blue blotch, and *T. violacea* (which is often classed as a sub-species of *T. pulchella*) crimson-violet or purple, but the gradations are so continuous and the range so wide that for garden purposes there is little to choose between them. In any form they are delightful sturdy little plants, hardy outdoors in a well-drained sunny bed although not always very long-lived, and their compactness and early flowering make them very welcome as pans in the alpine house. 3″–4″. February–March.

Tunica

*T. kaufmanniana. The Water-lily Tulip. From this species a whole race of flamboyant and giant-flowered beauties in every shade of yellow, pink, and brilliant red has evolved, by selection and hybridization. The only member I would think suitable for the rock garden is the type plant, and that in as compact form as obtainable. This bears large solitary flowers, crimson stained in bud, but opening into very beautiful "Water-lilies" of solid creamy-white with a golden base. 6″–8″. March.

*T. linifolia. C. Asia. Rather tall, but of slender, graceful habit, with solitary, pointed-petalled flowers of glossy scarlet with black-purple blotch. 6″–10″. May.

*T. montana. N. Persia. A well-proportioned and brilliant tulip of glossy crimson-scarlet, with a black blotch. A lovely plant, especially in its more compact forms. A citron-yellow variety has been recently introduced into cultivation from the Elburz Mts., Persia. 6″–10″. April.

T. sylvestris is itself rather tall, but the sub-species, **T. s.** var. **australis** (*australis*) from S. Europe, especially the Mediterranean region, is an attractive and good-tempered late-flowering tulip, with rather small golden yellow flowers, opening into wide stars, but pendent and crimson-stained in the bud. 6″–8″. April–May. *T.s.* var. *celsiana* is very similar.

*T. tarda (*dasystemon* of gardens). E. Turkestan. Attractive and very prolific, with short stems of little more than 2″, each bearing five to six flowers, opening out to bright gold, white-tipped stars. 2″–4″. May.

*T. urumiensis. N.E. Persia. A charming dwarf, with reddish and dull green buds, opening to rather urn-shaped clear yellow flowers. 2″–3″. April. (Pl. 32)

Among many others, distinctive species are *T.T. griegii*, scarlet and with very characteristic leaves, glaucous with dark purplish stripes and mottlings, *hageri*, coppery scarlet, with buff and green outer segments, late flowering, *orphanidea*, an attractive, almost indescribable blend of dull orange, coppery-green, and pinkish purple, and *turkestanica*, much branched, with as many as seven white, starry flowers, tinged outside with reddish-green. These are more appropriate to the alpine house than the rock garden. All may grow to 12″ or more.

TUNICA *Caryophyllaceae*

A small genus nearly allied to *Gypsophila*.

T. saxifraga. S. Europe, east to Persia. A herbaceous plant which forms a cloud of much-branched wiry stems, set with small, narrowly linear leaves, and bespangled with tiny, rose-tinted, five-petalled flowers from June–September. Likes a warm, sunny position, where it will persist for some years, and mildly self-seed around. 5″–6″.

UVULARIA *Liliaceae*

A small genus of rhizotamous woodland plants, superficially suggestive in habit of Solomon's Seal.

U. grandiflora. N. America. Forms a single upright stem (occasionally branched into two), with few, basal, sheath-like leaves. Upper leaves sessile, very long-pointed, heart-shaped; flowers solitary or twin at tips of branchlets, pendent, long-petalled, pale yellow, narrowly bell-shaped. 8″–10″. May.

U. perfoliata. N. America. Similar but less robust and variable in shade and size of flower. May.

VACCINIUM *Ericaceae*

A large genus including deciduous and evergreen shrubs, many very dwarf or prostrate and all bearing urn-shaped flowers from white to pale or deeper pink. All require a lime-free, cool, woodland soil. Among those suitable for the rock garden or alpine house are:

V. delavayi. Yunnan. A delightful evergreen shrub of 12″ or so, with many oval, glossy, leathery leaves, about ½″ in length, and terminal (occasionally axillary) clusters of small, pink-tinged, five-lobed, almost globular flowers, fruit a purplish-black berry. June.

V. mortinia. Ecuador. Also evergreen, this varies in height with its position, but in an open, exposed site makes an attractive bushy shrub of 12″ or so, with many small oval leaves which tend to take reddish-bronze tints in winter, and dense clusters of small five-lobed narrowly urn-shaped flowers in June, followed by glaucous purple fruit. Of borderline hardiness in a severe winter. June.

p*V. nummularia. Sikkim, Bhutan. Perhaps the most lovely of the dwarf Vacciniums, but of suspect hardiness, except in the most sheltered districts. Forms a compact evergreen bush, with bristly short growths, and many leathery, rounded leaves which are almost hidden in April–May by the dense clusters of pendent, pink, five-lobed, narrowly urn-shaped flowers. About 12″.

V. vitis-idaea. Europe, N. Asia, N.E. America. The Cowberry or Mountain Cranberry makes an evergreen spreading mat by means of underground rooting stolons. The wiry arching stems bear many oval, glossy, dark green leaves and, in May–June, clusters of white or pinkish, four-lobed, urn-shaped flowers. Dark red, rounded fruits, about ⅓″ across. 4″–10″.

Other rather similar Vacciniums may be found in nurseries specializing in ericaceous plants, and all, when growing happily, have an attractive sturdy air of well-being, by means of their glossy little leaves, and ample clusters of flowers.

Valeriana, Vancouveria, Verbascum

VALERIANA *Valerianaceae*

Although the Common Valerian in red, pink, or white is found in the Alps at considerable heights it is, unless starved, too tall and coarse for anything but for covering a worthless bank. There is, however, one dwarf species which, although inconspicuous, is prized for its history of fragrance:

V. celtica. European Alps. Spike or Spikenard is about 3″ high, with basal rosettes of rather wedge-shaped leaves, and small heads of small, reddish-yellow flowers. Known from antiquity for its perfume, which is present throughout the plant, and especially in the root. 2″-3″. May–July.

VANCOUVERIA *Berberidaceae*

A W.N. American genus of three rather similar species, related to Epimedium, but six- (instead of four-) petalled. All are graceful woodland plants, with about nine basal, slender-stalked, heart-shaped leaves, usually three-lobed. They make a charming ground cover for small bulbs in the half-shady woodland suitable for Wood Anemones.

V. chrysantha. Oregon, California. Soft yellow flowers, larger than in the following species, are borne well above the foliage. Almost evergreen. 8″-12″. May.

V. hexandra. Washington to California. The species most usually obtainable; can grow from 4″-12″ or more. White flowers in May. Dies back in the autumn.

V. planipetala. Redwood Ivy. Oregon, California. White or lavender-tinged flowers and firm, leathery foliage. 7″-12″. May.

VERBASCUM *Scrophulariaceae*

The Mulleins are mostly much too large for the rock garden, but there are a few dwarf bushy species which are most suitable, being attractive even when not in flower by means of their dense habit and (usually) woolly foliage. Well-drained, sunny position.

*V. dumulosum. Asia Minor. Forms a rounded bush of up to 12″ or more, with many oval, almost round leaves, the whole plant light grey-green with woolly hairs. Short spikes of clear yellow mullein flowers in early summer. (Pl. 31)

295

*V. pestalozzae. Asia Minor. Very similar to the foregoing, but rather more dwarf, with slightly larger, more solid flowers. 12″. Early summer.

*V. spinosum. Crete. An intricately-branched bushlet with lanceolate, slightly-toothed grey-green leaves, the shoots ending in narrow spiny branches. Short spikes of yellow flowers. 8″–10″. Summer.

Hybrids are obtainable between the first two, and also between *V. dumulosum* and *V. spinosum*.

VERBENA *Verbenaceae*

Only one Verbena is really suitable for the rock garden, and that is the prostrate:

V. chamaedryoides. Southern S. America. Really a strain of *V. peruviana*, this provides throughout the summer an exotic display of its flat heads of small, five-petalled flowers of such a flaming scarlet as to overshadow all the usual occupants of the rock garden. A wonderful plant if an appropriate place can be found. Not quite hardy, so cuttings should be over-wintered under glass as a precaution. Trailing.

VERONICA *Scrophulariaceae*

This very large genus is invaluable in providing many prostrate or dwarf shrubby species, with spikes of small but delightful flowers of shades from white to purple and deep clear blue. The Speedwells flower in early summer, are quite hardy, and most are easy in any soil or position. Some of the compact and prostrate species make charming pans for the alpine house. Their very near relations from New Zealand, formerly found under Veronica, are now listed as Hebes (q.v.).

*V. armena. Armenia. A very distinct little plant, far too seldom seen, with trailing stems and small leaves cut into *linear* segments. Flowers bright blue. 4″. Summer. (Pl. 31)

V. bidwillii. See **Hebe bidwillii.**

ᴾ***V. bombycina.** Lebanon. A delightful plant for the alpine house, which its densely white woolly foliage demands. Quite prostrate, with tiny oval sessile leaves, and few-flowered spikes of reddish flowers. 1″–2″. July.

Veronica

V. bonarota (*Paederota bonarota*). S. Europe (especially the Dolomites). A charming plant forming dense clumps of 5″ sprays set with glossy oval leaves, more or less deeply toothed, and slender terminal spires of fluffy purple-blue flowers. Good for a sink or wall but too seldom seen. Procumbent. 2″–3″. July.

V. buchananii 'MINOR'. See **Hebe buchananii** 'MINOR'.

V. filiformis. Asia Minor. Makes an entrancing carpet in May, of wide, clear pale blue flowers over a mat of thread-like stems and tiny circular leaves, but should be avoided, as it must be the most invasive of all plants, even taking possession of a lawn.

V. fruticans (*saxatilis*, under which name it is usually found). Mts. of Europe (including Scotland). One of the most attractive species, with sprays of 4″–6″ bearing many oval, slightly-toothed leaves and terminal sprays of deep clear blue flowers, with a conspicuous red eye. Summer.

V. fruticulosa. Mts. of Europe (including Scotland). Very similar to the foregoing, but with veined, soft pink flowers. 6″. July.

V. gentianoides. Caucasus. From tufts of solid lanceolate leaves, resembling those of *Gentiana acaulis*, rise graceful 10″ spires of pale blue flowers. There is a variegated form and also a dwarf, *V. g.* 'NANA'. June.

V. incana. Russia. Another erect Veronica with narrow, lanceolate basal leaves of deeply-plated silver, as is the foot high stem bearing a slender spike of intensely blue flowers. July.

V. lutea. (*Paederota lutea, P. egeria*). E. Alps. An undistinguished little plant, with toothed, lanceolate leaves, but mentioned because of the unusual (for the genus) colour break; the rather dull yellow flowers are borne in a short, few-flowered spike. 6″–9″. Summer.

V. 'PAGEANA'. See **Hebe pinguifolia** 'PAGEI'.

V. prostrata (*rupestris*). Europe, N. Asia. One of the easiest rock plants, with oval to linear toothed leaves on 2″–8″ stems, and spikes of deep blue flowers. Several selected forms are offered in catalogues, of which *V. p.* 'ALBA' (white), *V. p.* 'ROSEA' (pink), and *V. p.* 'SPODE BLUE' (clear pale China blue) are the most distinct.

V. rupestris. See **V. prostrata.**

V. saxatilis. See **V. fruticans.**

V. teucrium. S. Europe, N. Asia. An extremely variable species, of which the dwarf members (6″–10″) are invaluable for their good temper and thickets of more or less erect, slightly hairy stems with many slightly or deeply-toothed leaves and sprays of comparatively large blue flowers. July. (Pl. 21) Several forms appear in catalogues under varietal names, of which one of the most distinct is *V. t.* 'TREHANE', which has golden yellow foliage.

Of the many other dwarf Veronicas none is more beautiful than our native Germander Speedwell (*V. chamaedrys*). Several small species are

Vinca, Viola

found universally in the European Alps, especially *V. alpina, V. aphylla, V. bellidifolia,* but, although charming for a few days, these have too short a flowering period to be counter-balanced by their undistinguished green mats during the rest of the year.

VINCA *Apocynaceae*

The dwarf Periwinkle, *Vinca minor* (Europe), is an indestructible plant for any partly-shaded spot, which it will soon colonize. There are many named forms; all have opposite, glossy dark-green, pointed elliptic leaves, bearing in their axils in early summer a succession of the familiar, five-petalled, slightly whorled flowers, blue in the type but also varying from white to purple. Within the corolla tube, the stigma forms a perfect fairy paint-brush. Among the varieties are

V. m. 'ALBA', white.

V. m. 'ALBOPLENA', double white.

V. m. 'BURGUNDY', wine-red.

V. m. 'COERULEA' and **'COERULEA FLORE PLENO',** deep blue, single and double respectively

and forms with silver or gold variegated foliage.

VIOLA *Violaceae*

The violets and miniature Pansies include a large number of delightful plants for the rock garden, alpine house, or woodland. Some are short-lived perennials, but seed is usually plentiful, although in some species only produced by cleistogamous flowers—i.e. flowers without petals, usually developing after the display of normal flowers is over, and therefore liable to be overlooked unless one is looking out for them. Leaves usually of the typical heart-shape of the Common Violet, but in a few species beautifully cut into narrow radiating segments.

V. aetolica. See **V. saxatilis** var. **aetolica.**

V. beckwithii. W. N. America. A charming small species with upright purple velvety back petals and pale, pencilled lip and wings. First year from seed makes dormant plants. 3″. Summer.

Viola

V. biflora. The whole of the northern hemisphere. This delightful small violet, with dancing flowers of clear, bright yellow, finely veined with brown, lights up crevices and shady spots throughout the Alps, but is also, surprisingly, occasionally found growing happily in open ground above tree level. Long flowering from early summer. 2″–3″.

D**V. calcarata.** Alps of Central Europe. This miniature pansy, although sky-blue in the type plant, may be found in a wide range of colours. In one particular square mile of high alpine turf in E. Switzerland, colour forms from white to yellow, blue, purple, or parti-coloured can be seen in their thousands. This is difficult to establish in the garden, and not long-lived. Seed would seem to offer the best chance. Long-flowering in the wild. 2″–3″. Summer.

V. canina. Dog Violet. N. Temperate Region (including Gt. Britain). Variable in form and not to be despised for an out-of-the-way corner. A variety from the Dolomites, completely prostrate, with round flat flowers of vivid blue has proved a good perennial. 2″–4″. Late spring.

D**V. cenisia.** European Alps, on limestone. A charming viola, even more elegant than *V. calcarata*, with more rounded foliage and lavender blue flowers, beautifully veined. Difficult to establish. 2″–3″. Summer.

V. cornuta 'MINOR'. Pyrenees. This form of the type plant makes a close mat of fresh green foliage, above which the lively butterflies of clear blue are held on 2″–3″ stems from July onwards. (Pl. 31; white form, Pl. 20)

D**V. delphinantha.** Greece, Bulgaria. A difficult, but delightful plant, spasmodically in cultivation, and very distinct by means of its upright almost shrubby growth, narrow to linear leaves and deep pink flowers, held erect on long stalks, with narrow petals and long, slender, curved spurs. 3″–5″. June–July.

V. eizanensis. Japan. An elegant plant with many radical leaves, long-petioled, having three leaflets much cut into linear segments. The large white (rarely rose) flowers are borne singly just above the foliage. Leafy soil. 4″–5″. April.

V. gracilis. Asia Minor. Balkans. The true plant is a dainty little plant of 4″–6″, with entire, oval basal leaves, and pinnately divided stipules at the base of the upper slightly-toothed leaves. Large, deep violet flowers of graceful shape, with long spurs. The true species is less often seen than coarser hybrids masquerading under the name. Summer.

V. jooi. Transylvania. A particularly cosy little violet, with long, heart-shaped leaves, and rounded flowers of pinkish mauve. 2″–3″. May onwards.

V. labradorica 'PURPUREA'. N. America, Greenland. An easygoing violet for any soil in semi-shade. with slightly elongated heart-shaped leaves, suffused with bluish purple, and mauve flowers. 4″–5″. Early summer.

V. lutea. Europe (including Gt. Britain). A leafy little plant with oval basal leaves, upper lanceolate and all slightly toothed. Comparatively large flowers (over ½″) of clear yellow, with brown veins. Throughout the summer. 4″–5″.

D*V. pedata.** Bird's-foot Violet. E. N. America. One of the most lovely species, but difficult to grow and keep. An open position in leafy sandy soil offers the best hope of permanence. Leaves all basal, divided palmately into many narrow segments. A large rather rounded flower (but variable in shape) with the two upstanding petals of deep velvety purple, and three lower ones of light purple with fine veining. 4″–5″. Spring.

V. p. var. **concolor** has flowers of uniform light purple.

V. pinnata. European Alps, N. Asia. A delightful little plant, also requiring leafy soil and part shade, rather suggestive of a miniature form of the foregoing and the only European species with leaves palmately cut into linear sections. The early spring solitary flowers of blue violet are sterile, but later in the year cleistogamous flowers are formed, i.e. without petals, but bearing fertile seed. Not easy, but a charming little plant. 2″. Spring.

V. sagittata. E. N. America. A rather coarse plant, with roughly arrow-shaped leaves and medium-sized violet flowers. Woodland. 4″–6″. Spring.

*V. saxatilis** var. **aetolica** (*aetolica*). E. Europe, Asia Minor. One of the most delightful species, making leafy tufts, with many much-branched stems bearing myriads of tiny yellow pansies throughout the summer. 3″–5″. (Pl.10)

V. septentrionalis. N. America. Quickly forms mats of rather coarse violet foliage in any cool spot, which are transformed in spring by the large, solid-petalled white violets held well above the foliage and delicately pencilled with purple. 6″.

V. tricolor. Heartsease, Love-in-idleness, Pink o' my John, Garden Gates, etc. Europe (including Gt. Britain). This widespread British species is immensely variable, and when it occurs as a welcome "weed" in gardens may flaunt, all through the summer, its galaxies of tiny pansies in cream and yellow, fading to mauve and purple (the true Love-in-idleness) blue, dark blue to almost purple-black, and many bicolors. But it is hardly ever without an odd flower even in the depth of winter. With *V. lutea* the parent of the Garden Pansy. Once obtained it will mildly seed itself for ever, in various forms, but is easily controlled if one has the heart to do so. (Pl. 31)

V. yakusimana. Japan. The smallest viola and one of the smallest flowering plants. A perfect violet in miniature, with tiny heart-shaped leaves and ⅓″ white flowers, with finely purple-veined lip, the whole well under 1″ in height. Perfect for alpine house or trough garden. Summer.

VISCARIA *Caryophyllaceae*

V. alpina. Now **Lychnis alpina** (q.v.)

Wahlenbergia, Waldsteinia

WAHLENBERGIA *Campanulaceae*

A genus very similar to *Edraianthus*, both being small tufted, often mat-forming plants, with rather narrow campanulate flowers, usually of rich blue or purple, but, whereas in *Edraianthus*, the flower-stem bears either a dense cluster of flowers or a single flower with bracts immediately below it, *Wahlenbergia* has a single flower on a fairly long pedicle, with no bracts immediately beneath it.

W. dinarica (*Edraianthus dinaricus*). Dalmatia. Forms a dense intricate mat of silvery, needle-shaped leaves, and bears in July solitary, deep purple, bell-shaped flowers on 2"–3" stems. Scree.

W. hederacea. Europe (including Gt. Britain). A fairy-like little plant, completely prostrate, with tiny light green, ivy-shaped leaves, and, in June–July, many upturned, pointed-petalled, bell-shaped flowers of light clear blue. Requires a cool damp situation, and is entrancing when growing, as it does on Dartmoor, among the equally small and prostrate pink flowered *Anagallis tenella*.

W. pumilio (*Edraianthus pumilio*). Balkan Peninsula. A mat-forming species with short ($\frac{1}{2}$") linear silvery leaves, and, in June–July, lavender bells on 2" stems. Scree. May–June.

W. serpyllifolia (*Edraianthus serpyllifolius*). Balkan Peninsula. Another mat-forming species with deep green, narrowly lanceolate leaves. The form usually offered is:

> **W. s.** var. **major.** One of the most sumptuous of all rock plants when it is seen as a patch in perfect health, covered with upturned, solitary, bell-shaped flowers of deepest imperial purple. Scree or very well drained bed. 2". June. (Pl. 31)

WALDSTEINIA *Rosaceae*

This small genus lies between Geum and Potentilla, and provides a couple of charming ground coverers, of easy temper in any soil, which are too seldom seen. They are suggestive in habit of a woody, creeping Potentilla with dark green, three-lobed, jaggedly-toothed leaves, and bear $\frac{1}{2}$", five-petalled flowers of golden yellow. Early summer. The one most usually met with is

W. ternata (*trifolia*). E. Europe, Siberia, Japan. Small yellow Dog-Rose-like flowers. 4". April–May.

W. fragarioides. E. United States, is very similar, but slightly larger.

Weldenia, Woodsia, Wulfenia, Zauschneria

WELDENIA *Commelinaceae Monotypic*

*W. candida. Mexico and Guatemala. A beautiful and distinctive plant, with basal strap-shaped leaves, and open bowl-shaped, three-petalled, snow-white flowers, whose purity is enhanced by the white pedicels. Continuous in bloom from early summer, although each individual flower is short-lived. Needs the shelter of an alpine house in all but exceptionally dry and sheltered spots. Difficult to increase, but root cuttings of the fleshy roots, in peaty sand in September, offer the best chance. 4″–6″. May onwards.

WOODSIA *Polypodiaceae*

These charming little tufted ferns are most suitable for a cool, rather moist corner in leafy, sandy soil. Their delicate 3″–4″ fronds have alternate ovate or triangular leaflets.

W. alpina. Arctic Europe (including Gt. Britain).

W. ilvensis. Alpine regions of N. America.

W. scopulina. Rocky Mts.

These three are very similar. All are variable according to position, but *W. ilvensis* has more oblong leaflets and *W. scopulina* is slightly larger in all its parts.

WULFENIA *Scrophulariaceae*

The Wulfenias, although rather coarse-looking plants, are a little suggestive of the ubiquitous purple Horminum of the European Alps, but they provide colour in July, and are interesting because of their rarity in the wild. The species usually grown is:

W. carinthiaca. E. Alps, Balkans. From flat rosettes of sturdy oval leaves, crinkled, and with scalloped edges, rise the erect flower-stalks, terminating in a dense cylindrical 2″–3″ head of small, deep purple-blue lipped flowers. 8″–9″. June–August.

ZAUSCHNERIA *Onagraceae*

This small genus of sub-shrubby perennials tend to be rather large and spreading for the small rock garden, but should be included where possible for their graceful spraying habit, and, especially, the gaiety of their many small, tubular, flame-coloured flowers in late summer, when their lively colouring is particularly welcome, and there are few, if any, other flowering plants to be overwhelmed by their brilliance.

Z. californica (*mexicana*). Californian Fuchsia. California, Mexico. The 12″ high spraying branches, with many linear-lanceolate willow-like leaves, bear at their tips loose spikes of narrow tubular 1″ scarlet flowers in late summer and early autumn. (Pl. 31)

*****Z. c.** var. **angustifolia** is rather more compact, with narrow, silvery-grey leaves. Both appreciate a sunny position in well-drained soil. To ensure against loss in an exceptionally severe winter cuttings should be taken from side shoots in September, and over-wintered in cool greenhouse or frame.

ZEPHYRANTHES   *Amaryllidaceae*

These charming bulbs, with narrowly strap-shaped leaves and crocus-like flowers include only one species which is reasonably hardy. Even this, however, is not free-flowering in some gardens, but where it flourishes and flowers freely, as it *can* do, it is one of the most delightful autumn flowering bulbs.

*****Z. candida.** Argentina, Uruguay. From tufts of almost evergreen rush-like leaves of 6″–8″, arise in September–October the many pure white goblets, often flushed green at the base. Hardy in a sunny sheltered position.

DWARF CONIFERS

Very few conifers are naturally dwarf, if this is taken to mean growing to a height of 6″ or so in a reasonable number of years and not much above 12″ in a long life. Above the tree line, it is true, low bushes may be found, such as *Juniperus communis* var. *saxatilis*, not exceeding 12″ in height under the rigorous conditions in which they live, but their habit is prostrate and spreading so that the ground space they would eventually cover makes them impermissible except for a landscape on the grandest scale. The true dwarfs obtainable have almost all originated in one of the two following ways. Nurseries specializing in raising coniferous plants have found, among many thousands of seedlings, an odd plant here and there of a very compact and congested habit. This has been notably so in the genus Chamaecyparis, very closely related to the true Cypresses, especially among seedlings of the species *obtusa*. These include many delightful rather similar forms making close buns or cushions which never attain a height of more than a few inches. The other source of origin is the Witches' Broom, that congested tuft of very short twigs sometimes seen on a conifer (or, in fact, other trees), and at a distance suggesting a small bunch of mistletoe. This is caused by a parasitic fungus, but if cuttings are struck from it the resultant plants perpetuate the stunted growth of the original Witches' Broom. But, whatever the source, these truly dwarf conifers are exceedingly slow-growing (for example, the average yearly growth of *Picea abies* 'GREGORIANA' may be only $\frac{1}{4}''$) and, since they can only be propagated by cuttings if they are to retain their character, when buying them it should be remembered that a sizeable plant must have spent some years in a nursery, and a specimen piece may easily be twenty years or more old without being at all exceptional. As a result, these miniatures are bound to be expensive and, in fact, a "miniature" offered at a low price is extremely suspect, and may well make such growth each year as speedily to leave that category.

Although hardy in any but the most exceptional winter, they are usually grown in pans, where their delightful habit and satisfying proportions may be most readily appreciated. It must be confessed that this mode of growth helps to keep them compact without any artificial "Bonzai" treatment. In the open garden they do tend to grow slightly larger than their potted contemporaries, but in any case they are seldom grown out of doors as they resent snow settling on their foliage. The following short list contains the cream of these delightful shrublets, which are attractive all the year round, especially when their new spring growth of light apple-green contrasts with their permanent more sombre tones or, in some instances, when their winter foliage takes russet or almost plum-coloured hues.

In most species, cuttings from the present year's growth root easily if planted in the autumn. They must be taken from the shortest, most congested growths, usually from the base of the shrublet; the longer and more feathery shoot which occasionally occurs will not perpetuate the desired dwarf habit.

Any good alpine nursery will supply a representative collection and

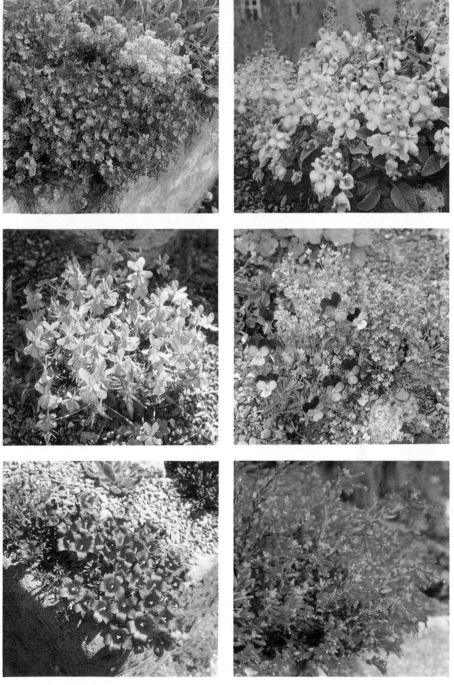

Veronica armena
Viola cornuta minor
Wahlenbergia serpyllifolia var. major

Verbascum dumulosum
Viola tricolor, Saxifraga cymbalaria
Erinus alpinus
Zauschneria californica

Allium oreophilum var. ostrowskianum BULBS   *Colchicum speciosum* 'Atrorubens'
Lapeirousia (Anomatheca) cruenta   *Muscari macrocarpum*
Tecophilaea cyanocrocus   *Tulipa urumiensis*

Dwarf Conifers

the few firms specializing in these plants offer a large selection from which to choose.

A selection of species which will not outgrow their position
for many years, if at all.

Abies balsamea 'HUDSONIA'. Dwarf balsam fir of spreading habit, having narrow, stiff, deep green, straight leaves with two sunken blue lines beneath. Rare.

> **Abies b.** 'NANA'. Differs from the foregoing in having curved, rather shorter leaves, with two sunken white lines beneath. More easily obtainable than and often supplied as *A. b.* 'HUDSONIA'.

Cedrus libani 'NANA'. A variable but attractive dwarf form of the Cedar of Lebanon, very slow growing but eventually reaching 3–4 ft.

> **C. l.** 'COMTE DE DIJON'. An even more compact form with finer leaves. Eventually 2–3 ft. Rare.

The dwarf cypresses (*Chamaecyparis*) appear in many delightful dwarf and congested forms, of which the following are a representative selection:

Chamaecyparis lawsoniana 'ELLWOODII'. An upright torch-shaped conical bush, with glaucous blue foliage. Eventually 4–5 ft. but very slow growing.

> **C. l.** 'MINIMA AUREA'. ('MINIMA AUREA ROGERSII'). A lovely golden pyramid with slightly twisted branchlets. Eventually 2½–3 ft.

> **C. l.** 'PYGMAEA ARGENTEA'. A delightful almost globular bushlet, with blue-green foliage, silvery-white when young. Eventually 2–2½ ft.

C. obtusa 'CAESPITOSA'. A tiny tufted bushlet of dense dark green. One of the smallest, rarely reaching 12″ in many years.

> **C. o.** 'JUNIPEROIDES COMPACTA'. A dense tuft with crowded short pointed branchlets of medium green. Less than 12″.

C. pisifera 'COMPACTA VARIEGATA'. A congested rather feathery bushlet with silver and green foliage. The light tips are rather susceptible to frost. Up to 2½ ft.

> **C. p.** 'PLUMOSA AUREA COMPACTA'. A dense feathery bush with golden foliage. Up to 2 ft.

> **C. p.** 'PLUMOSA COMPRESSA'. The smallest form of *C. pisifera*, and very slow growing. In its early years like a tight, glaucous moss, and always a dense bushlet. Up to 2 ft.

> **C. p.** 'SQUARROSA CYANO-VIRIDIS'. May eventually reach 4–5 ft., but remains a bushy feathery dwarf for several years. Notable for its brilliant glaucous-blue foliage in summer. Dull grey-green, plum-shaded, in winter.

Dwarf Conifers

The Japanese Cedars include a few distinctive dwarf forms:

Cryptomeria japonica 'ALBA-VARIEGATA'. The dense dark green bushlet produces white tips to many of its shoots. These age to pale green, and are apt to be browned by frost. A seventy-year specimen has reached 6 ft.

    C. j. 'KNAPTONENSIS'. In effect a very congested version of the foregoing, with conspicuous very dense white shoots. Rare. The previous plant is often sent out under this name.

    C. j. 'VILMORINIANA'. A very slow growing form, with minute leaves on crowded branchlets. Deep green. A forty-year specimen has reached 2½ ft.

Juniperus communis 'COMPRESSA'. The Noah's Ark tree. A slender, erect, pointed column, eventually reaching 3 ft., but so slow growing that it may even be admitted to a trough garden for some years.

    J. c. 'ECHINIFORMIS'. One of the most delightful of all dwarf conifers, making a dense, spiky ball of short branches thickly covered with small spiny leaves. Rarely attains more than 1 ft. in many years.

Picea abies 'CLANBRASSILIANA'. A dwarf spruce with very short and crowded branchlets, eventually making a rather flat-topped globular bush. Eventually 5–6 ft., but very slow growing.

    P. a. 'GREGORYANA'. A satisfying dense, rounded bushlet, particularly attractive when its new light green foliage in spring contrasts with the darker green of the old. Seldom more than 1–1½ ft.

    P. a. 'NIDIFORMIS'. A particularly congested form with densely crowded branchlets. Up to 4 ft.

P. albertiana 'CONICA'. A sturdy, shapely plant, making a dense pyramid. Eventually 3–4 ft.

Pinus sylvestris 'BEAUVRONNENSIS'. The best of the dwarf pines, making a thick, densely branched bush. Takes many years to reach 12".

Thuja dolabrata 'NANA'. (*Thujopsis dolabrata* 'NANA'). One of the most useful dwarf conifers, rarely reaching 2 ft., and extremely hardy and slow growing.

T. occidentalis 'RHEINGOLD' (*T. o.* 'ELLWANGERIANA RHEINGOLD'). Valuable for its bright golden foliage, especially in the winter months. Forms a slow growing, compact pyramid. Eventually 3 ft.

Thujopsis (*Thuja dolabrata*).

GLOSSARY

Alkaline	Of a limy nature.
Anther	See **Stamen.**
Auricles	The small recurving tips at the base of the flowers of some cyclamen species, owing to their suggestion of tiny ears.
Awn	Usually applied to the stiff, thread-like termination to some seeds, e.g. *Erodium* species.
Axil	The angle at the junction of a leaf and stem.
Axillary	Arising in the axil.
Biennial	A plant which flowers in its second year from seed and then dies.
Bract	A leaf-like structure at the base of a flower cluster. It may be green, or coloured (both are seen in certain spurges) or white, as in *Cornus canadensis*.
Calcifuge	A name given to plants disliking lime. In many cases this antipathy is so great as to cause death in alkaline soil, in others a yellowing of the foliage.
Calyx	The outer system of the flower structure, usually green. It is generally divided, either wholly or partially, into segments. These are called **sepals.**
Capitulum	See **Composite.**
Carpel	One of the divisions of the pistil (q.v.).
Clone	A collective name for all plants which have been propagated vegetatively, i.e. by cuttings, layerings or division, from a single plant. These will have all the qualities of the parent plant, whereas with seedlings there is always the possibility (and often the probability) of variation.
Composite	Having many florets massed on a flat base, giving the appearance of a single flower, as in the daisy. In this example the outer, ray florets are sterile and the inner, disc florets are tiny complete flowers and produce the seed. In some cases, as in the tansy, the flower head (**capitulum**) has only disc florets, and appears button-shaped.
Cordate	Heart-shaped.
Corolla	The inner, and usually more showy process of the perianth. It is generally divided, either completely or partially, into sections and may be of any colour or white (or, exceptionally, green). Each division of the corolla is called a **petal.**
Cotyledon	The first seed-leaf of a plant. The first large division of flowering plants is into **Monocotyledons,** having only one seed leaf on germination, such as most bulbs, and **Dicotyledons,** having two seed leaves.
Crenate, Crenulate	Having rounded teeth, usually with reference to leaf edges.

307

Glossary

Deciduous	Losing its leaves in season, usually in the winter.
Dentate	Toothed, usually referring to leaf edges.
Dicotyledons	See **Cotyledon.**
Digitate	See **Palmate.**
Evergreen	Not losing its leaves during the winter or at any season.
Farinose	Covered with a mealy coating (farina), as in the case of the leaves of some auriculas.
Filament	See **Stamen.**
Glabrous	Without hairs, referring to the surface of a leaf.
Glaucous	Having a bluish-grey bloom, usually referring to the surface of a leaf.
Herbaceous	Perennial but dying down each winter to or below the surface of the soil.
Hirsute	Hairy.
Inflorescence	The name given to the individual groups of flowers on a plant, e.g. a single head as the poppy; a spray in various arrangements, as veronica; or a capitulum, as aster.
Involucre	A collection of bracts enclosing an inflorescence. Present in most composites.
Lanceolate	Lance-shaped. Applied to leaves which are considerably longer than broad and taper to each end.
Linear	Name given to long, narrow leaves, often with parallel edges.
Lyrate	Lyre-shaped.
Monocarpic	Dying after flowering.
Monocotyledons	See **Cotyledon.**
Monotypic	Applied to a genus containing only one species.
Ovary	That part of the flower which contains the **ovules,** which, if fertilized, will develop into seeds.
Ovate	Oval.
Palmate	Of leaves. Formed with radiating sections like the fingers of a hand. If they are divided into completely separate leaflets they are often said to be **digitate.**
Partite	Divided.
Pedatifid	With feathered edges.
Pedicel	Flower-stalk.
Perennial	A plant which lives for at least three seasons, and is not monocarpic.
Perianth	A collective name for the outer parts of a flower; in general this comprises the calyx and corolla, but in a few flowers one or the other is missing.
Petals	See **Corolla.**
Petiole	Leaf stalk.
Pinnate	Of leaves with opposite pairs of leaflets, suggesting the feather of a bird.
Pistil	The central system of a flower, consisting of a seed-box (**ovary**) and a slender stem (**style**) arising from it with

Glossary

terminal area (**stigma**) which is receptive of pollen. This is the basic pattern, but the relative sizes and shapes vary very greatly from species to species, and the divisions of the pistil (the **carpels**) may be joined or free.

Pollen   See **Stamen.**

Procumbent   Almost prostrate.

Radical   Arising more or less directly from the crown of the root.

Rhizome   An underground stem, producing roots and fresh shoots, and often acting as a storage organ when the plant is dormant.

Scape   A flower stem arising directly from the ground, and bearing no leaves upon it.

Sepals   See **Calyx.**

Sessile   Without stalk.

Spatulate   More or less spoon-shaped.

Stamen   The process of the flower which produces the pollen, by means of which the ovules are fertilized to become viable seeds.   It consists of a slender stem, the **filament,** bearing a head (the **anther**) which contains the pollen grains.   When ripe the capsule splits, distributing the pollen.   Any grain alighting on a stigma of the same species commences to grow down the length of the style until it reaches an ovule in the ovary, where fertilization takes place.

Stigma   See **Pistil.**

Style   See **Pistil.**

Tepal   In the case of many Monocotyledons the place of calyx and corolla is taken by a single set of petalloid growths, as in the tulip.   The correct botanical name for each section is tepal, but in this book the word petal is used, as it is the most general description in common use.

Tomentum,   Applied to the dense woolly surface of some plants, caused
  Tomentose   by close white hairs.

Umbel   When the inflorescence is composed of flowers or groups of flowers on stems radiating from the top of the flower-stalk like the ribs of an umbrella it is said to form an umbel.

Whorl   An arrangement of flowers or leaves in sets, each placed closely around the flower-stalk in a ring.

SOME FAMILIAR NAMES AND
EQUIVALENT LATIN NAMES

Where the generic name only is given, more than one of its species are loosely called by the familiar name.

Alpine Rose (alpenrose)	*Rhododendron ferrugineum,*
	R. hirsutum
Apple-blossom Anemone	*Anemone narcissiflora*
Auricula	*Primula auricula*
Barrenwort	*Epimedium*
Bedstraw	*Galium*
Birch (dwarf)	*Betula nana*
Bird's Foot Trefoil	*Lotus*
Bistort	*Polygonum bistorta*
Black Sarana	*Fritillaria camschatcensis*
Bleeding Heart	*Dicentra*
Blue-eyed Grass	*Sisyrhinchium* (the blue species)
Blue Buttercup	*Anemone obtusiloba patula*
Bog Asphodel	*Tofieldia calyculata*
Bog Pimpernel	*Anagallis tenella*
Bramble (dwarf)	*Rubus arcticus*
Broom	*Cytisus, Genista*
Bugle	*Ajuga*
Buttercup	*Ranunculus*
Butterwort	*Pinguicula*
Campion	*Silene*
Candytuft	*Iberis*
Cheddar Pink	*Dianthus gratianopolitanus* (*caesius*)
Chinese Balloon Flower	*Platycodon grandiflorum*
Christmas Rose	*Helleborus niger*
Creeping Jenny	*Lysimachia nummularia*
Creeping Wintergreen	*Gaultheria procumbens*
Crowberry	*Empetrum nigrum*
Cuckoo Flower	*Cardamine pratensis*
Daffodil	*Narcissus*

Familiar Names and Equivalent Latin Names

Daisy	*Aster, Erigeron*
Day Lily	*Hemerocallis*
Deadnettle	*Lamium*
Dog's Tooth Violet	*Erythronium dens-canis*
Dutchman's Breeches	*Dicentra*
Dyer's Greenweed	*Genista tinctoria*
Edelweiss	*Leontopodium alpinum*
Evening Primrose	*Oenothera*
Fairies' Thimbles	*Campanula cochlearifolia (pusilla)*
Flax	*Linum*
Foam Flower	*Tiarella*
Forget-me-not	*Myosotis*
Foxglove	*Digitalis*
Fruiting Duckweed	*Nertera granadensis (depressa)*
Funkia	*Hosta*
Garland Flower	*Daphne*
Gentianella	*Gentiana acaulis*
Globe Flower	*Trollius*
Glory of the Snows	*Chionodoxa*
Golden Drop	*Onosma tauricum*
Golden Rod	*Solidago*
Grape Hyacinth	*Muscari*
Grass of Parnassus	*Parnassia palustris*
Grim the Collier	*Hieracium aurantiacum*
Hawkweed	*Hieracium*
Heather	*Erica, Calluna*
Holly	*Ilex*
Holly Fern	*Blechnum spicant*
Houseleek	*Sempervivum*
Ivy	*Hedera*
Jacob's Ladder	*Polemonium*
Kaffir Lily	*Schizostylis coccinea*
Kingfisher Daisy	*Felicia*
King of the Alps	*Eritrichium nanum*
Knot-grass	*Polygonum*

Familiar Names and Equivalent Latin Names

Lady's Mantle	*Alchemilla*
Lady's Slipper	*Cypripedium calceolus*
Lady's Smock	*Cardamine pratensis*
Ladies' Tresses	*Spiranthes autumnalis*
Lavender	*Lavandula*
Lilac (dwarf)	*Syringa velutina (palibiniana)*, *S. microphylla*
Ling	*Calluna vulgaris*
Lousewort	*Pedicularis*
Love-in-idleness	*Viola tricolor*
Lungwort	*Pulmonaria*
Maiden Pink	*Dianthus deltoides*
Mallow	*Malva*
Mayflower	*Epigaea repens*
Milfoil	*Achillea*
Milkwort	*Polygala*
Mint	*Mentha*
Monkey Flower, Musk	*Mimulus*
Moss Campion	*Silene acaulis*
Mountain Ash (dwarf)	*Sorbus reducta*
Mullein	*Verbascum*
Myrtle (prostrate)	*Myrtus nummularifolia*
Nasturtium	*Tropaeolum*
Oregon Sunshine	*Eriophyllum caespitosum*
Partridge Berry	*Mitchella repens*
Pasque Flower	*Pulsatilla vulgaris*
Penwiper Plant	*Notothlaspi rosulatum*
Periwinkle	*Vinca*
Pimpernel	*Anagallis*
Pink	*Dianthus*
Plumbago	*Ceratostigma*
Poor Man's Weather Glass	*Anagallis arvensis*
Poppy	*Papaver*
Primrose	*Primula vulgaris*
Primrose (Bird's-eye)	*P. farinosa*
Prophet Flower	*Macrotomia echioides*
Pussy Paws	*Spraguea multiceps*
Rest Harrow	*Ononis*
Rock Rose	*Helianthemum*
Rosemary	*Rosmarinus*

Familiar Names and Equivalent Latin Names

Scarlet Fritillary	*Fritillaria recurva*
Scarlet Pimpernel	*Anagallis arvensis*
Sea Heath	*Frankenia laevis*
Sea Holly	*Eryngium*
Self-heal	*Prunella*
Skull-cap	*Scutellaria*
Snowdrop	*Galanthus*
Snowflake	*Leucojum*
Solomon's Seal	*Polygonatum multiflorum*
Speedwell	*Veronica chamaedrioides*
Spikenard	*Valeriana celtica*
Spindleberry (prostrate)	*Euonymus farreri*
Spurge	*Euphorbia*
Squill	*Scilla*
Squinancy-wort	*Galium*
Star of Bethlehem	*Allium umbellatum*
Stock	*Matthiola*
Stonecrop	*Sedum*
Sweet Woodruff	*Asperula odorata*
Sundew	*Drosera*
Tansy	*Tanacetum*
Toad Lily	*Tricyrtis hirta*
Trefoil	*Trifolium*
Vanilla Orchid	*Nigritella niger, N. rubra*
Vegetable Sheep	*Raoulia eximia*
Viper's Bugloss	*Echium*
Virginian Cowslip	*Mertensia virginica*
Wake Robin	*Trillium*
Wallflower	*Cheiranthus, Erysimum*
Willow	*Salix*
Willow Herb	*Epilobium*
Winter Aconite	*Eranthis*
Wintergreen	*Pyrola*
Wood Anemone	*Anemone nemorosa*
Wood Sorrel	*Oxalis*
Yarrow	*Achillea*

A HUNDRED OF THE MOST CHARACTERISTIC ALPINE PLANTS TO BE FOUND FROM 6,000 ft. UPWARDS IN THE CENTRAL EUROPEAN MOUNTAINS

Achillea nana
Ajuga pyramidalis
Androsace carnea
A. glacialis
A. helvetica
A. imbricata
Anemone baldensis
Antennaria dioica rosea
Aquilegia alpina
Artemisia glacialis
A. mutellina
Astrantia minor
Aster alpinus
Biscutella laevigatus
Campanula allionii
C. barbata
C. cochlearifolia (pusilla)
C. excisa
Chrysanthemum alpinum
Daphne striata
Dianthus alpinus
D. carthusianorum
D. neglectus
D. sylvestris
Draba aizoides
Dryas octopetala
Erigeron uniflorus
Erinus alpinus
Eritrichium nanum
Erysimum pumilum
Gentiana clusii ⎫ *G. acaulis*
G. kochiana ⎭ group

G. alpina
G. bavarica
G. brachyphylla
G. nivalis
G. verna
Geum montanum
G. reptans
Globularia cordifolia
Gymnadenia conopsea
Leontopodium alpinum
Linaria alpina
Loiseleuria procumbens
Moneses uniflora
Myosotis alpestris
Nigritella niger
Orchis sambucina
Papaver alpina
Phyteuma comosum
P. hemisphaericum
Pinguicula alpina
P. vulgaris
Polygala chamaebuxus
Potentilla aurea
P. nitida
Primula auricula
P. farinosa
P. glutinosa
P. halleri
P. integrifolia
P. minima
P. rubra
P. viscosa

Characteristic Alpine Plants

Pulsatilla alpina
P. halleri
P. sulphurea
P. vernalis
Ranunculus alpestris
R. glacialis
R. parnassifolius
R. pyrenaeus
R. seguieri
Rhododendron ferrugineum
R. hirsutum
Rhodothamnus chamaecistus
Rosa alpina
Saxifraga aizoides
S. aizoon
S. aspera
S. bryoides
S. caesia

S. oppositifolia
S. retusa
S. squarrosa
Sempervivum arachnoideum
S. montanum
S. wulfenii
Senecio carniolicus
S. incanus
S. uniflorus
Silene acaulis
Soldanella alpina
S. minima
S. pusilla
Trifolium alpinum
Veronica aphylla
V. saxatilis
Viola biflora
V. calcarata

BIBLIOGRAPHY

A SELECTION from the many books of interest to the alpine gardener.

The English Rock Garden. (2 vols.) (1918) Reginald Farrer. T. C. & E. C. Jack.

The New English Rock Garden. (1937) Sampson Clay. T. C. & E. C. Jack. (These two are indispensable to any alpine enthusiast.)

General Reading

My Garden in Spring. (1914) E. A. Bowles. T. C. & E. C. Jack.
My Garden in Summer. (1914) E. A. Bowles. T. C. & E. C. Jack.
My Garden in Autumn and Winter. (1915) E. A. Bowles. T. C. & E. C. Jack.
Alpine Gardening. (1963) Roy Elliott. Vista Books.
My Rock Garden (1907). *Alpine and Bog Plants* (1908). *In a Yorkshire Garden* (1909). All by Reginald Farrer. Edward Arnold.
Garden Terms Simplified. (1962) A. J. Huxley. Collingridge.
The Living Garden. (1935) E. J. Salisbury. Bell.
(Full of interesting information on plant life and enjoyable reading for any plantsman, alpine or otherwise.)

Alpine and Rock Gardening. (1961) (Chapters by various writers.) Ullswater Library of Gardening. Seely Service.

Cultivation

The Propagation of Alpines. (1950) Laurence D. Hills. Faber & Faber.
Alpine House Culture for Amateurs. (1938) Gwendolyn Anley. Country Life.
The Alpine House. (1938) Stuart Boothman. Rush & Warrick.
Alpine Plants Under Glass. (1951) Royton E. Heath. John Gifford.
Miniature Rock Gardening in Troughs and Pans. (1957) Royton E. Heath. Collingridge.
The Scree Garden. (1933) Alpine Garden Society Publication.

Books on Separate Genera

Campanulas. (1951) H. Clifford Crook. Country Life.
Crocus and Colchicum. E. A. Bowles. The Bodley Head.
Dianthus. (1949) Will Ingwersen. Collins.
Fritillaries. (1953) C. Beck. Faber & Faber.
Gentians. (1936) David Wilkie. Country Life. The classic on this genus.
Gentians in the Garden. (1951) G. H. Berry. Faber & Faber. (Includes experiments in cultivation.)
Miniature Daffodils. (1955) Alec Gray. Collingridge.

316

Bibliography

Orchids of Europe. (1961) A. Duperrez. Trans. by A. J. Huxley. Blandford Press.

Primulas in the Garden. (1948) Kenneth Charles Corsar. Lindsay Drummond.

Primulas for Garden and Greenhouse. (1928) E. M. Cox and G. C. Taylor. Dulau.

The Primulas of Europe. (1923) John Macwatt. Country Life.

Sedums. (1921) R. Lloyd Praeger. R.H.S. Publication.

Sempervivums. (1932) R. Lloyd Praeger. R.H.S. Publication.

A succession of monographs are being issued by the Alpine Garden Society, of which volumes on Sedums, Dionysias, Saxifrages, Lewisias etc., etc., have already been published.

Bulbs

Dwarf Bulbs for the Rock Garden. (1959) E. B. Anderson. Nelson.

Collins Guide to Bulbs. (1961) Patrick M. Synge. Collins.

Shrubs

Dwarf and Slow-growing Conifers. (2nd edition, 1938) Murray Hornibrook.

Shrubs for Rock Garden and Alpine House. (1954) Royton E. Heath. Collingridge.

Dwarf Conifers. (1964) H. G. Hillier. Alpine Garden Society and Scottish Rock Garden Club. Obtainable from the Secretary of either Society.

Books on the European Mountain Flora

Among the Hills. (1911) Reginald Farrer. (French Alps.) Swarthmore Press.

The Dolomites. (1913) Reginald Farrer. Adam & Charles Black.
(Both of these are delightfully readable, and abound in descriptions of plants and their habitats.)

Plant Hunting in Europe. Dr. Hugh Roger Smith. Alpine Garden Society.
(An invaluable small book for a companion when visiting the regions described.)

Alpine Plants of Europe. (1911) H. S. Thompson. Routledge.

Sub-Alpine plants of Europe. (1912) H. S. Thompson. Routledge.
(Both good, especially the former, but a little bulky for the suitcase.)

Alpine Flora. C. Schroter. Raustein, Zürich. Probably the best general flora at the moment of small bulk in English.

(*Alpine Flora* (1903), Hoffmann, Longmans, and *Alpine Flowers* (1930) Hegi, Blackie, are very similar in format, and can often be found second-hand. The Hegi, which has the best illustrations of the three, has just been republished but with German text.)

Mountain Flowers of Europe. A. J. Huxley, Blandford Press. (In preparation.)
A very comprehensive Flora in handy size, with many excellent illustrations in colour and black and white.

317

Bibliography

Two other slim volumes are unfortunately not available with English text. They are:

Unsere Alpenflora (1960), by Elias Landolt, Schweizer Alpen-Club, with text in German and excellent colour photos of 316 mountain plants. Worth taking for these alone.

Taschenatlas der Schweizer Flora (1951), by Eduard Thommen, Birkhauser, Basel. In two volumes, one containing the text, in either German or French, and the other small but distinct line drawings of 3,055 plants. Available separately.

The Italian flora is beautifully illustrated by colour and black and white photographs (over 400 of which are of alpine plants) in the large quarto volume *La Flora* (Conosci L'Italia, volume II) published by the Touring Club Italiano, text in Italian (1958).

American Mountain Plants

Western American Alpines. (1932) Ira N. Gabrielson. Macmillan Co., New York.

Wild Flowers of North America. (1961) R. N. Lemmon and C. C. Johnson. Hanover House, New York.

Californian Mountain Flowers. (1963) Philip and Munz. University of California Press.

(Both of these have many colour photographs.)

American Alpines in the Garden. (1931) Anderson McCully. Macmillan Co., New York.

Hardy Californians. (1936) Lester Rowntree. Macmillan Co., New York.

Several interesting older American Floras may be found second-hand from time to time.

Asian Plants

Beautiful Flowers of Kashmir. (1930) (2 vols.) Ethelbert Blatter. Raithby, Lawrence.

Wild Flowers of Kashmir. (3 vols.) B. C. Coventry. Staples & Staples.

On the Eaves of the World. (Kansu–Tibet border). (1926). Reginald Farrer. Edward Arnold.

Plant Hunter's Paradise. (1937) P. Kingdon Ward. Jonathan Cape.

Plant Hunting on the Edge of the World. (1960) F. Kingdon Ward. Gollancz.

Pilgrimage for Plants. (1960) F. Kingdon Ward. Harrap.

The first two of these are illustrated in colour and are Floras of the district. The last three describe plants found in the course of exploration.

New Zealand

Rock Garden Plants of the Southern Alps. (1962) W. R. Philipson and D. Hearn. Caxton Press.

Several of the above books are out of print but can be found from time to time among the second-hand shelves at bookshops and elsewhere.

SOME SOURCES OF PLANTS AND SEEDS

Plants

Ballalheannagh Gardens, Glen Roy, Lonan, Isle of Man (dwarf shrubs, conifers, rhododendrons, Ericaceae).

Barton Alpine Nursery, Barton House, Pooley Bridge, Penrith, Cumbria, CA10 2NG (heathers, conifers, shrubs, alpines).

Walter Blom & Son Ltd, Leavesden, Watford, Herts. (bulbs).

S. W. Bond, Thuya Alpine Nursery, Glebelands, Hartpury, Gloucester (rare items in small numbers).

Broadleigh Gardens, Barr House, Bishop's Hull, Taunton, Somerset (dwarf bulbs).

Bulls Green Nursery, Knebworth, Herts. (pulsatillas and gentians).

P. J. & J. W. Christian, Pentre Cottages, Minera, Wrexham, Clwyd, N. Wales (rarer dwarf bulbs, orchids).

Jack Drake, Inshriach Alpine Plant Nursery, Aviemore, Inverness-shire, PH22 1QS.

Edrom Nurseries, Coldingham, Berwickshire.

Joe Elliott, Broadwell Nursery, Moreton-in-Marsh, Glos.

Peter J. Foley, Holden Clough Nursery, Bolton-by-Bowland, Clitheroe.

Hartside Nursery Garden, Low Gill House, Alston, Cumbria CA9 3BL.

Hillier & Sons Ltd., Winchester, Hants. (dwarf shrubs).

W. E. Th. Ingwersen Ltd., Birch Farm Nursery, Gravetye, East Grinstead, West Sussex.

Reginald Kaye, Waitman Nurseries, Silverdale, Carnforth, Lancs LA5 0TY (hardy ferns and alpines).

C. J. Marchant, Keeper's Hill Nursery, Stapehill, Wimborne, Dorset (Ericaceous plants especially).

The Orpington Nurseries Ltd., Rocky Lane, Gatton Park, Reigate, Surrey (iris species).

J. & E. Parker-Jervis, Martens Hall Farm, Longworth, Abingdon, Oxon OX13 5EP (specialists in snowdrops and colchicums).

Perry's Hardy Plant Farm, Enfield, Middlesex.

John R. Ponton, Old Cottage Gardens, Legerwood, Earlston, Berwickshire (dwarf conifers, dwarf rhododendrons, heathers).

Potterton & Martin, The Cottage Nursery, Moortown Road, Nettleton, nr Caistor, Lincoln LN7 6HX (dwarf bulbs, cyclamen, carnivorous plants).

Robinson's Hardy Plants, Greencourt Nurseries, Crockenhill, Swanley, Kent BR8 8HD.

W. H. Rogers & Son, Red Lodge Nursery, Cheshunt Avenue, Eastleigh, Hants (dwarf conifers).

Alan Smith, 127 Leaves Green Road, Keston, Kent BR2 6DG (sempervivums).

Wallace & Barr, The Nurseries, Marden, Kent (bulbs).

Wansdyke Nursery, Devizes, Wilts (dwarf conifers).

Washfield Nursery (Elizabeth Strangman), Hawkhurst, Kent.

Several other specialist nurseries advertise in the Bulletins of the Alpine Garden Society and the Journals of the Scottish Rock Garden Club. It is an advantage if one can be found which is readily accessible.

Some Sources of Plants and Seeds

Seeds

Messrs. Thompson & Morgan, Ipswich.
Major V. F. Howell, Firethorn, Oxshott Way, Cobham, Surrey. (Unusual and Rare Seeds.)

The Annual Seed Exchanges of:
*The Alpine Garden Society
   (*Secretary:* E. M. Upward, Lye End Link, St. John's, Woking, Surrey.)

*The Scottish Rock Garden Club
   (*Hon. Subscription Secretary:* Mr. D. J. Donaldson, Morea, Main Road, Balbeggie, Perth PH2 6EZ.)

*The American Rock Garden Society
   (*Secretary:* Donald Peach, Box 183, Hales Corner, Wisconsin, 53130, USA.)

Offers seeds of many species collected in the Rocky Mountains and elsewhere.

Second-hand Books

Ashwell Books, Ashwell House, Baldock, Herts SG7 5AZ.
Greenacre Books, Stancliffe Avenue, Marford, Wrexham, Clwyd, N. Wales.
Peter Kennedy, 702a Christchurch Road, Bournemouth, Dorset.
Daniel Lloyd, 4 Hillcrest Avenue, Chertsey, Surrey.
Rudge Books, Swanspool, Loudwater, Herts WD3 4JE.
Watch House Rare Books, 43 Belsize Park Gardens, London NW3.
Wheldon & Wesley Ltd., Lytton Lodge, Codicote, nr. Hitchin, Herts.

* Further particulars on page 16.